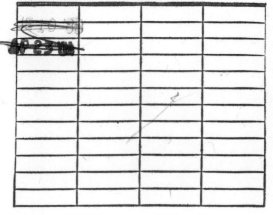

DISPUTES
AND NEGOTIATIONS

A CROSS-CULTURAL PERSPECTIVE

STUDIES ON LAW AND SOCIAL CONTROL

DONALD BLACK *Series Editor*
Center for Criminal Justice
Harvard Law School
Cambridge, Massachusetts 02138

DISPUTES
AND NEGOTIATIONS

A CROSS-CULTURAL PERSPECTIVE

P.H. Gulliver

Department of Anthropology
York University
Downsview, Ontario, Canada

ACADEMIC PRESS

A Subsidiary of Harcourt Brace Jovanovich, Publishers

New York   London   Toronto   Sydney   San Francisco

ACADEMIC PRESS, INC.
111 Fifth Avenue, New York, New York 10003

United Kingdom Edition published by
ACADEMIC PRESS, INC. (LONDON) LTD.
24/28 Oval Road, London NW1   7DX

Library of Congress Cataloging in Publication Data

Gulliver, P.   H.
    Disputes and negotiations.

    (Studies on law and social control)
    Bibliography: p.
    Includes bibliographical references.
    1. Negotiation––Cross–cultural studies.
2. Decision–making––Cross–cultural studies.
3. Law, Arusha. 4. Arusha (African tribe) I. Title.
II. Series.
BF637.N4G8   301.15'54   79–22735
ISBN 0–12–305550–4

PRINTED IN THE UNITED STATES OF AMERICA

79 80 81 82   9 8 7 6 5 4 3 2 1

To Marilyn
who helped make this a better book

CONTENTS

1

THE PROCESS OF NEGOTIATION 1

2

THE STUDY OF JOINT DECISION-MAKING 35

vii

7

MEDIATORS: TRIADIC INTERACTION IN THE NEGOTIATION PROCESS   209

8

TWO CASES STUDIES   233

9

CONCLUSION   265

LIST OF FIGURES

PREFACE

Negotiation is one kind of problem-solving process—one in which people attempt to reach a joint decision on matters of common concern in situations where they are in disagreement and conflict. In its simplest and most general form, this book is a study of the way in which two parties negotiate with each other in the endeavor to resolve a dispute between them and to discover a mutually acceptable, tolerable outcome. In their disagreement or competition with each other, they neither seek the deciding judgment of a third party nor resort to the sheer force of violence against each other. Rather, by the exchange of information, they explore the nature and extent of their differences and the possibilities open to them, they seek to induce or persuade each other to modify their expectations and requirements, and they search for an outcome that is at least satisfactory enough to both parties. If negotiations are to be "successful"—that is, if an outcome can be discovered that each party can accept and agree to—then initially at least, one of the parties must have been mistaken in his assessment of what he would be prepared to accept. It is more probable, however, that both parties come to modify their initial demands and their responses to the other's demands. Thus the outcome is frequently some kind of compromise. However, compromise is not at all inevitable: The negotiators may be able to discover some acceptable outcome that they had not originally conceived of or considered, which offers advantage to both of them.

The study of negotiations has attracted the attention of a diverse variety of social scientists. The result is that there has been a gradual accumulation both of materials—conceptual, experimental, and empirical—and of general or partial explanations and theory. Game theorists and some decision theorists have sought to get at the essentials of decision-making and the associated strategies in situations where two or more parties are interdependent, and where, therefore, the outcome of their conflict and competition must be a product of their joint requirements and the interaction of their separate choices. Such theorists have deliberately concentrated on the logical and hypothetical conceptualization of problems and processes wherein many of the variables of the real world are held constant or ignored. Bargaining theorists, mainly economists, have sought to develop theory that would enable them to predict the outcome of negotiations, chiefly with reference to wage rates. Social psychologists, concerned with interpersonal behavior and the nature of interaction under conditions of conflict, have been especially active in devising and carrying out experiments and laboratory simulations of real-life conditions in order to investigate and to reach generalizations about particular aspects of negotiations. Political scientists studying international conflict and industrial sociologists studying labor–management disputes have inevitably been more concerned with the patterns of real-life negotiation and their explanation. In addition, a growing number of sociologists and social anthropologists have come to recognize that negotiation is one means by which social relationships and even whole institutions, such as a hospital or school, are organized and adjusted. So far, however, the theoretical dimensions and implications have been poorly developed.

Partly because of this diversity of intellectual background, concerns, and approaches, but also because of the marked complexity of the many variables involved in negotiation, there has been relatively little consensus. The study of negotiations is still in the formative stage of tentative conceptualization and hypothesis, with a paucity of specifically directed data collection and analysis.

Social anthropologists have contributed very little to the study of this area of human behavior and interaction, although they inevitably confront it in their field research. This may explain why the acknowledged specialists in other social sciences have almost entirely ignored the cross-cultural dimensions and empirical data that undoubtedly would raise questions about some of the assumptions and preconceptions that are current in the investigation of negotiations. Moreover, it has been overlooked that the reference to cross-cultural data provides a useful test-bed of hypotheses and ideas.[1]

As a working anthropologist, my own approach to the investigation of negotiations is frankly and obviously cross-cultural. My interest in the subject was originally aroused as a result of my research in non-Western societies and cultures. It so happened that I worked in a number of African societies in which judicial institutions were little developed (or they had been rather ineffectively imposed by alien government) and where, therefore, interpersonal and intergroup disputes were dealt with by a variety of other processes. Principal among those processes was negotiation. It became a major preoccupation to discover and to understand how people negotiated and how in consequence they resolved their disputes.[2] Seeking to generalize from my own field materials and particularist analyses and conclusions, I found little assistance from my fellow anthropologists. It seemed sensible, therefore, to go to the work of social scientists who appeared to be studying the same kinds of problems in the Western context. In their work I found a great deal of illumination, insight, and stimulus. I also found that it was possible, tentatively, to generalize across diverse societies and cultures. In this recourse to the work of Western-oriented social scientists, I brought not only the cross-cultural approach inherent in anthropology, but also an expertise in the study of microsociological relations and processes and a concern for empirical, real-life data as these have been developed in social anthropology since the time of Malinowski.

The endeavor in this book, therefore, is deliberately cross-cultural: to show that patterns of interactive behavior in negotiations are essentially similar despite marked differences in interests, ideas, values, rules, and assumptions among negotiators in different societies. That endeavor is supported by data from rather intensive investigation of particular cases where people were in dispute and conflict with one another and where they sought a negotiated resolution and outcome. Much of this empirical material comes from my own research in Africa although continually I attempt to complement and, as it were, match my African examples with comparable data from Western instances. The latter are drawn chiefly from

---

[1] The neglect of cross-cultural reference and pertinent data is quite obvious, for example, in three symposia of writings by scholars working in the field of negotiation: Young, *Bargaining: Formal Theories of Negotiation* (1975), and Zartman, *The Negotiation Process* (1977), which contain papers by economists, political scientists, and sociologists; and Druckman, *Negotiations* (1977), which contains papers by social psychologists.

[2] My data and analysis for two East African societies—the Arusha and the Ndendeuli—are given in Gulliver (1963 and 1971, respectively).

industrial negotiations, without doubt the area of richest empirical materials.

I do not attempt in this book to produce theory that is either predictive of the outcome of negotiations or prescriptive of the behavior of negotiators. Probably the majority of specialists assume that the major concern should be with the outcome of negotiations and how it is determined. There is a good deal of faith that sooner or later it will be possible to develop understanding and theory to the point of being able to predict what the outcome will be in particular cases. "A theory of negotiations is a set of interrelated causal statements which explain how and which outcomes are chosen [Zartman 1975:70]." In that sense this book provides no theory. I have little expectation that such theory is likely to emerge in the near future, except perhaps for very limited, largely artificial cases. Such predictive theories as there are remain untested and the theories themselves intrinsically depend on conceptual assumptions that certainly cannot be made in the context of actual, concrete cases. The complexity of variables involved in real-life situations (some of which are scarcely knowable, such as negotiators' mental processes) and the high degree of uncertainty with which actual negotiators must cope, make it unlikely that we can predict with any useful degree of reliability. Since we are unable to predict, it is obviously difficult to prescribe behavior that negotiators should follow. I prefer not to attempt what seems presumptuous in view of the present state of our understanding.

My principal intention is to identify some common patterns of behavior and interaction among negotiators and to present these in the form of general models. With the use of these models, I hope to make some advance in the explanation of what happens in negotiations, how it happens, and why. Various parts of these models are illustrated and exemplified by reference to recorded, real-life cases but I am mindful that my data are neither plentiful enough nor altogether complete. There are irresolvable problems in knowing and recording what happened in specific cases. In consequence some social scientists eschew the reference to concrete reality and instead concentrate on logical conceptualization. There is some usefulness in so doing, of course, but ultimately, to be more than intellectual puzzle games, theory and concepts must be brought back to some kind of real-life context if they are to explain anything at all. Despite the genuine problems of data collection and the possible accusations of naive empiricism, I prefer to start from a real-life context, not because this is necessarily the only or even the best approach, but because I have come to this study directly as a result of attempting to understand what happened in specific, actual cases.

Whether my models of negotiating behavior are "correct" is not the principal issue. What I intend and hope is that they may prove useful in directing inquiry and in developing understanding in the study and explanation of negotiations. These models are based on certain assumptions, which will become clearer in the main body of the book. I briefly outline them as follows: Negotiations comprise a set of social processes leading to interdependent, joint decision-making by the negotiators through their dynamic interaction with one another. These processes involve the exchange of information (and its manipulation), which permits and compels learning by each party about his opponent, about himself, and about their common situation: that is, about their expectations, requirements, strengths, and strategies. As a result of learning, there is modification of expectations and requirements such that the negotiators may shift their demands to some point at which they can agree. Negotiators continue to exchange information and to explore possibilities so long as they consider that they may gain an outcome that is more advantageous than the status quo. Negotiations are thus a dynamic process of exploration in which change is intrinsic: changes in each party's assessment of his requirements, in his expectations of what is possible, preferable, and acceptable, and changes in his understanding of the opponent's assessments and expectations. Analysis of negotiation is necessarily the analysis of process and change within the ineluctable interdependence of the negotiating parties.

This study begins with the identification of negotiation as a distinctive social process of decision-making. For this purpose, in Chapter 1, the contrast is drawn between negotiation and adjudication. I argue that although scholars have proposed a number of characteristics that tend to distinguish these two major processes, none is altogether decisive, especially in a cross-cultural perspective. The focal distinction is shown to lie in the locus and nature of decision-making: joint, interdependent decision-making by the parties themselves in negotiation and decision by a third party in adjudication.

In Chapter 2, I examine some of the dimensions of the study of joint decision-making. First, I look at the contributions of theorists working in abstract, logicoconceptual terms. The intention is not primarily to make a sustained critique but rather to discover the significant variables to be considered. The theorists themselves have proposed certain key variables; in addition, however, it is most revealing to examine the limiting and simplifying assumptions that the theorists have made, which, being inapplicable to real-life situations, are therefore in effect variables to be considered. Second, I look at the problem of multiple criteria. Most disputes concern several issues and most issues involve several attributes by which they are assessed. This multiplicity, in which these various criteria are necessarily interdependent in some degree, has largely been ignored in problem formation, theoretical conceptualization, and analysis. The proper study of joint decision-making must, however, take full account of multiple criteria and of the ways by which actual negotiators attempt to cope with them. Finally, there is an outline of the approach adopted in this book—historico-ethnographic. It concentrates on real-life situations and takes as full account as possible both of the variables identified in conceptual theory and of empirical data concerning actual negotiators dealing with their disputes.

In Chapter 3, I define and distinguish certain terms that have been confused in the literature and are critically used in the analyses that follow. These terms are *negotiation* and *bargaining*, *disagreement* and *dispute*, and *outcome*.

The core of the book is contained in Chapters 6 and 7. There I describe and discuss two interconnected, processual models of negotiation. First, there is a model of the repetitive, cyclical exchange and interpretation of information through which negotiators develop and adjust their expectations and preferences and attempt to influence and alter those of the opponent. Presentation of this model involves consideration of the nature of information exchange, the formation and modification of a negotiator's preference set, expectations about the opponent, and the choices of strategy and tactics. Second, there is a model of the progressive development of negotiating interaction from the initiation of a dispute to the affirmation of some agreed outcome. This model constitutes a flexible sequence of overlapping phases, in each of which there is a distinctive kind of interaction and effective purpose. Each phase makes the succeeding one possible in a patterned progression toward an outcome. These phases are considered separately, though the tendencies for overlapping are noted. They are (1) the search for an arena of confrontation; (2) agenda compilation and the definition of issues in dispute; (3) the emphasis on differences and the exploration of the limits of the field of dispute; (4) the narrowing of differences and the reduction of issues, thus revealing the obdurate issues in the context; (5) preliminaries to bargaining; (6) final bargaining to an outcome; (7) the symbolic affirmation of that outcome and of the negotiators' accord; and (8) perhaps the execution of the terms of agreement.

The propulsive dynamics of negotiation are discussed in Chapter 6. First, I reexamine the internal dynamics of negotiation, giving particular attention to the intrinsic contradictions of antagonism and coordination between the negotiators. These dispositions, though continuously present throughout negotiation, alternate in predominance and each promotes the resurgence of the other. Second, I consider the potential power that each party possesses, which may be transformed into negotiating strength as each attempts to induce or coerce the other to shift his expectations and demands. Such power and associated weaknesses reside in material resources and normative claims; both are liable to be affected by the impingement of third parties whose interests and values are touched by the dispute and the disputants. An operational scheme is suggested by which to incorporate the notion of power into the study of negotiations and decision-making. In Chapter 7, the direct intervention of a third party as a mediator is considered in the context of the processual interaction of the negotiations.

The concepts, arguments, and general framework of analysis presented in this book are illustrated at relevant points by examples drawn from actual cases. Further empirical exemplification is given in Chapter 8 with the presentation in detail of two recorded cases of the negotiation of disputes: one from the Arusha of Tanzania and the other from labor-management relations in the United States.

In conclusion, I point to some further aspects of negotiation that require investigation, and I briefly examine the process of the negotiation of a dispute in a public arena and two comparable processes: private, dyadic negotiation of disagreement and conflict in interpersonal relations, and the more or less continuous negotiation of conflict in social relations by which whole institutional complexes are organized and adjusted.

ACKNOWLEDGMENTS

My thanks are due to Canada Council for a research grant in 1972 which allowed me to undertake library and archival research away from my own university, thus enabling me to have access to materials otherwise unavailable. The Faculty of Arts, York University, Toronto, awarded me a Faculty of Arts Fellowship for the academic year 1977–1978, during which time the bulk of this book was drafted. To many colleagues in North America and Britain, I wish to express real gratitude for their collegial encouragement, comments, and suggestions in a variety of seminars and discussions. In particular, I wish to thank Marilyn Silverman who gave me invaluable editorial assistance in addition to acting as an excellent sounding board and frank critic for my ideas and exposition. Elsewhere I have previously published my personal gratitude to various peoples of East Africa among whom I have worked; but it is appropriate for me, as an anthropologist, to reemphasize my appreciation of their tolerance of an outsider's intrusions and their help to me during field research, without which I could not have begun to write this book.

1

THE PROCESS OF NEGOTIATION

In all societies, regardless of their location in time and space, there is a wide variety of modes by which disputes are handled and resolution sought. In general terms, the range of these procedures and their variation can be comprehended within a few broad categories.

One such category is the duel: the institutionalized, organized contest or fight between disputants, or their supporters or champions, in which the winner supposedly proves the rightness or superiority of his case. The contest may be fought with physical violence or by stylized competition (e.g., wrestling matches) or by verbal confrontations (e.g., Eskimo song contests). A second category is violent self-help. This has been widely reported by anthropologists, particularly from noncentralized, acephalous societies where there are no obvious means for the peaceful resolution of those disputes that occur beyond the limits of fairly small groups. Where such groups are well organized and integrated, self-help may develop into feuding. This suggests that the groups involved can manage, at least for a time, without other peaceful and useful interaction between them. However, where such groups are more dependent on each other, where their individual members have valuable, persisting relationships with each other (e.g., through marriage, kinship, or economic exchange), and especially where members of the groups are residentially intermingled, hostilities cannot long be tolerated. In such situations, the resort to violent self-help may be a regular means not only to express the strength of dissatisfaction and determination but also to precipitate a crisis so that other procedures can be initiated or resumed. Thus there are, for example, the raid on the opponent's home, the seizure or spoliation of property, and the industrial strike. All lead to efforts for peacemaking.

Third, there is avoidance: the more or less deliberate curtailing or limiting of further relations with the other person, letting the matter rest, accepting the status quo (at least temporarily), seeking no specific decision on the dispute, and endeavoring to prevent the continuation or escalation of conflict because of the perceived difficulties that would result. In societies where residential mobility is fairly easy one party may move away so as to evade the possible consequences of his actions or to avoid further trouble. Later, the importance of the dispute and its attendant emotions may wane and it may be possible to deal with it more easily. Alternatively, the offender may improve his behavior so that his former actions can be forgotten. However, in some circumstances disputes may not be resolvable without unacceptable repercussions and so, in avoidance, they are allowed to lapse.[1]

Fourth, when effective, practical means are unavailable or unavailing, or where their use might bring about intolerable complications or threaten social relations, a dispute may be transformed and redefined in symbolic and supernatural terms—witchcraft accusations, performance in the ancestral cult or some other religious system, but also perhaps sporting contests or getting to the moon first. As with avoidance, the dispute is not so much resolved as deflected. Yet burying the dispute in the symbolic process may be effective. In the opinions of the people involved, the renewal of relationships and the reemphasis of group unity—potentially important features of dispute resolution—can be accomplished.

Finally, despite the prevalence of the foregoing modes of treating disputes—procedures that are not at all confined to so-called "primitive" or simpler societies—there are two other modes that are far more common, indeed virtually universal. These are negotiation and adjudication. Although each of these two terms refers to a considerable range of behavioral patterns and cultural forms, each is characterized by certain fundamental features of process and interaction that are valid cross-culturally. Although this present study is concerned only with negotiation, this mode of treating

---

1. As Felstiner (1974:76) has pointed out, this mode of dealing with disputes has been little studied. He notes its probably frequency and importance in the United States. Examples from other societies are given by Schwartz (1954:471), Koch (1974:74), and Yngvesson (1976). Avoidance in nomadic societies is mentioned, without detailed analysis, by Furer-Haimendorf (1967:22), Goldschmidt (1971:135), and Gulliver (1975b:377–378).

disputes can be usefully introduced and initially identified through a discriminating contrast with adjudication. The conceptual distinction is not new and indeed it has sometimes been too much taken for granted. On the other hand, it is not one that has acquired universal acceptance. In making the distinction in the following section, certain similarities between the two modes are also noted.

NEGOTIATION AND ADJUDICATION: (A) PROCESS OF DECISION-MAKING

As a first description, the picture of negotiation is one of two sets of people, the disputing parties or their representatives, facing each other across a table or from opposite sides of an open space. They exchange information and opinion, engage in argument and discussion, and sooner or later propose offers and counteroffers relating to the issues in dispute between them, seeking an outcome acceptable to both sides. The comparable picture of adjudication is that of two parties (each including one or more persons) who, separated from one another, face an adjudicator who sits in front of, apart from, and often raised above them. They address him, offering information, opinion, and argument. Each seeks to refute the other's presentation and to persuade the adjudicator to favor his own case. Eventually the adjudicator pronounces his decision on the issues, often sorting out and summing up the information given to him and explaining his judgment.

Although these pictures are simplistic and merely intended to be suggestive by way of introduction, it is clear that a fundamental characteristic of negotiation is the absence of a third-party decision-maker. It is my contention that the paramount distinction between the two modes—negotiation and adjudication—comes from that fact. This is because the absence or presence of an authoritative third party produces an essential difference in the nature of the decision-making process. The locus of decision-making, together with the process leading to it and affected by it, is taken to be crucial because it is directed to the end result of dispute treatment; that is, some outcome. That outcome may be specific, conclusive, and, at least in intent, more or less permanent, or it may be quite vague and temporary, even leaving things much as they were initially. Furthermore, the outcome may be capable of practical execution or it may be no more than a matter of general intention and orientation. The range of kinds of decisions and their efficacy is, of course, enormous. Yet it is not the kind of decision-outcome that is distinctive but rather the process by which the decision is reached. Although there are a number of other characteristics that tend to be more associated with one or the other mode, I show later that these cannot form the basis for a clear distinction.

In adjudication, the decision-maker is typically a third party who is not himself directly a disputant.[2] That third party—a single individual or a set of persons—holds the acknowledged right, that is the legitimate authority and responsibility, to reach and enunciate a decision that is the outcome of the dispute and is in some degree binding on the disputing parties. Compulsorily or voluntarily, the disputants surrender the ability to decide for themselves. They become petitioners or supplicants. Therefore, the primary concern of a disputant is to focus on the adjudicator: to present information and argument to him in the attempt to persuade him to give a decision that is favorable, or less unfavorable, to the disputant. The adjudicator is, at least for the moment, in a superior role, the disputant is in an inferior one. The disputants themselves are separated from one another as each directs himself to the adjudicator.

It is most common, of course, that disputants attempt to bring persuasion, even threat and promise, to bear on each other in the endeavor to affect each other's presentation to the adjudicator. Although important, this is a secondary matter, because in the end neither disputant himself makes the decision. Those attempts are, in intent and effect, part of the persuasion directed to the adjudicator. They are efforts to influence, alter, and diminish the presentation to him by the opposing party. The adjudicator may be quite open to persuasion on fact, interpretation, application of rules and norms, recognition of extenuating circumstances, and the like, but he may choose to disregard parts of either party's presentation. Furthermore, the adjudicator may be more or less wise and perceptive, more or less conscientious, more or less constrained by rules, values, and pragmatic considerations, more or less concerned for justice and equity, and more or less influenced by his own and others' interests. Moreover, the procedural "rules of the game," the sociocultural milieu, and the situational context of the dispute and the disputants may affect the process leading up to decision making. However, the central fact remains that the adjudicator makes the decision and that, therefore, the disputants and the process are directed toward and subject to him.

To be sure, the degree of authority held and exercised by an adjudicator ranges from the virtually absolute to no more than the ephemeral, accepted ability to propose an outcome. He may represent the

---

2. Pospisil (1978:99–100) has pointed out that in some instances the recognized authority (e.g., king, chief, or lineage head) may be or may represent a party to the dispute, as plaintiff or defendant. Yet he still acts as adjudicator in the case. That is to say, he exercises his authority and power to give a decision, however partial he may be.

legitimate, stable political order—he may be the political authority and an autocrat to boot—or he may be the unchallenged holder of practical power in the situation. Alternatively, he may be no more than the exponent of opinion, the fleeting representative of neutrality or of the "public interest." Although the degree and nature of authority are of considerable practical and sociological importance, they do not in themselves alter the essential structuring of the process and the patterning of interaction among the participants. It is unlikely and seems not to have been demonstrated that there is any direct correlation between the degree of authority and the nature of the decision. For instance, an autocratic adjudicator, well supported by organized, coercive powers, may imperiously disregard the disputants' presentations and perhaps flout rules and values. But he may, on the other hand, for political, religious, moral, or symbolic reasons, be as much constrained as, say, the elderly villager who seeks no personal advantage but who is willing to arbitrate between quarreling neighbors. Conversely, that village arbitrator too might ignore rules and values when he is far more concerned about village interests, or those of some section of the community, than he is about the interests of the disputants or about justice. In short, differences in the authority of adjudicators are matters of degree rather than of kind.

In negotiations, by contrast, the decision is made by the disputing parties themselves. *It is a joint decision.* Each party can only obtain what the other is in the end prepared to allow. Since the two parties necessarily began with some kind of difference between them, as they perceived the situation, the process of decision-making therefore involves a convergence. At least one party, but usually both, must move toward the other. Although there may be a compromise of some sort, this is not inevitable since one party may be induced to move altogether to his opponent's position or, alternatively, there can be the joint, integrative creation of something new that is acceptable to both parties.[3]

In the process of seeking a joint decision, the disputing parties are inherently interdependent if an acceptable outcome is to be obtained. Their primary concern is to influence or coerce each other. The course of negotiation therefore involves the exchange of information: alleged facts and proffered interpretation of them, argument, appeals to rules and values, threat, promise, demand, offer, counteroffer, and so on. The flow of information permits a continuous process of learning by each party about the requirements, preferences, expectations, perceptions, attitudes, feelings,

---

3. On the distinction between compromise and integrative outcome, see Walton and McKersie (1965:128, passim). I discuss the notion of convergence further on pages 160, 162–164.

5

strengths, and weaknesses of both the opponent and himself. A party may initially consider himself clear and well prepared, although often (and perhaps necessarily so) he is vague about his real preferences and aims and about the possibilities available. In any case, what he learns from and about the opponent, and about his own position, compels reconsideration, clarification, and adjustment of expectations. As a result of learning, that is, there are modifications (maybe including reinforcement) in preferences and demands by each party. This interaction continues. There is, and must be, a gradual willingness to coordinate and collude. Negotiators may never achieve amity, sympathy, or trust but they have to attain sufficient coordination, however reluctantly, so as to work toward and ultimately achieve a joint decision on the issues in dispute. The alternative, always an available option, is to accept the status quo or status quo ante, which is also in effect a joint decision, as preferable to anything else that appears possible.

There is no third party to determine what the outcome is or should be. The only outcome is one to which both agree, which is, therefore, in the opinion of each party, the most satisfactory (or at least satisfactory enough) that can be obtained in the circumstances. The reasons for acceptability are, of course, likely to be different for each party. Moreover, one or both may be mistaken in assessing acceptable adequacy—just as they may be mistaken about many other features of the dispute between them. One party may gain nearly all he orginally desired because of overwhelmingly superior power vis-à-vis his opponent, whether that power comes from coercion, moral strength, persuasive skill, or whatever. That, however, would be an uncommon situation, if only because the various kinds of power are unlikely to be so monopolized. In any case, as Schelling (1960:22 ff.) has convincingly shown, even the weak or "powerless" party may be able to turn his position into one of quite effective strength. Each party is also subject, in varying degrees, to considerations concerning the expectations, interests, and pressures of outsiders and the prospect of future relationships with them.

Third parties—mediators—are often, but certainly not always, involved in negotiations. They are not, however, unilateral decision-makers but rather facilitators of the process leading to the parties' joint decision. In various ways they help to increase or orient the exchange of information and to expedite the learning and adjustment process. Their presence does not deprive the disputants of the final ability, or need, to make their own individual choices and to reach an agreed decision.[4]

The crucial distinction then, between adjudication and negotiation is

---

4. Mediators and mediation are examined in Chapter 7.

that the former is a process leading to unilateral decision-making by an authoritative third party, whereas the latter is a process leading to joint decision-making by the disputing parties themselves as the culmination of an interactive process of information exchange and learning. Let me be clear: My concern here is to emphasize that distinction. I do not wish to deny that there are also certain similarities and, in real life, sometimes an overlapping of the two processual modes.

Several additional points must be noted. First, decision-making is not limited only to the final outcome of a dispute. Throughout both kinds of process, there is a necessity for decisions on both procedural and substantive matters. Procedural decisions relate to such things as the time and place of proceedings, agenda compilation and item definition, rules of procedure in general and particular, ad hoc matters (e.g., when to adjourn, whether certain evidence is admissible, whether to hear a particular witness). Substantive matters concern, inter alia, agenda items as these are partly or wholly resolved prior to the final outcome, and the specification, interpretation, and application of rules and values. Under adjudication, all these kinds of decisions, minor or more substantial, are made by the adjudicator, even when he listens to and is prepared to accept a joint proposal by the disputants. In negotiation, each procedural and substantive issue must be resolved by the joint agreement of the parties through their interaction. There is, though, more to this than keeping the game going. Just as the adjudicator's decision on each issue confirms and symbolizes his authority, so each joint decision by the negotiators contributes to the development of a coordination between them that is essential to the ultimate end of an agreed outcome.

Second, the distinction being made here is not a matter of formal, more institutionalized processes as against informal, weakly institutionalized ones. For example, some industrial arbitration is quite informal, as are proceedings in small-claims courts or a village headman's hearing under a convenient shade tree. On the other hand, some negotiations occur in a quite formal manner, in accordance with a good deal of protocol, particularly in those contexts where negotiations are frequent and repetitive. Third, it is not helpful to make the distinction between "in court" and "out of court" proceedings, if only for the reason that this begs the question of the definition of "court" and raises possible ethnocentric assumptions.

NEGOTIATION AND ADJUDICATION: (B) SOME OTHER DISCRIMINATING FEATURES

A number of theorists in the social sciences and jurisprudence have made a conceptual and processual distinction between negotiation and adjudication (or their near equivalents such as arbitration and collective bargaining or meditation in negotiation and adjudication). Many of these writers, however, have emphasized distinguishing characteristics other than the locus of decision making. It would seem, on reflection, that although none of these other characteristics is as fundamentally discriminating as the locus of decision-making, they do contribute to a general syndrome for each mode. These other characteristics, significantly enough, have generally been proposed as paired contrasts, although the pairs tend to overlap a good deal in mutual reinforcement.

These features are briefly reviewed in the present section with the intention of bringing them together within a single pattern. The purpose is not only to indicate the differences between the two modes but to establish the viability of negotiation as a manifestly separate, social process. The treatment of adjudication is therefore rather superficial, especially as it will appear to a lawyer; nor is there consideration of the various types of adjudication.

One contrast distinguishes between interests and values. In its simplest form the argument goes something like this: Negotiation occurs and may even be required in disputes over interests, in a situation of scarcity when both parties seek the same resources without there being enough to satisfy both. On the other hand, adjudication occurs, or at least is most appropriate and effective, when the dispute concerns values, norms, and the assessment of facts. It is easy to see that few, if any, disputes involve only interests or only values; some mixture of both is almost inevitable. Therefore Aubert, for instance, has suggested that

> as long as a conflict of interests remains relatively pure it is amenable to solution through bargaining and compromise [i.e., negotiation] on the condition that there is something to give and something to take on both sides. (This condition need not always be fulfilled, however.) When a clash of interests has become associated with dissensus [i.e., conflict of values] bargaining and compromise may be hard to achieve, while the conflict has, on the other hand, become amenable to a solution through the intervention of law in the broadest sense [Aubert 1963:30–31].[5]

Later Aubert modified his argument. "Where interests are partly incompatible and partly overlapping negotiation presents itself as a normal procedure to resolve the conflict [1969:283]." Whereas, if interests are totally incompatible, or if the conflict is over values and facts, then negotiations are inadequate to deal with the matter and it may be "solved by delegating

---

5. Reprinted from "Competition and Dissensus: Two Types of Conflict and Conflict Resolution" by Vilhelm Aubert in *Journal of Conflict Resolution*, Vol. VII, No. 1 (March 1963) by permission of the publisher, Sage Publications, Inc.

the decision to a court of law [p. 283]." Although this is a more weakly discriminating statement, it is suggestive of something in the contrast between the two modes. It is pertinent to note, however, that in some societies, and in many situations in all societies, all kinds of disputes, with whatever mixture of interests and values, are successfully dealt with by negotiation; for example, in industrial disputes in Western countries, or among the Arusha of East Africa. Conversely, a judge in his court may be faced with cases largely comprising a conflict of interests, which he must and does decide with the full authority of his role. In most particular cases of dispute, however, it is virtually impossible to disentangle interests and values.

To deal with such objections, it has been suggested that "when a conflict of interests is turned over to the law it must from now on be formulated as . . . a conflict of values or belief [Aubert 1963:33]." The implication would seem to be that, conversely, a dispute over values and fact might be reformulated as one over interests when it becomes subject to negotiation. There is some validity in this argument, especially as it relates to certain kinds of adjudication. The nature of the arena and its ground rules must surely influence the kind of presentation, including definition, of the issues in dispute. Nevertheless, it is undeniable that during actual negotiation in concrete cases, both values and facts are often strenuously disputed, are seldom taken for granted, and are commonly a real source of conflict. This remains true even though a lot of such contention is a form of rhetoric, a language of dispute, rather than the dispute itself. Moreover, whatever the formulation before him, an adjudicator may still be dealing in effect with problems of interests.

Something of the same distinction, and an extension of the general argument, lies in the assertion that adjudication can only occur when there is the possibility of the application of rules, values, and principles in reaching a decision. For example, Fuller has written that "a judge is one who applies some principle to the decision of the case; if there are no principles the decider cannot be a judge—the case is not justiciable [Fuller 1963:28]." Similarly, Eckhoff wrote, "The judge is distinguished . . . in that his activity is related to the level of norms rather than to the level of interests [1967:161]." The implication is that negotiations occur in disputes that do not, or cannot, involve the application of principles and norms. There is the further implication, it would seem, that negotiations are stereotypically of the order of horse-trading, marketplace haggling, and the like, where "principles" supposedly matter little or not at all.

In discussing this view I shall, for convenience and simplicity, use the term *norm* to include principles, norms, values, rules, laws, and the like. Although these may, in other contexts and for other purposes, be usefully discriminated, here I wish to emphasize their common characteristic as standards containing a marked "ought" quality.[6] In that general sense, the relationship between norms and negotiations is problematic and has been insufficiently studied.

What can be said, briefly, is that first, virtually all negotiations involve the consideration of norms. Most disputes originate in the claim by one or both parties that rights have been infringed or denied; and rights logically imply norms, even though the parties may disagree as to the relevance, content, and applicability of the norms they cite. Second, it is doubtful that even marketplace haggling altogether disregards norms: for example, the notion of the going price at the time (the norm of what other people are paying), the principle of making offers in good faith, and certain standards of behavior drawn from the local culture. Third, some norms are so intrinsic to the culture that they are scarcely articulated. They are taken for granted in tacit agreement, yet they considerably affect both the process and the content of joint decision-making. Fourth, negotiators often take a stand on certain norms for ideological and symbolic reasons, but this too may sensibly affect the process, as it is probably intended to do. On the other hand, the fact that claims and complaints are made in terms of alleged rights, and therefore norms, does not necessarily mean that this is in reality the core of the dispute. It may be that a claim or rejection of a claim is merely rationalized by reference to norms, though that is not insignificant.

The whole question of the interrelationship of norms and interests and their connection with decision-making in disputes is one of great complexity and not a little confusion.[7] Consideration of this question is not helped by the sometimes dogmatic assertions about the ideology of norm usage and norm (rule) dominance in certain adjudicatory systems, as if that represented an unequivocal as well as universal empirical condition. Cross-culturally, or even within any single judicial system, it is unlikely that all adjudication operates primarily, much less solely, by the application of norms by the decision-maker. It is clear that norms may be ignored by the adjudicator for various reasons. For instance, he may not consider them

---

6. This inclusive definition is a simplistic one that ignores the several meanings that have been given to the term *norm*. It is hoped that it is adequate for present purposes. At least it allows me to avoid entanglement in jurisprudential and philosophical argument about the nature of "rules," such as Dworkin's distinction between "legal rules" and "principles" in his attacks on legal positivism (cf. Dworkin 1977).

7. It is worth noting that in political anthropology and political science there is quite similar confusion concerning the relation of norms and ideas (often as opposed to power) to political action and outcomes.

adequate for a particular case in hand, or his own interests (political, economic, ideological, or emotional) may persuade him to disregard them, or he may believe that existing norms are no longer useful in changed sociocultural conditions. Sometimes there may be no applicable norm.

An example is a dispute, over a piece of land, that came before an African subchief in the Songea District of Tanzania in 1954. Each disputant claimed the whole of the land, basing his claim on alleged facts about the original pioneer who had cleared the woodland and who therefore had established rights to it for himself and his lineal descendants. Each claimant asserted that his grandfather had been the pioneer some 60 years previously and denied the claim for his opponent's ancestor. Each backed his claim with elaborate argument and circumstantial evidence, but no firsthand witnesses were alive and there was no documentary evidence. The two claims were contradictory on vital points and the indirect evidence was inconclusive. However, the essential norm was clear to all: Unless pledge or gift of the land had occurred (and this was not claimed), its ownership went to the legitimate, patrilineal descendants of the pioneer. The subchief (the adjudicator) could not determine the facts of a very tangled case, yet he believed that he had to reach a decision. First, the piece of land was important in an area where good, cultivable land had quite recently become scarce and valuable as a result of population growth, immigration, and an increased demand for land for food and cash crops. Formerly, the subchief said, had two men become locked in such a dispute (an unlikely event), he would have declared that the land not be held or used by either party. But that was when land was still plentiful so that neither party would suffer. In the novel, modern conditions, it was considered wrong to leave good land unused. Second, the subchief not only was the local magistrate but also was administratively responsible for the maintenance of order in his area. The disputants had already failed to reach a negotiated agreement; some violence had occurred and more was threatened. Third, the subchief could not, for administrative reasons, allow the case to lie unsettled. He did not wish to risk reprimand by the supervisory officer, nor did he wish to suggest his own inability by referring the case to his superior chief (holder of a superior court), for he was jealous of his local autonomy and of his reputation. In short, the norms could not be applied in the absence of clear evidence and under new social conditions, yet a judgment in the case was thought to be essential.

The court's decision was to divide the land along a small stream that ran through it—a clear boundary but one that apportioned roughly two-thirds against one-third. The subchief stated that the prime consideration was to make a settlement and to make one that was obvious so as to preclude later argument. Each disputant was to take that portion that adjoined the land already held by him.[8] This was a novel decision in that region at that time; no such case had hitherto come to the court. The judgment was accepted by both parties, although they remained antagonistic toward each other. It was a pragmatic decision for which there was no existing norm or precedent. It is not sufficient to treat it merely as an administrative decision for it was the adjudicator's finding.[9]

Fuller (1963:32) illustrated his assertion of nonjusticiability without norms by reference to the case of the will of Mrs. Timkin of New York, who left a valuable collection of art to be divided "in equal shares" between the Metropolitan Museum and the National Gallery of Art. Because of the obvious difficulties of reaching a decision by itself, the court allowed the two museums to negotiate an agreement between them, which it then formally ratified. This was no doubt most sensible in the circumstances. Nevertheless, the court could have made a decision, and might have been compelled to, had the parties not been able to find agreement; it might even have come to a more or less similar settlement. As Fuller himself noted, "Confronted by a dire emergency or by clear constitutional direction, a court may feel itself compelled to do the best it can with this sort of problem [1963:34]." This seems to have been the situation for the United States federal judge who, in the school desegregation and busing case in Louisville, Kentucky, ruled that the percentage of black students at any school should not be more than 40 nor less than 12. Here, apparently, the judge had to invent the specific rules within the more general framework of the earlier decision of the United States Supreme Court that racial segregation in schools is unlawful.

The conclusion must be that although there is a marked tendency for adjudicators to make decisions by reference to and through the application of norms, this is not always done, nor is it always possible, even in societies where the rule of law is heavily emphasized. In many societies, for political and economic reasons, this must often be the case. On the other

---

8. In fact, this division gave the larger portion to the disputant whose kinsman was the local headman under the subchief. Whether this influenced the decision, I do not know, but it was afterward alleged to have done so by the other disputant.

9. Although legal rules were not and could not be applied in this case, neither is it really clear that here there was a resort to legal and moral principles in Dworkin's sense (1977). There may have been, but I neglected to inquire. Other possibilities are that (a) the subchief's decision was pragmatic, being that which, in his opinion, would at least be acceptable to the parties and most readily enforceable; (b) the subchief was motivated by his own interests and those of his closer associates; (c) the subchief was attempting to give a decision that would not be objectionable to the supervising officer who represented to colonial government and its alien, poorly understood ideas. It is probable that all these considerations had some bearing on the outcome.

hand, it is fairly obvious that negotiators (in comparison with adjudicators) can more easily operate where norms are nonexistent, vague, or outdated; and they can, if they so agree, sometimes ignore even quite specific norms in order to protect their common interests or to reach an outcome without delay and expense.

Related to the matter of norms is the contention that "all or nothing is a characteristic feature of the ordinary judicial method. An action is proven and sustained or not proven and dismissed [O. Schmidt 1969:63]." Similarly, the "verdict of the court has an either/or character; the decision is based upon a single, definite conception of what has actually taken place and upon a single interpretation of the legal norms [Aubert 1969:286]." This implies that adjudication operates largely in terms of black and white: This is the rule, that is not; this rule is superior to or more compelling than that one and therefore the latter is overridden; these facts are more probably correct, those are less probably, and therefore the latter are rejected; this disputant is in the right, the other is in the wrong. Conversely, it is implied, negotiators are able to, indeed almost must, take less of an either–or stance. They can compromise and take account of a spectrum of shades between extremes.

This is a distinction that can usefully be made so long as it is not pushed too far or too dogmatically. Clearly the all-or-nothing mode is typical of some kinds of adjudicatory process, particularly where the adjudicator is socially remote from the disputants. Conversely, in negotiations, even where interests are severely opposed, the negotiators are inclined to be flexible precisely because each party is dependent on the other in obtaining an outcome. This distinction, however, rests only on a tendency, which is often modified to some degree in practice. For example, judges must sometimes take account of degrees of culpability, factual correctness, and applicability of norms.[10] Undoubtedly there are many adjudicators who do not, even cannot, work with so inflexible a procedure as all or nothing. Many would consider it neither moral nor practicable, especially where some kind of reconciliation is a goal. Nor are negotiators invariably flexible and seeking compromise. For instance, given sufficient bargaining power or sufficient hard evidence of one party's offense, there can be considerable hardening to the point where the other party insists on taking everything.

---

10. In some instances this directly affects the judgment given; in other instances it appears not in the decision making for judgment but in the subsequent ordering of what shall be done thereafter. For example, a defendant may be found guilty of libel but only nominal damages are awarded to the plaintiff.

Fuller makes the point that, under a system of state-made laws, adjudicators find a strong compulsion to rule maintenance as such, irrespective of particular disputes before them. "As between black and white, gray may sometimes be an acceptable compromise, but there are circumstances in which it is essential to work hard towards keeping things black and white. Maintaining a legal system in functioning order is one of those occasions [Fuller 1971:328]." Otherwise, not only would the judicial system be jeopardized, but also there would be a danger that "no one could know precisely where he stood or how he might get where he wanted to be [p. 328]." Undoubtedly, many adjudicators are genuinely concerned with maintaining the system, sine qua non, but not all adjudicators and probably few of them all of the time. Some adjudicators have a rather fuzzy conception of "the system" in any case, and many find their security and operations grounded in more fundamental political and sociocultural conditions. Fuller's argument seems therefore to be something of a rationalization in the context of one particular judicial system, that of the United States, and perhaps it is chiefly directed to the system's higher, appellate levels. It should be clear, however, that under a pervasive system of negotiation (as in Western industrial relations or in some African societies) men appear to find no especial difficulty in knowing where they stand, what to expect, or what to do. Most probably such men have been socialized to live with a degree of uncertainty to meet this very condition, but they could be similarly socialized, and indeed often are, to accept uncertainty in social contexts governed by adjudicatory decision-making.

A rather different discrimination between negotiation and adjudication is indicated by Gluckman's suggestion that there are limits to adjudication and that these limits are imposed by the nature of the relationship between the disputants. In the conclusion to his study of adjudication in the Barotse kingdom, he wrote,

> I myself, in the text of this book, have indicated that in industrial conciliation and marriage guidance counselling were two methods of attempting to adjust relationships involving not limited, and possibly ephemeral, interests, but multiple interests, and *hence courts could not lay down decisions* to maintain the relationships in effective functioning [Gluckman 1967:396; italics added].

Although he did not follow up this line of argument, he appears to have had in mind an assumption that disputes within permanent, multiplex relationships are not (or at least not easily) susceptible to adjudication. That assumption cannot be true without considerable special qualifications and it is probably not generally valid at all. It is strange that Gluckman should have argued this way, for he amply demonstrated that Barotse judges were sometimes compelled, and were able, to deal with such disputes. For example, two of his more detailed cases—"The Biassed Father" and "The Headman's Fishdams" (1967:37–45 and 178–87, respectively)—were dominated by such relationships and their complex interests, but they were dealt with by the courts, apparently with much success. A senior judge in the latter case asserted that "we are moulding peace among you," which, commented Gluckman, "sums up the judicial task" in such cases (p. 196).

It may be that negotiation (or some other mode of treatment) could have dealt with those kinds of cases more effectively, though it is hard to see what the criteria of assessment might be. We are not told why a nonjudicatory mode was not used in those particular Barotse circumstances or if it was in other, similar ones. On the other hand, Gluckman had a point that relates to the distinctions previously discussed and to what I consider to be crucial to negotiation. In disputes within multiplex relationships, the outcome can, of course, be decided by an adjudicator who may try to ensure that careful account is taken of the complexity of the relations and issues. Yet under adjudication, the disputants, and those intimately associated with them, do not necessarily have the opportunities that are available in negotiation to work through that multiplexity and its implications, to learn about their own and each other's interests, expectations, and emotions, and to make their adjustments accordingly. Thus, negotiators with their associates can arrive at a mutually acceptable accommodation both of the immediate issues and of their ongoing relationships. This is probably more effective than an imposed outcome, however careful, tolerant, and empathetic the adjudicator might be. Yet the difference must be a matter of degree, a general tendency, rather than any absolute distinction. For example, it could be, for a number of reasons, that the negotiators are unable or unwilling to learn from their interaction and, as it were, have to be taught a lesson by a third party or have to be given an outcome of immediate problems, whether or not that gets down to underlying issues and relationships.

It should be added that it would not be correct to say that negotiation is only used, or only effective, in disputes that concern multiplex, enduring relationships. Negotiation occurs in all kinds of disputes, whatever the relationship between the disputants. That is to say, the nature of the parties' relationship, if any, and the kind of issues in dispute do not necessarily determine which mode is used on particular occasions, nor are the two modes properly distinguishable in those terms.

A related distinction is that between norm (rule) making in negotiation and norm using in adjudication. This has come from a comparison between industrial collective bargaining, on the one hand, and judges and arbitrators on the other.[11] In that context, in Western countries at least, the distinction is valid and useful. Industrial negotiators are concerned with setting up a new contractual arrangement between workers and management in a socioeconomic field where, for a number of reasons, the state has done little more than establish some broad, limiting rules. Thus the negotiated settlement creates the rights and obligations of both parties for a specific or indeterminate period. In many countries (e.g., Canada, France, the United States) the agreed terms become a legal contract enforceable by the courts.

Those industrial disputes significantly occur between parties who are locked in a persisting relationship and who are virtually bilateral monopolists. They must somehow get along together in their interdependence. Many of their disputes relate to the way they are to accomplish this in the future and therefore these disputes are naturally concluded by the effective establishment of some of the norms for their continuing association. Even where a particular dispute arises over the alleged failure by one of the parties to meet obligations (e.g., an employer has not provided certain facilities expected of him by his workers), it is likely that the major concern is to establish that such obligations be, or not be, provided in the future. In other social contexts where there is no expectation of, or desire for, future relations between the parties—they are strangers or they desire an end to their previous association—there is no intent of establishing norms; there is only the wish to settle whatever lies between them. This can be and is done by either mode of treatment.

It so happens that the majority of industrial disputes in Western countries are dealt with by negotiation (collective bargaining) and this gives the impression that it is negotiation, rather than the context of the disputants and their disputes, that requires the emphasis on norm making. In some cases, however, adjudicators (formal court or arbitrator) do sometimes have to make decisions on, say, wage rates or working conditions where not only is there no applicable norm but the adjudicator is in effect creating the norm. Therefore it is the nature of industrial relations—for instance, bilateral monopoly—which requires that special emphasis be given to norm making, rather than to norm using, and not the particular mode of dealing with disputes. Yet it is not quite so clear-cut as that. One industrial sociologist has pointed out that

> there is a difference between an action brought by a worker for wages due and a claim by his union that his rate of overtime should be raised. But between the two there is no simple chasm. There is a spectrum of delicate color. Many conflicts are carried on beneath the guise of one color when in fact the agreed prin-

---

11. See, for example, Flanders (1970:248) and Fuller (1971:308).

ciple of relevance could have led to their appearance under a slightly different hue [Wedderburn 1969:89].

Parties will, that is, seek the mode of dispute treatment that seems most advantageous in the circumstances, whether or not there are norms governing the matter at issue.

It is useful to recognize situations in social life comparable with that of industrial relations, where disputing parties are linked in persisting relationships: kinsmen, neighbors, co-members of an association or group, and the like. We may assume that here, too, negotiators and adjudicators are much concerned—though not altogether so—with the creation of norms for the continuation of the relationship.

Linked with this consideration is the suggestion that adjudicators are concerned only, or at least primarily, with the specific issues put before them but have little or no interest in the disputants' relationship as a whole or its future. Additionally, adjudication has been characterized as retrospective in that it concentrates on the past behavior of the disputants and assesses it against the prescribed standards. In contrast, it has been said that negotiation is concerned with the total relationship between the disputants, that the primary focus is on future rather than past arrangements, and that negotiators take account of the effects of any possible outcome on relations between the parties themselves and between them and other involved persons.

These distinctions must at best be a matter of relative emphasis. In some judicial systems, especially in higher appellate courts, there can be an intense focus on specifically defined issues and little concern for associated matters or for the future relationship of the disputants. Yet this is not the case for all adjudicators; it need not be so and therefore it is not an intrinsic characteristic. To a greater or lesser degree, adjudicators often do seek to discover the ramifications of a dispute within its wider relational context and they often take care, in framing a decision, to take into account the disputants' future relations as these seem likely to be affected. This is often a strong cultural and moral precept, as Gluckman showed for the Barotse:

> Throughout a court hearing [concerning permanent ties between disputants] the judges try to prevent the breaking of relationships, and to make it possible for the parties to live together amicably in the future. . . . The judges constantly have to broaden the field of their enquiries, and consider the total history of relations between the litigants, not only the narrow legal issue raised by one of them [Gluckman 1967:21].

To take account of underlying relations and their future and so to enlarge the scope of the hearing may even be a formal requirement, as in some divorce courts.

Negotiators are themselves parties in their relationship (or representatives of the parties) and therefore have an inherent concern for its future
where that is relevant—that is, where it must or can usefully be continued.
They are, the argument runs, unlikely to agree to an outcome that, though
immediately satisfactory, threatens the future of their relationship or their
relations with others. There is much truth in this, of course. Negotiators
have to live with their joint decision and its results, unlike some adjudicators. Should one party forget or ignore this, he is likely to be reminded
by his opponent. Indeed, it can be an effective stratagem to do so in order
to influence the party, making him more amenable, both because the opponent is aware of the future implications and because he may be able to
threaten to withhold future advantages from the party. Nevertheless, the
contrast with "irresponsible" adjudicators[12] can too easily be overdrawn.
There are shortsighted negotiators out for immediate advantage, there are
many who have no future relations to worry about, and sometimes the
future implications and consequences are so obscure that it becomes more
or less impossible to try to take account of them. It also may happen that
negotiators find it impossible to sort out their relationship and the more
fundamental conflicts it contains, although they can agree that some,
almost any, immediate outcome is preferable to continued disputation.

Negotiators do not ubiquitously, let alone necessarily, ignore past
behavior and past events. It is true that they can agree to ignore almost
anything, if they both wish to do so, and concentrate on what they consider to be principally important to them. For instance, the culpability of a
thief can be played down in cases where to do otherwise would prejudice
the continuation or reestablishment of a worthwhile relationship between
the parties. To forgive and forget may not only be a moral maxim but also
good tactics by the offended party who perceives it to be to his own advantage to do so. The offender can use this expediency, and be allowed to, in
order to avoid the disgreeable consequences of his past behavior. An adjudicator may not be able to forget, at least not if he is to apply norms. But
once again the empirical facts show that adjudicators sometimes can and
do forget (i.e., ignore) norms and past behavior when they consider this to
be helpful and practical in settling particular disputes. An adjudicator's
desire to promote reconciliation or to foster adequate norms for the future
does not necessarily mean neglect of the past or of the initial issues, but it
may, in his opinion, seem desirable to neglect them and therefore he does so.

Summing up, it can be said that there is no strict correlation between
negotiation and norm making or concentration on the future; nor is ad-

---

12. Compare this statement by Julius Stone: "the judge is often adjudicating conflicts of
interest . . . but without feeling responsibility for the choice which he makes [1964:229]."

judication inevitably linked with norm using or concentration on the past and on specific and narrow issues in dispute. There are only general tendencies of that kind to which there are many exceptions.

Somewhat similarly, it has been argued that

> whereas mediation [in negotiation] is directed towards *persons*, judgments of law are directed towards acts; it is acts, not people, that are declared proper or improper under the relevant provisions of the law . . . in deciding, for example, whether a man has committed a crime or broken a contract, the standards of legal judgment are derived from rules defining the consequences of specific acts or failures to act; these rules do not attempt or invite any general appraisal of the qualities or dispositions of the person [Fuller 1971:328–329].

This statement was made with specific reference to the judicial system of the United States. Even in that context there must surely be real doubts as to its universality in, for example, the lowest courts or in cases of divorce, child custody, and the like where the qualities of the disputant are quite often taken into account. Cross-culturally, however, such a distinction is not clear at all. On the one hand, norms prescribing the consequences of acts are sometimes too fuzzy for such precise application. On the other hand, and more important, adjudicators in many societies would think it most improper to ignore the qualities and dispositions of the disputants before them, thus reflecting the ethos of their culture. This must be particularly so when adjudicator and disputants are co-members of the same small-scale community, group, or class and where, therefore, the disputants' dispositions are well known and almost necessarily become an integral part of the matter.

One other suggested distinction between these two modes of dispute treatment must be mentioned here if only because I myself once proposed it and several anthropologists (e.g., Moore, Gluckman) have rejected it. Now, partially as a result of their influence, I regard it as invalid. The attempt involved the construction of polar, ideal types of process: judicial and political. In a judicial process, decision settlement is made by a judge in accordance with the established norms (rules) of the society; in negotiation, by contrast, there is a "purely political" process in which "decision is reached and a settlement is made as a result of the relative strengths of the two parties to the dispute. . . . [The] accepted norms of behavior relevant to the matter in dispute are but one element involved, and possibly an unimportant one [Gulliver 1963:298]." It has been obvious to me for some time (cf. Gulliver 1969, 1973) that this is far too simplistic a distinction. The notion of a continuum with "pure judicial" and "pure political" at the extremes merely obfuscates both concepts and reality. The pervasiveness of both norms and power in all kinds of dispute processes in all societies is too subtle and complex to be treated in this crude fashion. Negotiation certainly involves issues and contests of power, although power is itself too monolithic a concept to be analytically useful without further discrimination.[13] Equally certain, however, is that negotiation is concerned with norms (and rules, values, and morals). On the other hand, power and politics are intrinsic in all adjudicatory processes. Adjudicators, whether official and formal or not, are in some sense representatives of the group and of its political organization and ideology. They are in some degree, therefore, concerned for its maintenance and for the persistence and reinforcement, more or less, of the distribution of power and interests within it. Adjudicators also have their own interests, overtly or not, including concern for their own role within the system. Moreover, adjudicators are, sometimes at least, subject to the power of disputants and their supporters; they may be induced to acknowledge this and perhaps bend before it.

S. F. Moore (1969a) has ably demonstrated the political dimensions of adjudication in one small-scale society and, by extension, in all societies. Following her, Gluckman has asserted the essentially political character of adjudication in courts in that it relates directly to the organized state and its predominance over private concerns: "In a system with forensic institutions (i.e., with courts in a hierarchical structure), a private dispute becomes political when it comes to court, since it involves the power of the state; and the power of the state in this public arena brings in interests other than those of the immediate disputants [Gluckman 1974:35]." He went on to argue that, within corporate groups, with or without courts, disputants are subject to the interests and pressures of the group if they cannot or choose not to keep their dispute private. If they belong to different groups, then the matter is affected by relations between those groups. Gluckman was here concerned with the "transformation"[14] of a dispute when it is shifted from a private context to some public arena "where interests other than their [the disputants] own narrow and selfish interests may control the process [1974:40]." He recognized that such a transformation occurs both when an adjudicator enters the scene and when the dispute is put into some public forum of negotiations.[15] In either case the treatment of the dispute is then affected by political factors.

In summary of this brief survey, my assertion is that adjudication is essentially characterized by the fact that decision-making and the outcome

---

13. The concept of power and its contribution to the outcome of negotiations are discussed in Chapter 6.

14. This notion was borrowed from S. F. Moore (1975b:111; see also 1972:70).

15. It is argued later in this book (page 75) that a "dispute proper" does not begin until and unless a "disagreement" (Gluckman's private dispute) is put into a public domain (cf. Gulliver 1969:14).

of the issues in dispute are controlled by a third party exercising some degree of accepted authority. The disputants surrender their own ability to decide an outcome and they direct their attention, presentation, and argument primarily to that third party. In negotiation by contrast, the disputants are interdependent in the absence of authority. The outcome results from an interactional process of information exchange and learning that leads to joint decision-making by the parties themselves, so that both must accept the outcome as adequate in the perceived circumstances at the time.

To this fundamental distinction may be added contrasting syndromes, each comprising mutually reinforcing tendencies or possibilities. In adjudication, there is more likely to be concern for values and a definition of disputes in terms of values, an emphasis on the application of norms, and a concern for all-or-nothing decisions, for acts (rather than actors) and past behavior, and for less multiplex relationships. In negotiation, there is more likely to be a concern for interests and a definition of disputes in terms of interest, an emphasis on the making of norms, and a concern for the personal qualities and dispositions of disputants, for the future of their and others' rights and relationships, and for multiplex, persisting relationships. There is also the probability of greater flexibility in negotiation. These emphases are relative, suggesting what on the whole is more likely; for as I have indicated, albeit summarily, in concrete reality any of these tendencies may appear in some degree in either mode. The wide variety in sociocultural patterns and in the particular contexts of dispute and disputants precludes any firmer generalizations. Given a particular society, then clearer specification is probably obtainable.

A number of supplementary points can be briefly added in order to clarify the foregoing argument.

First, there are a number of factors that, when both options are available, encourage disputants to choose negotiation rather than adjudication. These include the relative ease and lower costs (time, money, effort, etc.) of negotiation, the wish to avoid publicity or precedent-making outcomes, the disinclination to become involved with officialdom and with what may be perceived as rapacious or biased judges, the desire for face-saving outcomes, and the antipathy of authorities toward certain kinds of issues.[16] An important factor is that disputants may be unwilling to surrender to a third party their abilities to participate in and so to affect deci-

---

16. For example, the general policy of Western governments and legislatures has been to leave industrial disputes to collective bargaining negotiations, excluding these from adjudication except where dangerous deadlock occurs (when arbitration is an option). In a number of African societies, judges were disinclined to become involved in disputes within kin groups.

sion-making. Even where a party is in a weak position, he can hope (perhaps too optimistically) to exercise some direct influence on the outcome and to salvage some advantage (cf. Macauley 1963).

Second, I have been concerned about making a deliberate contrast between adjudication and negotiation, primarily by reference to the decision-making process and at a most general cross-cultural level. Therefore, what may be significant dissimilarities within each of the two generalized modes are knowingly ignored. For instance, there are some obvious distinctions between arbitrational and judicial processes, and between relatively informal procedures where this is no written law and highly formalized procedures associated with written law and recorded, binding precedent. Similarly, there are, for example, significant differences between negotiations that are part of a series of recurrent disputes between parties in a persisting relationship, and negotiations that are, so to speak, unique encounters between otherwise more or less unconnected parties. Actual processes are, of course, inevitably shaped by particular sociocultural milieux. To make an obvious point, there is no intention to deny important variations in actual manifestations of either mode as these occur in myriad contexts. My intention has been to emphasize the primary distinction between the two modes and to link that with the associated, secondary distinctions and with differences in processes of information exchange, learning, adjustment, and interaction between the parties. My principal purpose is to establish the validity of negotiation as a specific, distinctive social process of interaction for decision making between disputants. That process is not to be subsumed under or confused with the process of adjudication.

Similarly, I do not deny that there are similarities between the two modes and between their actual manifestation in particular contexts. For instance, both may be concerned with conciliation between, or reconciliation of, the disputants, although neither is necessarily so. As already argued, both are involved with power and the political system. Guiding reference to norms and values occurs in both, often quite similarly, and may sometimes be more or less ignored in either. Cross-examination usually occurs in both as a means of eliciting the validity of facts and the significance of witness, and this can be essentially the same in either mode (Glickman 1973). However, these and other correspondences and parallels, although decidedly important, are not my concern here.

Third, the two modes are sometimes applied consecutively, or simultaneously, in the course of a single dispute so that they become equivalent to phases of a total case history. Epstein (1974:24) has questioned the validity of the analytical distinction on these grounds, with reference to Melanesian data, but his criticism misses the point. Either mode provides a means of moving toward an outcome but the particular outcome reached may be unacceptable (immediately or in retrospect) to one or both parties and therefore they turn to the other mode in the hope of obtaining something more satisfactory. Alternatively, recourse to one mode may be a strategical move by a party to persuade or coerce his opponent in their participation in the other mode. For example, a party might seek the intervention of a third-party adjudicator in order to compel his opponent to reply to his demands, to be more open in response, to eschew private threats, or in order to explore public opinion and the kind of outcome a third party might propose. Such action could strengthen the party's position or induce a recalcitrant opponent to enter or to continue negotiations. Moreover, the party might become better aware of outside interests, applicable norms, and potential outcomes. Similarly, while their dispute is before an adjudicator, the parties might agree to negotiate (with or without the knowledge of the adjudicator) so as to clarify their common situation or to modify their future presentations to him or to remove the dispute from his control and supervision. An adjudicator sometimes requires or recommends that the parties negotiate between themselves and he is prepared to consider giving his formal endorsement to whatever they agree as a result.

These kinds of strategies are quite common in all societies and their use indicates that disputants themselves in practice recognize and appreciate the different possibilities and the situational opportunities that each offers. That is, disputants perceive (and demonstrate in their actions) that the two modes involve different procedures and different kinds of interaction.

Finally, the distinction that has been made between negotiation and adjudication is empirically quite clear in the large majority of instances. For example, there is no confusion between the two for trade union leaders considering collective bargaining (negotiation) and arbitration (adjudication), or for lawyers and their clients choosing between going to court and engaging in out-of-court negotiation, or for Arusha comparing action in a moot and in a local court, or for Arab or New Guinea villagers participating in interlineage negotiation as against handing over their dispute to some respected outsider or big man. They see, rightly, essential differences of behavior, interaction, and potential results. On the other hand, as in virtually all analytical distinctions within the complex and varied phenomena of human society, there is no absolutely clear and neat dividing line in all cases. Anthropologists in particular delight in producing ethnographic instances where the line is obscure or perhaps altogether absent. Although this is quite valid procedure, usefully cautioning against over-rigid discriminations, such particular instances cannot deny the value of the more generally applicable distinction. Lord Coleridge C.J. expressed the point thus: "The Attorney General has asked where we are to draw the line. The answer is that it is not necessary to draw it at any precise point. It

23

is enough to say that the present case is on the right side of any reasonable line that could be drawn." Most instances of the treatment of dispute are clearly on one side or the other of the "reasonable line" that can most usefully be drawn for analytical purposes.[17] This is discussed further in the following section where some apparently marginal cases are briefly examined in order to see on which side of the line they fall.

MARGINAL PROCESSES: A COMPARISON OF SOME EMPIRICAL INSTANCES

The question remains, nevertheless, whether the negotiation–adjudication distinction is an either–or categorization with potentially dangerous rigidities for sociological analysis. Part of the answer to this has already been indicated in the preceding discussion; the distribution of many of the identifying characteristics is not of an either–or kind but is rather a matter of more or less and some of both. This means that the two modes share in some degree the same characteristics and that a particular instance in a given society will exhibit a particular mix. It also means that to a considerable extent the analysis of each mode is concerned with some of the same kinds of features and therefore there is a good deal to be learned from studies of varieties of one mode for the understanding of the other. Nevertheless my decisive criteria—the locus and the nature of the process of decision-making—and their implications definitely propose an either/or definition. I cannot and do not wish to escape that. There is a crucially significant difference between joint decision-making by the parties themselves (however much or little affected by a third party or by outside influence) and decision-making by a third party (however much or little that party is affected by the disputants or by outside influence). It means that the dynamics of interaction in the two processes are essentially different. But this need not gainsay certain kinds of similarities when these are present—for instance, similarities between an active mediator in negotiation and a weakly authoritative adjudicator who is intimately associated with the disputing parties.

The question may be put in another way. Are there empirical instances of the treatment of disputes in some societies that are not unambiguously either negotiation or adjudication? An approach to the answer can be made

17. Lord Coleridge's statement is quoted by Williams (1945:184) and is given in Gluckman (1967:343–344). In a different but comparable context, Heath has cautioned against the foolishness of "saying that, since nature has not seen fit to draw a line down the side of men's heads, we cannot say anything about the back of one's head or the front [1976:126]."

through an examination of some ethnographic cases. I cannot claim to be exhaustive in the following selected examples nor are they held to be "typical"; the anthropological literature is too broad and, at the same time, unfortunately, too often vague on some critical features.

First, let me take a fairly straightforward example that presents little problem but may serve as a useful reminder that the issue is neither formality against informality nor impersonal remoteness against a high degree of personal involvement by the decision-maker. The example is from the traditional East African kingdom of Bunyoro in Uganda, as described by Beattie (1957).

In Bunyoro there was a hierarchy of chiefs under the hereditary king of which the two higher ranks (county and subcounty chiefs) held official courts and clearly acted as adjudicators. The area of the lowest-ranked chief contained some half-dozen local communities or neighborhoods in which face-to-face relations dominated and which the people themselves perceived as distinct social units with fairly clear boundaries. Disputes between co-members of a local community were commonly dealt with internally by the friendly intervention of other neighbors rather than by taking them to an official court.[18] This local treatment of a dispute was "through an informal local Tribunal, a *rukurato rw'enzarwa* . . . a group of neighbours summoned ad hoc to adjudicate upon the matter in issue [Beattie 1957:190]." The composition of this tribunal was not fixed and almost any man could participate. Beattie insisted that the objectives of the tribunal were to hear and settle the dispute, to reintegrate a delinquent into the community, and, if possible, to reconcile the disputants with one another (p. 195). It is clear that members of the tribunal sought a decision that would be acceptable to the disputants and, therefore, the tribunal was attentive and sympathetic to the disputants' own suggestions. It is also clear, however, that the tribunal—typically, it seems, one or two leading members—did reach a decision and make a judgment prescribing what should be done. The tribunal had no official sanctions at its disposal and so the decision could be (and presumably sometimes was) ignored by a disputant who would, however, put himself in jeopardy with his neighbors upon whom he depended a great deal in ongoing, everyday social life. Beattie gave examples of hearings. In one, a man was found guilty of physical violence against a neighbor and was ordered to bring beer and meat for a

---

18. Although Beattie does not say so, my own experience in East Africa strongly suggests a disinclination to have recourse to an official court in order to avoid the costs, uncertainties, and authoritarian interference inherent in court proceedings and to keep disputes and their social implications within the bounds of the local community.

commensal feast; in another case the decision was that a man had falsely "spoiled the name" of another and he too had to contribute to a feast; in a third case it was decided that a divorce should occur and that bridewealth should be returned to the husband.

Most probably the proceedings of these tribunals were more informal and flexible than what the people expected and experienced in an official court of a chief under regulations prescribed by the then colonial administration. Yet certainly the tribunal adjudicated and proposed settlements. Members of a tribunal represented the local community and gained authority to act as they did through common, tacit consent that the community and participation in it were important, that quarrels should not persist, and that neighbors should live in good relations with one another. Proceedings were not of the order of mediation by co-neighbors but of adjudication where third parties (albeit neighbors and so closely associated with the disputants) came to a decision. It seems quite possible that negotiations could occur before resort to a tribunal, but it is reasonable to assume that disputants commonly preferred to obtain the active involvement of their neighbors and to surrender their own abilities to make the decision. For example, the father who accused his adult son of unfilial conduct presumably wanted the judgment of their neighbors in order to reinforce his traditional parental superiority.

The Bunyoro procedures, distinguishing between informal, local-level processes and impersonal, official-level processes, are examples of what must be quite widespread practices in centralized states. Although the differences of process are important to the understanding of patterns of adjudication, those differences are matters of degree and not of kind. Much the same can be said with reference to a comparable local-level institution in North America: the rabbinical court (*Bet Din*) operating in Jewish communities. A *Bet Din* comprises one or more rabbis who hear disputes between Jews, or sometimes between a Jew and an outsider. It is reported that rabbis allow, indeed encourage, disputants to speak freely and fully, without imposing narrow limits of relevance on their evidence and argument. Rabbis take care to consult texts of Jewish law and precedent and seek openly to apply them to the case in hand. There is emphasis on the reestablishment or reordering or relations between the parties, as against the mere assessment of rights and wrongs. That is, rabbis look to the future and are concerned with making decisions that will promote and encourage disputants to remain accepted members of the community. The rabbis themselves are members of that community; they may well have some relationship with the disputants, and at other times they are consulted for practical and religious advice and guidance by members of the community. Yet in the *Bet Din* they are adjudicators and recognized as such, however considerate they are (and that is said to vary) of the disputants' own suggestions for a settlement.[19]

Both the active members of a Bunyoro local tribunal and the Jewish rabbis make decisions that are authoritative. Both are able to do this, and are expected to do so, because they are recognized as the representatives of the community—although a rabbi has the additional qualities of being learned in Jewish law and of having spiritual leadership. In both cases the authority of the decision-makers is otherwise poorly sanctioned. Disputants can, therefore, ignore a decision and institute a suit in the available civil courts. Yet there is, apparently, a low rate of "failure." The decision is, as it were, that of the community itself, judging the issues and wishing to continue to embrace the disputants thereafter. The disputants themselves recognize and accept this. A similar conclusion can be drawn from processes of dispute treatment within Chinese-American communities (Doo 1973) and within other such groups that seek to preserve their autonomy from the enveloping, larger society.

A somewhat comparable but, on the face of it, less clear example of marginality comes from the Tolai of New Britain, a Melanesian people, as described by Epstein (1971). There, each village has a Councillor who, with a "committee" (presumably of leading villagers) regularly meets in open assembly with those villagers who care to attend in order to deal with matters relating to "the government of the village." Having attended to those, the assembly turns to the "hearing" of intravillage disputes. On other occasions, however, the Councillor may summon an assembly by blowing the conch shell: "In this way he proclaims the jurisdiction of the moot [1971:167]."[20] The task of the Councillor and committee (*tena varkurai*) is to maintain conditions for orderly debate and freedom of argument by the disputants and by anyone else who wishes to express opinion. The *tena varkurai* may intervene during the presentation of evidence and argument "but the questioning does not amount to an interrogation or cross-examination," and it is intended "to elicit further information . . . rather than to probe what has already been said [p. 167]."

It is significant that, in the illustrative case given by Epstein, the Councillor sat in a chair with his committee next to him while the complainant sat on a mat before him. This is a typical way of distinguishing the ad-

---

19. On rabbinical courts, see *Columbia Journal of Law and Social Problems* (1970), Kirsh (1971), and Starkman (1975).

20. It is unfortunate that Epstein should use the term *moot* in this connection after it had earlier been used by anthropologists (e.g., Bohannan 1957; Gulliver 1963) specifically to exclude notions of a court and adjudication.

judicator and symbolizing his superiority. Information is presented directly to the *tena varkurai*, rather than to the opponent or to the assembly in general.[21]

Epstein gave an account of a case in which a woman complained of the failure of her mother-in-law to look after the grandchildren. Her presentation to the *tena varkurai* soon developed a number of other complaints about the behavior of her mother-in-law, which were set in contrast with her own allegedly model behavior as a daughter-in-law. Supported by an elderly, matrilineal kinsman, she raised the issue of a canoe belonging to her mother-in-law that had been frequently used by the latter's son (husband of the complainant). The Councillor asked the defendant to explain this. As a result it became clear that the old woman resented its use but that in order to regain full control over it she would have to leave his house. The case became transformed into one between mother and son, the latter demanding that she move from his house, where she had been living. In response to questioning by the Councillor, both mother and son agreed that she should leave. The committee, however, said that it wanted "to make peace between you and not have you living apart." At this point a leading elder of the village and brother of the defendant angrily denounced her eviction and the unfilial contempt it showed. A member of the committee, son of the defendant's sister and matrilateral cousin of her son, then intervened and suggested the impropriety of the mother's eviction and spoke of a son's obligation to care for his mother. The son remained silent and the same committee member went on to propose that the mother remain in her son's house, that the canoe was relatively unimportant, and that henceforth the defendant should care properly for her grandchildren. The Councillor endorsed these proposals and, in reply to his specific question, obtained the son's agreement. "Very well, let the case finish now," said the Councillor, and so it did.

Epstein, in his analysis of this case, clearly found the process "a mode of adjudication" but also "a settlement by consensus [1971:168]" with the aim of creating conciliation between the disputants as well as settling their dispute. Furthermore, "settlement can only be reached when the parties are persuaded that their behavior was in conformity with the norms to which they themselves subscribe [p. 169]." It should be noted that the parties seemed unable, or at least unwilling, to settle their dispute by themselves and that they sought others to do it for them. Eventually, after con-

---

21. A contrast can be made with negotiations in Arusha parish assemblies. Although there is a "chairman" to keep order, the disputants do not address him but direct their arguments to each other or, where public opinion is sought, to the assembly in general (Gulliver 1963:223).

siderable airing of grievances and opinions, the Councillor and his committee proposed a specific decision, showed that it conformed to accepted norms, and pronounced it as the outcome. That the *tena varkurai* worked for an outcome that was agreeable to the disputants, though certainly not unimportant in the context, seems to have been a secondary matter. Indeed, there appears to have been some assumption by the people that a settlement in accordance with the norms should be acceptable to the disputants.

Another ethnographic example is the mode of treatment of interpersonal disputes in the Mexican village of Ralu'a where a judge (*presidente*) sits in the official municipal court (Nader 1969b). It seems clear that the process was adjudicatory, yet there are close parallels with the processes described in the preceding instances. The *presidente*, in reaching his judgments, not only took careful account of the disputants' opinions but sought to be guided by what was acceptable to the disputants and allowed them to come to agreement, if possible, concerning the terms of the settlement.

In one case, a woman laid a complaint before the *presidente*. She alleged that her small son had been beaten and injured by a young man while she and the boy had been working in the field of that man's grandmother. On being summoned to the court, the defendant denied the allegation and counterclaimed that the boy was a mischief maker who had called him "miserable names; he said very ugly things." In reply to the *presidente's* questioning, the plaintiff said that she and her son worked in that field at the request of the defendant's grandmother, not the defendant himself. The *presidente* asked the plaintiff how much she wanted from the defendant to pay the costs of her son's treatment. She demanded 30 pesos. The defendant rejected that and offered 20 pesos. The *presidente* asked the plaintiff if she would accept that amount. She did and thus the case ended.

The *presidente* was the focus of proceedings and of the plaintiff's complaint. She sought a decision from him in her favor. He acted with authority in summoning the defendant and seems to have controlled the hearing. He did not overtly make a judgment of the guilt of the defendant, although such is clearly implied in his action when he asked the plaintiff what payment she wanted. The defendant did not contest that implication but, following the *presidente's* lead, also turned to the matter of the size of compensation. Yet it appears that the *presidente* wished to reach a result agreeable to both parties, quite like Nyoro and Tolai adjudicators. To this end he encouraged the disputants themselves to propose offer and counteroffer so as to reach an agreed outcome, which he approved. Thus the *presidente* administered the proceedings, exercised authority, and made a judgment, but he merely endorsed the parties' agreement on the amount to be paid. From the rest of Nader's account, it seems clear that the *presidente* could have followed up his judgment by determining the size of compensation and he might well have done so had the disputants themselves been unable to agree. In that context of a small village, characterized by multiplex, face-to-face relations, he preferred that the disputants discover agreement. Nader's other cases exhibit more obvious judgments. In her Case 1, the *presidente* decided that a driver was responsible for damages caused by his truck, saying, "It will be most convenient in this case if the chauffeur paid for the damage [1969b:75]." In Case 3, the *presidente* "pronounced" his decision in a marital dispute: that the couple should come together, forget the past, and take joint concern for their sick child. In Case 4, the *presidente* "dictated . . . [that] the lost coffee should be restored to the plaintiff [p. 79–80]."

Finally, a contrasting instance is taken from the Ifugao people of the Philippines, as reported by Barton (1930). Here there were neither courts nor neighborhood tribunals. Disputing parties sought to settle matters strictly between themselves. Argument and offers were not conducted in a face-to-face manner but through a go-between (*monkalun*), a man of acknowledged presitige who carried messages, adding his own interpretations and advice, and who met with each party separately in their own houses.

Barton described a case in which a man demanded the payment of a debt of pigs from another man. Ample notice was given of the requirement since the plaintiff needed the pigs for use in connection with his son's impending marriage. The two men disagreed as to the number of pigs resultant on the natural rate of increase of the two pigs originally loaned. The plaintiff asked for five; the defendant offered four and raised a counterdebt of a chicken (and its expected progeny), a debt left over from their grandfathers' time that, it was claimed, reduced the present debt to three pigs. In a later direct confrontation, the defendant severely insulted the plaintiff by a reference to malpractice by the plaintiff's ancestor, a great-grandfather.

The plaintiff now initiated a formal dispute by sending his demands with a prestigious go-between to the defendant's house. There the go-between emphasized the enormity of the insult and made a demand for payment of 11 pigs. After much discussion with the go-between, the defendant's brother offered 4 pigs, which were to be repayment of the original debt only. During the next few days each disputant sought the support of his own kinsfolk. Then the go-between met with the plaintiff and his kin. He emphasized the earlier, unpaid debt of the chicken and its progeny, condemned a proposal to seize a valuable gong from the defendant in lieu of payment, spoke of possible violence by the defendant's party, and pictured the defendant as a poverty-stricken youth who would find it hard to pay 5 pigs. Finally he talked of the need for harmony in the community and the need for unity against its threatening neighbors. What the plaintiff and his supporters replied to all this is not reported by Barton, but the go-between left with an offer to accept 4 pigs for the debt, 1 pig for the insult, and 1 pig for the go-between's fee, plus cancelation of the debt of the chicken. This was an "ultimate" offer on their part.

Meeting next with the defendant and his kin, the go-between told of the large number and unified determination of the plaintiff's party explained their offer, and advised its acceptance. After discussion, the counteroffer was four pigs, plus one for the go-between and annulment of the charge of insult. The go-between departed, saying that the offer was inadequate and promising to return when the party had reconsidered the matter.

Next day, the plaintiff's son came and took the gong (of considerable ancestral value and especially prized by the defendant's mother), leaving deliberate proof of his identity. The go-between returned to the defendant's home, declaring his anger at the seizure but demanding that the dispute be settled forthwith so as to avert further trouble. The defendant's brother demanded four pigs in compensation, but the mother declared that they should pay the debt and regain the gong. Her proposal seems to have been accepted by the defendant's party. The go-between immediately visited the plaintiff, saying that the latter must return the gong and pay four pigs indemnity. After further discussion, the go-between proposed the return of the gong in return for five pigs from the defendant—three for the plaintiff and two for the go-between. The plaintiff agreed to this after some argument and the go-between took the gong to his own house. He sent a message to the defendant saying that the gong would be returned on receipt of five pigs. The defendant's party considered this propsal, agreed to it, and completed the transaction straightaway. The go-between passed on three of the pigs to the plaintiff.

Here there was clearly a bargaining process, the exchange of offer and counteroffer to the point of reaching joint agreement. The influence of the go-between was considerable in the framing of the offers and in their interpretation to the other party. Only the last offer (by the defendant) was precisely the same as his own suggestion (which included his own increased fee!). The go-between could not judge the issues involved and in fact he told different stories to each party. Nor could he order what the outcome should be. He could only propose terms. He expressed his views of the parties' behavior with reference to applicable cultural rules and to his estimates of the parties' strengths. Finally he gave a kind of ultimatum to the defendant. This was not an order so much as a proposal that was calculated to succeed because of the weakness of the defendant after the loss of the gong.

According to Barton, a go-between could fail altogether to bring the two parties into an agreed decision, in which event he withdrew from the case as he declared a temporary truce. Later another go-between would be invited to start fresh negotiations.

Other similar marginal instances could be taken from the borderline area between negotiation and adjudication but mere number would not necessarily offer improved understanding of the conceptual issues. Therefore I summarize and attempt to generalize from these few instances.

Indubitably, the Bunyoro local tribunals were engaged in adjudication. Decisions, judgments, and ordered outcomes were given by third parties and not by the disputants themselves. Mutatis mutandis, the same is true of the Jewish rabbinical courts and of the Mexican village court. It is important to note that in these instances the adjudicators sought, with some flexibility, to gain the agreement of the disputants and to promote their reconciliation and their reintegration in the community, but this does not alter the fact that adjudication occurred. I note also that these adjudicators claimed that they applied the accepted normative rules to the cases before them.

As Van Velsen has argued, "judgment by decree" and "judgment by agreement" are not mutually exclusive. He observed that the former refers to the "decision as to the relevant facts and the appropriate legal rules to be applied" in order to reach a verdict, whereas the latter refers to "the decision as to the appropriate sanction" and so to the award or sentence (Van Velsen 1967:144). In the instances described, the adjudicators issued the verdict, overtly or tacitly. Regarding the award or sentence, they were prepared to accede to the joint decision of the disputants if that could be obtained, although otherwise they made the decision themselves following the interests of the disputants and of the community as they saw them. In either event, however, the adjudicator issued the decision and completed the process comprising the two kinds of judgment.

With Tolai we approach the limits of the adjudicatory process, for there the adjudicators were particularly susceptible to the disputants' opinions and particularly concerned, perhaps, to promote outcomes acceptable to the disputants—but also outcomes that were acceptable to the community at large. It may be cheese-paring to try to distinguish the operation of the councillor and his committee from that of a forceful mediator of the type that later in this book I describe as a "leader" (page 225). Yet there was third-party decision-making, with the endeavor to accord with normative rules. The disputants themselves sought the decision of the committee as a way of settling an intolerable situation that, apparently, they could not deal with alone, and they were prepared to accede to the decision. That is, they placed themselves in a subordinate position before the committee, although (like most disputants) they sought to influence it in their own favor.

There remains an important contrast with the decision-making process among the Ifugao. There the disputants retained the ability to define the issues, reach a verdict, make offers, and reject or accept the offers. They were affected by the influence, persuasion, and pressures of the go-between acting as facilitating mediator. Although the go-between backed his varied suggestions by reference to allegedly accepted norms, he shifted his emphasis and reference according to his audience and the desired responses he sought. Both in the particular case and from Barton's other accounts, it seems clear that for the Ifugao people there was no question that a go-between himself should, or in fact did, make the decision (Barton 1919, 1930; see also Hoebel 1954:114 ff.). The disputants retained that ability, in practice as in normative expectation, so that the outcome came from their interdependent decisions.

In this section I have deliberately described a few marginal cases in the light of the analytical distinction between negotiation and adjudication. Let me be clear: Purely within the context of an ethnographic analysis of these particular cases it may not much matter what we call the processes of the treatment of disputes. It might be sufficient to understand them as well as possible and to discover their significance in the ongoing life of the local community and the wider society. Nevertheless, both observation and analysis might be improved by a keener appreciation of the distinction between third-party judgments and the disputants' interdependent decision-making, and by a more perceptive regard for the locus and dynamics of decision making.[22] My primary concern here, however, is to make cross-cultural, sociological comparison in the search for sharper conceptual tools as a preliminary to the detailed examination of the process of negotiation. I think that it has been shown that in these marginal instances the distinction is both valid and usefully suggestive. If this is so in these instances, then it is even more so in other instances where the contrast is more marked—say, between formal, largely impersonal courts and their judges, on the one hand, and collective bargaining or unmediated negotiations among the Arusha, on the other hand.

There is one other advantage to be gained from the examination of these marginal instances. Although the sociological dichotomy holds good with reference to the key criterion of decision-making, the distinction is

---

22. For example, it would be possible to avoid the conceptual error of defining negotiation as the promotion of conciliation (which may also be a purpose of adjudication and is sometimes not a goal of negotiation) and by reference to an award given by a third party. Such was the definition given by Allott et al. (1969:31; cf. Gulliver 1978:33).

shown to be less draconic for other characteristics of the two kinds of process, such as the concern of decision-makers for the future relations of the disputants and others, flexibility of procedures, the search for reconciliation, and the application of norms. Because one makes a decisive distinction in terms of a critical variable—as I emphatically do—there is good reason not to overlook similarities in other variables and the ranges of variation.

2

THE STUDY OF JOINT DECISION-MAKING

The central topic of the previous chapter was that negotiations comprise processes of interaction between conflicting parties, leading to and including joint or interdependent decision-making on the issues between them. The conflict or dispute between the parties occurs within a range from pure competitiveness (where interests in the outcome are, or seem to be, diametrically opposed) to pure cooperation (where the parties are prepared to seek an outcome in their common interest). Usually there is some picture of competitiveness and cooperation.

Before presenting my own accounts and explanations of these processes of interaction and my examination of joint decision-making, it is useful to clear some ground in preparation. Scholarly concern for these processes is well established and substantial work of a variety of kinds has been produced. In particular, game theorists, certain economists, and some other social scientists have sought to deal with joint decision-making through deductive, logicostructural argument and conceptualization. It is to the work of these scholars and I turn first because of its highly abstract character and especially because of its very considerable influence on almost all writers who have been concerned with negotiations, conflict resolution, and decision making.

It is not my intention to attempt any comprehensive review of what has since the 1940s become a complex field of intellectual activity. Nor do I endeavor (which would probably be futile) to produce something like a distillation of the results of this work. Rather, I intend to extract some of the more important concepts and guidelines, and also hazards and unresolved problems, which seem valuable and stimulating to my own alternative approach in the present study.

Second, I consider some of the problems of multiple criteria (multiple issues and their multiple attributes) that are intrinsic to negotiations and decision making but have been largely and strangely neglected by theorists. It is not possible to examine processes of real-life negotiations without regard for these problems because negotiators themselves continually have to take account of them.

Finally, with these lessons and clarifications in mind, I discuss the general approach to the study of negotiations and joint decision-making that informs and orients my own analyses and explanations. This is a historico-ethnographic approach, the basis of which is the use of and reference to empirical data from actual cases of negotiations in the real world.

ABSTRACT SIMPLIFICATION: GAMES AND BARGAINING MODELS

The abstract, deductive study of joint decision-making has been described by Oran Young (1975) as comprising three more or less distinct approaches. First, there is that of the game theorists. This is the most abstract and is characterized by tight, logical closure of hypothetical situations of decision making. The models used are essentially static ones in which it is assumed that "each player decides *in advance*, before the game actually starts, what move he will make *in any possible situation* that may arise. A full description is called a *strategy* [Harsanyi 1977:94; italics in original]." In pure game theory the players are merely notational, for it is the theorist who attempts to deduce what, in given circumstances, the strategy of a player should be, taking account of the fact that an outcome is the result of the interdependent strategies and choices of two or more players. Consequently there is an endeavor (not always realizable) to indicate determinate solutions, or predictions, in respect to the issues between the parties. The concern is not with particular problems that occur in the real world, but with highly generalized situations.[1]

---

1. The somewhat endearing convention of attaching real-life lables (e.g., *prisoners' dilemma, chicken, trucking*) to particular games does nothing to introduce real-life conditions and complexities into the considerations of game theorists.

Second, according to Young, there is the approach of economists, principally in bargaining theory under conditions of bilateral monopoly. Here there is reference to real-life problems, such as the determination of wage rates in industrial negotiations or of prices between isolated buyer and seller. The substantive contribution of such reference is in effect, however, insubstantial because argument and analysis remain hypothetical, abstract, and deductive. Bargaining theorists, in contrast with game theorists, seek to develop dynamic models of process, involving offers and counteroffers and interdependent concession-making. Thus there is no concern for the discovery of once-and-for-all strategies but rather an intention to examine how the bargainers (the players) should interact in terms of their expectations of each other. To a greater extent than in game theory, the bargaining theorists are concerned with attempts to produce hypotheses relating to determinate solutions of conflict.

Third, there is the approach of some social scientists who are critical of some of the deliberately limiting assumptions of game and bargaining-theory models. They have sought to emphasize the importance of players' expectations of one another and their manipulation of opponents' perceptions of possible outcomes and assessment of costs and risks, and even of basic objectives. Consequently, much attention is given to the nature of changing expectations and players' tactics and to the significance of uncertainties of information, perception, and evaluation—all matters that tend to be ignored by game theorists. All this involves a closer approximation to the real world, although a great deal of the argument is still concerned with suppositional circumstances and quite limited ranges of variables. Moreover, exposition tends to be in terms of models of game-theory type.[2]

These three approaches are not absolutely distinct, for they shade into one another. Certainly bargaining theory and manipulative theory have borrowed considerably from game theory and all tend to use some similar concepts and notations. In the present section the concentration is on game and bargaining theory, and for expositional simplicity some of the important distinctions between them are blurred or ignored.[3]

One way or another, most game theorists and virtually all bargaining theorists have been concerned with discovering determinate solutions to problems of conflict between interdependent parties. Some games will not yield such a solution—for example, "prisoners' dilemma" on single plays—and some theorists have chosen to concentrate on the conditions of

---

2. See, for example, the work of Schelling (1960); see also Young (1975:303 ff.).

3. Insights gained and ideas borrowed from manipulative models, as from the work of social psychologists, are used more pervasively in the presentation of my own theoritical models and are, therefore, dealt with as relevant in later chapters.

strategy formation. Nevertheless, it is in general not unfair to say that the ultimate aim of theory has been to devise logically correct solutions. In attempting this there has been a most sophisticated exercise in simplification and abstract argument in which variables are severely limited in number; other variables are ignored, held constant, or carefully controlled. The viewpoint is not that of the hypothetical players so much as that of a disengaged observer examining what is possible and optimal.

Earlier economic theorists, starting with Edgeworth (1881), regarded price or wage rate as being necessarily indeterminate under bargaining conditions. But, following the work of Zeuthen (1930) and Hicks (1932), this view has come to be rejected. To a noneconomist it appears to be almost an act of faith that the result of bargaining must be determinate, at least theoretically. There has been a succession of proposed solutions, although as yet none seems to have become generally accepted. Indeed, to the contrary, each theorist tends to be quite critical of previous proposals, though building on them to some extent, and it remains difficult if not downright impossible for the outsider to choose among them. I have in mind the solutions of such theorists as Nash (1950), Pen (1952), Bishop (1964), Coddington (1968), Cross (1969), Stahl (1972), and Harsanyi (1977).[4]

In any case, despite increasing sophistication, including attempts to introduce factors of uncertainty and to take account of larger numbers of variables, none of these theoretical solutions provides a result in any exact, predictable form that can be referred to negotiations and interparty problem-solving in the real world. Some theorists have claimed that their solutions are applicable to real-life situations and to bargaining of a "noneconomic" kind, for instance in political affairs. None has, to my knowledge, been successful in demonstrating this claim by applying a theoretical model to concrete, empirical data, predictively or retrodictively. Some theorists disclaim any such intention, including most game theorists.

In the years following the publication in 1944 of *Theory of Games and Economic Behavior* by von Neumann and Morgenstern, there were lively anticipations that game theory would begin to provide a scientific framework that would allow the prediction of outcomes as well as the explanation of bargainers' behavior and decisions in real-life economic and political situations. It was hoped that the developing theory would even permit practical application by prescribing proper strategy or at least advising negotiators what best to do. Few if any people have seriously continued so to hope and certainly most game theorists themselves have disclaimed

---

4. Useful reviews of these and other theorists' work can be found in Stahl (1972:231 ff.) and Bartos (1974:75 ff. and 196 ff.).

such pretensions. The continued endeavor therefore has been to clarify conceptual problems, specifically and deliberately divorced from reality, in order to understand more about some of the variables and their interconnections. This has meant a strict, logicostructural analysis of a limited number of variables that are assumed to be unambiguously determinable. This would seem to be about the best that can be done in the painfully but ineluctably slow process of seeking to develop theoretical generalization in the social sciences. Game theory is but one use—a most elaborate one mathematically—of models or abstract constructions of human behavior and interaction.

Only 10 years after the appearance of that seminal work by von Neumann and Morgenstern, two prominent scholars in this field could write that in

the present state of game-theory analysis, we are indeed sceptical that many such problems [of real life] can be given a realistic formal analysis; rather we would contend that a case can be made for studying simplified models which are suggested by and related to the problems of interest. The hope is that, by analogy, their analysis will shed light—however dim and unreliable—on the strategic and communication aspects of the real problem [Luce and Raiffa 1957:115].

This statement probably continues to represent the majority view. There is little reason yet to entertain greater, or lesser, expectations. As Bartos has put it,

although we found that some predictions were remarkably accurate [at the experimental level], their practical value was relatively small: in order to make those predictions, we had to have information one does not usually have . . . [and] it turns out that to make such predictions possible, we must simplify our conceptions of the process [of negotiations] even more than we have done so far [Bartos 1974:273].

In contrast, however, Harsanyi (1977) deliberately based his whole conceptual theory and analysis on the notion that a determinate solution in game thoery is both essential and possible. Moreover, he went further by asserting that, with his own solutions as part of a general theory, there can be nontrivial application to the social sciences and related disciplines in their study of human behavior (p. 3 ff.). With all due respect, it is difficult to agree. There does not appear to by any convincing formulation—his or any other—that offers reliable explanation or prediction, even at a probabilistic level, of the outcome of negotiations and joint decision-making in the real world. Harsanyi himself did not attempt to demonstrate his assertion by the application of his prediction theory to empirical data. He contented himself with the declaration that "once the required factual assumptions have been made . . . one obtains unique predictions for *all* specific economic, political, and other social situations on the basis of the *same* general theory [p. 5; italics in original]." He did not tell us how to make "the required factual assumptions" and therefore how to translate his general theory to the analysis of empirical conditions.[5] If determinate solutions are to be acceptable, other than as abstract, logical formulae they must ultimately by applicable to and tested against real-life data.

Typically, the theorists' solutions are embodied in mathematical formulae. That is, they are highly abstract. This raises two general problems in regard to their potential validity and applicability, which it is instructive to consider. One is the inevitable inclusion of abstractly defined components and determinant variables; the other is the nature of the simplifying assumptions that are incorporated.

On the first of these problems, Pen, for example, was careful to disclaim the notion that his theoritical solution could provide "the result of the bargaining in an exact, predictable way. . . . The formulas are exact indeed, but prediction is not [Pen 1952:39]." He gave two reasons for this that are, mutatis mutandis, also pertinent to other solutions of a game-theoretical type. First, his formulae present a static representation of what is essentially a dynamic process in which components and their interrelations are intrinsically subject to change, thus affecting their contribution to and the nature of the outcome. Although some theorists have attempted to take account of dynamics, especially in bargaining rather than game thoery, none appears to have done so successfully. So far, the full flexibility and variability, especially of subjective assessments by the parties, seems to have proved too complex to be wholly comprehended. Theorists have needed to resort to the device of holding some variables constant as a way out of this dilemma.

The second reason given by Pen is that his formulas include components that are clearly not measureable nor ascertainable even in broadly acceptable approximations.[6] Thus Pen included such opaque concepts as "ophelimity" (a bargainer's satisfaction from the attainment of a certain outcome), "propensity to fight" (the maximal risk of conflict that a bargainer will accept), and "correspection function" (the relation between one party's "factual net contract ophelimity" and the other party's estimate of the risk of conflict). Similarly, for example, both Foldes (1964) and

---

5. This comment does not purport to assess the general theory of his book in which he confines himself to game-theoretical situations of a specifically limited kind.

6. Problems of calculating and giving numerical values to a person's subjective satisfactions, utilities, and the like are examined later. See page 90.

2. The rules of play are known and fixed.

3. There is perfect knowledge by each player in many or even all matters, such as the complete range and commensurable sizes of all possible outcomes, the preferences of each player, the probabilities attached to choices and outcomes.

4. There is no interference from the outside world.

5. There is no (or very little) opportunity for players to use tactics (quite typical of actual negotiations) such as bluff, coercion, persuasion, rationalization, and misrepresentation.

6. There is little or no scope for a player to develop and adjust perceptions, expectations, and preferences, or to manipulate those of his opponent.

The precise assumptions in a particular case depend, of course, on the nature of the game or the bargaining scenario. In fact, it is the specifics of the assumptions, together with the specification of the rules, that actually create the game or scenario.[8]

Central to the construction of almost all game-type models is the assumption of rational behavior by the players, defined in terms of maximization of expected outcome. That the general notion of rationality in human behavior is highly complex is clear from the lengthy controversies and discussions that have occurred among philosophers, logicians, game theorists, and social scientists. Any attempt at a thorough reexamination of the concept and its manifold implications would necessarily take us far beyond immediate requirements. Rather, I am content to make a few observations in order to suggest that the convenience and optimism of an oversimplification of "rational" does not and cannot adequately deal with, or dispose of, the problems relating to actual negotiations and negotiators. An agnostic approach seems preferable, although that is, as always, unsatisfactory to those who dislike doubt and loose ends and instead seek to develop a tidy, consistent, theoretical framework.

It is quite valid, no doubt, to say that a negotiator, like people in general, endeavors to obtain an outcome that is, in his opinion, most satisfactory to him. At least he chooses an outcome that is no less satisfactory than any perceived alternative possibility, taking into account his interests, values, and concern for self and others. To say that, however, is to say very little at all. It is a tautological truism. Such universalistic behavior can, if one so wishes, be called "rational." The problem is that this axiomatic truth becomes transformed into an equation between "rational" and

---

8. A complex but clearly specified example is Stahl's game model for labor–management bargaining. He lists 20 assumptions that lead to a bargaining game characterized by 14 other assumptions (Stahl 1972:202).

Bishop (1964) included a "maximum delay time": the longest period a bargainer will wait in order to obtain a certain outcome rather than accept an available alternative immediately. This is a component to be calculated *before* bargaining begins; it is not a retrospective evaluation on the facts as they have turned out. Cross (1969) used as a critical component the rate at which a party expects his opponent to make concessions. Coddington had, inter alia, "a pair of 'learning rates' . . . which express how sensitively each bargainer revises his expectations in response to the discovery of errors in them [1972:51]."

With these and similar concepts, and the models in which they are included, a severe problem is how such immeasurable components of interactional behavior can be used to obtain, or at least to understand, a more or less determinate, measurable outcome. More important, despite the apparent plausibility of such models, in the face of the differing emphases (and absence of emphasis) given to them by various theorists, do those variables really affect and even determine the outcome? Are they more or less consciously perceived and taken account of by negotiators, or are they part of the structural context of which the participants are unaware? How do we know? How can we know? And how can we be persuaded of the validity of the proffered answers? Such questions and the implied critique are often met by the assertion that these formulations relate only to inquiry and explanation of a conceptual kind. They do not pretend to explain particular empirical circumstances and results; they are useful insofar as they are fruitful of better understanding and illumination of the important variables. Thus, it is contended, such conceptualization should be treated only in terms of abstract deduction.

This kind of answer and defense is certainly not without merit, for we do need to speculate on and pursue the logical consequences of suppositional premises and concepts. Thus, there is much value to be gained from these abstract procedures. Granting that and recognizing the stimulus that is to be obtained, nevertheless the question persists: How can we know? To put it another way: What are the sources of these conceptualizations and are they valid? The sources may be in the fertile imaginations of the theorists, but even the most abstract conceptualizer relates somewhere to his experience of reality, his assumptions of what it is and what its critical features are. For instance, those who assert that some notion of risk taking is influential on outcome must surely have been persuaded, by egoistic or wider experience, of its importance even though that is not explained in exposition. After all, why risk and not something else? Why does one theorist give priority to risk taking whereas another emphasizes the expected rate of the opponent's concessions? If we are to contemplate whether or not to attribute some degree of importance to such components, we must apply not only logical reasoning but, consciously or not, some reference to our experience of reality.

To say that is not to ignore the immense difficulties of discovering what empirical reality is. The perceptions of participants and observers obviously give different realities, or rather different aspects of some possibly, or ideally, ultimate reality. But, accepting the gross imperfections of our perceptions of the real world, it remains inevitable that sooner or later the abstract conceptualizations and the explanations they offer must be brought to and set against some of the events and processes of that world.

Game theorists quite explicitly eschew any such responsibility, leaving it to others to undertake this task if they will. As Rapoport has written, "The mathematical model [of game theorists] is a set of assumptions. We know that every one of these assumptions is false. Nevertheless we make them, for our purpose at this point is not to make true assertions about human behavior but to investigate consequences of assumptions, as in any simulation or experimental game [1964:147]." On the other hand, there are possible bridges between such abstraction and the facts of the real world, between the pure theorist and the scholar who desires to understand actual human behavior. Rapoport has written, quite without irony, that "the chief value of game-theoretical analysis is that it points to questions beyond its scope [1970:41]"[7] Another reviewer of the achievements of game theory came to a similar conclusion:

> It is my contention that a knowledge of the theory of games provides a useful bench mark and a fundamentally important methodological approach to the study of situations involving potential conflict. The insistence of the game theorist on having a completely specified game to study, i.e., a rigid rule game, provides a device for the behavioral scientist to classify and analyse his own models of men, so that in contrasting his models with the frequently unsatisfactory but well defined models of the game theorist, he can isolate key factors with facility [Shubik 1975:157].

Bargaining theorists sometimes take a similar position. Nevertheless these theorists are dealing with phenomena and variables of interaction that do have empirical reference to what people do or seek to do. They are not dealing with symbolic, theological argument about something that by definition can never be experienced—such as angels dancing on the head of a pin. Yet so many of their proposed concepts are extemely difficult, if not impossible, to evaluate, to refer to reality and therefore to rely on and use for the understanding of people's actions. This can be exasperating and

---

7. One reason for Rapoport's own interest in game theory is evidently the hope that it will indicate ways of understanding and dealing with international conflict and warfare.

frustrating. The various theoretical formulations do contain an array factors and their interconnections that negotiators experience. Negotiato do indeed take some account, however vaguely and inconsistently, of ris the cost of delays in reaching agreement, the possible future actions of opponent as indicated by his past behavior, and so on. At the very lea such components of negotiations can and must be taken into account du ing the examination of real-life situations and behavior. Even though I a unpersuaded of the precise validity of any or all of these theoretical forn ulations, there is inducement to perceive and to consider possibilities an notions that might otherwise be ignored. Although that is, no doubt, fa less than any theorist desires for his own conceptualization, it comprises most genuine and valuable contribution. The stimulus and insights gaine from purely theoretical proposals permeate the analytical exposition of thi book, whether or not they are specifically acknowledged. To take a single important example: My own emphasis on information exchange and learning in negotiations owes much to the work of Coddington and Cross, among others. These crucial features of their models appear to be highly pertinent to my experience of the real world. I do not attempt to prove that those factors are dominant, though I believe they are, because there seems to be no satisfactory way to do so. But their use is fruitful in trying to make sense of what happens in practice; they give form and pattern to interactional processes and they help to clarify many concomitant features of recorded cases of negotiation.

I turn now to the second major problem associated with the theoretical formulation of negotiation processes. In real-life circumstances, the dynamic complexity of the apparent component variables is enormous—forbiddingly so. Yet procedures of abstract simplification, by reducing and controlling many of these variables, inevitably alter the very conditions and processes we seek to understand. Again, there is a wide gap between actual circumstances and the artificial conditions of conceptual inquiry. But again, also, there is the opportunity to gain valuable insights that might otherwise be missed. In this case, the inducement is to reexamine the assumptions and prescribed limitations made by game and bargaining theorists. In so doing, it is possible to come to an improved understanding of some of the components of actual negotiations when, in real-life conditions, those limitations do not obtain and the assumptions cannot be made.

The principal assumptions and limitations are examined next. In brief, and generalizing quite broadly, they are as follows:

1. The players think and behave rationally, with complete skill and competence (personal and social characteristics being ignored) to calculate the best possible or maximal outcome.

"maximization," where what is maximized is quantifiable (or can be treated as if it were).

For instance, Bartos has written,

> Defined in the simplest terms, rationality refers to maximization of payoffs: a negotiator is rational if he prefers high payoff to low payoff. . . . [This makes] good sense substantively, by corresponding to the concept of motivation. To say that a negotiator maximizes his payoffs amounts to saying that he is motivated to do something: he is motivated to strive for X, where X is a goal with the highest payoff attached to it [Bartos 1974:39].

The trouble with this quite typical statement is not that it is untrue but that it is largely irrelevant and unhelpful in tackling the interesting and vital questions as to how negotiators can know the so-called payoffs, how they attempt to alter them and to assess their relative attractiveness, and how, therefore, they can make choices. Presumably people do indeed prefer, and so seek, an outcome that is better rather than one that is worse. But what *is* better? Moreover, do negotiators have clear and consistent standards of assessment either of the relative attractiveness of possible outcomes or of their expectations of the opponent? Are possible outcomes, in any case, unequivocally discernible? The answers in real life must be that there are inevitably huge gaps in knowledge, inconsistencies of multiple criteria of assessment, and a great deal of uncertainty.

Obviously it is seldom, if ever, a simple matter of a higher quantity (of material goods, wages, prestige, leisure, or whatever) being inherently "better" than a lower one. The payoffs—and note the quantitative, even monetary, implications of that favorite term—are seldom presented to a negotiator such that 10 is clearly preferable to 9. Yet ultimately that is what game and bargaining theory comes down to: a gross oversimplification.

The problems are immensely increased when the components of possible or envisioned outcomes and the criteria by which they are assessed are multiple and in some degree incommensurable and contradictory. I show this later in this chapter. Moreover, in actual negotiations we have to take account of the hard facts that goals, preferences, possible outcomes, costs, and much more, do not remain stable. They are more or less continuously subject to change and to manipulation by the parties in interaction. Nor are negotiators always able consciously, and therefore deliberately and rationally, to articulate and organize their interests and values, their wants and preferences, and their assessment of probabilities.

Nevertheless, the common conceptual solution has been to stick to an assumption of rational choice and rational behavior in terms of maximization, typically maximization of expected, subjective utility. Harsanyi, for example, has asserted that under risk and uncertainty (which are, after all, perfectly usual in actual life) this can be conceptualized as "maximization of the mathematical expectations of [a decision-maker's] cardinal utility functions [1977:39]." Like others employing the concept of utility, he assumed that all of a person's interests, values, goals, and preferences can be collapsed into a single cardinal index of his stable, subjective evaluations. Convenient though this may be—even essential to abstract theory—it ignores the interesting but thorny problems of how a decision-maker, a negotiator, does this, or if he does it, or how we (the observers) might perceive him doing it.

Confronting this general problem of rationality and maximization, Diesing has suggested four possible solutions. One is to accept "irrationality," that people are just unable to achieve their goals. The second is that "people attempt to follow rational procedure but—because of difficulties of information processing, communication or calculation—find it too complicated and fall short." The third possibility is "to complicate the [economic notion of] rational by adding factors of uncertainty, or by substituting satisfying for maximizing, or by complicating the goals." Fourth, we might "substitute some non-economic rationality model. For instance, to drop the notion of transitivity or consistency of preferences . . . gives . . . a different concept of rationality, not merely a complication of the model."[9]

Each of these possibilities needs to be held in mind while attempting to build a model of negotiation and analyze processes of interaction leading to an outcome. However, it is probable, as Diesing thought, that the fourth solution may be the most useful in the end. This is so because it is imperative that we continue to move away from the simplistic "economic" model, as in fact many social scientists have been trying to do.[10] However, it is doubtful that any alternative model has acquired general recognition despite the growing volume of criticism of the old one. Frankly, I have no comprehensive and coherent proposal to offer here, although the rough outlines of one are reflected in the analyses that are given in later chapters. There, my approach to an alternative model is guided by the empirical content of real-life negotiating behavior as it occurs in various sociocultural contexts and in various situations of interaction. Therefore, instead of making untested and unprovable assumptions about behavior, we may instead inquire, for example, how and how far negotiators tolerate and cope

---

9. Diesing's suggestions were made in a seminar discussion on "The Concept of Rationality," published in Archibald (1966:153–154).

10. The seductive attractiveness of the "economic" model remains strong, however. In one symposium by social psychologists, almost every contributor seems to have been prepared to accept it with little questioning (Druckman 1977).

Bishop (1964) included a "maximum delay time": the longest period a bargainer will wait in order to obtain a certain outcome rather than accept an available alternative immediately. This is a component to be calculated *before* bargaining begins; it is not a retrospective evaluation on the facts as they have turned out. Cross (1969) used as a critical component the rate at which a party expects his opponent to make concessions. Coddington had, inter alia, "a pair of 'learning rates' . . . which express how sensitively each bargainer revises his expectations in response to the discovery of errors in them [1972:51]."

With these and similar concepts, and the models in which they are included, a severe problem is how such immeasurable components of interactional behavior can be used to obtain, or at least to understand, a more or less determinate, measurable outcome. More important, despite the apparent plausibility of such models, in the face of the differing emphases (and absence of emphasis) given to them by various theorists, do those variables really affect and even determine the outcome? Are they more or less consciously perceived and taken account of by negotiators, or are they part of the structural context of which the participants are unaware? How do we know? How can we know? And how can we be persuaded of the validity of the proffered answers? Such questions and the implied critique are often met by the assertion that these formulations relate only to inquiry and explanation of a conceptual kind. They do not pretend to explain particular empirical circumstances and results; they are useful insofar as they are fruitful of better understanding and illumination of the important variables. Thus, it is contended, such conceptualization should be treated only in terms of abstract deduction.

This kind of answer and defense is certainly not without merit, for we do need to speculate on and pursue the logical consequences of suppositional premises and concepts. Thus, there is much value to be gained from these abstract procedures. Granting that and recognizing the stimulus that is to be obtained, nevertheless the question persists: How can we know? To put it another way: What are the sources of these conceptualizations and are they valid? The sources may be in the fertile imaginations of the theorists, but even the most abstract conceptualizer relates somewhere to his experience of reality, his assumptions of what it is and what its critical features are. For instance, those who assert that some notion of risk taking is influential on outcome must surely have been persuaded, by egoistic or wider experience, of its importance even though that is not explained in exposition. After all, why risk and not something else? Why does one theorist give priority to risk taking whereas another emphasizes the expected rate of the opponent's concessions? If we are to contemplate whether or not to attribute some degree of importance to such components, we must apply not only logical reasoning but, consciously or not, some reference to our experience of reality.

To say that is not to ignore the immense difficulties of discovering what empirical reality is. The perceptions of participants and observers obviously give different realities, or rather different aspects of some possibly, or ideally, ultimate reality. But, accepting the gross imperfections of our perceptions of the real world, it remains inevitable that sooner or later the abstract conceptualizations and the explanations they offer must be brought to and set against some of the events and processes of that world.

Game theorists quite explicitly eschew any such responsibility, leaving it to others to undertake this task if they will. As Rapoport has written, "The mathematical model [of game theorists] is a set of assumptions. We know that every one of these assumptions is false. Nevertheless we make them, for our purpose at this point is not to make true assertions about human behavior but to investigate consequences of assumptions, as in any simulation or experimental game [1964:147]." On the other hand, there are possible bridges between such abstraction and the facts of the real world, between the pure theorist and the scholar who desires to understand actual human behavior. Rapoport has written, quite without irony, that "the chief value of game-theoretical analysis is that it points to questions beyond its scope [1970:41]"[7] Another reviewer of the achievements of game theory came to a similar conclusion:

> It is my contention that a knowledge of the theory of games provides a useful bench mark and a fundamentally important methodological approach to the study of situations involving potential conflict. The insistence of the game theorist on having a completely specified game to study, i.e., a rigid rule game, provides a device for the behavioral scientist to classify and analyse his own models of men, so that in contrasting his models with the frequently unsatisfactory but well defined models of the game theorist, he can isolate key factors with facility [Shubik 1975:157].

Bargaining theorists sometimes take a similar position. Nevertheless these theorists are dealing with phenomena and variables of interaction that do have empirical reference to what people do or seek to do. They are not dealing with symbolic, theological argument about something that by definition can never be experienced—such as angels dancing on the head of a pin. Yet so many of their proposed concepts are extemely difficult, if not impossible, to evaluate, to refer to reality and therefore to rely on and use for the understanding of people's actions. This can be exasperating and

---

7. One reason for Rapoport's own interest in game theory is evidently the hope that it will indicate ways of understanding and dealing with international conflict and warfare.

frustrating. The various theoretical formulations do contain an array of factors and their interconnections that negotiators experience. Negotiators do indeed take some account, however vaguely and inconsistently, of risk, the cost of delays in reaching agreement, the possible future actions of an opponent as indicated by his past behavior, and so on. At the very least, such components of negotiations can and must be taken into account during the examination of real-life situations and behavior. Even though I am unpersuaded of the precise validity of any or all of these theoretical formulations, there is inducement to perceive and to consider possibilities and notions that might otherwise be ignored. Although that is, no doubt, far less than any theorist desires for his own conceptualization, it comprises a most genuine and valuable contribution. The stimulus and insights gained from purely theoretical proposals permeate the analytical exposition of this book, whether or not they are specifically acknowledged. To take a single, important example: My own emphasis on information exchange and learning in negotiations owes much to the work of Coddington and Cross, among others. These crucial features of their models appear to be highly pertinent to my experience of the real world. I do not attempt to prove that those factors are dominant, though I believe they are, because there seems to be no satisfactory way to do so. But their use is fruitful in trying to make sense of what happens in practice; they give form and pattern to interactional processes and they help to clarify many concomitant features of recorded cases of negotiation.

I turn now to the second major problem associated with the theoretical formulation of negotiation processes. In real-life circumstances, the dynamic complexity of the apparent component variables is enormous—forbiddingly so. Yet procedures of abstract simplification, by reducing and controlling many of these variables, inevitably alter the very conditions and processes we seek to understand. Again, there is a wide gap between actual circumstances and the artificial conditions of conceptual inquiry. But again, also, there is the opportunity to gain valuable insights that might otherwise be missed. In this case, the inducement is to reexamine the assumptions and prescribed limitations made by game and bargaining theorists. In so doing, it is possible to come to an improved understanding of some of the components of actual negotiations when, in real-life conditions, those limitations do not obtain and the assumptions cannot be made.

The principal assumptions and limitations are examined next. In brief, and generalizing quite broadly, they are as follows:

1. The players think and behave rationally, with complete skill and competence (personal and social characteristics being ignored) to calculate the best possible or maximal outcome.

2. The rules of play are known and fixed.
3. There is perfect knowledge by each player in many or even all matters, such as the complete range and commensurable sizes of all possible outcomes, the preferences of each player, the probabilities attached to choices and outcomes.
4. There is no interference from the outside world.
5. There is no (or very little) opportunity for players to use tactics (quite typical of actual negotiations) such as bluff, coercion, persuasion, rationalization, and misrepresentation.
6. There is little or no scope for a player to develop and adjust perceptions, expectations, and preferences, or to manipulate those of his opponent.

The precise assumptions in a particular case depend, of course, on the nature of the game or the bargaining scenario. In fact, it is the specifics of the assumptions, together with the specification of the rules, that actually create the game or scenario.[8]

Central to the construction of almost all game-type models is the assumption of rational behavior by the players, defined in terms of maximization of expected outcome. That the general notion of rationality in human behavior is highly complex is clear from the lengthy controversies and discussions that have occurred among philosophers, logicians, game theorists, and social scientists. Any attempt at a thorough reexamination of the concept and its manifold implications would necessarily take us far beyond immediate requirements. Rather, I am content to make a few observations in order to suggest that the convenience and optimism of an oversimplification of "rational" does not and cannot adequately deal with, or dispose of, the problems relating to actual negotiations and negotiators. An agnostic approach seems preferable, although that is, as always, unsatisfactory to those who dislike doubt and loose ends and instead seek to develop a tidy, consistent, theoretical framework.

It is quite valid, no doubt, to say that a negotiator, like people in general, endeavors to obtain an outcome that is, in his opinion, most satisfactory to him. At least he chooses an outcome that is no less satisfactory than any perceived alternative possibility, taking into account his interests, values, and concern for self and others. To say that, however, is to say very little at all. It is a tautological truism. Such universalistic behavior can, if one so wishes, be called "rational." The problem is that this axiomatic truth becomes transformed into an equation between "rational" and

---

8. A complex but clearly specified example is Stahl's game model for labor–management bargaining. He lists 20 assumptions that lead to a bargaining game characterized by 14 other assumptions (Stahl 1972:202).

"maximization," where what is maximized is quantifiable (or can be treated as if it were).

For instance, Bartos has written,

> Defined in the simplest terms, rationality refers to maximization of payoffs: a negotiator is rational if he prefers high payoff to low payoff. . . . [This makes] good sense substantively, by corresponding to the concept of motivation. To say that a negotiator maximizes his payoffs amounts to saying that he is motivated to do something: he is motivated to strive for X, where X is a goal with the highest payoff attached to it [Bartos 1974:39].

The trouble with this quite typical statement is not that it is untrue but that it is largely irrelevant and unhelpful in tackling the interesting and vital questions as to how negotiators can know the so-called payoffs, how they attempt to alter them and to assess their relative attractiveness, and how, therefore, they can make choices. Presumably people do indeed prefer, and so seek, an outcome that is better rather than one that is worse. But what *is* better? Moreover, do negotiators have clear and consistent standards of assessment either of the relative attractiveness of possible outcomes or of their expectations of the opponent? Are possible outcomes, in any case, unequivocally discernible? The answers in real life must be that there are inevitably huge gaps in knowledge, inconsistencies of multiple criteria of assessment, and a great deal of uncertainty.

Obviously it is seldom, if ever, a simple matter of a higher quantity (of material goods, wages, prestige, leisure, or whatever) being inherently "better" than a lower one. The payoffs—and note the quantitative, even monetary, implications of that favorite term—are seldom presented to a negotiator such that 10 is clearly preferable to 9. Yet ultimately that is what game and bargaining theory comes down to: a gross oversimplification.

The problems are immensely increased when the components of possible or envisioned outcomes and the criteria by which they are assessed are multiple and in some degree incommensurable and contradictory. I show this later in this chapter. Moreover, in actual negotiations we have to take account of the hard facts that goals, preferences, possible outcomes, costs, and much more, do not remain stable. They are more or less continuously subject to change and to manipulation by the parties in interaction. Nor are negotiators always able consciously, and therefore deliberately and rationally, to articulate and organize their interests and values, their wants and preferences, and their assessment of probabilities.

Nevertheless, the common conceptual solution has been to stick to an assumption of rational choice and rational behavior in terms of maximization, typically maximization of expected, subjective utility. Harsanyi, for example, has asserted that under risk and uncertainty (which are, after all, perfectly usual in actual life) this can be conceptualized as "maximization of the mathematical expectations of [a decision-maker's] cardinal utility functions [1977:39]." Like others employing the concept of utility, he assumed that all of a person's interests, values, goals, and preferences can be collapsed into a single cardinal index of his stable, subjective evaluations. Convenient though this may be—even essential to abstract theory— it ignores the interesting but thorny problems of how a decision-maker, a negotiator, does this, or if he does it, or how we (the observers) might perceive him doing it.

Confronting this general problem of rationality and maximization, Diesing has suggested four possible solutions. One is to accept "irrationality," that people are just unable to achieve their goals. The second is that "people attempt to follow rational procedure but—because of difficulties of information processing, communication or calculation—find it too complicated and fall short." The third possibility is "to complicate the [economic notion of] rational by adding factors of uncertainty, or by substituting satisfying for maximizing, or by complicating the goals." Fourth, we might "substitute some non-economic rationality model. For instance, to drop the notion of transitivity or consistency of preferences . . . gives . . . a different concept of rationality, not merely a complication of the model."[9]

Each of these possibilities needs to be held in mind while attempting to build a model of negotiation and analyze processes of interaction leading to an outcome. However, it is probable, as Diesing thought, that the fourth solution may be the most useful in the end. This is so because it is imperative that we continue to move away from the simplistic "economic" model, as in fact many social scientists have been trying to do.[10] However, it is doubtful that any alternative model has acquired general recognition despite the growing volume of criticism of the old one. Frankly, I have no comprehensive and coherent proposal to offer here, although the rough outlines of one are reflected in the analyses that are given in later chapters. There, my approach to an alternative model is guided by the empirical content of real-life negotiating behavior as it occurs in various sociocultural contexts and in various situations of interaction. Therefore, instead of making untested and unprovable assumptions about behavior, we may instead inquire, for example, how and how far negotiators tolerate and cope

---

9. Diesing's suggestions were made in a seminar discussion on "The Concept of Rationality," published in Archibald (1966:153–154).

10. The seductive attractiveness of the "economic" model remains strong, however. In one symposium by social psychologists, almost every contributor seems to have been prepared to accept it with little questioning (Druckman 1977).

with unavoidable ignorance, how they assess and reassess expectations and preferences about quantifiable and nonquantifiable components, and how in practice they make some kind of choice under risk and uncertainty. There is no need to assume "maximization," although we need not deny its sometime possibility in effect or in the intention of a negotiator. We should be prepared to find circumstances where maximization is impossible and where there are alternative intentions and strategies, along with intransitivities, incomparabilities, and contradictions. A more diligent scrutiny of the real world and a toleration of its obscurities, fragility, and untidiness are well overdue.

It must be emphasized most strongly, however, that in practice negotiators do in fact attempt to simplify the conditions under which they come to make final choices and reach a joint decision on the outcome. They do not and cannot attain the "simple" conditions of theoretical games although the gap between game and reality is narrowed. Indeed, I argue that it has to be narrowed for quite practical reasons. During the phases of negotiation that lead to final choices, the parties try to clarify and establish the effective rules for their interaction and seek to obtain fuller knowledge of all aspects, including potential outcomes and their satisfactoriness. They endeavor to determine and readjust their preferences and expectations and to discover those of the opponent, however, vaguely and inconsistently. They seek to take account of the nature and extent of external forces and interests so as to adjust their expectations accordingly. One can confidently say that the final result is never complete knowledge; it is no more than the roughest approximation to it and seldom or never eliminates inconsistency. In fact, it seems preferable to assume that negotiators may well end up with some kind of distorted perception of the circumstances, possible outcomes, and available choices. Nevertheless, negotiators do come to some kind of overall assessment, even if it be a thing of bits and pieces not altogether articulated, which stands in lieu, as it were, of an ideally precise cognition.

In the pattern-models presented later in this book, negotiation is portrayed as a set of processes in which the parties begin with a degree of assumed knowledge but also, both consciously and unconsciously, with a considerable degree of uncertainty and downright ignorance. That knowledge is tested and altered, augmented and refined as a result of the developing interaction between the negotiators themselves and between them, third parties, and others (the outside world). I wish to emphasize that what is largely or wholly assumed by the theorists has to be laboriously pursued and discovered as far as possible by the negotiators. They do this with dissimilar, variable abilities and certainly with limited skill to perceive and appreciate the possibilities, to assess them, and to cope with the opponent's stratagems that affect perception and preference. In some negotiations the significance of disparate skills is empirically obvious and clearly pertinent to the outcome that is achieved. In other cases it is a subtle, less easily recognizable and accountable factor, though none the less relevant.

In all but the very simplest disputes, the magnitude of calculations that would be necessary to make a so-called rational choice is likely to be well beyond the negotiator's abilities, even if all the variables were clearly and correctly known. Some indication of the enormity of the problem can be gained from a familiar, game-like setting, namely chess. Rapoport has noted that "the number of outcomes (i.e., positions) following the first exchange of moves in chess is $20 \times 20 = 400$. But the number of strategies available to Black *on his first move alone* is 20^{20} [Rapoport 1966:90; italics in original]." In a three-party game with only six strategy options, something like a million calculations are required to reach a "best" decision for the parties (Keirstead 1972:166). Negotiators obviously cannot make these kinds of calculations. In any case, the difficulties are hugely compounded when the rules about moves are far from definite (unlike chess) and when the objectives and the possible options are neither clear nor altogether capable of quantitative assessment. In these matters, as in so much else that the theorists neatly assume away, *negotiators can at best attempt to cope reasonably with the impossible.* Somehow, in real life, they do manage to cut their way through, however, crudely, effectively reducing the number and range of calculations required, comparing the incomparable and making some choice. To understand how they do all this, we must take account of the operational significance of those factors that actually confront the parties. Regardless of theoretical convenience, we cannot assume that we know what the parties themselves cannot know. However, by examining the theorists' assumptions it becomes possible to identify more clearly what the parties have to contend with.

In reviewing theoretical approaches to the study of joint decision-making, it is useful to look at the main types of nongame models that have been proposed and the particular sets of phenomena they emphasize. Patchen (1970) has most helpfully surveyed the field of what he calls "conflictful and cooperative interaction," and his results provide a working base. He found that theoretical models are of two principal kinds. One is concerned with the processes of bid and counterbid by which parties attempt to reach an agreed outcome. These are in effect bargaining models of the kind I have already discussed. The second kind of model concentrates on processes in which the parties influence each other's expectations, assessments, and behavior during the search for an outcome, thereby affecting the outcome itself. These are manipulative models, and they are of three general types.

First, there are *cognitive models* that purport to explain interaction in terms of the assumption that each party's actions depend on his perception about the *future results* of those actions—generally, the probable utility they will produce. A party's cognition of future results is partly affected by his expectations about the opponent's future actions. Therefore each party is concerned with attempting to influence his opponent's expectations in his own favor. Such influence may be exerted through coercive threat—the behavior emphasized in the particular examples referred to by Patchen (e.g., Porsholt 1966; Russett 1963; Timasheff 1965)—but it can also be induced by promise of advantage to the opponent; the presentation of information on relevant issues (including, of course, calculated misinformation); persuasive reference to the opponent's own best interests; claims to superior understanding by virtue of alleged superior ability, experience, and status; reference to rules and ideology; and much else. There is no special difficulty in accepting this kind of model, at least as far as it goes. This essentially future-oriented approach is not concerned with the question as to when agreement is reached or what the outcome might be; rather, it deals with the processes leading to that end. This allows an examination of the succession of moves as each party (*a*) influences the other's expectations of future possibilities and (*b*) reassesses and readjusts his own expectations.

Second, there are *learning models* in which it is assumed that each party's actions are largely dependent on his experience of the results of *past* actions by the two parties. What has occurred previously is used as a standard of assessment by which to choose what to aim for and what to do next. This assumption surely accords with both common sense experience and empirical case data. It may be true that, as Patchen suggests, in negotiations where the parties have little or no previous experience of each other, there might be little to go on. However, each party will have had some experience of other, somewhat similar opponents and situations and there is a fund of precedent on which to draw. More important, as negotiations continue, each party accumulates an experience of his opponent and of what has occurred between them.

Third, there are *reaction process models* in which a party's actions are assumed to be an almost automatic response to his opponent's last action and to be based on the party's own characteristics and propensities. As Patchen points out, such models appear to focus on what people would do if they did not stop to think—and sometimes people do simply react in that way. It may also be the case that a negotiating party has already established a stable set of preferences and expectations that he is unwilling, even unable, to modify. For instance, trade union leaders, committed by their constituency and by the necessity to exhibit firmness in the face of a mistrusted management, may be virtually compelled to make something like an automatic response to the management's actions. However, this focus is generally too narrow since it largely ignores the palpable processes by which parties modify expectations and preferences and make more or less deliberate decisions about strategy and action. Yet we cannot ignore the fact that in some cases—or at certain times in most cases—actions are in effect nearly automatic responses, sometimes (as in arms races or race conflicts) leading to a progressive escalation of conflict. The questions then are these: Under what conditions and for what reasons does this sort of thing occur? What are its limits? How is it stopped?

It is not clear if the theorists who proposed these various manipulative models were choosing to concentrate on a particular feature with the assumption that it is the crucial variable. Such assumption is unacceptable. However, insofar as these theorists have explored and clarified certain features, they have provided valuable insights and raised useful questions. In particular, they have shown that we need to take account of a negotiator's assessments of the future results of actions and of the effect of past experience. They are two sides of a coin. Both direct attention to the development and clarification of expectations, preferences, and strategy, and both emphasize the intrinsic interactional quality of negotiations. There is a process of modification and adjustment of expectations in the light of experience of each other, subject to the various influences each exerts, and affected by a developing appreciation of what is and is not possible in the future. There is a process of exploration and discovery by each party separately and by both together. It is a process that does not necessarily lead to some real and final truth. Both parties are limited in their assessments and anticipations. They are limited by each other's influence; by each party's characteristics, propensities, and abilities, by their working definitions of what the issues are, and by the multiplexity of the situation in which they operate. Nevertheless, the parties seek—and succeed in a restricted but operational sense—to discover more about the opponent, about themselves, and about whatever else seems relevant, such as outside forces and interests. Discovery is a continuous process that produces adjustments by at least one party, but probably both, so that eventually some outcome can occur.

Finally, in this brief survey of some theoretical approaches to the analysis of joint decision-making, I draw attention to four features of negotiations that have been given relatively little attention by any of the theorists and have often been virtually ignored. One comprises rules, norms, values, and beliefs. Sometimes these are described as "institutional factors," or some similar blanket term is used, which neither clarifies their nature nor encourages examination of their significance in the process. They are frequently assumed to be held constant or somehow to be incorporated into the rules of play or the utility functions of the parties. Some models include rather naive, ethnocentric assumptions to the point that negotiators almost appear to be crude stereotypes of North American, middle-class suburbanites. Few models are concerned with the implications of cross-cultural variation and in many cases, sometimes fairly explicitly, negotiations are assumed to occur in a cultural vacuum such that perceptions, learning, and choices are unaffected by cultural milieu and by the social status of the negotiators.

The second feature is power. Few models take this into account, with the exception of some coercive models of the cognitive, manipulative type previously mentioned. Game and bargaining theories almost universally ignore the distribution of power or, what amounts to the same thing, they assume that, like skills and knowledge, power is equally distributed to the parties. Some theorists, more positively, deny the possibility of taking account of power on the grounds that it is knowable only in the eventual outcome of bargaining.[11] A disinclination to treat power as a variable is, of course, particularly associated with the prior disinclination to examine the processes by which one party attempts to manipulate the other's perceptions and preferences.

The third feature comprises the influences, the limitations, and the effective compulsions brought to bear on negotiators by persons who are not directly participant in the negotiations. Theoretical models generally assume that negotiations occur in a social vacuum. It is, of course, highly convenient to make that simplifying assumption because, like cultural factors, these external forces are most diverse and diffuse and not easily handled. Yet obviously they exercise some—probably considerable—effects on both process and outcome; so much so, indeed, that some social scientists have, contrariwise, asserted that these external forces are the decisive ones in determining outcome, rather than the actions of the negotiators themselves.

Fourth, virtually all the models have failed to take account of a characteristic that is almost universal in actual negotiations. This is that disputes and conflict concern multiple issues or items that are in some degree interconnected and are evaluated in terms of multiple attributes. I turn now to an examination of this and of its significance.

---

11. Some theorists (e.g., Cross 1969) see a chicken-and-egg situation: Is a negotiator more successful because he is more powerful, or is he more powerful because he is more successful? This is examined later; see pages 189–190.

MULTIPLE CRITERIA IN JOINT DECISION-MAKING: ON CHALK, CHEESE, AND HONOR

In the relatively impersonal, urban societies of the Western world, with a predominance of single-interest or single-stranded relationships, "simple" disputes are not uncommon, whether subject to adjudication or negotiation. By "simple" is meant that the two parties in the dispute are concerned with a single, readily definable issue between them that is assessed in terms of a single attribute. For instance, a shopkeeper claims payment from a customer for goods received on credit; a city demands payment of overdue taxes by a resident; an employee seeks payment of standard wages for work performed.

In most cases, however, disputes turn out not to be so simple. Take for example a plaintiff's demand for payment of the costs of repairs to his car, which, while parked in the street, was damaged by the car driven by the defendant. The defendant could be clearly and admittedly responsible and the costs of repairs verified by a competent mechanic. Commonly the case would be more complicated than this. The defendant may be willing to pay for the damage he has caused but he also has to consider the effect of his admission of fault on his financial resources and on his reputation as a driver (say, liability to a fine for careless driving, a less favorable record with his insurance company, the imputation about his driving skill) or his reputation as a person (say, suggestions of drunkenness, or stigma on his image of aggressiveness). Or, being prepared to pay, the defendant might contest the criteria by which his liability is assessed. Was he inattentive or driving too fast? Did he really need to swerve so violently to avoid a child? Was the plaintiff's car parked too far from the curb or partly hidden by a tree? Or he might contest the criteria by which his expenses are assessed: the age of the plaintiff's car, already existing damage, the amount of work to be done, and the repair rates of the mechanic. The defendant might have to consider the costs of contesting his liability or the exact payment to be made, and perhaps he would also wish to take into account his relationship with the plaintiff (or a close associate of the plaintiff) who, it turns out, is a neighbor or a member of the same church or a notable in local politics. The plaintiff too might need or wish to take account of these and similar matters. Moreover, it is not inconceivable to imagine that another issue could arise: say, the defendant's claim for damages caused by the irate plaintiff who assaulted him or slandered his character at the scene of the accident.[12]

This familiar kind of example is intended merely as an introductory

---

12. In such frequently occurring incidents as automobile accidents, many of the issues and criteria relating to them are routinely decided by established rules and precedents, of

illustration of an important characteristic of disputes and their negotiation. Commonly they are not "simple." Most often they involve a multiplexity of two distinguishable kinds. There are multiple issues (objectives, goals, more or less discrete items to be settled) and there are multiple attributes (characteristics, qualities, variables) by which a particular issue is evaluated. This might only produce a multiplication of problems if (a) each issue could be dealt with and settled separately and (b) the various attributes could be summed by simple aggregation. That is not usually the case, however.

On the one hand, satisfaction on one issue (attainment of one objective) commonly affects and interferes with gaining satisfaction on another. It may be that two issues are more or less contradictory so that satisfaction on one precludes or at least limits satisfaction on the other. To gain one issue or objective a party may have to be prepared to forfeit part or whole of another. On the other hand, the various attributes of an issue often do not lead to quite the same evaluation so that some choice must be made between an outcome containing much of desirable x, a little y, and some of undesirable z, and one containing much y, a little z, and some x. There is the difficulty, not always readily susceptible to neat solution, of what relative values to give to x, y, and z.[13] Thus there are likely to be problems of choice between the different issues being negotiated, between the attributes of each issue, and, perhaps, between some issues and some attributes.

The proverbially irreconcilable differences between chalk and cheese may, for the sake of more useful analogy, be further complicated by adding the highly qualitative issue of honor. If all three are in dispute between two parties it is most probable that neither will be able to obtain as much, or as little, of each as he wishes. A party will be compelled to consider how much of one—say, cheese—he might be prepared to cede to his opponent in order to gain a somewhat vaguely comprehended amount of another — say, honor. There are the problems of knowing how much is available, or could become available under certain conditions, and of deciding how much is desired. When, for example, does the accumulation of cheese raise problems of increasingly intolerable smell for a sensitive nose (or a neighbor's sensitive nose), and when does too much honor become a liability in its demands on life-style, moral responsibilities, and material resources? One's desire for chalk may be quickly satisfied, thus affording the possibil-

---

course. But the frequency of negotiations in these cases indicates their continued importance as sources of disputes and the problems of decision-making (cf. H. L. Ross 1970).

13. The objective might be a new car and the attributes, x, y, and z, might be safety of operation, seating capacity, and expenses of maintenance.

ity of offering the bulk of available chalk to the opponent in the hope of his yielding on the honor issue, but he too may want only a little chalk and be indisposed to forgo honor in order to obtain more. Indeed, the difficulty may be not in obtaining chalk but in getting rid of it when neither party desires to hold it. It might be possible to accept the chalk (having a convenient place to store or dump it) if it is accompanied by considerable amounts of cheese and honor; though contrarily, the party that can profitably use the chalk, that may even be in need of it, may find his position weak on cheese and honor, which he would also like to have.

A major difficulty is that these three items (issues) are not altogether commensurable and that in some senses they are not measurably comparable at all. A monetary index may be available by which to compare chalk and cheese, though most probably not honor, but monetary value may well be a poor guide to the prestige and power gained from cornering the chalk supply in the community or to the disapprobation received from storing too much malodorous cheese. In any case, not all cheese is the same, for there are innumerable varieties and qualities (attributes) offering different combinations of flavor, color, storage quality, culinary use, price, and cultural esteem, and these do not all point to gorgonzola as preferable to Camembert. Indeed, a party may want some of both, though just how much of each is hard to determine. The attributes are not readily ordered in simple priorities, let alone measured; moreover, the most flavorful cheese may also be the one that is liable to quick damage in storage.

Whether or not issues are interconnected in ordinary social life, they necessarily become so in some degree when they become co-issues in a dispute. It becomes difficult if not impossible for the parties to agree to settle, say, the cheese issue first, then the chalk, and finally the matter of honor, for it is obvious to the participants that advantages may be gained or lost in respect to one by the ways in which the others are treated. Moreover, and apart from the problems of assessment of issues singly and comparatively, a party's tentative evaluation is not necessarily by the same compound of attributes as his opponent's evaluation. It is advisable, then, for a party to try to discover what he can about his opponent's evaluations and preferences. It might be that, on inquiry, the two sets of preferences are more or less complementary and, after a little mutual adjustment, not really in conflict. However, a party may perhaps discover that, despite his initial preference for the flavorful cheese, it is wise and advantageous to forgo that in the face of his opponent's obdurate insistence on that variety. Thus a party may be constrained to alter his preferences and objectives either to prevent a breakdown of the negotiations, or to exact a large concession from the opponent on another issue. That is to say, not only are there severe difficulties in assessing various combinations of the multiple issues and attributes, but the preferences and expectations are liable to change in the light of further understanding of the possibilities offered or denied by the opponent's preferences and expectations.

From this discussion, it will probably be evident also that the distinction between issues and attributes is not altogether clear. An attribute may turn into an issue as negotiations proceed where, for instance, the attribute is a value attaching to several of the initial issues, such as prestige. Conversely, it may come to be perceived that some of the ostensible issues are but attributes of an underlying and overtly unrecognized issue, such as power or status. In particular empirical cases, the parties themselves declare and define the issues and consider the relevant attributes so as to reach some kind of evaluation. As the negotiations develop, and as the parties acquire better understanding of the possibilities and implications in the context, there are likely to be adjustments and even quite radical changes of evaluation. The distinction between issues and attributes is thus subject to change. Therefore, although the distinction can still be analytically useful, there is no need to insist on it since so much depends on the interactional context. It may be sufficient simply to take account of the complexity, the conflict, and the irresolution of multiple criteria, without introducing possibly misleading discriminations of the kinds of criteria (i.e., issues and attributes). It remains absolutely essential, however, to maintain analytical regard for multiplicity.

These trite observations on matters of seeming common sense and everyday experience would scarcely be necessary but for the palpable fact that they represent two orders of complexity in decision making that have very largely gone unrecognized, or at least have been ignored or assumed away, by theorists. In particular they have been ignored in connection with processes of interdependent decision-making in the context of conflict and dispute between two parties. Bargaining theorists have generally limited themselves to something like a single, readily measurable, divisible item. For example, Cross (1969) quite typically focuses his analysis on the distribution between two parties of a finite quantity, M, which is homogenous and divisible into small portions, without diminishing marginal utility.[14] Bargaining "solutions" of the Nash type involve similar emasculating limitations.

It is only fairly recently that constructive criticism has mounted against the general assumption made by economists and other theorists that decision-making can be treated as if it referred to a single issue (profits,

---

14. Let me reiterate that there is no need to deny the usefulness of reducing the variables and thus simplifying problems of interest as a first approach. Nevertheless, it becomes a major defect persistently to ignore quite fundamental characteristics of bargaining and negotiation.

wages, etc.) that is adequately measurable on a single, ordinal scale, usually money. Included in that assumption has been the notion that evaluation is linear, transitive, and stable. Diminishing returns from regular increments have, of course, long been recognized, but again in measurable, linear, transitive, and stable forms. This is implicit in the indiscriminate use of a blanket concept such as "profits," which, it is said, an entrepreneur seeks to maximize. But in reality profits are "really a *surrogate* for a number of complex variables—such as earnings per share, stock price, debt–equity ratio, market share, goodwill, labor relations, product quality, ecological impact of operations, and so forth [Cochrane and Zeleny 1973:xiii]." To gain profits, let alone to maximize them, is not the straightforward thing it is too often taken to be.

Where bargaining theorists have concentrated on the determination of wages they have used another blanket concept, similar to "profits." For example, Pen does not explicitly recognize or take account of the complexity of the object that is his prime concern. He does note that "the bargaining on the labor market may be about the wage rate [*sic*] and, let us say, a pension scheme"—that is, a multiplicity of issues. He concludes, without further inquiry, however, that "this kind of double criterion bargaining is not dealt with in a satisfactory way in our theory [Pen 1952:41–42]." So much the worse for the theory. In actuality, of course, management–labor negotiations are deeply concerned with the multiple criteria of "the wage rate," and the number and complexity of other issues simultaneously negotiated are generally great.[15] Some issues, though scarcely formulated specifically, are very much present, pervading negotiation on most others: for instance, the independence and prestige of the trade union and its leaders, management prerogatives, and political ideologies.

A theory of bargaining and decision-making that does not specifically take account of interconnected, multiple issues and of the multiple attributes by which issues are assessed must assuredly fall short in both explanatory power and prescriptive ability. Although theorists are now increasingly revising their assumptions and theoretical analyses to include multiple criteria in economic behavior, there appears to be a continued reluctance to extend this to the area of joint decision-making. Indeed, there is probably not yet a thorough attempt to make an integrated treatment in this way. There continues to be disproportionate attention given to in-

---

15. Industrial negotiations deal with all matters relating to the conditions of employment and, nowadays, with issues relating to the operation of the business. Thus in addition to the manifold criteria of a range of wage rates, there are issues of pension plans, paid vacations, hours of work and overtime, toilet facilities, the powers of supervisors, complaints procedures, leisure facilities, rules of operation of certain machinery, employee information about and participation in business decisions and ongoing administration, and the like.

dividual decision-making as if a businessman, say, or a political leader were effectively isolated and in control of all variables of importance—or that those beyond an individual's scope can be allowed for statistically in terms of calculated probabilities.

This conclusion is encouraged by, for instance, an examination of the voluminous symposium, *Multiple Criteria Decision Making* (1973). The editors, Cochrane and Zeleny, approvingly and with admonition to their discipline, quoted a passage by Morgenstern:

> Virtually all economic activity . . . is described by the fact that none of the parties completely controls the outcome (not even statistically, as in the case of a—presumably—indifferent nature). The seeming argument that of, say, 100 variables, only one is under someone else's control and could therefore be neglected . . . is conceptually incorrect and hence inapplicable [Morgenstern, 1972:1166].

This authoritative warning went almost unheeded by the contributors to that symposium. For instance, in an otherwise valuable review of theories and methods relating to decision-making with multiple criteria, Mac-Crimmon (1973:19–44) made no reference to problems of joint decision-making.

On the other hand, in his editorial conclusion to a compilation of key theoretical papers on bargaining, strategic interaction, and interdependent decision-making, Young (1975) recognized the failure to take account of multiple criteria as one of the persisting problems in that field. He pointed to the inadequacy of at least one, too facile solution:

> In principle, it is possible to collapse a multiplicity of issues into a single set of utility functions (that is, one for each of the players) by treating all possible combinations of outcomes for the issues or separate alternatives for the players and expressing the expected values associated with those alternatives in terms of some common unit of utility. In reality, however, this procedure is apt to prove well beyond the capabilities of the players [1975:394].

Nevertheless, neither Young nor any of his authors dealt with this severe problem of bargaining theory. Young's only reference was to the brief, unhelpful comments of Pen previously quoted. Young's only solution was that "interactions involving several issues at the same time will often have to be represented in terms of a multidimensional payoff space [1975:394]." He did not suggest how this might be done, nor did he refer to the multiple attributes of the "several issues."

The theoretical problems and analytical difficulties are, admittedly, formidably complex, but they arise from the concrete reality that we wish to understand (and even predict). That reality is that *decision-making com-*

monly involves multiple criteria that are in some degree subject to control by a second party. The implications of both characteristics and of their interconnections sorely need careful study.

Although economists are not the only culprits in the neglect of these fundamental considerations, they have probably had the major responsibility in setting and maintaining the orientation and assumptions that induced that neglect. Nevertheless, it has largely been the criticism made by some economists that has led to increasing recognition of the unfortunate consequences of such oversimplification and to serious attempts to rectify theoretical inadequacies. Most social scientists, all of whom are in some way or other concerned with human interaction rather than a social isolation, are open to similar criticism. The truth is that we still do not know much about the ways in which parties reach their interdependent decisions over poorly apprehended and scarcely comparable issues.

Anthropologists have contributed little to the understanding of these processes. Despite some pioneering work in extended case histories, these studies have tended to concentrate on the environing structures of rules, values, groups, roles, and the like, which establish the conditions within which people evaluate and act. In describing and analyzing dispute causes, anthropologists too have tended to treat them as if they involved but single criteria, single issues and attributes. "Inheritance," "bridewealth," and the "status of village headman" are no less surrogates for complex multiple criteria than "profits" or "wage rate." Ironically, it is most probable that disputes in the small-scale societies that anthropologists have studied are particularly characterized by interconnected, multiple criteria. In such societies, the principals and their associates in a dispute are often intimately involved in some network of multiplex relationships, rights, and obligations. Thus there is additional reason for disputes to involve numerous related issues, and often the emergence of overt dispute brings out other issues that have hitherto lain dormant or have been suppressed. My complaint is not that anthropologists have failed to indicate these kinds of phenomena, but rather that they have inadequately explored them and have not incorporated them into analysis and explanation.

The complexity of multiple criteria is diminished under a process of adjudication. Not only are joint decision-making problems avoided in that process but, to be acceptable to the adjudicator and to meet judicial requirements, issues often have to be reduced to more or less standardized, limited categories. That is, issues have to be formulated in certain justiciable forms. Those that cannot be so presented and argued are more likely to be dropped. Thus, there is a simplification process such that adjudicators and jurists can afford to ignore much of our complex problem. In negotiations, however, there is much less simplification—it would be wrong to say none at all—so that multiple criteria flourish. It is curious, therefore, and an example of the blindness of presupposition, that cases have been reported as if this were scarcely so.

Let me be particular in my criticism. It has become clear to me in retrospect, and confirmed by reexamination of my own field records, that many of my reports of dispute cases among the Arusha and Ndendeuli (Gulliver 1963, 1971, 1975a) have not adequately described and taken account of multiple criteria. For example, a so-called bridewealth case also involved other issues as well as diverse attributes of those issues and was, in the event, negotiated and decided *only* in the context of such multiplicity. That the relative status, prestige, and rights of the wife and of her husband, father, and children, together with some allocation of resources, were all under consideration is, of course, usually apparent in the description of the case. Yet analysis did not include sufficient emphasis or consideration of those issues and their interdependence.

It seems that my perceptive selectivity was encouraged by the practical simplifications of the peoples whom I studied. Arusha and Ndendeuli commonly described their dispute cases as the plaintiff's claim for bridewealth, say, or for a piece of land. Yet, in the actual negotiations, that was but one of the issues; the claim itself often comprised a set of interconnected issues. The people themselves were applying conveniently simple labels. Those labels were not intended for analytical purposes, of course, but they became unintentionally misleading. No less important, the observer can be in error by a too narrow search for what a dispute is "really about," leading to underemphasis of some of the issues involved. It would be better to assume that a dispute is "really about" all the issues involved and to inquire how they are dealt with in their interconnection in the negotiations.

For example, in an Arusha case (more fully described later in Chapter 8), participants and others spoke of the dispute as being one between neighbors over a field. In fact, however, there were at least eight other identifiable issues, two of which in the event proved more intractable than the question of land ownership. My own assumption at the time was that this was a land dispute to which secondary issues had accreted. Later reassessment designated the case as one about the relationship between neighbors but focusing around the land issue in a society where land was desperately scarce. Still later, further consideration led me to abandon that evaluation in order to understand how the whole dispute was negotiated and joint decisions reached. At that point, it became possible to see a "chalk, cheese, and honor" situation. However "important" the land issue was—materially and otherwise—its treatment and settlement sensibly affected and was affected by the other issues. From this perspective, rather than examining how far the conflict over valuable land precipitated other issues, or whether the land might not have become an issue of dispute had other disagreements, quarrels, and alleged slights not occurred, it seemed preferable to examine the multiple criteria as these were dealt with in the actual negotiations. To my mind, this gave the most satisfactory understanding of what happened and how.

To conclude this discussion of multiple criteria, let me note that my principal concern is for the ways in which negotiators themselves deal with problems of multiple criteria. Obviously, negotiators do usually manage to cope somehow to their own acceptable satisfaction as—again—they attempt to deal reasonably with an apparently impossible situation. No comprehensive theory is to be suggested. In general, however, and in line with the approach to similar problems relating to uncertainty, ignorance, and complexity the experiential assumption is that, in real-life negotiations, people are compelled to resort to gross acts of simplification in order to reduce the intricacy of the variables they have to handle. Negotiators gradually become prepared (as they were not at first) to ignore a great deal and to adopt an assumed certainty in the face of otherwise intractable uncertainty that could, and sometimes does, lead to frustration and impotence. However, the simplifications of practical negotiators are not necessarily the same as those of the abstract theorists.

A HISTORICO-ETHNOGRAPHIC APPROACH

In the study of processes leading to joint decision-making, there is a somewhat neglected alternative to conceptual, deductive analysis and to laboratory simulation that investigates theoretical notions under tightly controlled conditions. That alternative is to concentrate on, or at least to start from, inquiries in and information from "the real world." One possible procedure here would be to attempt to put into operation and thus test hypotheses generated by theoretical work, seeking to validate or invalidate them against empirical data drawn from actual cases. This is certainly something that needs to be done, and it has been strangely neglected by the proponents of theoretical analysis. It is not, however, the approach to be adopted here. This is partly because it would require the deliberate collection of empirical data specifically for the purpose, with particular hypotheses in mind—something that I have not done. In any case, my own interests and experience as an anthropologist have lain elsewhere.

The endeavor in this present study is to use available empirical materials provided by reports of real-life instances of negotiation. Eschewing attempts at discovering predictively firm solutions to joint decision-making or at formulating prescriptive models, at least for the immediate future, I concentrate instead on what actually happened in known cases in order to make first-level, provisional analyses of the variety of factors involved and to attempt to produce a synthesis of the apparent patterns of behavior, interaction, and process. The methodology begins inductively, therefore, but with a recognition that the blank spaces and some of the interconnections can usefully be treated, tentatively, by deduction. Processual patterns can be developed into something like ideal types and/or "as if" models whose explanatory characteristics may be, as it were, fed back to particular cases in order both to demonstrate and further refine them against the facts.

The apparent difficulties and inherent problems of a real-life, empirical approach are indeed formidable. They are so great that some scholars have explicitly denied the validity and usefulness of an empirical base and even the possibility of any success.[16] Many others have merely ignored such an approach, presumably because it appears so hazardous.

Case studies are inevitably trapped in the particular such that is most difficult to disentangle what is relevant and significant from the situational fortuities, the peculiar sociocultural context, and the individual personalities of the participants. Case studies produce uncontrolled, once-and-for-all materials where replication is never wholly possible and where experimental modification of apparently critical variables is impossible. Comparison of cases is obviously problematic, especially so because of the uncertainties coming from the observer's bias, poor recording, and plain ignorance of significant details. Many of the features of key interest are in fact scarcely observable directly, such as the largely unconscious motivations and evaluations of which the participants themselves are unaware, or the more conscious deliberations and ideas that a negotiator attempts to keep hidden from outsiders, including the observer. What is witnessed and recorded by an observer is subject to the carefulness and skill of the research and to his or her perceptiveness and presuppositions as these are unavoidably affected by intellectual, cultural, and personal experience and knowledge. Most certainly it cannot be assumed that any report of a particular case, however detailed, is either complete or altogether accurate, whatever that might mean. Moreover, there is undoubtedly a shortage of reasonably detailed case studies to which comparative reference can be made.

---

16. See, for example, the comments of McGrath (1966:105 ff.) and Coddington (1972:55 ff.), a social psychologist and economist respectively, whose views probably reflect those of many of their colleagues. Works such as those by Iklé (1964) on international negotiations or Douglas (1962) on industrial negotiations have been characterized as descriptive and anecdotal (e.g., Druckman 1973:5), implying a good deal of theoretical dissatisfaction. One suspects, however, that many theorists are simply unprepared to go out and collect real-life data, preferring the secure coziness of the study or laboratory.

There is no need to deny these and similar difficulties. Indeed, we must constantly be aware of them in order to avoid naive error and overconfidence. We must try to take account of them and to encourage improved observation and recording. For instance, I am most conscious of deficiencies in my own reports of Arusha and Ndendeuli cases of dispute and negotiations. Detail is often insufficient; rather crude summary obscures subtleties of complex interaction; verbatim reports are incomplete; there is too little information on intraparty discussion and strategic planning; and so on. Those cases that have been published are, of course, edited versions of lengthier field notes that could be reviewed and re-presented. There is little doubt that, were it possible to observe these or comparable cases now, both my field notes and published versions would be somewhat different. This would be so partly because of much reconsideration of my materials since they were originally collected in the field, and partly because I have in mind concepts and hypotheses that had not occurred to me earlier.

Take the example of what is probably the most detailed record of a single case of industrial negotiations—the 463 closely printed pages provided by Douglas (1962). The verbatim detail, from tape-recorded sessions of negotiations, is so profuse that perhaps few readers have been able or willing to work through it. Yet there remains a need for further information that is not available from a tape transcript. This is not to suggest that Douglas's presentation is inconsiderable; we could do with more of that kind. Rather, the point is that full information is an impossiblity and that, in any case, the detailed material must inevitably be subject to processing from its raw state before it can be used.

Now these kinds of criticisms are nothing new to historians, anthropologists, and others who gather, synthesize, and present empirical data about social life and behavior. Despite genuine attempts to be objective and to check and validate the data they collect, anthropologists are generally well aware of the deficiencies of their performance. These deficiencies arise not only from the inelucitable limitations and subjectivity of the field anthropologist, but also from the immense complexities of human social behavior, which are greater and less amenable to control and examination than those of the nonhuman world.

In this chapter and elsewhere in this book there is frequent use of the terms *real life* and *the real world,* as well as synonymous phrases such as *empirical reality, concrete social life,* and *hard data.* It should be obvious, but I wish to emphasize it in order to avoid charges of naivete, that these usages do not imply that it is possible to know "reality" in any complete, fully coherent, incontrovertible way. Indeed one must accept that there is no ultimate "reality" out there waiting, as it were, to be observed, recorded, and examined. Our comprehension must necessarily be partial, influenced as it is by our senses, our perceptions, and our cognitive abilities. Thus "real life" can only refer to what we imperfectly know and understand of what occurs behaviorally and mentally among people. My usages may appear to suggest more certainty and comprehensiveness than can or should be claimed. The only defense is that there seem to be no more satisfactory alternatives when it is desired to make the contrast with abstract conceptual and experimental data.

Yet it should go without saying that these problems and defects cannot constitute an acceptable argument against the collection and use of real-life data. Particular cases, however, imperfectly known, in themselves raise questions of interpretation and explanation. These questions, and such answers as develop, can be transferred to the examination of other cases. More important, the comparison of cases, both within the same sociocultural context and cross-culturally, should enable us to perceive common features that transcend situation and culture or correlate with definable, concomitant conditions. This leads to tentative generalization and to the development of hypotheses that can be considered further at an abstract, analytical level or can be taken back to real-life circumstances to enlighten fresh observations.

Let me be clear. There is no intention at all to deny the legitimacy or the usefulness of abstract, inductive conceptualization nor of controlled, artificial experiment and simulation. Neither is it desired to promote a methodological approach in some kind of opposition, as it were, to those intellectual procedures. Historico-ethnographic data are valuable (outside of some anecdotal interest) only insofar as they are subjected to analysis, synthesis, and interpretation. Each case, apart from its importance to the participants in it, becomes significant only as it contributes to the general understanding of the phenomena of interest. This exploitation of real-life data requires tools—concepts, ideas, hypotheses—that in part are obtained from the theorists and in part are generated through the handling of the materials themselves, deductively and inductively. There should be a kind of dialectical relationship between different methodological approaches. The need for abstract theory to aid understanding and generalization is patently obvious. Yet that understanding, apart from its intrinsic intellectual appeal, is in the end useless unless and until it is referred to reality, both to test and refine it and to obtain an improved comprehension of social behavior. That is neither a novel statement nor one that ought to require emphasis; yet the fact is that the use of historico-ethnographic data and the approach derived from their examination have been relatively, even grossly, neglected. Indeed, it is fair to say that the theorists are uncomfortable with real-life data and they seem uncertain about how to use them. These data appear as messy, incomplete, unvalidated, and not readily amenable to the neat control that is taken for granted with abstract concepts and laboratory data (cf. Zartman 1976:6).

The present study is grounded in historico-ethnographic materials, without making unjustifiable claims that they are sufficient in quantity or adequate in quality. The problems of knowing what "really" happened in particular cases are left aside, if only because too critical an inquiry in terms of validity would be, as it sometimes has been, stultifying. Let us, instead, acknowledge that real-life data are but rough approximations, partial and exiguous, and that they may sometimes be misleading, but let us see what can be done with them nevertheless. At a minimum there will be some suggestiveness to be derived from their examination, confirming, contradicting, or modifying some of the ideas and stereotypes prevalent in current theory. Additionally it should be possible to generate hypotheses and to indicate interconnections between various relevant factors. The true test will then be not so much whether the results are true or false, or whether the empirical base is adequate, but whether the results are suggestive of useful ideas and fruitful of some increased understanding. If they are in some degree, then on the one hand, they should stimulate other field researchers toward improved exploitation of their data and better and fuller collection of empirical materials. On the other hand, they will contribute to conceptualization and the development of theory.

THE CROSS-CULTURAL STUDY OF DISPUTES AND NEGOTIATIONS

My concern in this book is with negotiations and joint decision-making, both in Western societies and in those small-scale, non-Western societies that have been the orthodox interest of anthropologists. Thus I am equally concerned with the negotiation of industrial wage rates and working conditions and with the negotiation of bridewealth and the claims of kinship. Moreover, in both kinds of cases, there are associated, vital, and even overriding issues relating to such imponderables as honor, status, self-image, prerogative, morality, and ideology. Such issues are dealt with simultaneously by the same processes within negotiation. A regard for the real world, Western or other, compels us not to neglect them, and this book attempts to give them due consideration.

With an approach based on historico-ethnographic data relating to actual cases of negotiations in various societies, my aim is to propose generalizations. *My premise is that negotiations and joint decision-making, in any society, deal with any kind of issue over which dispute occurs, that is with anything at all. My working hypothesis is that there are common patterns and regularities of interaction between the parties in negotiation irrespective of the particular context or the issues in dispute.*

The center of this book contains an extensive presentation of two models that together describe the processual patterns of negotiation. One is the model of the repetitive, cyclical interaction between two negotiating parties, briefly characterized as the exchange and manipulation of information. The other is a model of the development of interaction from the initiation of a dispute to the conclusion of an agreed outcome. These models are presented and discussed in the first instance as if they were something like a closed system, relatively unaffected by the situational context within which they occur.

In presenting these patterns in simplified, model form, I do not claim any high degree of methodological sophistication. The methods of the social sciences are not well developed in any case, but a tenuousness of the empirical data seems to preclude too fine a procedure here. The genesis of the models lies in ideas and hypotheses of scholars concerned with negotiations and joint decision-making, in my own experience as a field anthropologist, and in the experience of model building in the social sciences at least since the time of Weber's ideal types. The models are partly inductive—what is in fact common to cases of negotiations as far as we can see, given the quality of the real-life data. The models are also partly deductive. This is because there are lacunae in the empirical data, especially concerning private and mental processes, motivations, calculations, and expectations of negotiators. To create anything like a prima facie, plausible model, it seems essential to fill in the gaps by deductive procedures.

These models of processes are presented in their finished form. Real-life data are used merely to demonstrate and to attempt to make clearer particular features of the processes. These data are not intended to, nor can they, prove the "correctness" of the models. Indeed, the models should not be assessed as correct or incorrect. Rather, the test is whether or not they are useful and illuminating toward further understanding. Essentially, any model "is an abstraction from, not a replica of, the real world. Its 'validity' depends entirely upon its utility in furthering fruitful research or in increasing our understanding of reality [Murphy 1964:32]." My claim is that the models in this book are capable of such usefulness. The intention is to improve understanding of what goes on in negotiation, how it goes on and why, and to identify the interaction of some of the variable components involved.

The models are not inflexible representations. In the real world, absolute uniformities of even the basic features of negotiation are not to be found. Flexibility is therefore deliberately built in so as to allow for a degree of variation and, at the same time, to permit the application of the models to particular cases embedded in their own peculiar contexts. They are, of course, observer's models, although the subjective perceptions and intentions of the actors are included as far as seems possible.

Finally, these models are intended only to be *descriptive*. That is, they are not normative or prescriptive in the sense of claiming to lay down what negotiators should do in order to achieve a "best" result or any result at all. My concern is with the patterns of what people do and how they interact in their own endeavors to negotiate outcomes.

A variety of real-life data has been used in the construction of the models. Some of these are specifically used as illustrative material. However, the contemplation and analysis of a great deal more underlie the constructions and the general and particular arguments. Unfortunately, from a "scientific" viewpoint, no satisfactory way seems to be available by which to present the whole body of evidence on which this study depends. This may appear as a signal defect to some readers who wish to see all of the evidence and who will, with some reasonable objection, be dissatisfied with more or less casual, apt illustrations that in themselves prove nothing. The only answer to such objections lies in the usefulness of what can nevertheless be achieved.

As a result of the development of this book, stemming from my own anthropological experience, the first and last resort tends inevitably to be to the materials that I collected firsthand in East Africa. Particular attention is given, without apology, to the results of this research, and especially to case histories among the Arusha and Ndendeuli peoples of Tanzania, some of which have been previously published in analytical ethnographies. The probable bias of this experience is acknowledged since continually, and not always deliberately, I have come back to those personally vivid materials to test and reformulate my ideas and conclusions.

The other richest and most useful source of real-life data is undoubtedly the reported cases of industrial negotiation in Western countries, particularly in the United States. Sociologists, political scientists, economists, and experienced practical negotiators have provided a considerable body of material. It was, in fact, my initial examination of this material that stimulated the notion that the processes and patterns that I detected in East African societies are similar to those that occur in societies with markedly different sociocultural conditions. Moreover, the analytical results and conceptual ideas coming from studies of management–labor disputes and negotiations provided the most helpful stimulus to my theoretical formulations.

The anthropological literature has been less helpful. Negotiation as a field of inquiry has generally been ignored by my fellow anthropologists, although some useful materials are, of course, available from a variety of non-Western societies. Too often, however, the lack of detail in reported case studies is frustrating. On the whole, the most rewarding stimulus from anthropologists has come from those working in the associated, partly overlapping fields of law and adjudication and of local-level politics. Some data are also available on nonindustrial negotiation in Western countries—for instance, concerning disputes over claims against insurance companies. Unfortunately, the lawyers, who spend so much of their time in practical negotiation, have given us exceedingly little from what must be a most rich source of empirical materials.

Another obvious supply of both empirical data and analyses of negotiations lies in the field of international relations. Frankly, I have scarcely ventured into that field. Both the apparent abundance and complexity of the material, requiring considerable specialized knowledge, and the inevitable lacunae imposed by the requirements of secrecy in diplomacy and politics, have seemed a deterrent.[17] Neither are adequate justification for gross neglect and I can only admit to this deficiency.

---

17. According to Roig (1973:52),

It takes something as unexpected and accidental as the publication of the *Pentagon Papers* (as published by the *New York Times*, New York, Bantam Books, 1971) to show just how fragile and incomplete is the information upon which the most serious and apparently best documented interpretations are based. One of the editors of these papers rightly remarks: "The internal functioning of machinery of the post-World War II Executive Branch has been much theorized about, but only intermittently perceived in authentic details. Usually these perceptions have come in the personal memoirs of the policy makers, whose version of history has been understandably selective [p. XII]."

3

SOME BASIC CONCEPTS FOR THE
STUDY OF NEGOTIATION

The social science literature is somewhat confused and contradictory about the definition and application of some basic concepts that are used in the study of negotiations. It is necessary, therefore, to explain and clarify these and to indicate the usages adopted in this book. I wish to distinguish between *negotiation* and *bargaining* and between *disagreement* and *dispute* and to examine the nature and implications of the terms *outcome*. This is not, however, merely an exercise in definitions for the sake of clarity of exposition. The definitions and discriminations proposed here have an analytical significance that is critical for the understanding of negotiation and for the particular presentation in this book. With these concepts in mind, it is then possible to make a preliminary, summary statement of the pocesses involved in the negotiation of disputes.

NEGOTIATION AND BARGAINING

Some writers have not distinguished *negotiation* and *bargaining* at all but have merely taken them to be synonyms. Others have made a distinction but not always in the same way, and dictionary definitions are not sufficiently discriminating for technical purposes. The definitions proposed here may therefore appear arbitrary, as in a sense they must be. Yet there is a real need to make such proposals, not only for clarity of reference but especially for clarity of analysis. On that basis, it is most desirable to recognize a wider and a narrower process of interaction between the opposed parties as they seek to reach an agreed outcome; it is semantically convenient to denote these as negotiation and bargaining, respectively.

Following Sawyer and Guetzkow (1965:466), we may initially describe negotiation as a "process by which parties interact in developing an agreement." This must be refined; for as Bartos has pertinently remarked,

> In order to be realistic, a theory of process must assume that the participants start with only a hazy idea about what the opponents' payoffs may be. Hence, the process of negotiations is more than a sequence of concessions . . . it is also—and at times primarily—a sequence of attempts [by each party] to discover what the opponent's true interests are [Bartos 1974:167].

However, the scope of that sequence of attempts, referred to by Bartos, is wider than he indicated. It is also necessary to include each party's efforts to discover what he can about all potentially significant matters, not only those concerning his opponent. These matters include the interests, goals, expectations, strategies, and psychological concomitants (attitudes, perceptions, emotional dispositions, etc.) of both parties; the ambient reality of the situations and changes in it that indicate the result of nonagreement; an appreciation of the costs of the possible outcomes to each party; the limits of the effective range of consideration for the issues between them; whether and where respective expectations overlap; relevant and potentially useful norms and rules and overarching principles; areas of relative strength, weakness, and tenacity; the nature and strength of outside interests and influences; and much more, depending on the particular parties, their interconnections, and the issues in dispute. Not infrequently, to start right back at the beginning, the parties may not be agreed, or at least are not at all clear, about what issues they are tackling or how they are to be defined in the context—that is, the agenda—let alone what each more or less wants and hopes to obtain.

Throughout the process of interaction, the parties give each other information, directly and indirectly. Each engages in learning about the other, about himself, and about the possibilities and impossibilities of their common situation. Negotiation is a process of discovery. Discovery leads to some degree of reorganization and adjustment of understanding, expectations, and behavior, leading (if successful) eventually to more specific discussion about possible terms of a final, agreed outcome.

There is not only discovery, but also attempts to manipulate the opponent's understanding and preferences. The exchange of information is not an objectively straightforward process. Therefore, while each party seeks to learn what he can, he attempts to implant a version on the opponent that is favorable to the party himself. Part of the exchange is probably coercive—threat and promise.

With this in mind, I propose to give the widest definition of *negotiation* so that it includes the whole range of interaction between the two parties in dispute. It embraces everything that occurs, from the initiation and recognition of the dispute proper[1] to the final outcome and, perhaps, its practical execution.

The narrower process of *bargaining* occurs within that comprehensive frame of negotiation. Bargaining consists of the presentation and exchange of more or less specific proposals for the terms of agreement on particular issues. I have first in mind the process of demand, offer, bid, and their counters, on the analogy of the marketplace or bazaar, relating to the settlement point on items in the dispute. Of course bargaining also occurs on other matters, for instance on the selection of an arena for the negotiation, on the definition of issues, on a variety of procedural arrangements, on applicable norms and rules, and in fact on any matter that arises where a joint decision is required so that the negotiations may continue reasonably effectively. Bargaining on such interim matters can be just as competitive as it may be on the particular issues comprising the dispute itself.

It sometimes happens that bargaining on the issues in dispute ultimately becomes unnecessary as the learning and adjustment processes come to reveal that the parties are not, or are no longer, in disagreement or that their disagreement is not still important. Not everything eventually has to be resolved by bargaining, not even issues of crucial importance to the parties. On the other hand, learning may confirm or reveal real differences that the parties consider can only be settled by bargaining.

It is not always clear, empirically, whether the parties are actually engaged in bargaining, particularly when they are involved in several endeavors at the same time. For example, it may be difficult to know whether an offer or demand is really a proposal for the terms of settlement—that is, a bargaining move—or if it is part of the wider negotiating process as a statement of general intent, an assertion of strength, a scenting of the wind, an attempt to induce a telling reaction from the opponent, an ideological expression, and so on. Conceptually, however, the distinction between the comprehensive process of negotiation and the more restricted, contained process of bargaining is clear enough and it is a useful one for expositional purposes.[2]

---

1. The meaning of "the dispute proper" is discussed on pages 75–77.

2. More or less the same, restricted definition and usage of *bargaining* have been made by Stevens (1963), Cross (1969), Shackle (1970), Coddington (1972), and a number of other

More significant, however, is that the distinction has analytical implications with respect to the identification and separation of processes. It is important to note, therefore, that theoretical work on joint decision-making has very largely concentrated on bargaining as here defined. Moreover, the interest has been focused on the final bargaining that leads directly to the ultimate outcome. This has meant a neglect both of the wider, formative processes and of bargaining on earlier, interim matters that in reality have to be determined if the negotiations are to continue.

Game theorists do not contemplate any wider, more prolonged process of interaction between the parties for, of course, it is the theorists themselves, rather than the parties, who determine the context, the rules, and the possible outcomes of a game. Although some bargaining theorists have acknowledged a phase or process of interaction that precedes bargaining, this has been given little attention. It has often been referred to, and in effect dismissed, as a prebargaining phase. Bartos (1967:482), for example, was frank in writing: "Whilst the problem-solving [i.e., prebargaining] phase has intriguing dilemmas of its own, of primary interest to the theory of negotiations is the bargaining phase: if it is assumed that the possible outcomes and the associated payoffs are already defined, how should one behave in order to get the best possible deal?"

A well-known case in point is that of Nash (1953), whose model contains a "threat game" that precedes the "bargaining game." The effect of the threat game is to establish the outcome that will occur in the event that bargaining is unsuccessful. It seems to be assumed that this can be quite a brief phase. A similar notion was suggested by Bishop (1963); for him, this phase may amount to no more than a matter of each party deciding (and informing his opponent) what he will do if bargaining fails to produce an agreed outcome. The extensive implications of this are scarcely examined: how a party so decides, the possibilities for manipulation and bluff, refusal to inform the opponent so as to promote uncertainty, inability to decide,

---

economists concerned with bargaining theory. Schelling (1956) appears to agree, although he sometimes used *negotiation* synonymously without discrimination—presumably, like some other writers, he saw no particular analytical importance between the two concepts. The use of *negotiation*, specifically or in effect, for the wider process was largely followed by Sawyer and Guetzkow (1965), McGrath (1966), Cross (1969), Stenelo (1972), Bartos (1974), and others. Iklé (1964) made essentially the same distinction but he applied *bargaining* to the more inclusive process. Patchen (1970) used *negotiation* for the narrower process but referred to the participant actor as a *bargainer*. Pruitt (1972) equated *negotiation* with purely verbal communication between the two parties and made *bargaining* include nonverbal communication as well. Further semantic confusion has stemmed from the conventional usage of the industrial term *collective bargaining* to include both of the processes without distinction. The listing could be continued but the foregoing should indicate the partial extent of consensus.

and so on. Similarly, other matters relating to the establishment of the conditions of bargaining have been conveniently assumed to be taken care of in the prebargaining phase. In effect, this has removed them and their problems from the processual context and hence from genuine examination. For example, in making the assumption that perfect information is available to both parties in bargaining, Stahl (1972:181) naively asserted that such a happy state is achieved in prebargaining; either "the parties might agree on an exchange of information" or a mediator supplies it.

Thus, even when it is acknowledged that something happens before final bargaining occurs, it has not been seen as particularly important. The results of prebargaining have been generally assumed, without special inquiry, to become built into the conditions (as "givens") within which bargaining takes place. This has meant a gross neglect of the wider processes and the dynamics of negotiations—a disregard for factors of crucial importance to the end game of bargaining. If, however, we are to understand real-life negotiations, it is essential to investigate how the parties actually get to that end game. This requires examination of the interconnected processes of information exchange, learning, and the recurrent adjustments of expectations and strategy. Involved in these processes are efforts to manipulate the opponent's perceptions. In the course of all this the parties accumulate an experience of each other and of the changing situation in which they are operating and interacting. They develop an appreciation (not necessarily objectively accurate, of course) of each other, of themselves, and of the apparent potentialities and impossibilities between them. There is likely to be some development of their immediate relationship as negotiators in terms of, for instance, competitiveness or cooperation, trust or mistrust, cautiousness or candor, respect or disdain.

In these ways, for the moment only briefly indicated, the conditions are created in which a final outcome may be achieved. In addition, there is a carry-over from earlier phases into the end game. Bargainers do not newly approach each other as if they were hitherto isolated game players. Rather, they bring a load of accumulated, direct experience of themselves and their conflicts, and this affects the way they engage in bargaining. In reality there is not usually a sharp distinction between earlier phases and final bargaining. Instead there is a continuity as the parties more or less gradually shift into the end game. This suggests that the rules and conditions of bargaining and the range of potential outcomes are less specific and more flexible than many theorists have been prepared to recognize.[3]

---

3. The preliminaries to final bargaining and the bargaining itself are considered as phases in the developmental model of negotiation. See pages 153–168.

DISAGREEMENTS AND DISPUTES

It is necessary, next, to define and elucidate the concept of *dispute* as it is used in this study of negotiation.

In ongoing social life, relationships and interaction between individuals and groups are oriented and guided by the generalized, customary standards current in the society or in some particular sector of it. The very definition of a relationship—the pattern of behavioral interaction, interests, rights, obligations, and affective content, and the extent of tolerable leeways in all these—depends on such accepted standards, more or less clearly understood by the members of the social unit. These standards carry some degree of moral imperative; they involve endogenous sanctions and perhaps exogenous and legal prescription, and they may be instrumental and technical in prescribing conventionally practical and practicable ways of behavior. In persisting or repetitive relationships, these standards and the associated expectations are, in varying degrees, modified and augmented by more or less idiosyncratic conventions and understandings, which become established and accepted by the particular individuals concerned. Thus there emerges the pragmatic pattern of the relationship between John Smith and George Smith, as distinct from, yet influenced by, their society's cultural definition of the relationship between brothers. That pragmatic pattern reflects the history of their interaction, their particular interests, and their relative strengths, and psychological factors within their social context. There are, then, two overlapping frameworks composed of cultural and idiosyncratic standards respectively—they might be called the "rules"—within which specific interaction occurs. More often than not, presumably, a person conforms adequately to these rules, with little deliberate or conscious reflection. Indeed it is a truism to say that regular social life would be impossibly cumbersome were people not to accept and work within the rules.

Problems and disagreements inevitably arise in any relationship, ephemeral or persisting, if only because no set of rules can prospectively provide for every eventuality. These problems are of two basic, though not entirely distinct, kinds: those concerning the nature of the relationship itself or some important feature of it, and those concerning what to do (and how, where, and when) in particular matters of interest to the individuals. On the other hand, what right or obligations, and with what strength, does either party have vis-à-vis the other? For example, should two farmer-neighbors assist each other in plowing, or should two friends give up some other activity in order to play golf together—or is cooperative plowing or golfing not to be involved in those relationships? On the other hand, if such activities are involved, then there are such problems as whose field the farmers shall plow first, or when and where the two friends shall play golf.

Dynamically, a social relationship constitutes a problem-solving process as well as a rule-patterned process. Some problem solving occurs through the toleration of a persisting disagreement—one farmer disliking but accepting that he gives more help to the other than he himself receives. Resolution can often be accomplished quite quickly once the problem is confronted—for instance, a reminder that it is your turn now since I contributed last time, in a situation in which reciprocity or alternate action is the rule, or a reminder that my need is greater than yours, or more conveniently met, at this time. But problem solving may not be that easy, particularly where the rules are unclear or ambiguous or where one party in his own interest wishes to change the rule to the possible disadvantage of the other. Novel circumstances occur, new interests arise or old ones change; relative power, values, and goals shift, so that a more conscious deliberation may be required.

In short, the obvious point is that *disagreements*, large or small, are commonly resolved within a relationship (sometimes by terminating it) by dyadic and private problem-solving between the parties themselves. There is a general, repetitive process of dyadic adjustment, whether that leaves the relationship more or less as it was or whether it changes or reinforces the status quo.[4] The point to be emphasized here is that disagreements are resolvable (and/or tolerated) within the relationship and no dispute arises.

A *dispute* becomes imminent only when the two parties are unable and/or unwilling to resolve their disagreement; that is, when one or both are not prepared to accept the status quo (should that any longer be a possibility) or to accede to the demand or denial of demand by the other. A dispute is precipitated by a crisis in the relationship. That crisis comes from the realization by at least one party that dyadic adjustment is unsatisfactory or impossible and that the continued disagreement cannot be tolerated. That person therefore attempts to take the disagreement out of the private, dyadic context and to put it into a public domain with the intent that "something must be done." Going into a public domain offers the possibility of appealing to other people and to the interests and norms of the community, which, it is thought, may be advantageous to, and supportive of, the party's demands. Sometimes going public is an attempt to avoid

---

4. For simple convenience it is assumed that a social relationship concerns only two parties (individuals or groups), principally because the present study of negotiation is specifically limited to two-party situations (see page 268). There are, of course, often three or more parties (e.g., father, mother, child), so that problems and their resolution involve multiparty adjustment.

further deterioration of the relationship and of the situation, including perhaps a threat of violence or some other unpleasant result (Starr 1978:128).

To put the disagreement into a public domain[5] is to put it into a different frame of reference and action. There is, in effect, an announcement that there is disagreement that is not resolvable by normal, dyadic adjustment and is considered in some sense to be serious and therefore requires special treatment.[6] There is some kind of public recognition and cognizance of the matter and of the desire for attention. Some other people become involved as supporters, advocates, or representatives of each of the parties and perhaps as third parties. There is a publicized proposal that the matter be dealt with through some recognized, overt procedure that is routinized in some degree. Minimally, the proposal is for an arranged meeting, or for time in a meeting already in prospect, when discussion, the exchange of information and offers—in short, negotiations—can take place with respect to the issues. The term *public* is used here in specific contrast with *private* and *dyadic*. It does not imply that the disagreement, now a potential dispute, invariably becomes a matter of knowledge, interest, and concern to more or less everyone in the community, for the public is often quite limited.

The fact that a person seeks to shift a disagreement to the level of a dispute does not necessarily mean that it will thereafter be dealt with in a public domain. For one thing, the other party may now become willing to resolve the disagreement through dyadic discussion, not wishing to meet the implications of going public. Indeed, the threat to initiate a dispute may be a stratagem by one party to induce the other to come to terms privately. Apart, from that, however, the other party may have to be persuaded or compelled to enter the public domain when otherwise he might merely refuse to do so or to do anything else in the matter. Much depends on the institutional arrangements of a society and what form of public treatment is sought. Public domains usually include an adjudicatory system wherein, once a complaint is lodged and is accepted as prima facie legitimate, the other party is more or less compelled to appear and to meet the complaint. It is sometimes more difficult when the complainant seeks to enter into negotiations and if there is no formal authority to persuade or compel a recalcitrant party to participate, particularly if the latter considers non-cooperation to be to his advantage. (See Chapter 5, page 123.)

Thus, to convert dyadic disagreement into a dispute two things are re-

---

5. The useful term *domain* is borrowed from Fortes (1958:6).

6. In most societies there are regular, even dramatic, ways of making the announcement, such as beating a gong, calling out the news in the quiet of the evening, or making a formal declaration to news media or at some assembly of potentially concerned persons.

quired. First, one party precipitates a crisis and seeks to put the matter into a public domain. Second, the other party must be willing or be induced to agree to and to participate in negotiations.

This distinction between the dyadic adjustment of disagreement in the private domain and the negotiation of a dispute in a public domain is conceptual and analytical. In the large majority of cases and in most societies, the distinction is clear enough since there is a definite social and cultural shift from one process and one domain to another process in a different domain. Even though negotiation as a social form may be only weakly institutionalized, the distinction is emically recognized. Nevertheless, the distinction is not altogether unproblematic. I am reserving the term *negotiation* for a process in a public domain where the two parties, with supporters of various kinds, attempt to reach a joint decision on the issues in dispute. Yet ordinary as well as scholarly usage commonly describes dyadic adjustment also as negotiation. Moreover, although a distinguishing characteristic of the public nature of negotiation is the involvement of a team of some kind in support of each principal or as representative of a constituency, such as the lineage, village, or workers in a firm, supporters or interested third parties may also intervene and participate in dyadic adjustment. For instance, a wife might intervene in disagreements between father and child or a common neighbor vis-à-vis two friends. Thus the distinction is by no means an absolute one; there are features common to both dyadic adjustments and negotiation, although these features take on rather different emphases in each case. Indeed, I shall argue later that the process of public negotiations can be perceived as an extension and elaboration of the mode of interaction and problem-solving adjustment in all social relationships. For the moment, however, for purposes of a first analysis, it remains useful to emphasize the distinction.

THE OUTCOME OF NEGOTIATION

The beginning of the process of negotiation, the initiation of a dispute proper, has now been described in general terms. The pattern of the process is described in Chapter 5. The culmination of that process is the outcome. As I have argued earlier, one outcome is a joint agreement by the two parties on the terms for the issues in dispute. Those terms are, in the opinion of both parties, satisfactory enough under the circumstances, and better than no agreement. Since the parties began with some differences between them, it follows that, at the conclusion, at least one but probably both have been induced to accept less than originally desired and/or something different. Each party expresses overt or tacit acceptance of the joint decision outcome. This does not mean that there is necessarily a final resolution of the issues in dispute. That might happen though it is not easy to know, perhaps not for a long time afterward. In any event, the outcome represents the end of the particular negotiations and thus, for the time being at least, the end of the dispute.

In many instances, negotiations run on to a culmination even though the final agreement deals with only some of the issues in dispute. Other issues, by joint consent, are withdrawn from consideration or left as being incapable of resolution. The parties achieve only limited joint success. Those other issues lie dormant or revert to dyadic disagreements; they may fade out altogether or become subject to fresh negotiations in the future. Nevertheless, there is an outcome.

Negotiations may be cut short, ending in a stalemate. The parties are unable to gain genuine consideration of the issues, let alone an agreed outcome. Neither party is willing to shift his demands, and their expectations remain quite divergent. There is merely repetitive declaration of set positions and, perhaps, increased mistrust, anger, and anxiety. As Iklé (1964: 59–61) has shown, negotiators continually have three choices: to accept the other party's offer, to propose a preferred alternative, or to accept the status quo. One party may force the matter by refusing to consider the issues further, by refusing to hear the other's views, or by walking out and refusing to return. That party therefore prefers the status quo or status quo ante to anything else that appears possible. The other party, in not accepting the first party's offer, must perforce concede to that and in a sense agree to it. Both parties may agree in effect to disagree since they see no way to come to mutually acceptable terms. Here again, however, there is an outcome.

It is important to note that, quite often, the overt issues in negotiations are not the "real" issues causing conflict in the relationship between the principals. The outcome, therefore, does no more than deal with currently overt problems, and the parties cannot or do not wish to deal with others that may be more fundamental for them. The current negotiations may then provide a partial confrontation or a symbolic encounter in the ongoing conflict between the principals. For instance, particular negotiations may be one way of, and a phase in, conducting a political or economic struggle. Yet, whatever the intended purpose of the negotiations, they culminate in some sort of an outcome.

My simple point, emphasized merely to prevent misunderstanding, is that, once begun, negotiations lead to some result. With Felstiner (1974:63) and others, I wish to avoid the use of the word *settlement*, which seems to carry a notion of finality and completeness. Outcomes vary tremendously in their degree of settlement and, in any case, it is generally impossible to know this until some time after the negotiations are over. To be sure, the outcome is frequently the result of a positive joint agreement on the terms relating to at least a number of the issues in dispute. It is because such an outcome is the end result of a total process of negotiation that the movement toward it and the total process are the principal concerns of analysis in this book. It nevertheless remains of interest to show how and why some negotiations "fail" or are cut short and what the outcome then is.

DISPUTES AND NEGOTIATIONS:
A SUMMARY STATEMENT

A *dispute* begins when two parties become unable or unwilling to deal with problems and disagreement in their relationship by dyadic adjustment in private and when, therefore, one or both put the matter into a public domain. At that time, other people take cognizance and they become involved, as supporters, representatives, or third parties, in one or more meetings in some agreed arena. Some result, an *outcome*, is eventually reached. This may be positive agreement on some or all of the issues in dispute, but it may be a deadlock or an uncontrollable default by one party from which the outcome is the retention of the status quo.

Negotiations are processes of interaction between disputing parties whereby, without compulsion by a third-party adjudicator, they endeavor to come to an interdependent, *joint decision* concerning the terms of agreement on the issues between them. This joint decision is one that, in the end, is agreeable to and accepted by both parties after each has brought influence and persuasion to bear on the other and, most probably, after both have experienced influence from other sources. The outcome is essentially one that, in each party's opinion in the perceived circumstances, is at least satisfactory enough and is perhaps considered to be the best that is obtainable. It often represents a compromise between the parties' initial demands and expectations, but there may be, in part or whole, the joint creation of some new terms not originally conceived of by either party. The outcome reflects the relative strengths of the parties in terms of their resources of material and symbolic power and the constraints of moral and practical rules and values in the society.

Negotiations proceed through the *exchange of information* between the parties, and between them and third parties. Information is verbal and nonverbal, including evidence, argument, appeals to rules and ideology, expressions of strength and proposals of terms for agreement. This exchange permits a *learning* process by which each party formulates, modifies, and readjusts expectations, preferences, and proposals. In consequence, the parties are able to approach agreement on an outcome.

The key terms are italicized in this summary statement. They have been initially discussed in this chapter and they will be examined further in succeeding chapters as account is taken of their implications and of their appearance in conjunction with other relevant factors.

4

PROCESSUAL MODEL OF NEGOTIATION, 1: THE CYCLICAL MODEL— INFORMATION EXCHANGE AND LEARNING

> *Some problems are just too complicated for rational logical solutions. They admit of insights, not answers [Jerome Weisner; quoted in Lang 1963].*

As we have already seen in preliminary fashion, when a dispute emerges and negotiations begin, the two parties[1] start at a distance from one another, in disagreement, opposition, and conflict, with disparate ideas and expectations about an acceptable outcome. Through the processes of negotiation the parties gradually may be able to come together into coordination and collusion and, in the end, to some agreement on the issues between them.

In essence—and this is to be emphasized—the process of negotiation is one of information exchange and of consequent learning and adjustment by the parties. Ultimately, if agreement is reached, "the position of each [party] has been subtly changed not only by the terms offered, but by its experience of the other and exposure to the other's persuasion [Vickers 1972:151]." That experience and exposure are the content and effects of

---

1. In this and succeeding chapters the terms *party* and *opponent* refer either to a principal disputant or to a team. The team may be recruited by a disputant in order to obtain supporters, advisors, and advocates, or it may comprise representatives of a constituency (some group or category of people involved in dispute). For general analytical purposes it does not matter much which particular meaning applies, though where it has importance a specific distinction is made in the text. For simplicity, third-person pronouns (he, him, his, etc.) are used throughout. This usage does not imply that the referent party is a single individual nor only male.

negotiating interaction. In the end, for any particular issue in dispute, when "a bargainer knows 'that is all' means that, it is not that the opponent has told him so but that he has personally *experienced the futility of seeking more* [Douglas 1957:79; italics in original]."[2]

In negotiation there are two distinct though interconnected processes going on simultaneously: a repetitive, cyclical one and a developmental one. A simple analogy is a moving automobile. There is the cyclical turning of the wheels (linked to the cyclical action of valves, pistons, etc., in the motor) that enables the vehicle to move, and there is the actual movement of the vehicle from one place to another. The latter process depends on the former but the raison d'être of the automobile is its spatial movement. In negotiation, somewhat similarly, there is a cyclical process comprising the repetitive exchange of information between the parties, its assessment, and the resulting adjustments of expectations and preferences; there is also a developmental process involved in the movement from the initiation of the dispute to its conclusion—some outcome—and its implementation.

The model of the developmental process is presented and examined in detail in Chapter 5. Briefly, it comprises a series of overlapping sequences or phases, each with its particular emphasis and kind of interaction and each opening the way for the succeeding one in a complex progression. Summarily, these phases are (1) the search for an arena for the negotiations; (2) the formulation of an agenda and working definitions of the issues in dispute; (3) preliminary statements of demands and offers and the exploration of the dimensions and limits of the issues, with an emphasis on the differences between the parties; (4) the narrowing of differences, agreements on some issues, and the identification of the more obdurate ones; (5) preliminaries to final bargaining; (6) final bargaining; (7) ritual confirmation of the final outcome; and, in many cases, (8) the implementation of the outcome or arrangements for that.

It is logically appropriate to discuss first the model of the cyclical process since by analogy it is the turning of the wheels that makes movement of the vehicle possible. Because the two processes are intimately interconnected, references to the developmental process are unavoidable in the following exposition, though they are kept to a minimum so as to avoid confusion. The reader should keep in mind, however, the developmental phase pattern just outlined.

---

2. This and all subsequent quotes cited to Douglas (1957) are reprinted from "The Peaceful Settlement of Industrial and Intergroup Disputes" by Ann Douglas in *Journal of Conflict Resolution*, Vol. 1, No. 1, (March 1957) by permission of the publisher, Sage Publications, Inc.

THE CYCLICAL MODEL

Briefly, the pattern of repetitive exchange is that, in turn, each party receives information of various kinds from the other and in response offers information to him. There is, however, more than merely communication. There is cognition and learning. Received information is interpreted and evaluated by a party and added to what he already knows or thinks he knows. Thus a party may be able to learn more about his own expectations and preferences, about those of his opponent, and about their common situation and possible outcomes. Learning may induce changes in the party's preference set and his strategies or it may reinforce his existing position. Learning may raise the need for more information from the opponent and/or the need to give further information to him so that he may be induced to learn and therefore be persuaded to shift his position to something more favorable to the party. Depending on the kind of learning, the party makes a tactical choice concerning the purpose and content of his next message, which is then proffered to his opponent. In turn, the other party goes through the same procedure and then offers his information to the first party . . . and so on. Thus, one might say, the wheels turn and the vehicle moves.

A diagrammatic model of the cyclical process is given in Figure 4.1. In the following exposition of this model and its implications, I deal first with the exchange of information and the intrinsic dynamics of the interaction. Second, I examine the inherent problems facing a negotiator as he establishes and adjusts his set of preferences relating to the issues in dispute and their possible outcomes. Third, there is discussion of the operational strategies adopted by a negotiator to deal with these problems. Fourth, there is consideration of the expectations built up by a party concerning his opponent's preferences and future actions as these affect his own preferences and choices. Fifth, I briefly discuss the tactical choices a party must make before he offers his own messages and further information to his opponent. This exposition thus embraces a half-cycle of the repetitive process, from the receipt of a message from the opponent to the offer of a message to him in return.

THE EXCHANGE OF INFORMATION

In negotiation there is a continual need both to give and to receive information. There is a need to give it in order to tell the opponent about one's own demands and strengths and to attempt to induce him to shift his

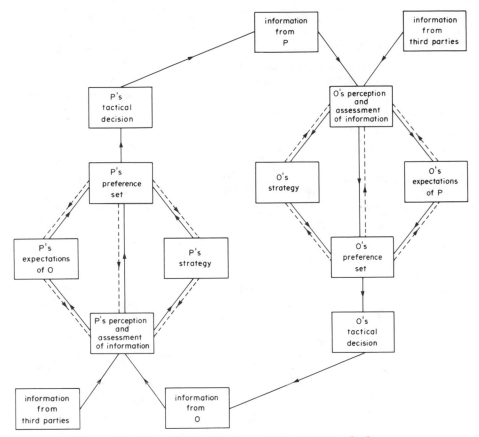

Figure 4.1. The cyclical model of negotiation: P, Party; O, Opponent.

demands toward one's own. There is a need to obtain information in order to get a better understanding of the opponent—his expectations and demands, his attitudes, strategies, strengths, and weaknesses, together with any changes in all these matters. In order to obtain needed information, a party has to give information to his opponent. In order to give information, he needs to receive information from his opponent. Receiving information creates the opportunity, but also the necessity perhaps, to learn and to adjust expectations and demands. That in turn induces the party to offer further information and to seek to obtain more.

Thus there is and has to be exchange of information, or more accurately, of messages. Strictly speaking, information is not exchanged but shared since the giver himself retains that which is given, in contrast with economic exchange of goods. A party must respond and wishes to respond to the receipt of messages by giving his own in return. As in other kinds of social reciprocity, a party offers messages in order to obtain a response and to be able to claim a respor.se, or at least some kind of reaction that carries a message. Refusal to exchange messages may, in the short run, draw further messages from the opponent and may be intended to do so. Continued refusal—or what is effectively the same thing, mere repetition of previous messages—leads to impasse and the possible breakdown of negotiations.

Yet these desires and needs to give and to receive information create a persisting dilemma for each party. How much information should be given and when? What information is required and how can it be obtained? Moreover, as Iklé has pointed out, "It is an essential feature of negotiations that the process of finding out the opponent's terms (and of revealing one's own) is also part of the process of inducing him to soften his terms (and of making one's own more acceptable to him) [1964:191]." While seeking to persuade or coerce his opponent, a party lays himself open to persuasion and coercion. He may, therefore, attempt to defend himself by the offer of further information and his opponent proceeds likewise.

Thus reciprocal giving and receiving information is reinforced and continued by new needs to give and to receive. Kelley has written of the "tension between *information needs* and *information restraints* that constitutes the central motivational force for negotiators' behavior [1966:58; italics in original]." There is, however, a wider range of motivational force than that, as I have indicated, and therefore a stronger and more complex one, the elements of which feed each other. All of these reciprocal needs and desires to receive and to give continually generate interaction in a cumulative fashion. There is a marked potential for persisting motivation to continue the negotiations. I wish to give the strongest emphasis to this at the outset of my exposition because it is crucial to the understanding of the process of negotiation.[3]

An inherent problem in these exchanges is that each party tends to edit in his own favor the information he offers. He wishes to show and substantiate his demands and to emphasize his strengths and determination but without disclosing his weaknesses, his truer expectations, or his minimal requirements. Thus he usually stresses and exaggerates the more advantageous features of his case while discounting or ignoring the disadvantageous ones. A party must expect that the messages he receives are similarly edited. The flow of information is therefore distorted in some degree. Moreover, the exchange of messages always carries the possibility that

---

3. A second and connected major motivational force is evident in the repeated alternation of antagonism and coordination between the parties throughout negotiation. This is examined later, on pages 181–186.

unintended information will be conveyed at the same time. On the one hand, a party may not say what he intended, or he may say more than he intended as information is carried between the lines and, as an affectual penumbra, colors what is said. On the other hand, his opponent may misreceive and misinterpret messages and obtain wrong information.

Information is carried by any and all kinds of messages from one party to the other—and by messages from third parties also. These include both the intended and unintended, the overt and covert, and the linguistic and nonlinguistic. Silence too sends a message of some kind, according to context and cultural norms.[4]

The kinds of information exchanged depend a good deal on the current phase of the negotiation: that is, on the mode and focus of interaction and purpose at the time (as explained in the developmental model). Some kinds of subject matter are more likley to be confined to particular phases. For instance, information concerning procedural rules is more pertinent to earlier phases when procedure is being established, although it is never altogether excluded from later phases if the parties consider it important. Factual information similarly is more emphasized in earlier phases, whereas messages carrying threats, promises, and other persuasion are likely to be more common in later ones. Yet the subject matter and even the overt content of messages are often much the same in different phases even though the information transmitted can be quite different. "This is my best offer," or "We cannot agree to your claim," carry and are more or less intended to carry different information in earlier and later phases. During final bargaining a "final offer" may indeed be just that or something very near it, but earlier it is nothing like so definitive and usually it is not intended to be so. Earlier, the information is something like a show of the importance of the particular issue in dispute and of the strength of resistance intended. It may in fact be little more than putting a toe in the water to test it, an attempt to get reaction and response from the opponent in order to learn more about his expectations and preferences. It relates, in the earlier phases, to attempts by parties to perceive where the main differences lie and what the maximal limits are to the range of reference on the issue in question. That is to say, messages are to be understood, and are so interpreted by the receiver, depending on what is already known and not known by the parties about each other. A message and its information are

---

4. In some societies silence has a particular significance. For example, among the Arusha it unequivocally means agreement with the last message received, since it is assumed that a party would otherwise express his disagreement (Gulliver 1963:228). Elsewhere and according to context, silence can mean refusal of a message, expression of frustration or of mistrust, acceptance of inferiority, and so on.

very largely contextual, as of course is the case in most ordinary conversation.

Assessment of messages is necessary to complete the transference of information and so make it usable. Some or even all of a message may not be received. What is received is subject to appraisal. For instance, what is its content, overtly and covertly? What is the probable degree of validity of fact, opinion, affectual state, and ignorance? What did the opponent intend to convey and with what force? What did he convey unwittingly and why in the fashion he used? What is absent from the message and why? Such assessment can be carried out quite carefully and analytically or, at the other extreme, it may be largely unconsidered gut reaction. Some messages are highly complex, containing information that cannot be immediately assessed or its implications understood. Such information may have to be set aside for the moment until more information is accumulated or until a later phase of the negotiations. Other messages are so simple that, in one sense, their content is clear; yet the alert negotiator is prepared to acknowledge that the simplicity may be deceptive, deliberately or not on the part of the sender. "No" can indicate or be understood to indicate a variety of information: "yes" or "yes but" or "I do not know" among others, or it can indicate a less certain denial than hitherto and so reveal some degree of change in the sender's expectations or determination.

For instance, an observation on the weather or a humorous anecdote may—though it may not—carry an expression of friendliness and willingness to be cooperative or an expression of antagonism and derision. It can show a desire to break tension, to pause awhile, or to change topic and tactics. It can be a sign of a lack of further ideas or of frustration, and many other things, according to the current phase of the negotiations and the relationship between the parties. Though seemingly trivial, it affords a party a possibility of indicating something about his position, attitude, and expectations. It may, at a particular point in the negotiations, be quite crucial to an improvement of understanding that in context is no less significant than the party's forthright declaration on some matter. Yet the message may be unimportant, offering little that is new or helpful to the other.

There is no need to suppose that assessment of messages is complete or correct, whatever that might mean. Nor is it suggested that the receiver is altogether aware of what he receives and how he assesses it. For the sake of the conceptual model being presented here, I merely wish to refer to and indicate the kinds of problems inherent in the process of information exchange. I am not concerned with attempting to develop any elaborate theory of that exchange. Such theory does exist, although much of it seems to require development and testing against empirical data. For present purposes, such theory is scarcely required and I can afford to be brief and simplistic.

In terms of the cyclical model, the supply of more or less assessed information can be seen as flowing in two directions. First, received information may affect a party's behavior as a result of causing changes in knowledge, preferences, attitudes, and strategy—in brief, as a result of changes in his preference set. Second, the information may affect a party's behavior as a result of his assessment of his opponent's future behavior— his expectations of his opponent. Both are liable to be affected and changed by each new piece of information received. In the following exposition, these two features of the model—the preference set and the expectations of the opponent—are dealt with separately in that order, although they are closely interconnected.

THE PREFERENCE SET: (A) THE NEGOTIATOR'S PROBLEMS

In discusing the preference set, it is useful to consider, first, the problems that confront a party in his attempts to construct and adjust his set and, second, the operational strategies he may employ to deal with those problems. These are examined separately in this and the following section respectively.

A party's preference set ideally comprises ordered evaluations of issues and conceivable outcomes. First, there is an ordering of the issues in dispute and their various attributes as a result of assessment of the expected, relative satisfactions that might be obtained from them with reference to basic objectives and requirements. This ordering allows an assessment and ordering of possible outcomes that can be contemplated as tolerable or as potentially unavoidable in view of expectations of the opponent's preferences. The preferential ordering of those conceivable outcomes is further modified by consideration of the anticipated costs of obtaining them and of the relative strengths of the two parties. Commonly, there is emphasis on three particular levels of evaluation for the issues, singly or in packages: the conceivable maxima that might be obtained, the anticipated minima below which anything is thought to be unacceptable, and the targets that are aimed for above the minima.

Three points must be made immediately about real-life conditions, although they are elaborated later. First, evaluations of preferences are often imprecise and even quite vague. Second, preferences are not necessarily altogether consistent with each other; objectives and evaluations may be established by different criteria and with varying frames of reference.

Third, evaluations and preferences are not fixed and static but more or less continuously subject to change during the course of the negotiations.

Game and bargaining theorists, and other social scientists influenced by their models, have usually conceived of a fixed, limited number of finite outcomes, which is assumed to be known to the parties. In their models, the parties are able to evaluate outcomes and their costs quantitatively against a single, numerical standard. Thus comparison and ordering are fairly straightforward. When uncertainties of outcome or evaluation are fed into the model, there remains the ability to calculate and use probabilities, again in concert with quantitative measures. Moreover, as previously shown, these models have virtually ignored conditions of multiple issues and multiple criteria of evaluation (pages 52–60).

In the desire to avoid these unrealistic simplifications and to acknowledge the much more complex conditions of real life, I am presenting a model that is closer to the messiness of reality, no more susceptible to mathematical manipulation than are the shifting, approximating assessments of actual negotiators. It is a model that accords with the general notion of negotiation as an exploratory interaction between the parties. Thus, initially, each party has some vagueness and uncertainty in his preferences. He may well be unclear about what he wants or prefers, what the possible outcomes might be and how to compare multiple, disparate issues and their attributes. In any case, the set of issues in dispute is not yet established since that, in part, depends on the ideas and aims of the opponent. It is commonplace that the issues over which dispute begins are not necessarily those that are, or become, most important for either party, that further issues are precipitated as negotiations begin and that quite new, hitherto unanticipated outcomes may become available. A party usually enters negotiations with some goals in mind that he hopes to achieve—though these are not always clearly perceived, nor are their implications fully understood at that point. Deliberately or not, he begins privately to compare and evaluate issues and possible outcomes and to clarify his aims and intentions. As information comes from the opponent, the party is able, and also compelled, to gain some better appreciation of what is probable, possible, and impossible and what the opportunity costs might be.

Thus the party refines and adjusts his preference set, and he continues to do this until the end of negotiations. It is unlikely, however, that he can reach and maintain complete clarity and certainty, for in any but the simplest of disputes the variables to be taken into account are not altogether known; for many variables only the roughest kind of evaluation is possible. Not even near the end of negotiations is such an ideal attained or attainable, nor is the preference set likely to be totally consistent. The principal sources of uncertainty and inconsistency are inherent in a range of problems that, singly and together, are not completely resolvable by the time of the culminating outcome. These are (a) the evaluation of preferences for anticipated outcomes for the various issues and the assessment of probabilities for potential outcomes and for the opponent's actions; (b) incommensurability between multiple issues and their various attributes, or between packages of them; (c) expectations about the opponent's preferences and the assessment of the strengths (and weaknesses) of each party that support (or undermine) their demands; (d) assessment of the directions and strengths of outside interests and influences; (e) the interpretation, applicability, and strength of normative rules and values; and (f) the assessment of the costs of attaining potential outcomes. These problems are briefly considered in the rest of the present section.

Evaluation of Preferences and Probabilities. It would scarcely need to be said that many issues and possible outcomes are not readily evaluated in quantitative terms were it not that so many prescriptive theorists have obscured the problem, either by ignoring it or by attributing numerical values to immeasurable phenomena. It is necessary, therefore, briefly to examine the problems, proposed theoretical solutions, and the kind of practical procedures that actual negotiators employ to evaluate preferences and probabilities.

Most decision theorists insist that it is possible to establish numerical values that are at least acceptable approximations to the true conditions. Often it remains unclear what criteria are used, whether they are or can be those of a real-life negotiator, and if there can be any such thing as the true conditions for him. One need only mention such issues as prestige, honor, moral probity, or ritual purity—commonly involved in disputes—to indicate the obvious difficulties. However, even where quantitative measures exist (as with monetary values in the market) these do not necessarily correlate with a party's subjective preferences. More money or a higher monetary value is not inevitably preferable; nor is more honor always chosen as against less. It is naive to assume otherwise.

To get over these kinds of difficulties, theorists have developed the concept of utility such that a negotiator's subjective preferences (whatever their basis and whether "rational" or not) can be expressed numerically in terms of "utiles." This has proved most attractive, even indispensable, to its proponents, for it has allowed them to avoid problems of measurement and comparison and to proceed with mathematical treatment of theoretical issues. So attractive has it become that some writers have claimed that relative utilities on a cardinal scale can be constructed for a party's actual preferences in real-life conditions. Briefly, one possible way of doing this is for an observer to present a negotiator with a series of choices of outcomes. The negotiator orders them by comparing successive pairs of options and in each case deciding which option is preferable, or indicating indifference between them. Eventually, the most preferred outcome can be designated as, say, 100 and the others are given appropriate cardinal numbers such that all are placed on a single scale of comparable utility.[5]

In the context of negotiation, at least, such a procedure has severe problems that do not seem to be resolvable. First, it requires that a negotiator is able to take time out in order to consider his assessments and choices meticulously. This is not always possible or at least it is often not done systematically. In any case, it cannot be assumed that a negotiator's evaluations during a time-out are necessarily the same as when he is under the stress of actual interaction with, and pressures from, his opponent and others. Second, a negotiator's subjective assessments and choices do not remain constant and consistent throughout negotiations. Thus a cardinal utility scale would have to be repeatedly reconstructed if it were to be useful and not misleading by its rigidity. Third, in most disputes there is a complexity of multiple issues and their attributes that renders the whole procedure exceedingly cumbersome and, given negotiators' unavoidable ignorance, uncertainty, and unwillingness to make commitment, seemingly impossible. In any case, however, there is little evidence to show that actual negotiators appreciate, create, and work with utility scales in order to cope with difficulties of preference and choice.

Confidence in that conclusion is strengthened by consideration of some of the assumptions required by utility theory that cannot be made in real-life circumstances. For example, Luce and Raiffa in their classic work, *Games and Decisions* (1957), made an essential presupposition to their mathematical exposition of utility theory. In a decision-making situation (they took choices of lotteries as their paradigm) they assumed "a finite set of basic alternatives or prizes . . . outcomes with certain known probabilities [p. 24]."[6] Now in real-life disputes, possible outcomes are fre-

---

5. A description of this kind of method for a single decision-maker against nature is given by P. G. Moore and H. Thomas (1976:169 ff.). Many theorists are not concerned with the practical construction of a cardinal utility scale; they assume its possibility and use the notion theoretically.

6. That this kind of assumption has been widespread can be illustrated by a comparable statement from a political scientist: "Decision-making is a process which results in the selection from a socially defined, *limited number* of problematic, alternative projects of one project intended to bring about *the particular future state of affairs envisaged* by decision-makers [Snyder *et al.* 1962:90; italics added]."

quently unclear and are seldom a finite set, and probabilities are generally indeterminate. Moreover, most negotiators are unable to assess and use probabilities in any technical sense.

There is, in addition, a theoretical argument against the assumption that probabilities can be determined in an essentially interactional situation, such as negotiation, as Young has pointed out (1975:14).[7] In that situation, the choices of the opposed parties are reciprocally interdependent. This means that a party finds it impossible to make an accurate prediction of the probable behavior, preferences, and choices of his opponent. The opponent's behavior depends in part on the party's own behavior (or the opponent's expectations about it), which in turn depends on the opponent's behavior, which in turn depends . . . in infinite regress. Probabilities therefore cannot be assigned to the choices of the opponent. Needless to say, in actuality, negotiators have to cut through that impossibility and this they do, somehow, crudely, but without particularly clear notions of the probabilities of the opponent's behavior and thus of particular outcomes.

Among the consistency requirements for the assignment of utility, Luce and Raiffa posited that any two alternative outcomes shall be comparable—one is preferred over the other or there is indifference—and that preferences and indifferences are transitive (1957:23). These two requirements are examined later in this section, but summarily I find that they are often not met in actual negotiations. This is an experiential conclusion from which Luce and Raiffa would not have dissented. They claimed, like other theorists, to create no more than what they called an "idealized model of human preferences."

One must remain unconvinced, as indeed are many of the theorists themselves, that negotiators think, assess, make choices, and act in the ways prescribed by utility theory and by models built upon it. Only in the very roughest fashion, with persisting inconsistencies, is negotiators' behavior at all compatible with that of the players in the models. The perception and assessment of outcomes, probabilities, and preferences are so crude, speculative, and inchoate that the theoretical refinements seem virtually irrelevant. Who ever heard of negotiators seeking to maximize the product of their utilities as prescribed by Nash's theory (Nash 1950), or seeking an agreement that is Pareto optimal? Negotiators do not know and work with utilities and, as far as I know, no one has attempted to show that in effect they do unconsciously operate in such ways. The fact is that

---

7. Luce and Raiffa, like so may decision theorists, were not concerned with interaction nor, therefore, with interdependence between two or more parties. Their players operated against an indifferent, unchanging nature.

negotiators have to work with a great deal of ignorance, admitted and unadmitted, which is scarcely mitigated by quantitative measurement and manipulation.

I appreciate that almost all theorists are not concerned with the processes (before the phase of final bargaining) by which negotiators try to sort out their preference sets, reduce ignorance and inconsistency, adjust expectations, and the like. The idealized models assume that all that has, somehow, been accomplished and that the parties therefore know the possible options, their probabilities, their preferences, and so their optimal choices and actions. Yet in that dynamic, sorting-out process, a lot of decisions as well as much of the pattern of the interactional relationship are determined such that the final agreement to a considerable extent flows out of what has been accomplished previously. However, even when the sorting out has been accomplished, at least sufficiently in the opinions of the two parties, the difference between the practical state of affairs and the theoretically prescribed state is great.

On the other hand, negotiators do not generally thrash around wildly and ineffectively, though there is sometimes a tendency to do that in the earlier phases. There is instead a fairly deliberate endeavor to clarify the preference set. The very process of negotiation as presented in this study is a process of discovery and clarification. Let me illustrate this with reference to possible outcomes and to probabilities and preferences.

Take, for example, a dispute between peasant neighbors that concerns, inter alia, a piece of farmland to which no clear rights are established by one party and accepted by the other. Some division of the land becomes a potential solution. The ideal, possible outcomes (leaving aside possible combinations with other issues in the same dispute) comprise everything between, on the one hand, the whole of the land going to one party and, on the other hand, it all going to the opponent. Perhaps, at the very outset, that is in fact the range, though it is likely that some of the logical possibilities will not be considered. For instance, 95% to one party and 5% to the other might not be seen as a conceivable outcome because 5% is so derisively small a share that such an outcome is impracticable. Perhaps, too, if 40%/60% were considered then 42%/58% would not be. In fact, of course, most peasant farmers would not measure accurate percentage divisions in that way; they would not conceive of so doing in a culture where measurement, as such, is unimportant.

What is much more probable is that a number of more obvious possibilities would emerge as these are given salience by the suggestiveness of natural features—a stream, a row of trees, soil differences, a line between two corners, and so on—that indicate potential divisions of the land. As negotiations continue, some of these divisions might become more prominent as further information is exchanged, reassessment is made, and improved appreciation is obtained regarding relative intensities of preferences and relative strengths of the two parties. For instance, the range now might come to extend from, on the one hand, a party obtaining about half the land (his readjusted, overt demand) to, on the other hand, his obtaining none of it and in addition paying compensation for making a malicious claim (the opponent's demand). The revised range would then exclude certain naturally prominent possibilities and give added weight to others. Nevertheless, the number of potential outcomes would remain somewhat vague and would, moreover, be confused by considerations relating to other issues in the dispute and opportunities for trading; for instance, a 50–50 division of the land might have to be considered in association with matters of water rights, honor, or debt.

When such a disputant is asked—as I have in fact done among the Arusha—what is the set of outcomes he perceives and what probability he gives to them, the answers are quite vague. They vary at different phases of negotiations and although they tend to become clearer, they never become altogether precise and firm. These perceptions and assessments are also likely to be confused by wishful thinking; there is a tendency to give a higher probability to certain preferred outcomes.

However, negotiators do gradually accomplish at least elementary ordinal assessments of probabilities and preferences—whatever errors and misconceptions they embody—but without developing these into coherent cardinal indices. The ordinal assessments remain tentative, much subject to change and not altogether consistent and transitive. Some fairly clear preferences and indifferences emerge, as do some fairly strong opinions about some probabilities. This may well be enough, as Ellsberg (1975) has indicated. Ellsberg was concerned with an opponent's threats, a party's attempt to assess the likelihood of their actually being carried out, and the effect on the party's own behavior. Inevitably there are uncertainties. If it is highly unlikely that the threat of punishment will be used it can be disregarded; if it is highly likely then it can change the party's preferences and behavior so as to avoid the punishment. It is not that simple, of course, since the degree of punishment and the relative attractiveness of outcomes with and without punishment are crucial. But as far as the probability issue is concerned, Ellsberg considered that a party can assess "reliable rough indications" or "likelihoods" of the order of "almost a sure thing," "more likely than not," "a long shot." These are sufficient to allow the party to make some decision whether to ignore the threat or not. However, the opponent does not have to persuade the party that the threat will certainly be carried out but only to convince him that it is "sufficiently likely," that the risk of disadvantage is too high, and that therefore it is preferable to avoid it.

This is an argument that seems to accord well with what negotiators actually do, without the ability and time to make the more complicated, precise calculations of probability theory. Mutatis mutandis, what can be said (and done by a negotiator) about assessing the probabilities of threats can be said about the probabilities of other uncertain features of negotiation such as possible outcomes or the opponent's preferences.[8]

A further point can be made here relating to the pragmatic clarification of a preference set. Luce and Raiffa assume that indifference between two possibilities is the only alternative to preference for one over the other. In practice, however, there is often plain inability to decide because of ignorance (insufficient information) and perhaps because there has been inadequate consideration of preferences and their implications. There may for the moment be no perceived necessity to decide and so the matter can be left open pending further enlightenment, or until circumstances compel some resolution. Indecisiveness, therefore, rather than indifference, is often unavoidable, or at least it is not avoided because it is considered good tactics not to commit oneself to a choice for the moment. This policy of wait and see can sometimes induce the opponent to commit himself more clearly (e.g., give signs that his threat is not likely to be carried out) and therefore offer advantage to the party.

There may, then, be a number of indeterminacies in a negotiator's preference set. Some are resolvable later but others may persist to the end. They may foster indeterminancy of strategy and action and they may, if apparent to the opponent, be sources of weakness for a party if the opponent is clearer about what he himself prefers. Conversely, a party's indeterminancy may impede the opponent in making his choices and may induce him to produce further information about his own position, which otherwise he might not have done.

Incommensurability among Multiple Criteria. It is rather seldom, however, that items in a dispute can be evaluated separately such that possible outcomes for each can be ordered in terms of probability and preference. As I have previously noted in Chapter 2, it is most likely that in a real-life dispute there will be multiple issues, multiple and interconnected criteria of

---

8. Ellsberg also suggested that a player's ideas about likelihoods can be clarified by an observer offering him side bets on the choices open to him, such that the odds the player insists on before the betting will produce "reliable *rough* indications" of his preferences (Ellsberg, 1975:348). See note 5, this chapter.

evaluation, and multiple objectives. Therefore, there is not the simple problem of assessing a single item and its anticipated outcomes but the far more complex problem of comparing and evaluating in terms of multiple interconnectedness—referred to earlier as the chalk, cheese, and honor syndrome. Because of these intricate complexities, contradictions, and intransitivities between preferences, it is clear that inconsistencies of decision and action, and whole areas of ignorance are even more likely to persist. This is especially the case since much of a negotiator's cogitation and decision making has to be done under the pressures of ongoing negotiations, with limited abilities, knowledge, and time. When a party is faced with inherently incomparable items, objectives, and options, intransitivity emerges because each option "invokes 'responses' on several different 'attribute' scales and . . . although each scale itself may be transitive, their amalgamation need not be [Luce and Raiffa 1957:25]."[9] Thus a party comes to prefer x over y, over z, but z over x. This may go unrecognized and be unresolvable by the negotiator and so become built into the preference set. Whether it is illogical is open to question. Sometimes it is and the negotiator may come to see it as such and therefore the preference set is readjusted accordingly. Sometimes it is not simply illogical, nor resolvable, but is the consequence of necessarily bringing together dissimilar criteria of evaluation, incomparable issues, and diverse objectives.

In part, these kinds of genuine problems arise out of ignorance—inadequate information and inadequate assessment of what is available. There is ignorance by a party concerning his own standards, preferences, and objectives, which, under the pressures of negotiations, come to be scrutinized, reconsidered, and readjusted. There is also ignorance of the opponent's preferences and the degree of congruence with one's own.

The Opponent's Preferences and the Parties' Relative Strengths. A party's preferences and demands do not exist in a vacuum nor apropos an indifferent environment. Clearly they are made and modified in a context that intrinsically contains the supposedly competing preferences and demands of the opponent, together with the relative strengths of commitment, persuasiveness, and coercion. A party's expectations about his opponent's preferences and probable actions are considered later in this chapter. All that need be said at this point is the obvious comment that a party's own preferences must be affected by those of his opponent, and vice versa. For instance, should the opponent appear to give high preference to issue p and to insist and strongly back his demand on it, that may induce the party to

---

9. Luce and Raiffa added that intransitivities "are an anathema to most of what constitutes theory in the behavioral sciences today [1957:25]."

raise his own preferences for issues q and r—say, to seek large amounts of chalk and cheese and to allow honor to go to his opponent. However preferable some outcome might seem to be, it can be ruled out if there is no way of achieving it when the party perceives that he cannot hope to impose it. A difficulty is that a party may often be unclear about his opponent's "real" demands and effective preferences, as distinct from those the opponent overtly declares. That difficulty is compounded when, as is so often the case, the opponent himself is not altogether sure of his own preferences. A second and perhaps greater difficulty lies in the reasonable assessment of one's own strengths and complementary weaknesses against those of the opponent. What, for instance, are the realities of threats and promises? Will they be carried out and, if so, what would be the effect? Moreover, is the opponent aware of one's own weaknesses so that he will take advantage of them in establishing and maintaining his preferences and exacting concessions? Sometimes the answers to these kinds of questions are, or appear to be, fairly clear, thus effectively closing off certain preferences and lines of action and perhaps opening up others. Often the answers are far from clear so that further uncertainty is engendered in the preference set.[10]

Assessment of Outside Influences.   Another factor to be taken into account is the influence, even downright coercion, exercised by outsiders to the dispute, in terms of their interests and preferences. There are people other than the negotiators who have some concern for the outcome because it touches their own interests and who consider they have the right or the strength to interfere. A party's assessment of this and whether he is prepared (in his own interest) or compelled to accede must affect the nature of the preference set. Certain outcomes may be seen as impossible, or at least impracticable, even ones that the opponent might be prepared to allow. An African villager, for example, might be willing to consider allowing his opponent to take a part of a disputed field (perhaps in order to obtain satisfaction over some other issue in a trade-off) but he is effectively deterred by the opposition of his kinsmen, who will not agree to what they see as the alienation of ancestral land. Conversely, certain outcomes become more advantageous, and thus more preferred, because they meet the requirements of outsiders and bring relaxation of their pressures and maybe additional benefits from them.

Normative Rules and Values.   In the formation and adjustment of preferences, a party needs to take account of the applicability and apparent

---

10. The significance of relative power and weakness and its contribution to an eventual outcome is considered more fully in Chapter 6 pages 200–207.

force of normative rules and values. Norms may rule out some potential outcomes as illegal, immoral, or at least undesirable, because the negotiator accepts those norms (consciously or not) and because of the sanctions that support them. Other outcomes are prescribed or seem more attractive for the same reasons. Some norms set standards for the evaluation and comparison of issues and objectives; indeed, they may establish the very satisfactions involved. Yet the precise applicability of norms and values is frequently unclear and may be quite vague. There would, of course, be no dispute at all were the norms clear, understood, and jointly accepted by both parties. Instead, there are, or are alleged to be, alternative norms or alternative interpretations and applications that give different evaluations, different courses of action, and different potential outcomes. Moreover, both parties may be inclined to ignore norms in favor of their own interests or to interpret them prejudicially if this seems possible. In brief, although norms and values offer guidance, more or less strongly sanctioned, they are seldom so clear and consistent as to prescribe the form of the preference set. They leave areas of vagueness and of indecisive alternatives. Because of this, allied to competing interests and affective states, the parties' preference sets differ. Account must be taken of this and adjustments made unless a party is able to persuade his opponent of the normative correctness and strength of his own preferences. In real life such persuasion is not merely of a normative kind, for a party uses whatever sources of power are available to him.[11]

Assessment of Costs.   Implicit in these endeavors to evaluate preferences in relation to anticipated outcomes is the assessment of costs that reduce the satisfactions to be gained. How much extra time and effort will be required to achieve a preferred outcome? Do time and effort matter and, if so, how much? A business firm can calculate the monetary value of lost production when its employees refuse to work, or when they work to rule pending a wage settlement. It may also calculate (though probably with less certainty) the effect on future profits of various sizes of wage increase, taking into account the gains from, say, more effective job rating or shift organization. Managements regularly make these kinds of estimates, with a high degree of accounting sophistication. Yet much necessarily remains vague, even quite incalculable. Can lost production be made up and how quickly? What are the advantages to business competitors meanwhile? How far can higher prices for the product be made to offset the wage increase? Will employees work more efficiently after a generous wage in-

---

11. Norms and values as potential sources of negotiating strength are further examined in Chapter 6, pages 190–194.

crease or can tolerable efficiency be expected at a lower rate of increase? What value is to be given to improved (or worse) labor relations in the firm?

An African farmer may consider it urgent to settle a land dispute so that he may obtain what land he can for immediate cultivation as the rainy season approaches. But what is the cost of lost produce if he refuses to settle quickly in the expectation of gaining the whole piece of land? Such a farmer does not have access to experts and computers that are available to Western businessmen, yet he too is compelled to attempt some assessment.

Honor may, in principle, be preferred to chalk and cheese but, in the actual situation, the cost of gaining or retaining it is in part the chalk and cheese in various combinations that might otherwise have been obtained. Here again are the problems of incommensurability, together with uncertainty of what the opponent might agree to—that is, how much chalk and cheese must be given up in favor of honor, and is that the amount worth it?

In some cases the cost may not be only what the party gives up for some advantage gained, but also what the opponent gains in terms of his interests and values. This may be unimportant (i.e., of low or negligible cost) if the party cares little or nothing for his opponent's gains and satisfactions, although he would be wise to understand them since he might be able to obtain more of his own satisfactions for the same cost. A party might not care how much approval his opponent receives from his (the opponent's) supporters and others as a result of an outcome that they endorse. However, a party might care a good deal. It might even be his principal concern to limit his opponent's gains. For instance, he may resent any advantage that a hated rival gains, or he may believe that gains acquired by the opponent will be used against him in the future. Conversely, there may be costs to a party if his gains leave an embittered opponent who is likely therefore to continue hostility and to harbor resentment in a persisting relationship. Similarly, account needs to be taken of the anticipated costs where an outcome adversely affects the concerns of other people whose relationships are important.

The assessment of costs is intrinsic to the establishment of a preference set, though analytically it is probably most useful to consider them separately, as indeed negotiators themselves tend to do. Like advantages and satisfactions, and in counterpart to them, the costs of different possible outcomes are not readily calculable and for the same kinds of reasons. Not infrequently, however, costs contain even more of the qualitative components and they tend to depend more heavily on the interests, preferences, and affective states of the opponent and of other concerned persons. They are, therefore, somewhat more problematic, both for a party and for an outside observer.

The purpose of this brief review of the inherent problems of establishing and adjusting a preference set is to indicate and to emphasize the unavoidable difficulties with which a negotiator must contend. These difficulties are never altogether resolvable in real-life conditions and this is why preference sets are inevitably incomplete, internally inconsistent, likely to contain intransitivities, and always subject to change. Although most or all of the problems can conceptually be delineated and treated more precisely in abstract, mathematical terms, this is only achieved through distortion of the reality that faces a negotiator. I have deliberately chosen not to attempt such treatment (nor to advocate the attempt) because negotiators themselves do not work in those terms, consciously or in effect. The relative vagueness of my description and the many unanswered questions posed are a recognized reflection of the obscurities and obfuscations that confront negotiators, nescient as we are of much of their mental operations, affective states, and motivations. Because many of these problems in actual situations are never wholly resolvable in a logical sense, this condition must be acknowledged in any analysis. Nevertheless, negotiators do endeavor gradually to clarify their preferences, however crudely, as further information becomes available and as they are virtually compelled to simplify and to reach some working conditions within the welter of uncertainty and complexity.

THE PREFERENCE SET: (B) THE NEGOTIATOR'S OPERATIONAL STRATEGY

There are at least three features of a working policy that negotiators use to simplify their problems, to help clarify uncertainties, and to allow them to make more reasoned choices. First, a party acknowledges some degree of ignorance and therefore his ability to be sure of his preferences. In recognizing his own ignorance he may recognize his opponent's probable ignorance and so the uncertainties in his opponent's preferences. Choices are therefore postponed until further information becomes available, offering more clarity, or until pressures from the opponent (or outsiders) demand some decision. Second, a party works with a tentative preference set in which there are indecisive parts but also some points of fairly firm decision, or at least they are thought to be so. Third, a party must be prepared to modify as well as to clarify his preference set in the light of new information, particularly on the opponent's preferences and strengths. For example, it will become necessary to discard "unrealistic" preferences and to accept less preferred options, to take account of costs that can be imposed by the opponent and the strengths of his preferences, and to consider and fit in hitherto unanticipated possibilities.

This wait-and-see, flexible policy is not, of course, necessarily the deliberate strategy adopted by a negotiator. He may be filled with self-righteousness, self-interest, and confidence in his negotiating strength, believing he knows what is available and what he wants and determined to obtain it. He may sometimes be proved right in the event. On the whole, it is more likely that he is not, certainly not altogether. As negotiations proceed, as further information is obtained and assessed and as he himself gives information, a party comes to appreciate, if he has not already, the inaccuracies or inappropriateness of some of his assumed preferences. He learns of his opponent's preferences and strengths and of his own relative weaknesses. New possibilities arise that have to be considered against ones already foreseen; some approximations become firmer and perhaps more accurate; some anticipated outcomes begin to be ruled out as impossible (or so unlikely as not to warrant further attention), impracticable, illegal, immoral, or abhorrent. Willingly or not, a party accepts the necessity of adjustment and the usefulness of calculated indeterminacy.

To some extent this flexible clarification of the preference set continues up to the point of final decision and outcome. Indeed, ignorance and uncertainty may go beyond that as a party remains vague about the gains and costs of what he has agreed to. Yet, if negotiations are not to break down, some choices are ineluctable before that, even though perhaps made arbitrarily. For instance, there has to be some kind of decision concerning issues on the agenda and their definition (though that can be modified later if desirable and agreeable with the opponent), on the relevance of some norm, whether to agree to withdraw some issue altogether or to accept the opponent's offer on another issue. If a party vacillates or procrastinates too much he may miss opportunities. He may find the decision made for him in effect by the opponent. Behind everything is the option of ceasing to negotiate and accepting the status quo. Should the status quo be scarcely tolerable, or should it be impossible to revert to it, a party is powerfully constrained to attempt decision despite the obscurity of his preferences and costs. There is, in that case, strong motivation to clarify and consolidate the preference set and so to focus actions and reactions more effectively.

With this kind of flexible approach, however incomplete his preference set is at any time, a negotiator is able to simplify his formidable problems further by particular concentration on three foci.[12] First, he seeks to set anticipated minima for the various issues and packages of issues below which

---

12. Here I follow the line of analysis suggested by Iklé and Leites (1962).

he hopes and expects not to go. A party may be convinced that he will not agree to anything considered to be less favorable, though he may still be compelled to do so or reassessment may allow him to reduce minima as preferences are modified later.

Second, there is a maximum (more exactly, a set of maxima for the various issues in dispute) that a negotiator conceives to be within the realm of the possible and/or allows him room for subsequent maneuver and concession. This sets the outer limits to his side of the negotiations. It could embrace virtually everything that could conceivably be gained from the opponent but usually it does not. Legal, moral, and practical considerations may prescribe or induce limits. Demand is subject to diminishing returns and there may be a point of negative satisfaction; in any case a limited amount may suffice, for various reasons. Imagination and ambition are often restricted so that a party thinks in terms of hundreds but not thousands of dollars, at the Volkswagen rather than the Rolls Royce level. For altruism or self-interest, a party may curtail his maximal demands so as not to ruin his opponent, cause him too great a loss of face, undesirably stiffen his resistance, or invoke his resentment. There may be fashions and trends in maximal demands in reaction to general conditions in a society. This is demonstrated, for instance, by changes in initial claims for wage increases in Western industrial negotiations in response to inflation rates, economic prosperity, and political conditions. Among the Ndendeuli, maximal bridewealth demands appeared to vary directly with annual receipts from tobacco cultivation (the principal source of income for many farmers).

The maxima are usually the overt demands and offers made to the opponent at any time in the negotiations. Negotiating "in good faith" is a widespread norm, often protected in law or well-entrenched custom. This includes the understanding that an overt offer will not be revoked for a higher one later. Although not invariably followed, it is difficult to avoid even when reassessment predicates a higher maximum.

The third focus comprises the anticipated outcomes that are to be aimed at, which lie somewhere between the minima and maxima. They are something like realistic estimates of what seem probably obtainable above the minima in the light of the party's understanding of the opponent's preferences and of the relative strengths of the two sides.

Put in the simplest way, a negotiator works with lower and upper limits and a target. Since the maxima must usually be stated to the opponent they tend to be clearest. Because of that there may be a good deal of hedging before a party commits himself. He often does not wish to set a maximum on an issue only to find later that the opponent would have been prepared to go higher if necessary, and he may wish to avoid setting so high a maximum that he soon has to reduce it and so appear to show weakness. An opponent seeks to pin down and to extract from the party what in maximal terms is meant by such statements as, "I demand full compensation for the injury you have done to me," or "We want a substantial increase in wages." Sooner or later a party has to be specific. In contrast, minimal and anticipated outcomes are usually less precise because of the problems of clarifying the preference set. Moreover, a party is likely to be most diligent in disguising what they are in order to deny advantage to his opponent. If the opponent is fairly certain what the party's minima are, then they may become effective maxima too, for it can be assumed that the party would sooner settle there than have no agreement at all. Similarly, to state one's targets is to give valuable information away. Since minima and targets are kept hidden they are often not precisely established. Therefore, in suggesting that a party works with these three levels in mind, I am not claiming that there is necessarily a fine precision about them. This is particularly the case in the earlier phases of negotiations, although increasing clarity develops as the negotiations continue.

It is important to note that these three working levels are not static. They are all subject to adjustment as more information is obtained and more realistic assessments are made. What was earlier a minimum, below which a party believed it would not go, turns out to be too high as the opponent's strength is understood and when it is appreciated that it is worthwhile to accept less in order to gain some other advantage. The target might be raised or lowered when more is known of the opponent. New potential outcomes can be suggested as a result of integrative coordination between the parties and these may make old targets irrelevant.

It would be unusual for target and minimum to come to be the same before the conclusion of bargaining. Considerable flexibility is lost if that occurs, and people tend to remain optimistic about obtaining something above the minimum. Only the very confident and the very strong party can afford to lose flexibility and maneuverability (or perhaps the one who does not care much whether agreement is reached or not). A good example of confident strength is shown in the strategy of Boulwarism as that was practiced in American industrial collective bargaining some time ago. Boulwarism, developed by the General Electrical Company, was a final-offer-first strategy. After careful preparation of its case, offers and demands were clearly decided by the company and presented early in the negotiations. There was adamant refusal to modify the package, which was presented in a spirit of take it or leave it. The strength of the management's position came not only from its meticulous prenegotiation preparation but also from the policy of direct communication with the employees (ignoring the union officials) and a great deal of propaganda before the negotiations began. A union party found itself, when its own preference set was still somewhat unclear, facing a well-organized ultimatum, while union members had been softened up and their allegiance to and faith in their leaders had been partly undermined.[13]

Such a show of strength can be most impressive to the opponent although there is a real danger that it will produce a powerful reaction of aggressive competitiveness or resentment, which only stiffens the opponent's stance and leads to breakdown or to more prolonged negotiations. The strategy is often considered unfair in that it is claimed to be tantamount to a denial of negotiations "in good faith." American industrial negotiators, like those in African rural communities, are supposed to be prepared to respect the opponent's views and needs, to make concessions toward compromise, and to join in cooperative search for fresh possibilities. Boulwarism was bitterly attacked on these grounds by trade union leaders.[14]

This concentration on the three working levels need not mean a complete neglect of other potential outcomes. It is particularly necessary to monitor and consider the opponent's demands, possible minima, and targets. Precedents from comparable negotiations can suggest other outcomes to be held in mind. The three-foci strategy only permits a simplification of problems and a relative concentration in certain potential outcomes and the areas around them.

Further simplification of problems is gained by adherence to some pervasive, general strategy. In intent and effect, this orients the determination of preferences and eliminates some of the possibilities from consideration. The strategy is not always deliberately nor altogether consciously established. There are a number of such strategies that can be briefly mentioned here.

One strategy is to seek to maximize advantage while conceding as little as possible to the opponent. Ideologically this is a cultural norm in some societies; it amounts to the rationalism assumed by game theorists and many economists. In such crude terms it is probably unusual, outside of rhetoric. Where there are multiple issues it is necessary to modify it because of the patent difficulty of attempting to maximize on every issue if the opponent has any negotiating strength at all. There will be issues that, for various reasons, are much preferred to others. There may be one or two issues that a party considers imperative to his interests so that his strategy consists of attempting to obtain as much (or to yield as little) as possible on

---

13. On Boulwarism, see McMurry (1955) and Northrup (1964).

14. Trade unionists saw the General Electric policy as an attempt to bypass the union and to weaken the workers' organization in defense of their own interests and aspirations.

those (e.g., honor in most Mediterranean societies). At least maximization on other issues is given secondary importance. Overall this could conceivably allow a party, in his intentions, to seek maximal total advantage or subjective utility. It is common, however, that a party cares rather little for some of the issues in dispute, other than perhaps their nuisance value and what he can get as a quid pro quo by yielding on them to an opponent for whom they are important. Often a party agrees to their inclusion on the agenda for that reason, as a kind of sweetener or to obfuscate his real interests and preferences. In any case he will probably be compelled, if not already so prepared, to yield on some issues—and not always those on which he would ideally prefer to do so initially. Moreover, it becomes increasingly difficult to be sure what the possible maximum might be in view of increasing understanding of the opponent's preferences. This will be so even on single issues but will be especially the case where several imcomparable issues and costs are involved. That is to say, a party begins in effect to modify his avowed maximization even though rhetorically he continues to advocate it.

Whether as a result of modification or as an initial, deliberate choice, there are other possible strategies. One is to seek options that minimize risk rather than maximize gains, something like the minimax of game theorists. Here both the assessment of risks and the psychological propensity to take or avoid risk are important. Risks are scarcely easier to assess than maximal gains, so that to minimax means in practice an orientation that tends to exclude certain possibilities as too risky and gives priority to others considered to be less risky. A variant of this strategy is to go for what appear to be "sure things," irrespective of maximization, leaving other issues to be settled as best they may, almost to the point of indifference. That strategy is associated not only with the avoidance of risk but also with the desire to complete the negotiations and to dispose of the dispute as speedily and with as little complication as possible. Sure things are those to which it is expected the opponent will agree fairly readily, although they are not trivial and they do offer at least some advantage.

Another strategy is to suffice: to be content with what seems to be enough, regardless of whether more could be obtained, or even positively eschewing a tendency toward maximization. What is sufficient may be fairly vague. Often it is linked with an estimate of minimal requirements or a target and a readiness to accept any offer by the opponent that meets it. For example, in several disputes among the Arusha, a claimant's aim was to obtain only part of a contested piece of land and he did not seek more than that. That part was sufficient to meet a particular need—to make a new coffee garden or banana grove. He simply agreed, after some negotiating, to an offer by his opponent that gave him the required area, although it was quite feasible (indeed, sometimes acknowledged by the claimant) that he might have obtained more without forfeiting other advantages had he been willing to persist with the negotiations.

Cultural standards may specify what is enough: for example, by emphasizing equality between peers such that a man avoids too great an advantage from negotiations—too much wealth or honor, say—and is prudently content with less than he might have obtained. He seeks enough to maintain his status as a peer. In all societies there are individuals who consciously or unconsciously limit their desires and ambition to sufficiency. Apart from the problem of unavailingly seeking to estimate and obtain maximal satisfaction, sufficing has the attraction of the quiet life, getting negotiations finished, avoiding tiresome bargaining or the reputation of aggressive rapacity.

In some cases, the strategy is concerned less, or hardly at all, with what a party can gain for himself but rather with the attempt to deny advantage and satisfaction to the opponent—either maximal or sufficient denial. This strategy arises out of strong competitiveness with, and probably acute animosity toward, the opponent. The endeavor may be as simple as causing him harm out of resentment or hatred, paying back an old score, or inflicting punishment. That is largely an affective motivation, touched perhaps by some notion of justice. But the intent may be to deprive the opponent of honor, reputation, or political support while keeping one's own honor or status intact.

It is unlikely that any of these general strategies can be followed quite consistently. In any case, it is possible that more than one is required, each relating to different issues in the dispute. Where this is so, the different strategies are not always coherently integrated into a single master strategy in this context of the confused business of real-life negotiations. Thus a party may attempt to maximize on certain issues, to minimize risk on another, and to inflict punishment on others. This can raise contradictions of both purpose and preferences. When that is recognized by a party, he will have to rethink and reformulate strategy and reassess priorities along with the continuous adjustment of his preference set. General strategies are equivalent to orientations by which the complexities of the preference set can be sorted out and reduced with some kind of consistency. They are not established once and for all (though negotiators sometimes assume that they are) any more than is the preference set that they help to organize and coordinate.

Nothing in progression can rest on its original plan. We may as well think of rocking a grown man in the cradle of an infant [Edmund Burke].

In summary, the preference set and its orienting strategy are likely to be incomplete and inconsistent. Although objective criteria are used, evaluation and preferences are inherently subjective and liable to fluctuate as circumstances and perception of circumstances change. The preference set is adjusted as continued negotiations bring further information and allow or compel reassessment. A fully coherent set may never be attained, but, as some issues are disposed of and others narrowed, there comes to be a less complex array of potential outcomes, probabilities, and choices.

EXPECTATIONS OF THE OPPONENT

Each bit of information received by a party from his opponent or from elsewhere may, inter alia, tell him something about his opponent's position and what may be expected from him. A party's expectations about his opponent are crucial to his interim choices, his cogitations, and his ultimate decisions. To reiterate for the sake of clarity and emphasis: In negotiations a party cannot assume preferences and objectives nor make choices as if he were in isolation or acting vis-à-vis an indifferent nature. These must inevitably be determined in relation to, and are therefore dependent on, the preferences and choices of the opponent. Therefore, it is imperative that a party endeavor to learn as much and as accurately as possible about his opponent's range of potential and actual choices, his preferences and their intensities, his strategy and tactics, strengths and weaknesses, and trends of change in all these. It is important, also, for a party to understand what the opponent expects of him. However filled with a righteous sense of the justice and morality of his own claims in the dispute, a party must fairly soon begin to take account of the opponent's preferences and demands, however unjust or extreme they may seem. To refuse to do so is to threaten a breakdown of the negotiations if the opponent has any strength at all in his position. So long, therefore, as a party continues to think that a breakdown and an acceptance of the status quo are less preferable than the possible terms of a negotiated outcome, he will, and indeed must be prepared to, temper his own preferences by taking account of those of his opponent.

Like the party's own preference set, his expectations of his opponent are probably incomplete, inconsistent, and, especially in the earlier phases of negotiations, rather vague. There are good reasons for this uncertainty. First, it is a result of insufficient information. Second, there are inevitable errors in the reception and assessment of information. Third, the opponent is generally concerned about disclosing only that information he considers advantageous to him and about hiding what is not. Fourth, the opponent may give false information. He just may not know or understand well enough, or his intentions may be to confuse the party. Fifth, a party may receive too much information about his opponent such that he cannot properly marshall and assess it. Sixth, in this interactional context, a party's expectations of his opponent depend on the opponent's expectations of him, so that indeterminacy and inaccuracy tend to engender confusion.[15]

Since jointly agreed decisions are required on all issues up to and including the final outcome, a party must aim at outcomes that are compatible with the preferences of his opponent, though attempting to modify those preferences at the same time. The simplest but most unusual way is to discover what the opponent minimally requires and accede to it. However, if the opponent's strength is sufficiently great to encourage that kind of reaction, then it is unlikely that he would be content only with the minimum or that a party could discover what his minimum is. In any case, even a weak party can salvage something. The difficulty really lies in getting behind the opponent's overt demands and discovering what he might be prepared to agree to, what his expectations and aims are. This requires understanding not only his real preferences but also his "exchange rates" between various issues (e.g., chalk for cheese) and the indeterminacies in his preference set. In addition a party needs to make some assessment of the potential power available to his opponent and how and when he may use it.

Moreover, a party is concerned not only to understand as much as possible about his opponent's preference set but also to assess what the opponent is likely to do in the future. This assessment is based both on experience of what he has done in the past, before and during the negotiations, and on what he can be expected to do as a consequence of his preference set, basic strategy, and potential power. A party needs to know as well as he can, for example, what his opponent's reaction will be to frankness of information, concession, threat, toughness, and other tactical approaches. Can a similar response be expected, an opposite reaction, or something else? Can the opponent be expected to continue in his current line of behavior (for instance, making concessions, emphasizing strength, showing cooperation), and in the same degree? What is required to encourage him to do so or to change? Such expectations, well or ill perceived, affect not only the party's own preference set but his tactical choices concerning further messages to his opponent and perhaps his longer-range strategy.

In terms of the present model, then, all incoming information is ex-

---

15. See my earlier reference to the regression built into interdependence, page 92.

amined for what it tells about the opponent so that an increasingly accurate understanding of his changing position can be developed. This includes an appreciation of his mental and affective states and of changes in them: for example, whether or not, and to what degree, the opponent is patient and careful in his deliberations, confident in his stand, well organized, able and experienced in negotiations, motivated by righteous indignation or by shrewd calculation, and similar attributes. Each increment of understanding can be, as it were, fed into the growing picture and from there fed into the party's considerations about his own preference set.

TACTICAL DECISIONS

Following the additions to and readjustments, if any, of a party's expectations of his opponent and of his own preference set, he then has to decide what response to make, what information to offer to his opponent. It is incumbent on him to make the next move. Usually this consists of some utterance, although silence—a refusal or inability to respond directly—carries its own message of antagonism, uncertainty, or imperturbability.

Tactical decisions relate to the relationship between the two parties and what might be called the tone of information exchange, to the kind of information to be offered, and to the reponse intended to be obtained. Insofar as a party is well prepared, he has, more or less consciously, an array of tactics he has already decided to use. These, or some of them, change acording to the phase of negotiations, in reaction to the opponent's tactics, and, in general, as the state of interaction is reassessed. Any attempt to describe all the possible tactics would be tedious and some further consideration of them is given in the exposition of the developmental model and elsewhere. Here I intend, therefore, only to be briefly illustrative of some of the more obvious kinds of tactics and to suggest the circumstances in which particular ones are chosen.

One possibility is to concentrate on obtaining further information from the opponent rather than giving information about one's own position. There may be a pressing need for information in order to attempt to clear up uncertainty that begins to be intolerable. It may appear that the opponent is prepared to be informative or is open to pressures to be so. There may be, for the moment, little need for a quid pro quo from the party himself. The message could then be on the order of "If I understand you, your assertion (demand, offer, etc.) is this and this. Am I right? It is not clear." Or, "You have told me about such and such but what about so and so?" Another tactic here is for the party to comment on what the opponent has previously said and ask, implicitly or explicitly, for additional comments and elucidation. In either case, the desire for information is directed with the intent of controlling the exchange of information for the moment. That is often the result of the opponent's previous unwillingness to give sufficient information, or it may be that the party's reassessment of his preference set indicates unacceptable ignorance hitherto unrecognized.

Conversely, a party may see usefulness in giving solid information and in emphasizing his openness (real or feigned). He may at that time wish to impress his opponent with the strength of his demands, the legitimacy of his claims, or the logic of his interpretation of the facts of the case. For instance, he may desire to correct apparent misapprehensions, to counter the opponent's case, to deflect his attention, or to appeal to third parties. Associated with this is the further tactical choice of being more or less frank or dissembling and bluffing, attempting a dispassionate assessment for his opponent or giving a strongly partial view on an issue. On the whole, frankness goes with believed strength, dissembling with weakness, but it may not be so straightforward, for a show of frankness may be a cover for weakness.

Another common tactic is to try to change the subject matter of the information exchange when a current issue seems threatening—perhaps because it tends to expose weakness or to demand decision when a party is not yet willing to commit himself. Especially in the earlier phases, but not only then, the tactic may be to persist in changing the topic in order to keep the whole range of issues under review and to maintain perspective, or in order to avoid commitment on any one issue. This tactic can be deliberately counteractive against the opponent who wishes to concentrate on certain issues for his own purposes, while the party is not clear about the implications of this concentration. It is a delaying tactic. Conversely, when continued concentration on an issue seems advantageous to the party— say, something on which he perceives strength or which is of particular concern—the tactic is to offer information on it with the intent of fetching direct response from the opponent.

Another possibility is temporarily to eschew giving and receiving information on fact and opinion and instead to focus on the opponent's affective condition or the state of the relationship being developed between the parties. The choice may be to ease strain or to increase it, to exasperate the opponent into anger or indignation (so inducing him to blurt out ill-considered, revealing responses), to placate him in a conciliatory, low-keyed fashion in order to gain his confidence, or to evince hostility or a willingness to be cooperative.

An avowed tactic is to reciprocate the manner of information giving by the opponent: to offer antagonism for antagonism, reciprocating ad hominem attacks or extravagances of speech and behavior—or, on the other hand, offering frankness for frankness, reciprocating friendliness, a strong moral tone, or a concentration on factual matters. This represents toughness or cooperativeness respectively. However, the tactic may be to refuse to allow the pattern to be set by the opponent and therefore to adopt the opposite approach, patently refusing to be influenced by the opponent.

The endeavor and tactical choice may be, at a relevant point in the negotiations, to focus less on one's own position and more on that of the opponent, not only to obtain more information about it but also with the intention of trying to persuade him that his own best interests would be served by a change in expectations and attitude. Thus the thrust might be to convince him that the costs of his objectives are dauntingly high, that certain outcomes will be less advantageous than he now thinks, or that morally or legally he is mistaken. In the face of a similar tactical approach by the opponent, the chosen tactic could be aggressively resistant or defensive, explanatory, and justificatory.

A final example of possible tactics is concession making. This takes on particular importance when the parties are approaching joint decision on an issue (on either a procedural or a substantive matter). A party must choose if he is to make concessions early, and whether in large or small amounts, or if he is to hold firmly to his existing position. This depends, of course, on his assessment of and expectations about that issue. Concession can be made in order to try to gain reciprocal concession or because it seems preferable to get the issue settled in order to move on to something else of more importance. Here the tactical decision comes directly from the preference set, seeking to get an agreement at an acceptable point.

In general, it should be clear that the tactical decision made by a party is closely related to the particular circumstances of the negotiations at the time (or the party's perception of them), to his needs for information and his desires to give certain kinds of information, to his intention to be tough or unyielding, to the state of his preference set, and much else. Moreover, the chosen tactical response and the message offered to the opponent can serve several purposes and comprise a number of stratagems together. For instance, the decision might be to change the topic, to give positive, frank information, and to express aggressiveness toward the opponent, all at the same time.

In using the terms *tactic* and *decision*, I do not mean to suggest that there is always shrewd calculation, considered intention, or deliberate action by a party. Such premeditation often does occur although a party does not necessarily foresee all the implications or effects of his decision. Partly this is the result of imperfect perception; partly it comes from limited abilities; and partly it is because parties often do not have time to consider their decisions fully under the pressures and stress of negotiations. The better prepared a party is, the clearer his preference set and his tactical program, the more effectively he can operate under pressure in furthering his interests and maintaining a consistent policy. In practice, a decision may not be made in any conscious fashion so that a party's response may be more of a gut reaction to the opponent's information: an immediate emotional retort, a sarcastic denial, an epithetic response. The opponent may be manipulating him to that end and the party may give away more information that he intends or even knows. On the other hand, such emotionally directed and laden messages may sometimes serve a better purpose than the cooler, considered response because of their immediacy and forthrightness. They need not necessarily be inconsistent with the party's preference set and strategy. Indeed, the tactical decision may be to allow indignation or conciliatory warmth to direct the response and the information offered. In that way, a marked sense of firmness and strength, or readiness or cooperate, can be conveyed in impressive fashion. The tactic may be to show, say, strength or anger and that can be simulated or at least exaggerated. However, if that is the tactic, then it becomes more convincing if in fact the party really does feel strong or angry.

Ultimately, of course, tactical decisions have to be made with reference to the tactics of the opponent in the strategic interaction between the two parties. Thus the opponent may be successful in forcing a party to go on the defensive, to concentrate on particular issues or to focus on explaining his own position, so that for the moment at least the party must give up his intention to extract information from the opponent. That is, a party has to cope with the same kind of tactical results that he himself is trying to impose on his opponent. He is not a free agent, able always to choose positively in his own interest. He may not be successful in imposing on his opponent. The later the phase of the negotiations and thus the more interlocked the parties have become and the narrower their focus, then the less the freedom in the choice of tactics. Each party imposes on the other and limits the other. Toward the end, tactical choice becomes almost a joint choice as coordination increases.

Having made his tactical choice (deliberately or unconsciously) a party then proffers a message to this opponent. Thus the half-cycle is completed. The opponent goes through the same procedures in his half-cycle and ends by proffering his message to the party. This brings the process to the beginning of a fresh cycle.

DISCUSSION AND ELABORATION

The model of interaction that has been presented and explored in this chapter was shown diagrammatically in Figure 4.1 (page 84). This model of the repetitive, cyclical behavior of the parties postulates a systemic, processual connection among a number of components, from the receipt of information and assessment of it, to learning and adjustment of preferences and expectations, to tactical decision and to the offer of information to the other party. Conceptually and analytically, my intention has been to separate the processual components or stages in order to reveal the process more clearly. Although primarily linear in form, there is capability for feedback within the central set of components, as indicated in the diagram.

In the model I am necessarily dealing with mental operations and changing affectual states of the negotiators, that is, with conditions that are often hidden from the observer and are often partly unrecognized by the negotiators themselves. Because of this, these conditions have not been well studied by social scientists. Therefore, a great deal must and fortunately can be deduced from negotiators' overt behavior, although it is patently subject to the observer's misapprehension and uncertainty. My own understanding has been enlarged by sitting in with participants during negotiations and by discussing their actions with them then and afterward. Nevertheless, a great deal remains suppositional and must be understood to be so. The results can at best be suggestive and illuminating, rather than definitive in any sense. I do not intend to present an integrated theory of psychological processes, however. Rather, and in more limited fashion, I wish to indicate how people behave, how they think and excogitate, how they come to make and remake choices as information is exchanged and processed, and how these things are necessarily linked together during the interaction of negotiations. This calls for an "as if" model. Although it is not clearly demonstrable by reference to empirical data nor altogether accurate in all probability, it may be useful as an approach to understanding what occurs and why. The alternative of merely relegating the whole process to an unknowable "black box" would be an unwarranted act of despair.

It is worth emphasizing that, although the content and significance of the information exchanged differs in different developmental phases of negotiations, the pattern of information exchange, preference adjustment, choice making, and interaction is in principle repetitively the same in all phases. The model is therefore applicable throughout and does not refer only to certain phases, such as final bargaining. I make this point largely because comparable cyclical models have been suggested or implied by some social scientists who have concentrated only on bargaining (see, e.g., Bartos 1974; Coddington 1968, 1972; Cross 1969; Pen 1959; Siegel and Fouraker 1960).

It is also important to note that the model says nothing about the absolute or relative time spans of a half-cycle or of each operation within it. In practice, a party's response to his opponent's offer of information ranges from the virtually instantaneous—a gut reaction—to lengthy deliberations perhaps requiring a pause in the negotiations while the party caucuses. For the sake of simplicity, the model assumes a more or less regular, more or less stable, cyclical interaction: first one party, then the other, in turn. In general and over a period this is reasonably accurate, for there has to be both giving and receiving of information, but such consistency is not always maintained in the shorter run. One of the parties may dominate the exchange as several of its members and supporting witnesses offer a mass of information before the other responds. The role of the other party is then, temporarily, largely a receptive one, either deliberately seeking further information or having it forced upon him. It is scarcely necessary to add that, in real life, straightforward reciprocal exchange is often interrupted and becomes inchoate. Members of both parties may offer information at the same time, talking simultaneously, maybe ignoring each other. Documents may be exchanged. Information from third parties may become available to both parties at the same time. Third parties or spectators interrupt, and members of either party may seek to create disturbance and diversion.

Frequently the information offered by a party is not a direct or relevant response to that previously offered by the opponent. Negotiators often talk past one another, deliberately or unconsciously. They ignore, or seem to ignore, each other's messages. They change topics arbitrarily or by tactical choice. They pursue a particular line or argument or persist in an affective state irrespective of what the opponent says or does. In short, there can be a good deal of confusion and rather little of the model's neat pattern of exchange and learning. There is not always a chairman to keep order, and a mediator, if present, can be ignored or can himself be caught up in the confusion. Yet it would be incorrect to emphasize this disorder to the point of denying order at all. The confusion may be more apparent to the observer than real to the disputants. There can be a "method in the madness" as negotiators relieve themselves of their feelings of righteousness or animosity or express their fears of being manipulated and outdone by the opponent. The whole process of negotiation is, in one sense, the gradual creation of order—that is, of coordination between the parties. Disorder is likely to be greatest in the earlier phases of the negotiations. Uncertainties are greatest then but they are often disguised in aggressiveness and in an impatience with the opponent's messages. To ignore the opponent's offers of information is, in those early phases, a refusal to be controlled or even influenced by him so as to prevent the field being defined or limited only by his interests and values. The confusion, real or apparent, tends to become less as negotiations continue. Issues are more clearly defined, narrowed in range, and reduced in number. Learning does occur. The possibilities of outcomes that are more favorable than the status quo ante grow in relative attractiveness. There is a wide and somewhat erratic oscillation at first, which gradually settles down to increasing concentration on limited dimensions of particular issues and potential outcomes. Moreover, the parties come to establish a working relationship that permits such concentration—a relationship that is not necessarily friendly or trustful but allows at least coordination of effort. Throughout the process of negotiation, periods of persisting antagonism alternate dynamically with periods of relative coordination.[16] Order and regularity in the repetitive exchange of information tend to be greater when coordination is emphasized and less when antagonism is marked.

The cyclical process, then, is much less tidy in practice than the model can indicate. It is necessary to bear this in mind, especially in the examination of particular concrete cases. This does not, however, invalidate the heuristic usefulness of the model. Like all such constructions, it is a simplified and generalized conceptualization of pattern within the untidiness of real-life behavior and interaction.

This cyclical model constitutes an attempt to demonstrate form and pattern in the repetitive exchange and interpretation of information. Therefore, it is useful to emphasize twin problems that continuously confront negotiators: what and how much information to give, and the significance of information received. It can be assumed that information can never become complete and that it is seldom given or received in wholly objective, impartial fashion. This raises the problem of the quality of information and the strategy of a negotiator. How far is information frankly offered or persuasively edited? Here I am not concerned with what a negotiator should do, morally or practically, in order to achieve the "best" results. Actual negotiators make their own choices and their policies vary. Cultural standards, the nature of relations between the parties, the kinds of issues in dispute, particular contextual difficulties, the kinds of information considered relevant, pressures from the opponent and from third parties—all vary a great deal and therefore preclude easy prescription. Consequently, the writer who advocates the fullest disclosure of informa-

16. This alternation and its dynamic consequences are examined later. See pages 181–186.

tion by both parties may in some circumstances be "correct," though probably naive in thinking it to be wholly possible. Similarly the advocate of Machiavellian tactics may be "right" in other circumstances.

"Perhaps the most frequent mistake which employers make in the field of labor policy is not to tell the union officers and members enough about the business [Sumner Slichter; quoted in Chamberlain 1958:155]." The supposition here was that if businessmen made it much clearer what their problems were—the state of the market, costs of production, profit levels, and so on—the union would be more perceptive in the size and timing of demands for wages and other benefits. At least, it is to be assumed, the union leaders would understand better when the employers are not in an economic position to agree to high wage claims or costly benefit schemes. Above all the workers would not feel that they are being deceived or belittled. Antagonism might be reduced and trust and accord strengthened so that coordination would be more easily achieved.

There is some support for this viewpoint from students of negotiation and from negotiators themselves. For instance, Walton and McKersie pointed out that in what they call "integrative bargaining"[17] the fullest disclosure of information is preferable because pragmatically it is most effective. Thus each party will be able to discover what kinds of possibility are available and can therefore coordinate with the other to achieve a mutually more satisfactory agreement than would be possible in antagonistic, mistrustful competition. Siegel and Fouraker concluded, from laboratory experiments, that "increasing the amount of relevant information available to bargainers increases the tendency to maximize joint pay-off [1960:41]," although in their cases the additional information came from the controller of the experiments rather then from the opponent—a rather different situation from that of real life. Bartos advanced the hypothesis that "dovish behavior is likely when information about the opponent is abundant; hawkish behavior is likely when it is scarce [1974:32]." "Dovish" implies a readiness to adjust expectations, to be cooperative and empathic, whereas "hawkish" implies toughness by a negotiator, an unwillingness to adjust or to reciprocate an opponent's concessions. Bartos' own experimental results indicated, however, that this may be only a weak, though fairly consistent tendency (p. 143).

Clearly, the better a party understands his opponent's position the better he is able to react to it and to make adjustments. However, better understanding is also likely to offer improved opportunity to give the op-

---

17. Integrative bargaining occurs in non-zero-sum contests where there are "possibilities for greater or lesser amounts of value which can be made available to the two parties [Walton and McKersie 1965:127]. See also page 150.

ponent selected information so as to persuade him to adjust his expectations and demands. In other words, the opponent may lay himself open to manipulation. The deisre to obtain as much accurate information as possible from the opponent is not necessarily always, or even generally, linked with an intention to give him equally reliable information. A party commonly wishes to disguise his own weaknesses and to exaggerate his strengths. Bluffs are not always perceived as such, or only too late to make a difference. There may be advantages in fostering doubt and confusion in the opposing party. As Shackle has written, "The deliberate cultivation of uncertainty and mistakenness by one party in the mind of the other [is] . . . the essence of bargaining [in Coddington 1968:vii]," though that is probably overemphasizing the case. Such tactics are one of many options open to negotiators.

In all this we need to remember that the two parties are in dispute. They want different things and they want them from each other. They are not necessarily reasonable men open to persuasion on the objective facts of the case, especially if more advantage can be gained by persistent unreasonableness. They are much inclined to be apprehensive of each other, mistrustful, and somewhat antagonistic. This is especially the case where something like a zero-sum condition obtains on some issue—what they get we lose, and vice versa. Interests are then diametrically opposed. In non-zero-sum conditions it is not clear, or may not be for some time, just how cooperation can be beneficial or whether one is being induced to take less than the opponent or less than otherwise might be obtained. Cooperation can be, or can seem to be, at the expense of one's own interests.

It cannot simply be assumed that in any case the more information a party has, and the better he understands his opponent's position, the more likely he will be to adjust and accommodate his demands. In an Arusha case, one negotiator told me that he perfectly appreciated his opponent's need of the piece of land that they were disputing. The opponent had only a small farm, the agricultural output of which was insufficient to feed and clothe his large family. The addition of the piece of land would have eased his problems considerably. My informant regretted his opponent's difficulties but had no intention of withdrawing his claim to the land, which would make a useful addition to his already prosperous farm by allowing a larger grazing area for his growing herd of livestock. In this case, my informant's good understanding of his opponent revealed the latter's weakness and therefore where his own strength lay. The desperate need for land dominated the opponent's preference set so that he was fairly easily persuaded to give way on the other issues in the dispute in order that he might obtain at least a part of the land.

Another factor inhibiting fuller information is that what seems to one party to be convincing support of his own position may be interpreted rather differently by the opponent. For example (and one directly pertinent to the optimistic dictum of Slichter), it is reported that the policy of General Motors for many years has been to obtain an annual return on investment of 20%.[18] The corporation was therefore unwilling to agree to increased labor costs that threatened that goal. This must have appeared rather differently to the production line workers and union officials who, less concerned for shareholders' interests or the financial leadership and prestige of General Motors, considered such a profit level as excellent evidence of the ability to pay higher wages and benefits. If, as seems most probable, the corporation's representatives perceived this, then there was good reason in their view not to furnish such information to the union. Instead they have refused to disclose financial details and have sought to argue their case (i.e., to offer information) in quite other terms. Just as reasonably in a negotiations context, the union has wished to avoid information relating to comparison with other, less favorable industries, and to attempt to concentrate on information about the corporation's ability to pay more. In this, as in most cases, the parties were seeking to control or restrict the kinds of information exchanged, but to restrict the giving of information is likely to produce reciprocal restriction by the opponent. Similarly, to dissemble and deceive may produce an escalation of deception, as well as the possibility of being caught and so losing credibility and potential for cooperation.

Solutions to these problems and dilemmas have, somehow, to be found by negotiators in actual cases unless failure to reach an outcome can be tolerated. Information from a mediator or outsiders often helps to fill gaps in negotiators' understanding of each other. In effect, as negotiations proceed, the stock of information grows, and demands and offers tend to become less extreme so as to come nearer to genuine and realistic expectations and preferences. Uncertainty is likely to persist right to the end, however. For instance, a party may not call his opponent's bluff because he does not perceive it as such or is unwilling to risk it. These and cognate matters are discussed further in the exposition of the developmental process in the following chapter.

One other aspect of information exchange must be mentioned briefly: the problem of "overinformation." Too much information can interfere with growing understanding and the capacity to adjust expectations and make choices. Too much detail can obscure the main issues and promote

---

18. From 1947 to 1969 General Motors "earned 24 billion dollars, more than 1.8 billion over the 20 per cent target rate [Serrin 1974:71]."

uncertainty as a negotiator tries to see his way through a plethora of economic and historical data, normative rules, genealogical facts, precedents, and much else. Indeed, it is sometimes a deliberate strategy to confuse an opponent with overinformation so as to hinder him from making assessments in his own interests. Elaboration of details, perhaps together with "irrelevant" minutiae on side issues, can be accompanied by seemingly reasonable solutions that favor a party's preferences but may not be in the best interest of the opponent. Technical experts on a disputant's team (e.g., on financial, technological, legal, or ritual matters) are used for this purpose as well as to provide protection against a similar strategy by the opponent.[19]

Apart from deliverate strategy, where a wide range of multiple items and multiple criteria are involved in the dispute, the range of possible outcomes can be so great that it induces vacillation, frustration, and a resort to arbitrary choice, which undermine confidence. Consequently, major decisions have been crudely made, sometimes by the toss of a coin or by the use of supernatural devices where no other way seemed possible or reliable. In these circumstances, negotiators become particularly susceptible to a mediator's suggestions or almost any suggestion at all. To make some choice and to stick by it may be unavoidable and increasingly desirable if negotiations are not to reach stalemate. One common policy, mentioned previously, is to attempt to delay decision in the hope that information becomes clearer. Although this policy hinders the development and adjustment of a party's preference set, it may nevertheless be all that a party can do.

C. F. Carter (1972) has outlined a prescriptive theory of decision making (but not under conditions of two-party interaction) in which he advocated "a stage by stage simplification of the issues." Thus possibilities to be entertained are successively reduced by omitting those that are abhorrent or extraordinary, involve highly unlikely circumstances, are difficult or unpleasant to contemplate, impose intolerable losses, deny essential minimal needs, and so on. "A very large and complex decision, involving anticipation of many circumstances over a long period in the future, requires a heroic degree of simplification [Carter 1972:41]."[20]

In practice, some such simplification must be and is made where overinformation threatens to produce mutual paralysis. In negotiations, however, although a party makes his own assessment and choices he can-

---

19. This piling up of technical details, neither fully comprehended nor easily controverted, was known as "blinding with science" in the R.A.F. in Britain during World War II.

20. Carter continued, "in an extreme case, a very big decision may be indefinitely delayed" and he gave the example of the case of the projected Channel tunnel between England and France.

not take a decision or choose a set of options unilaterally. He is ineluctably affected by the assessment and choices of his opponent, as far as he can know and understand them. He must take account of the effects of his own choices and his opponent's choices. Ignoring further regression—he chooses because I choose because he chooses—is one act of simplification. Simplification of complex issues and their many possible outcomes is quite essential, but it tends to introduce some distortion of the situation. It may be imperative to cut through to the possibility of some joint decision that is tolerable and sufficient, regardless of what alternatives might be potentially available if they could only be grasped.

5

PROCESSUAL MODEL OF NEGOTIATION, 2: THE DEVELOPMENTAL MODEL

The second of the two interconnected models of negotiation is concerned with the developmental progress from the initial recognition of a dispute to some kind of outcome.[1] This model is essentially one of successive phases in each of which there is a particular focus of attention and concern by the negotiators. It could be said that progress in one phase—that is, some accomplishment of the intent of its particular concentration—opens the way to the succeeding phase with a different concentration. That is too simple, however, both empirically and conceptually. These phases are not in practice, nor in conception, altogether congruent with linear, chronological time. It is not unusual for two, or even three, phases to overlap in time; nor is it desirable to ignore the possibility that negotiators may return to an earlier phase, in effect or by deliberate intent. They may wish to take up previously neglected matters, to clarify others, or to start afresh in the light of later experience. A precisely ordered development would make too limited and too rigid a model, because although there is a discernible common pattern the empirical reality of actual negotiation demands a recognition of considerable flexibility.

The phases are shown diagrammatically in Figure 5.1. For clarity of

1. The limited, specialized meaning of the term *dispute* as used in this book is explained on page 75. The notion of *outcome* is discussed on pages 77–79.

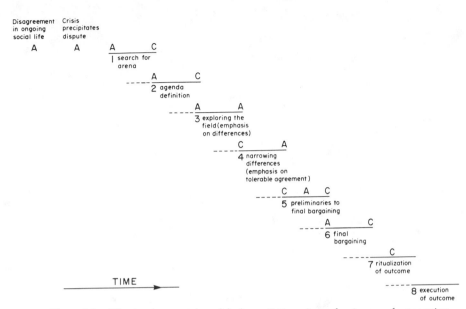

Figure 5.1. The developmental model of negotiation: A, predominance of antagonism; C, predominance of coordination.

exposition it seems most helpful to describe and discuss each phase more or less separately before considering the range of variation and the flexibility the model must encompass. In the following account, portions of actual negotiations are used to exemplify and to emphasize the kinds of behavior and interaction of negotiators in particular phases. These empirical examples are, however, no more than "apt illustrations." They may help to reinforce the conceptualization and they will suggest my persisting intent to retain the necessary connection between real-life conditions and analytical presentation.

PHASE 1: THE SEARCH FOR AN ARENA

When the two parties acknowledge the emergence of a dispute between them, there is a need to agree to some place where the negotiations may occur. This presupposes not only that the parties recognize that disagreement and conflict are not immediately resolvable, but also that they are prepared to enter into negotiations for the ostensible purpose of seeking to discover some tolerable resolution. Often there is little or no problem here, as both parties consider the disagreement less than tolerable and anticipate a negotiated outcome that is preferable to the status quo. Here the nature of the relationship between the parties and the particular problems within it are obviously important. The parties may have little choice but to accede to almost any attempt to deal with the problem in order to allow the continuation of what is an advantageous relationship, or to permit them to salvage what they can. The unresolved disagreement may concern interests that cannot easily be neglected, whether or not there is a relationship to sustain. It may be perceived as a matter of personal integrity, morality, honor, or reputation to meet the public complaint, though a sense of righteousness or an expectation of success may be sufficiently compelling.

Nevertheless, a potential defendant may attempt to ignore a complainant. He may be able to withstand such pressures as can be brought by or on behalf of the complainant. In such a case, negotiations do not begin at all. The potential defendant prefers the status quo to any other outcome he can foresee. The complainant may be quite unable to do anything, either because there is no recourse available or because the costs of bringing pressures are considered too heavy. For example, the abortive strike was a common feature of earlier industrial relations in Western countries—and sometimes still occurs—where a powerful, adamant employer refused to negotiate with the workers and held out until they acquiesced in economic privation. Anthropologists have reported cases, particularly from acephalous societies, where a complainant has been too weak to force a confrontation or where he just could not get at the other party because of geographical or social distance between them (see, e.g., Gulliver 1963:263–267).

There is a variety of tactics that complainants use to overcome such intransigence. They might attempt to interfere with the interests of the recalcitrant party or of some other person who can directly influence that party: for instance, the seizure of property, blocking a track, cutting off water supplies, or armed attack to inflict damage. The complainant might refuse to continue the relationship (if any) between them. He might appeal to or challenge the other to defend his case publicly, with the implication that he has a weak case should he refuse. The complainant may be able to appeal to influential persons to intervene or to general public opinion by referring to the public good, morality, honor, or whatever ideology seems effectively applicable. In some societies there are persons in institutionalized roles who can act as persuasive go-betweens, such as the head of a common kin group or association, a local member of the elite, a policeman, a politician, or an official of the Department of Labor. There may be people who have valued connections with both parties and who are therefore likely to be trusted by both and to have an interest in getting negotiations started: the common kinsman or neighbor, the co-member of an association to which both parties belong. There are sometimes established ritual and supernatural procedures for inducing compliance under threat of punishment and for publicizing a defendant's refusal. In many societies there are well-recognized means of public coercion that are hard to withstand: for example, the beating of the village drum or gong by the complainant to announce his grievance and his demand for negotiation, the calling of a press conference to obtain publicity in the news media, or the issuance of due legal notice to strike if negotiations are not undertaken (as in some industrial situations).[2]

Having agreed to begin negotiations, the choice of an arena may raise no difficulty. It may, for example, be the established norm for negotiations to occur in the village square, in the men's house, or under a convenient stand of shady trees. There may be ritually prescribed places where members of a lineage or clan meet to deal with their disputes. There may be a recognized rule that negotiations are held at the defendant's residence, at the house or office of a go-between or mediator, or in the business firm's boardroom.

Even though a conventionally recognized arena exists (and unless it is ineluctably prescribed), a party may wish to avoid it and choose some other. He might wish to avoid the expected publicity that the arena entails or, conversely, to seek greater publicity elsewhere. He might wish to avoid the probable intervention of a third party that the arena presupposes or to gain such intervention where the arena denies it. There may be, however, a range of possibilities, institutionalized or not, each one offering some particular ground rules, social context, and cultural arrangements. The range of choice is sometimes quite wide. For instance, among the Arusha of Tanzania the range included age-group conclave, parish assembly, intralineage conclave, patrilineal moot, mediation by the parish headman at his or the defendant's residence, and mediation in the office of the chief or of a magistrate. Normatively, particular kinds of dispute prescribed certain kinds of arenas. For example, a dispute between patrilineal kinsmen should have been handled in a lineage conclave or patrilineal moot, whereas a dispute between unrelated neighbors should have gone to the parish assembly. Yet for their own reasons of anticipated advantage negotiators could try to choose another arena that was thought to be more favorable (Gulliver 1963:178 ff.).

The preference for a particular arena, or the aversion to another one,

---

2. Some account of Arusha stratagems in these circumstances are given by Gulliver (1963:Chapter 11). See Charsley (1969:53) on the traditional Nyakyusa practice whereby a frustrated complainant seizes property belonging to a locally resident kinsman of the more distant, recalcitrant party. Colson (1953) has described the stratagems of the Tonga of Zambia in a specific case of homicide.

is not primarily a matter of the physical location of meetings, though that may have symbolic significance or offer certain kinds of facilities. Rather, the choice refers to the kind of social and cultural rules, assumptions, and predispositions an arena prescribes. The arena may affect the recruitment and composition of disputants' teams as well as the pattern of their interaction. For instance, where the parties meet at an ancestral site as members of linked lineages, the sociocultural context is probably quite different from a meeting in, say, the village square. In the latter case, there might be less emphasis on kinship and lineal differentiation but instead an orientation toward the commonality of neighbors and their enveloping community. There is also a difference between a completely public, and perhaps publicized, meeting and a smaller, semiprivate conclave. In the former there may be larger teams, negotiators' arguments are open to evaluation and comment by other people, and the intervention of third parties is more likely. In the latter case, smaller teams can meet with greater informality, outsiders can be avoided, and public scrutiny is less immediate. Similarly, there can be a significant difference between a meeting at the defendant's residence, or in the employer's office, and one on neutral ground, removed from the context of ongoing social life and where the relative status of the parties is less emphasized. To meet at a third party's place (e.g., the residence of a clan leader or village headman, the office of a government conciliator) may well involve acceptance of that party as mediator, or at least as a party with an acknowledged interest and privilege of intervention.

The important point is that when there is more than one possible arena, choice is available. The opposed parties must therefore, in this initial phase of negotiation, come to some joint decision. The supposed advantages and disadvantages of the options are weighed and the parties may differ in their preferences. The unwillingness of a defendant to acknowledge the dispute and to enter into negotiations may in part be an unwillingness to agree to a particular arena proposed by the plaintiff, or it might be a tactical move to persuade the plaintiff to accept an alternative. In any case, these early discussions are likely to reveal not only the implications of the options and the opponent's preferences but, through that, something about the opponent's expectations and preferences on the issues in dispute. That is to say, discussions about the arena can be used to start probing the opponent's initial stand. Moreover, it may be possible to gain tactical advantage by insisting on concession by the opponent or by making concession oneself.

In coming to an agreement the parties have begun to negotiate. They are in communication and they have exchanged some information, whether directly or through intermediaries. However, it is sometimes the case that, until the arena is agreed to, the recruitment of the disputants' teams cannot be completed because different arenas postulate different bases of recruitment.

Finally, although the parties reach agreement on an arena, this is not necessarily an irrevocable decision. For a number of reasons a party may find it disadvantageous to continue in an arena; both parties may agree that another arena is preferable. Indeed, the agreement on an arena may be, and may only be intended as, a temporary matter allowing the parties to come together to establish an agenda for their further negotiations. Part of the agenda agreement can be the choice of a more permanent arena.

PHASE 2: COMPOSITION OF AGENDA AND DEFINITION OF ISSUES

Although the parties have acknowledged the emergence of a dispute and, perhaps, an arena has been agreed upon, it cannot be assumed that the parties are each clear, let alone in agreement, concerning the exact nature of the dispute or what issues are to be negotiated.

As the dispute emerges, probably as original dyadic disagreement comes into the public domain, each disputant with his supporters takes stock of the situation and of the possibilities now open. The original disagreement may have been fairly clear—say, a rejected demand for repayment of debt or for a wage increase—but even so it may now be augmented by other, hitherto more or less dormant issues, new details, ideological considerations, and other matters. Seeming irrelevancies may get caught up, both material and affective. Other people join one or the other of the parties, as supporters and aides, and then introduce new issues, perhaps in terms of their own interests and potential advantages. Quite commonly the original disagreement was vague or in rather general terms: say, accusations of failure of cooperation or generosity stemming from some last-straw incident that might be of little importance in itself. Now, as the negotiations get under way, the underlying complaints and demands are raised and specified as a party clarifies and formulates his ideas and expectations in the light of the new situation. What began as a creditor's claim for repayment of debt comes to be, or to include, issues of relative status and other quite different rights; a boundary dispute between neighbors becomes transformed into a problem of inheritance or landlord–tenant relations or access to water; a complaint about general working conditions in a factory turns into a workers' demand for higher wages and an improved pension scheme. The original disagreement may continue and be more clearly articulated but antagonism, now aroused, spreads into other

126

matters. Decisions have to be made about which issues to press and in what form, and which are best left out. Emotions may run so high that virtually anything and everything are thrown in, regardless of relevance or possibility of resolution.

Since both parties engage in the same kind of activity, the choice of, and relative emphasis on, various issues are not usually at the volition of either party alone. There has to be some agreement, at least on a preliminary, working agenda. This could be a simple recognition that each party produces his own list of issues, as frequently happens in the negotiation of an industrial contract between workers and management. This establishes a loose framework that necessarily will be reduced and clarified in due course. Agenda formulation may occur through discussions specifically focused on that goal. In that event it is seldom a once-and-for-all agreement that precludes later additions and amendments (unlike a conference or committee meeting under parliamentary rules). More commonly, perhaps, the agenda in effect emerges out of the early exchange of information—that is, the presentation of demands, counterdemands, and complaints, and the reactions to them.

In any case, a party might refuse to consider an issue introduced by his opponent. The issue is regarded as nonnegotiable because it touches interests and values the party is unwilling to expose. Negotiations can hardly continue until the parties find some sort of agreement here. Perhaps the party admits negotiability or at least agrees to further discussion of the issue; the opponent may accept nonnegotiability and the issue is withdrawn; or the matter is reformulated in a manner acceptable to both parties. Often there is little difficulty as one of the parties gives way fairly easily. Either he considers the issue to be relatively unimportant or he believes his position to be so strong that he is not liable to make large concessions. Trading may occur. A party accepts an issue or a particular definition of it as proposed by the opponent in return for acceptance of one proposed by him. Failure to agree fairly easily indicates that the issue in question is a significant one for both parties and that therefore more serious and concentrated attention is required. Clarification and improved appreciation of the issue, of the dispute in general, and of each party's position, may result. There may be limited agreement to disagree temporarily until the issue can be reconsidered later when the negotiations have developed further. There may, however, be an early test of strength, and sometimes that leads to impasse and a breakdown of negotiations.

Strike at Pilkingtons.   An apt illustration of some of these agenda problems comes from an industrial dispute that occurred in 1970 at the Pilkington glass factories in St. Helens, Lancashire, England. Industrial relations at Pilkington had hitherto been stable and accepted by both employer and workers as satisfactory. The workers, in what was largely a company town, were seen by trade unionists in the nearby city of Liverpool as lacking militancy. Yet workers' dissatisfactions had been accumulating and little seems to have been done to acknowledge or deal with them, as a markedly paternalistic, puritan ethic management and a well-entrenched trade union bureaucracy continued in their established ways. The precipitating crisis was a sudden unofficial strike in one of the factories, following a complaint alleging underpayment of wages. Very soon afterward, as the first strikers were joined by workers from other Pilkington factories in the town, the dispute (as it had now become) widened to include issues concerning general wage rates and a demand for higher pay. Later, as more Pilkington workers joined in the strike (including some from factories elsewhere in Britain), the wage demand was increased and was claimed for all Pilkington employees.

Then a new issue developed between the workers on strike (local members of the trade union) and the national executive of the union (located elsewhere): whether or not the strike should be declared an official one, with full union support, strike pay, and other facilities. Gradually the employer, sticking to a wage offer below that demanded by the strikers, virtually withdrew to the sidelines as the immediate, principal conflict developed between the newly formed local strike committee and its leaders, on the one hand, and the out-of-town union officials on the other.

The fact that the strike lasted for 7 weeks—unique in that town and industry—is explicable by failures to agree as to what the dispute was really about and who should represent the workers or to discover an acceptable place where negotiations should occur. That is, neither arena nor agenda could be decided. The strike threw

> a number of pre-existing features of [the] situation into sharper relief. People [started] talking and thinking about things they [had] never really thought and talked about before. Or if they [had] thought and talked about them it [had] been in a desultory abstract way—the way people talk when there is no sense of urgency, no possibility of action [Lane and Roberts 1971:158].

Attempts were made to air and demonstrate the strikers' ideas and opinions, to reach preliminary agreement on the issues, and to find an acceptable arena. There were several mass meetings in the town, at some of which union officials were shouted down and even manhandled. There were also meetings between the unofficial strike committee and union officials. These were all quite unsuccessful; indeed, they stimulated misunderstanding and mistrust. The employer and the union officials were scarcely in disagreement, both coming to favor a general wage increase of £3, conditional on a return to work. In the end, workers, gradually decided that the loss of wage income was too severe to be accepted any longer and the strike faded out. In effect, negotiations ceased—or scarcely got under way—because the parties "were not agreed as to what to fight about. In withdrawing to positions based upon quite different issues, the parties were not deliberately attempting to be obstinate and intransigent. What was sincerely felt to be a real issue by one party was genuinely felt to be irrelevant by others [Lane and Roberts 1971:236]."

This was a complex affair, involving thousands of workers, unofficial (largely self-selected) strike leaders, dozens of shop stewards and union officials, employer's representatives, a national trade union and the Trade Union Congress, local and national news media, and national political figures. But it was not this complexity in itself that produced the principal difficulties. Both before and since, even more complex industrial strikes have been successfully brought to full negotiations and an agreed settlement in Britain, as in other countries. The failure to reach agreement on both arena and agenda was intimately connected with the adamant desire of union officials to preserve their prerogatives and leadership, as well as to maintain what seemed to them to be adequate union-management relations and procedures. The management, in little disagreement with union officials, was not prepared to negotiate about basic issues of employment conditions and industrial relations. The ad hoc strike leaders, on the other hand, wanted not only much higher wages but also changes in employment conditions and a radical alteration in management–employee relations. The latter included both an end to the employer's paternalism and a greater participation for local workers in union affairs and policymaking.

Negotiations were stalemated, therefore. It is important to note, nevertheless, that there was an outcome, though largely by default. The national union officials (supported by the management) proved themselves to be the stronger and more resistant party in the event. They were able to stand firm until the workers accepted the smaller increase in wages offered to them and acceded to the impossibility of obtaining changes in employment conditions or in union organization.

The problem of agenda formulation is not only a matter of what issues are to be negotiated. Some issues are capable of being defined in more than one way. Each party, insofar as he is aware of this, seeks the definition and the associated rules, values, and interests that seem most advantageous to him. Iklé, referring to international negotiations, has noted that the "formulation of an issue may stake out the starting points and limits for concessions, fix the bench marks for evaluating gains and losses, and circumscribe the areas where pressures, threats and inducements can be used [1964: 218]." Iklé also noted that a party may attempt to get on the agenda an issue that projects his basic goal into the negotiations and perhaps precludes consideration of some other issue. He cited the negotiations on a Free Trade Area in Europe when Britain attempted to make the implementation of such an area a principal agenda issue with the intent of avoiding discussion of its feasibility and desirability. In addition, however, a particular definition of an issue may prescribe certain rules and values that establish the context of its negotiation. Parties may therefore disagree in their proposed definitions because they see different advantages and disadvantages in them. Moreover, definition can affect the relative negotiating strengths of the parties. "The definition of alternatives is the supreme instrument of power. . . . [It] is the choice of conflicts, and the choice of conflicts allocates power [Schattschneider 1957:937]."

Some empirical case materials can illustrate these points and their significance in negotiations.

Wildcat Strike.   This well-known case, reported by Gouldner (1965), occurred in an American industrial plant in 1950. The workers had become dissatisfied with certain aspects of their working conditions, particularly some recent changes imposed by the management relating to the introduction of new machinery, new routines, and supervision. This dissatisfaction, gradually accumulating without amelioration, was the cause of the wildcat strike. The management was consistently concerned, in opening negotiations, with defining the relevant issues as what it called "grievances," in conformity with orthodox usage. These were demands by the workers that could be legitimated and negotiated in terms of the existing contract between management and employees. That is, the management wanted to take a stand on that contract, though it was, under pressure, prepared to discuss differing interpretations of parts of the contract. On the other hand, the management was not prepared to negotiate over what it referred to as workers' "complaints"; that is, matters falling outside the contract. This was partly because the management felt itself on safer ground in sticking to a legalistic basis and by limiting the number and kind of issues to be considered. It also wished to prevent the workers from raising issues that impinged on what were considered to be the prerogatives of the management in running the business enterprise efficiently. Such prerogatives included the "election and placement of supervisors, types of product manufactured, schedule of operations [Gouldner 1965:109]." In fact, at least some of the causes of the strike and some of the issues raised by the workers related to dissatisfactions in precisely those areas.

The negotiations and the eventual settlement had to deal with the appointment and competence of particular supervisors and with work rates connected with the management's investment in new machinery. The management was compelled to agree to those issues on the agenda because it wished to avoid a lengthier, more costly work stoppage. Yet the management was fairly successful otherwise in imposing its own definition of the issues in dispute and, therefore, in maintaining the right to run the enterprise as it saw best. The fundamental role, power, and prerogatives were, in consequence, hardly questioned or affected by the negotiated outcome.

It is not too early to ask why one party, in this particular instance, was able to gain the opponent's agreement to its choice of issues and their definition.[3] From Gouldner's account it seems clear that the workers were eventually persuaded to concentrate negotiations mainly on the issue of wages, even though this had not initially been their primary concern in deciding to strike. It is not unfair to say that the workers were bought off by the management and that their attention was distracted by a negotiable offer of increased wages. The wildcat strikers soon found themselves in financial difficulties without their regular wages, so that after letting off steam they become primarily interested in resuming work and earning money. They were attracted by the chance now to obtain higher wages and were convinced by both management and union officials that this was to their prime advantage. On the whole, these American workers were not inclined to question free enterprise and capitalistic business operations, or not seriously and at length, although some of their original strike claims threatened to do just that. By its definition of the chief issues, the management successfully headed off any real confrontation of that kind. After a time, then, the workers no longer perceived the need, nor perhaps the propriety, of pressing other issues to a logical or ideological end, especially when a few of the more immediately emotional, nonwage matters were dealt with. The management was able to appeal to and keep to a legalistic norm; the agenda of negotiations was defined in terms of the industrial contract that had previously been negotiated and was still the charter for working conditions in the plant. Union officials seem to have been influenced by this appeal, since their own role and functions were directly related to these established norms.

In an entirely different sociocultural context, a comparable problem of definition was dealt with in this phase of negotiations.[4]

An Ndendeuli Bridewealth Dispute. In an Ndendeuli local community in southern Tanzania in 1953, a young man had recently returned home after

---

3. Fuller examination of the general means of and reasons for reaching agreement on issues such as these is given later in this chapter.

4. A fuller account of this case was given by Gulliver (1971:145, Case 2).

an absence of a year or so as a migrant worker. His wife's father, a neighbor in the same community, sought a share of the money savings the young man was thought to have brought back. Apart from a courtesy gift to his wife's parents (a generalized obligation of generosity to his superior relatives-in-law), the young man refused to give anything else. The father-in-law initiated a formal dispute in a public moot comprising the two men and their respective local kinsmen–supporters. The father-in-law and his supporters argued that the principal issue was a legitimate demand for payment of a further installment of bridewealth. The son-in-law, however, argued that he had completed all bridewealth payments before leaving home as a migrant worker, and that what was in dispute was the nature and size of his gift to this affine.

In that society, bridewealth was intrinsically bound up with marriage and the legitimacy of the paternity of children. Marriage was considered to be fundamental and the compulsion to secure it by bridewealth payments was, therefore, especially strong. Despite this, completion of bridewealth payment (usually, as in this case, a series of cash payments) was not clearly identified in terms of a specified sum nor by any ritualized performance. A more or less tacit understanding would emerge that no further bridewealth was expected and that the marriage was fully established. A son-in-law did not always ensure that there were outside witnesses to such expression of final satisfaction by his wife's father. On the other hand, gifts from a son-in-law to his wife's father (or her other close kin) were related to the maintenance of affinal relations and scarcely touched on the established marriage itself. Affinal relations were certainly not unimportant in this society but there were usually, as in this case, many alternatives to any one affinal link; other affines (through the wife, sisters, sons, and daughters), as well as a wide range of cognatic kinsmen, all offered much the same relationships and social advantages. Therefore, the compulsion to secure any particular affinal relationship was rather less strong, both normatively and pragmatically, than the need to pay bridewealth. Thus, by defining the issue in dispute as one concerning bridewealth payment, the father-in-law could put himself in the stronger position; symbolically, and even practically, he could threaten the marriage. By defining the matter as one of affinal obligation and the maintenance of affinal relationship, the son-in-law would be less vulnerable (a less critical relationship being involved). This was especially so since he considered with some justification that his own record here was most satisfactory; he had met his affinal obligations as well as, or better than, his wife's father had. He could hope to show that the older man was making excessive demands on his resources and his generosity.

In the end, the definition of the father-in-law gradually came to dominate the negotiations. He was able to achieve this because of a combination of reasons. The son-in-law was unable to demonstrate adequately, beyond doubt, that there had been previous agreement that bridewealth was completed. At best he had, somewhat foolishly, failed to have this made abundantly clear in public, although he claimed that his wife's father was now failing to keep a private (and not unexceptional) understanding between them. Not only could he not demonstrate this to his opponent (though it seems to have been the case in fact) but he could not altogether convince his own supporters, to whom he seemed to have a weak, but not necessarily false, case. They supported him, but less strongly than they otherwise might. More decisively, however, the son-in-law came under considerable and concerted pressure from the mutual kinsmen of both disputants (some of whom were his own supporters) that he should neither prolong the dispute and the negotiations nor appear to be selfish and ungenerous. The disputants and their supporters, and also the mediator, were intricately coinvolved in a network of active social relationships (expressed in kinship terms), which were operative in a variety of important, practical matters. These men wanted a speedy conclusion of the dispute so that their valued relationships would not be threatened. They perceived that the younger man (a junior neighbor, much absent from the community as a migrant worker) was in a weaker position that his father-in-law and so more susceptible to pressure. This did not mean that he was deserted by some of his supporters; they helped him to gain advantages in the subsequent phases of the negotiations. Rather, they came to choose what seemed to them to be the more desirable definition of the issue in dispute in order to get it settled without delay.

An Arusha Bridewealth Case.   A contrasting case comes from the Arusha of northern Tanzania (cf. Gulliver 1963:243 ff.). There, bridewealth payments were in specifically named cattle and sheep, each of which was identifiable by symbolic penumbra and cultural significance. In this instance, in 1957, it was incontrovertible that bridewealth had not been completed and the son-in-law did not pretend to deny that three of those animals had yet to be handed over. His father-in-law precipitated the public dispute by demanding immediate payment and refusing any further postponement. In the negotiations, the son-in-law sought to define the issue not in terms of bridewealth debt but, rather, with reference to ongoing affinal kinship relations and the father's moral and practical obligations to his daughter and her children. In the face of his opponent's protestations of irrelevance, the son-in-law insisted, and claimed to demonstrate in detail, that hitherto he had acted as a good son-in-law should. He asserted that there had been no previous complaint and that their affinal relationship was an active, valuable one that should be preserved for mutual advantage. He also claimed that he had insufficient livestock with which to pay bridewealth without impoverishing his family (including the daughter and grand-children of the plaintiff) and that therefore to make an immediate claim was threatening to the relationships involved.

It came out, however, despite an attempt at concealment, that not only did the son-in-law have sufficient animals with which to pay bride-wealth but he was intending to use those animals to purchase a piece of land adjacent to his farm. The father-in-law had not known of this. Now he and his supporters renewed their insistence to define the issue as bride-wealth debt. At that point, in disagreement over definition, the negotia-tions broke down. At a second confrontation, this time in a larger, open meeting, the son-in-law continued to press his definition. He and his sup-porters argued that for the father-in-law to insist on making bridewealth the issue and so to demand immediate payment would prevent purchase of the land. The existing farm of the son-in-law was a small one, too small to provide a secure livelihood for his family under prevailing economic condi-tions. Land for sale, especially so conveniently located, was scarce and becoming scarcer. An enlargement of his farm was therefore now or perhaps never.

The father-in-law was gradually persuaded to accept the other's defini-tion of the issue and therefore to focus much of the negotiations on his (the plaintiff's) obligations to his son-in-law, daughter, and grandchildren. Thus, although the son-in-law was in effect rejecting the demand for bridewealth he was doing this in terms of the overriding affinal relation-ship. This gave him marked advantage in the subsequent negotiations because the affinal relationship was a most valuable one for both parties and the son-in-law could show that he had been diligent in his behavior there.

Let me be clear about what was happening in these last three cases of negotiations. In none of them was the matter of agenda and definition of issues pursued quite distinctly and separately from other phases of the negotiations. In the case of the wildcat strike, the arena could not be deter-mined until agenda and definition were more or less settled. Had the workers continued to insist on consideration of their full list of complaints about working conditions and management policies, then negotiations might have occurred between wildcat strike leaders and the management. With the legalistic, contract-based definition of the issues, centering on wage rates, as proposed by the management and accepted by union of-ficials, negotiations occurred between those two parties with the workers' tacit concurrence. Resolution of the issues brought about an agreed identification of the relevant parties, of the arena, and of the ground rules to be used. The two phases not only overlapped but were interdependent.

In the two African cases, there was little problem over the arena as the disputants in each instance resorted to standard procedures in their respective societies. There was really no alternative for the Ndendeuli: Since the disputants were neighbors they met in public moot at the defendant's house. In the Arusha case, it was initially agreed that the parties should meet in a small conclave (the disputants with a few supporters each); following the breakdown of the conclave it was again easily agreed that a second meeting should be in a larger, public moot. These choices were obvious and clear and scarcely affected the negotiations. However, the phases of agenda and issue definition in both of these bridewealth cases overlapped with the "next" phase: the concentration on and expression of differences, marking the outside limits of demands. In order to reach agreement on the definition of issues it was necessary to go on to make and justify demands and so attempt to show the validity of particular definitions. In the Ndendeuli case, the plaintiff was in effect saying (though without explicit articulation) that if his definition were not accepted, then lengthy and perhaps embittered negotiations would follow. In the Arusha case, the defendant successfully demonstrated that to treat the dispute as one principally about bridewealth debt was both unnecessary and most likely to be deleterious to valuable affinal relations and to the welfare of his family.

This kind of overlapping is not inevitable. With the arena agreed upon, the first consideration becomes that of agenda. Agenda formulation need not be too problematic and so can be resolved before proceeding further. On the other hand, even when the agenda is agreed between the parties, this does not necessarily mean that it is adhered to faithfully thereafter. Either party may later wish to introduce new issues or to redefine existing ones. Advantages in so doing are perceived after more exchange of information, which creates new understanding of the implications of the dispute. In that case the agenda may be renegotiated.

PHASE 3: ESTABLISHING MAXIMAL LIMITS TO ISSUES IN DISPUTE

This phase has sometimes been characterized by writers as the beginning of real negotiations. For example, both Douglas (1962:14) and Stevens (1963:59) have described it as the first stage. Yet it is clear that in practice a great deal of negotiating relative to crucial matters has already occurred, and usually it must occur, prior to this phase. Nor is it sensible simply to regard the two earlier phases merely as preparatory to the negotiators getting down to the business in hand. Rather, a great deal of the subsequent tone of the negotiations is often established during the first two phases. What the dispute is about, the ground rules, and the constitution of parties are determined by the agreed arena and agenda; the bases and something of the relative strengths of the parties are initially probed and demonstrated by the discussions and jockeying for position in respect to the agenda.

As problems of agenda are being resolved, with whatever degree of clarity, the parties begin to enter a new phase. In their respective offers of information, they start to range quite freely over the field that is being agreed to. Each party reiterates and develops his initial stands, both in general and on particular issues, and continues to elaborate on them. Typically, there are statements of what a party "absolutely" must have from and will not concede to the opponent, often at length and in oratorical fashion. These offers of information are not necessarily precise in detail. Indeed, often they are deliberately imprecise because a party may be unsure of just how much he can or should demand or refuse. His preference set and expectations are characteristically incomplete and inconsistent in this phase of the negotiations. There is often a desire to avoid too early or too restrictive a commitment so as not to set limits that later may seem to have been too narrow. A party might be unclear about his opponent's maximal limits and thus, as it were, about the size and shape of the field within which further negotiations are to occur. Therefore it is often considered prudent (say, by an employer) to make statements such as, "Your demands are quite impossible to meet," or "We can only consider a very small increase in wages." Such declarations are followed up, but without creating a definite commitment, by marshalled argument (often with a plethora of "facts") about business prospects, competitors' activities, costs, production schedules, and other problems. Mutatis mutandis, in an African bride-wealth case, the son-in-law acts in the same way apropos the demands by his father-in-law for further payments. In either situation and in others, a party's presentation is garnished with ideology, righteousness, and accusations.

In the course of these exchanges, each party attempts to extract greater precision and firmer commitment from his opponent. There are efforts, therefore, to probe more deeply and to provoke less guarded information. This kind of action is not usually vigorous, however, and there tends to be little attempt at argued rejection of the other's case. Assertive rejection is more typical. In this phase, each party is principally concerned with presenting his own case rather than with reacting specifically to the details of the opponent's case. There is little coordination still and overtly a good deal of expression of antagonism and competitiveness. The emphasis is on the establishment and embellishment of a maximal position—demands and offers and denials of those of the opponent.

There are shows of strength and suggestions or forthright assertions of resoluteness and threat. Comments are made on the alleged moral and practical weakness of the opponent and the errors or mendacity in his statements. Personal and group animosities are often brought into the open: animadversions to social, moral, and personal faults in ad hominem attacks on members of the other party, in contrast to the high motives and meritorious qualities of one's own party. Ideological banners are waved (e.g., workers' rights, the moral unity of the group, ideal norms of neighborliness) and supporting references are made to cultural rules, ethical standards, and evocative symbols.

There is a wide and free-ranging reference to, and partisan exposition of, everything on the agenda and, in effect, of more or less anything and everything touching the parties' statuses, relationships, past histories, and future prospects. In short, anything is brought into the arena that may conceivably be relevant and advantageous. It is not yet altogether clear to a party what might be useful and so it often seems preferable to bring in as much as possible rather than forfeit possible advantage through failure to do so. The point is, however, that all this is done in an extremist, antagonistic fashion, emphasizing differences and separateness. In this phase the two parties are not concerned with getting together to work out differences and seek acceptable outcomes of particular issues. That is to come later. For the moment, coordination, much less cooperation is eschewed.

Ann Douglas[5] has described this phase as having

all the outward signs of deep and irreversible cleavage between the parties. The speeches of participants have about them the qualities of public oratory: compared with the rest of the conference, they are exceptionally long; only main spokesmen carry the verbal load; there are few interruptions by others bidding for the floor; where interruptions occur, they are less likely to be acknowledged and responded to; speeches flow with unusual smoothness and rhythmic regularity as though they had been prepared and rehearsed in advance [Douglas 1957:72].

Douglas also noted the prevalent antagonism in this phase:

Each side shows prodigious zeal for exposing and discrediting its opposite, and sooner or later there almost invariably comes from each side a conscious,

---

5. I wish here to acknowledge my debt to and respect for the work of Ann Douglas and her analyses of industrial negotiations. They have probably been the most influential on my own thinking—in large part because of her persistent adherence to empirical, real-life data.

studied, hard-hitting critique of the other. These attacks are typically vigorous and spirited: not infrequently they are also derisive and venomous [Douglas 1962:15].

With some justification, Douglas pointed out that for "persons unfamiliar with [negotiations] this stage of the proceedings is probably the most difficult to understand [1957:72–73]." The parties are not only far apart but each is insisting on the inviolability and practical and moral strength of his own position, with a rejection of worth in the opponent's position or in the members of the opposed party. It looks as though there is not and cannot be any common ground, any concession, or any possibility of an agreed outcome.

What, then, is happening during this phase of free-roaming, antagonistic, and rhetorical behavior? There is communication of a kind. The parties are proffering messages and in effect desire information from each other. However, the general intent is not primarily to attempt to influence each other to shift toward some more acceptable position; rather, it is to explore the dimensions of the field within which further negotiations are to occur. Each wishes to discover what is contained within the field and what is not, relative to whatever agenda definitions have been established, and what the implications are. This can hardly be known at the outset, but in any case, it is important to make sure that the opponent learns one's own views. There is more than just exploration; there is the attempt to establish the maximal limits for claims and demands and for the relevance of associated matters. For example, is the range of disputed compensation to be from, say, nil to $100, from $25 to $75, or from $—100 (where the opponent counterclaims) to some positive sum? Similarly, what range of rules and norms is to be considered relevant? The parties represent and explicate opposite ends of each range for each issue on the agenda.

It is important to appreciate, as parties themselves more or less do in practice, that "real" demands, claims, and offers are not usually being made in this phase. By "real" I mean, first, demands or claims that a party has some calculated expectation of obtaining in the eventual outcome, and second, demands or claims by the opponent that a party accepts as representing the opponent's calculated expectations. Of course, there are instances where a party does in fact make demands that he believes to be at or near realistic expectations at this early stage. He is likely to do this when motivated by intensely emotional convictions of his moral and legal rightness or of his superior strength. Such instances are probably rather uncommon and they are likely to be unrealistic because a party can scarcely know enough about his opponent's preferences and strengths or even about his own. In this phase, neither party can be clear about what is possible. The negotiators are not talking about a possible outcome. To the contrary, each party is seeking to ensure that he does not set his initial demands too low, unduly restricting them before he learns about his opponent. Additionally, each party wishes to set up defenses and to leave room for maneuver against the opponent, not yet knowing quite where the opponent's thrusts will land.

This policy strongly inclines parties to make extravagant demands backed by extravagant justifications. American industrial negotiators sometimes refer to this as "blue sky bargaining." An Arusha informant described it to me as "talking to the mountain."[6] Most or even all of these demands will have to be relinquished in due course. It is significant that they are often freely and quite suddenly abandoned and forgotten once a party begins to obtain more information and an improved preference set. This is not a matter primarily of bluffing and deception; it seems unlikely that either party is or feels deceived by his opponent.

All of this tentative exploration and the setting of maximal limits on issues logically puts the two parties into extremes of opposition. It therefore emphasizes differences and antagonism. This is a matter of great processual and symbolic significance for at this time the parties are farther apart than at any other—farther, even, then where they were when their dispute began.

As already noted, this concentration on differences and the concomitant antagonistic opposition is commonly expressed in verbal rancor, direct attacks on individuals, and even personal abuse. Quite often harsh language and tone are employed (not necessarily deliberately)—perhaps profanity and other cultural connotations of disrespect, mistrust, and high emotion. Psychological considerations suggest a partial explanation. This kind of behavior seems to be expressive of the anxiety, insecurity, and uncertainty entailed in this phase of negotiations, as well as demonstrative of the distance between the parties. The cause for such stress later diminishes as information and learning increase and as the parties begin to move toward each other with a growing possibility of some agreement. Antagonism in this phase tends to lack focus, ranging widely and even wildly. Later, antagonism tends to be concentrated on particular issues. This kind of explanation would seem to conform to the fact that, later, each party tends to adopt a tolerant amnesia of the other's extreme demands and extravagances of emotion and language, implicitly accepting them as

---

6. The reference is to Mount Meru (14,979 feet). The Arusha live on its lower slopes and its conical peak dominates the physical environment.

the result of temporary stress. It may well be that, in addition, the open articulation of resentment, frustration, and anger allows members of a party more easily to deal with those emotions, or to dissipate them, so that later negotiations are less affected by them.

Nevertheless, however important such psychological considerations are in a total explanation, it is clear that in themselves they are not sufficient. The process of *social* interaction is such that, temporarily, separation, difference, and antagonism—that is, social distance—are to be emphasized in this phase. Were this not achieved, then the essential subsequent movement of the parties toward each other would be less clear, nor would they have adequately explored the field between them. It appears that negotiators can be fairly self-conscious of their behavior and intentions in this phase. Douglas and others have reported this from industrial negotiations, and my own observations in some African societies confirm it.

For example, in the Arusha bridewealth case previously cited (page 133), it was more or less deliberately arranged, in prenegotiation discussions, that the elder brother of the father-in-law would take the leading role of angry, intransigent extremist. It was he who, in this phase, repeatedly insisted that full, proper, and prompt payment should be made of all outstanding bridewealth owed by the son-in-law. He expressed resentment, injured morality, and righteous indignation.[7] This stratagem was useful, moreover, since the father-in-law did not have to express the extremist demands and emotional resentment. So he was more easily able to ignore them when their usefulness no longer existed in subsequent phases of the negotiations. Similarly, it seems not uncommon in industrial negotiations that the early, extremist position is taken by one or two members of the union party who are later superseded by others who have hitherto remained relatively quiet.

There is a ritualistic character to performance in this phase. Douglas (1957:72) has reported that members of both union and management parties often relished this kind of interaction, perceiving it as a kind of contest, admiring the skills of their opponents and holding little resentment against them even when the direct object of quite severe attack. Again, my experience of East African societies agrees with this. The rhetoric is appreciated and even praised. For example, among the Turkana of Kenya (for whom reticence and taciturnity were the everyday norm), this phase of the negotiation of bridewealth was marked by displays of most unusual

---

7. As Schelling has noted, if the stratagem is to express anger it helps if one is really angry. The elder brother was in fact resentful of what he genuinely considered to be ungrateful chicanery by the son-in-law. He was also a man of brusque manner, not noted for diplomatic subtlety.

rhetorical performance. Differences over issues between the woman's father and suitor, and their respective kin, were elaborately stressed. Social distance was emphasized by the brandishing of weapons and simulated aggressiveness. Each party allowed the other ample opportunity for this performance. The Arusha acted less dramatically; yet the eloquent acrimony of more or less set speeches was incongruous with the later, conciliatory approach to collusion and agreement. Spokesmen and counsellors, who were admired for their restrained diplomacy and quiet speech at other times, were expected to engage in fairly extravagant oratory. Arusha participants in negotiations appreciated the importance of this.

In addition to these expressions of differences and the exploration of extremes of demand and opposition, the parties are also taking up positions and demonstrating relative strengths that may sensibly affect subsequent movement toward an outcome. For instance, in that Arusha bridewealth case, the party of the son-in-law denied both the obligation and the ability to make any payment at all and argued this position forcefully. This established a different range and strength from an opening offer of, say, a limited payment together with a plea for tolerance by the father-in-law. The employer who now declares he can offer no wage increase at all is also saying that he is not seeking to reduce wage rates, but if he begins by stating that he can offer no more than a 5% increase he will almost certainly find it exceedingly difficult to give less than that, even if later he learns that the workers would have been prepared to take 4% rather than get no settlement at all. In either case the employer has set a limit on this issue in dispute. The limits are different and they create different ranges for the negotiations.

PHASE 4: NARROWING THE DIFFERENCES

This phase begins as there is a shift in orientation by the parties in the mode of interaction between them. The emphasis changes from differences, separateness, and antagonism toward coordination, collusion, and even cooperation. The shift may be gradual, as the new orientation supersedes the earlier one and as the parties come to be increasingly clear about the dimensions of their dispute and about their preferences and their understanding of each other. Instead, therefore, of emphasizing conflict and real or contrived intransigence, the parties begin to look toward the possibilities of approaching actual outcomes. There is often some confused overlapping of the successive phases as the rather radical change of orientation and purpose is achieved with difficulty and hesitancy. Sometimes, however, the transition is quite abrupt. Almost suddenly, the parties are coordinating

141

rather than acting separately in open antagonism. The change comes as one party (perhaps at the instigation of a mediator) makes what is perceived as a "real" offer on one or more issues—that is, one intended as, and taken to be, a possible outcome rather than expressive of ideal preferences. In any event, sooner or later the parties begin to propose real offers and demands, often with considerable modification of their previous assertions. Thus the parties begin to explore specific outcomes and to seek to discover if and where agreement might be feasible.

In those disputes where there is only a single issue, interaction in this phase of negotiations is simpler. It is not always easier to accomplish, however, for the parties may get locked in impasse because of the intensity of focus on the one issue. Yet, without the complications of multiple, interconnected criteria the parties can shift fairly easily to the exploration of real possibilities or of integrative solutions so that Phase 4 may be quite brief. It becomes a matter of reorientation leading to final bargaining.

Where, however, a dispute includes several or many issues and their several attributes, Phase 4 is generally more prolonged as the parties grapple with the considerable complexities necessarily involved. It is essential, therefore, to attempt to describe and elucidate what the possibilities are in these typical circumstances, or, more exactly, what the strategies are that negotiators employ in jointly dealing with these intricate problems and what the reasons are for their choices. This is particularly necessary because of the relative neglect of these strategies in the literature. As indicated previously (pages 55–57), theoretical concern has largely focused *either* on the procedures of a single decision-maker dealing (sometimes) with multiple criteria, or on joint decision-making with respect to a single, undifferentiated item. Interdependent decision-making in respect to multiple criteria has been largely overlooked. There seems to have been no thorough consideration of the possibilities under such conditions, either normatively or descriptively. The following examination is, therefore, a tentative, descriptive review of five principal, joint strategies used by negotiators in this phase, based on my knowledge of actual cases. It is not an exhaustive account of the methods employed and it will require further elucidation and discrimination in the light of additional empirical data and analytical insight. My account is thus intended to be suggestive. With no greater claims than that, it is presented here as a contribution to the understanding of how negotiators operate in this phase of negotiations.

Two points are to be emphasized in the presentation of these joint strategies. First, as given here, they may appear to be analytical ideal types that are mutually exclusive. In practice, however, strategies are likely to be less precise and clear and two or more may be used more or less simultaneously. Second, although a strategy may be overtly agreed to by the

142

parties as a modus operandi, it may be rather less deliberate, since the parties may simply drift tacitly into it in their endeavors to engender coordination and to move toward some kind of outcome.

One strategy is the simple agenda method. Issues in dispute are merely taken, one at a time, in the order already prescribed by the agenda and treated and settled separately. Although this may commonly succeed for decision making in committees and conferences, it can rarely work in negotiations. The chief reason is that it attempts to ignore the essential problems of multiple criteria: that issues are often interconnected in the social life of the negotiators and that, in any event, they are necessarily interconnected within the specific context of the negotiations in progress. Parties are aware of this and are unwilling to forfeit advantages that might be gained by getting better terms on one issue through concession (or refusal of it) on another. They wish to explore interconnections without the rigidity of a fixed agenda order. Neither can it be assumed that agenda formulation is always well accomplished. Indeed, to obtain agreement on a working agenda would be even more difficult than it usually is were it knowingly to include an inflexible order. Moreover, there is always the likelihood that some issues earlier in the order cannot be readily dealt with and must be left for renewed examination later. This opens the way to manipulative tactics, such as deliberately delaying progress on an issue in order to gain leverage on a second one or in order to induce the opponent's stronger commitment on a third. Agenda order tends to be subverted, perhaps almost immediately.

Yet the simple agenda method is sometimes used with some flexible modification. Where (as in industrial negotiations) there are many issues and little agreement between the parties on priorities, simply to start with one party's list, or with the numbered items in the old contract, is a means of getting away from the previous phase and its emphasis on differences and antagonism. This method may be thought to provide a way out of an impasse where neither party wishes an outcome to be delayed. Parties may be prepared to neglect negotiating advantages and to ignore interconnections between issues because of an overriding assumption that almost any outcome is preferable to none at all or to prolonged and costly negotiations.

More commonly, something like the simple agenda method is suggested by a party, or by a mediator, merely as a means of preventing a threatened impasse. This permits at least a start to coordinated discussion of issues. An alternative, sometimes adopted in labor–management negotiations, is for parties to take turns in raising issues for consideration and possible settlement. The evidence is that such procedures, though useful in keeping interaction going or renewing it, seldom persist for any length of time since one or the other party begins to insist on breaking the order. Issues begin to be tied together or the outcome on one is linked directly to that on another.

A second strategy used by negotiators to deal with multiple issues is for the parties to come to an agreement as to which issues are, for them, the one or two most important. They then concentrate on these in the expectation that, having reached agreement on them, the remaining issues can be more easily dealt with—if only because the parties will be unwilling to jeopardize the success already achieved. The major difficulty here is to gain agreement as to which are the most important issues. It may be far from obvious. Potential advantages may be seen by a party in pushing for his own preferences and obstructing those of his opponent. In any case, what is at first apparently more important may turn out not to be so after further exchange of information and reconsideration of the preference set. It becomes evident that expected satisfactions obtained on the earlier issues can be reduced or even negated by potential outcomes of later issues. For instance, in a peasant community, the allocation or division of a piece of land may appear, to the parties themselves, to be the major issue; yet the relative advantages of particular divisions of the land can be considerably affected by subsequent outcomes on, say, irrigation water or access paths. In any case, the whole set of issues may depend on less obviously linked matters relating to status and prestige, compensation payment, or the future relationship between the parties.

Probably the most effective application of the method of taking the more important issues first is in situations where no offense is alleged and no claims and counterclaims are made; rather, two parties are in dispute over the establishment of the terms of a new relationship or new rights and obligations between them. For example, the parties may wish to establish the terms of a new tenancy between landholder and tenant or the terms of business between supplier and purchaser. Although they may be in dispute over the several terms to be settled, the alternative to agreement is usually the status quo of no relationship and no transaction. Thus, where there are no claims for infringed rights or failed obligations, the parties may well seek to discover if they can reach agreement on the major items concerned—on the basic principles perhaps. Only if there is agreement on those is it worthwhile expending effort on less important matters, including matters of detail.

A third strategy is to reduce most or all issues to the effective attributes of a common objective, such as prestige, monetary profit, or a kin relationship. Each issue is now treated only in its possible contributions to the single objective. This probably requires a considerable degree of simplification in which some attributes of the issues are disregarded. If the reorganization can be achieved, then the new set of attributes can, perhaps with some kind of weighting, be aggregated so as to suggest a limited number of potential outcomes that the parties can consider and compare. In essence, this method, by its procedure of simplification, enables the parties to compare and measure what were initially perceived as unlike and incommensurable items. It requires, of course, that the parties must first agree on the common objective, and a difficulty may be that this simplification is seen as disadvantageous by one party. That party may suspect that in focusing on, say, monetary advantage or honor he may lose out on other objectives that are important to him. Profit-seeking businessmen who overtly declare their focus to be on monetary values are often, when the time comes to make real choices, much concerned with reputation, customer relations, and similar matters. Nevertheless, and particularly where a dangerous or costly impasse threatens, this strategy can work fairly effectively, either to deal with the whole dispute or to clear away some of the issues.

An approximate example of this strategy comes from one of the cases of dispute in a Jordanian Arab village recorded by Antoun (1972). Several issues of contention arose between members, individually and corporately, of two autonomous lineages. All these issues were transformed into matters of relative honor between the lineages. Relative honor could be expressed and compared in terms of the formal slaughter of sheep by each lineage. Antoun wrote that "honor, an abstract concept, is symbolized by material goods whose exchange serves as some sort of balance sheet for calculating the relative quantity of intangible resources (honor) held by each side in the dispute [1972:101]." Similarly, cost accountants attempt, sometimes successfully, to reduce multiple criteria to straight monetary terms that can be simply compared.

A fourth strategy to deal with multiple issues operates in the endeavor to discover the less difficult issues so as to deal with and dispose of them first. The less difficult issues are those, in context, where differences are found to be relatively small, where they are less encumbered with emotional and symbolical loads, and where concession comes to be considered less damaging and more tolerable. Such issues may always have been seen as relatively unimportant or the differences on them as relatively small, but others can be discovered by the parties as a result of their current exchange of information. Coupled with this, a party might withdraw issues, voluntarily or under persuasion, and so simplify the problems.

Issues that can be withdrawn are of two kinds in the assessments of the parties. On the one hand, there are those that are seen to be trivial. Perhaps they were originally included under emotional stress or for nuisance value, or a party may not have been clear at the beginning of the negotiations just what importance an issue had or what might be gained on it. Learning now

145

reveals its unimportance. Such trivial issues can be quietly dropped, merely by no longer referring to them. The decision to withdraw an issue may, however, be specifically announced to the opponent as a show of good will, generosity, and growing confidence, and also as an invitation to the opponent to make a similar move.

On the other hand, an issue can be withdrawn because it becomes clear that the difference between the parties is so great, and likely to remain so, that nothing can be done at the time to reach an agreed outcome. The status quo is jointly considered preferable and is allowed to hold because each of the parties agrees that further negotiation on the issue would only hinder movement toward outcomes on other issues. This, of course, indicates both a willingness to collude and a common expectation that useful agreements are possible and worthwhile on remaining issues. As well, there can be symbolic reasons for this move: to prevent and deny complete failure of the negotiations or to make some show (to each other or to the world outside) of accord—even suggesting the possibility of renewed negotiations later. Something may be salvaged if the intransigent issue is removed. For example, in negotiations aimed, inter alia, at a nonaggression pact between two countries, the parties might discover and agree on the impossibility of success. Therefore, for the moment at least they abondon that important objective. Yet they discover that agreement may be possible on other issues of some importance and wish to continue their negotiations—say, on matters of trade or navigational arrangements. This may appear to be the best that can be done but it has useful practical and symbolic advantages to each country.

This strategy of dealing first with less difficult issues (and withdrawing others) has positive advantages for the negotiators. Because of these, it is perhaps the most commonly used strategy. It can keep the negotiations going, preventing a deadlock on the more difficult issues which could lead to a breakdown. It allows some outcomes to be obtained, some success to be achieved together. In so doing, the parties gain some mutually beneficial experience of each other. They are able to express some readiness to understand and appreciate each other's preferences. The possibilities of making concessions or of jointly creating mutually advantageous outcomes are explored and shown to work, even if, so far, in a limited way. Conflict and opposition remain, perhaps mistrust and apprehension also, but the beginnings of useful coordination are established. If the negotiations are to be concluded in an agreed outcome, coordination is essential. It has to begin somewhere, somehow.

It cannot be assumed that the parties necessarily know and agree which are, in fact and in context, the less and the more difficult issues. Parties may think they know, only to find that some expected difficulties do not occur, whereas some seemingly simple issue bogs down in conflict. By ranging over the issues in dispute, the parties are able to discover together which issues can, with a little persuasion, compromise, and concession, be resolved and which others, therefore, are to be the obdurate ones requiring more careful and studied treatment.

The strategy becomes, then, one of gradual elimination.[8] In this connection, both Arusha and Ndendeuli drew on their familiar experience in making a new field in forest or bushland; they spoke metaphorically of this strategy as the clearing away of bushes and undergrowth. This, they said, then reveals the larger trees that have to be cut down in order to complete the task. They recognized, too, that some trees may be too large to fell, and must therefore be left untouched.

A fifth strategy for coping with multiple criteria is for the parties to engage in the trading of issues: We give way on this issue if you will concede on that one; we agree to compromise on one if you will agree to do the same on another. This simply means that the parties have, or come to discover that they have, differing assessments of the relative importance of some of the issues in dispute and their desired levels of satisfaction on them. That being the case, there is a possibility for trading, even for quite crude "horse-trading," which may be effective in clearing away some of the problems between them. The recognition and fulfillment of such reciprocity may be explicit and subject to some hard bargaining, though it is often tacit as one party offers a conciliatory concession in the endeavor to draw a comparable response from the opponent. This procedure requires an ability to evaluate and compare certain issues—which is more important and which is less—and a willingness to make concessions. It is common in industrial negotiations that, for example, the union party concedes to the management's desire, say, to revise the pension scheme in return for obtaining additional days of paid vacation and improved working facilities.

One form of this type of strategy lies in "packaging." This may be no more than the explicit, reciprocal linking of two issues. It can be more complex than that, involving a number of issues that are, or can be agreed to be, interconnected. Thus there can be trading of packages such that one party gets more or less what he wants on issues a, b, and c in return for the other party getting his demands on x, y, and z. Or the package might include compromises on the several items. The proposer of a package may be able, by his specific proposals, to control the outcome more closely than he otherwise could by piecemeal procedure. When a party remains rather

---

8. Whyte (1951:95) suggested this as a prescriptive strategy in industrial negotiations where the parties are strongly opposed on a vital issue. Schelling (1960:45–46) briefly noted its usefulness.

uncertain of his preferences and of the possibilities, the suggestiveness of the opponent's package proposal may be intrinsically attractive, offering a way out from the problems of multiple criteria.

It is even possible that a party may attempt to force the negotiations by proposing a package containing all the issues in dispute. This is unlikely to be acceptable to the opponent at this stage because of the possibilities of alternative and partial packages that require further exploration and because certain issues appear too problematic to be disposed of so quickly. Indeed, a single, or extensive package proposal is likely to be suspect; there is resistance against the attempt to force an outcome prematurely. Instead, smaller, less comprehensive packages offer the opportunity to clear away some of the issues where it becomes apparent that differences between the parties are relatively small or the issues rather unimportant.

The suggestion of a package is not necessarily a proposal for a particular outcome on the issues included. Instead it may be an invitation to the opponent to begin thinking in terms of one or more package deals and to make his own proposals in that mode. During this phase of negotiations, the parties are increasingly thinking of approaches to "real" outcomes. More extreme demands and offers begin to be modified, at least on some of the issues. Packaging and trading are potential means to those ends. Package offers are likely to contain some substantial concessions. Moreover, they have the advantage to the proposing party that, unless accepted as a whole by the opponent, they do not necessarily commit the party to settlement terms on any one of the issues alone. In contrast, an offer on a single issue strongly suggests that a party is prepared to agree to that as a minimum. Thus, package offers can be exploratory in nature, without commitment on single issues, at a time when a party still wishes to keep his options fairly open and flexible because he is still unsure of his opponent's preferences and even of his own.

I have now identified five main strategies that negotiators use to deal with the problems of multiple issues and to achieve a narrowing of differences in this phase of negotiations: (a) the simple agenda method, (b) concentration first on the one or two most important issues, (c) reduction of all or many issues to the attributes of a single objective, (d) elimination first of the less difficult issues, including the withdrawal of some, and (e) trading and package deals. It is clear from this list that these strategies do not altogether deal with the intrinsic problems of the complex interconnections of multiple issues and their multiple attributes. Indeed, it is fair to say that, through these strategies, negotiators avoid the problems rather than positively resolve them. This is because the intricacies, uncertainties, and incomparabilities are so great that they just are not capable of a fine resolution in the conditions of actual negotiations. Nor are the solutions of the abstract theorists of much help here, for however ingenious and elegant their hypotheses and formulas, these are certainly far beyond the capacities of real-life negotiators. In effect, what happens is that the parties are compelled to make considerable simplifications. Some of the possible interconnections between issues and attributes are merely ignored and particular issues are dealt with separately. In other instances, interconnection is rather crudely recognized and treated by trading and package deals; the parties have to content themselves with rough sufficing. To act otherwise would invite serious delay and frustration. On the other hand, the quite commonplace practice of repeatedly ranging over the issues in dispute does allow the parties to take account of interconnections by a kind of trial-and-error procedure.

As we have seen, issues are dealt with, singly or in packages, in two ways: either by their withdrawal and acceptance of the status quo or by reaching some positive outcome in joint decision. Such positive outcomes can be of two kinds which have been usefully called "distributive" and "integrative" by Walton and McKersie (1965). Distributive outcomes occur in something like zero-sum conditions where the gains of one party entail corresponding losses by the other. An outcome is achieved by concessions and compromise by one or both parties. Walton and McKersie, like a number of other writers, assumed that this procedure is typical, even unavoidable, where limited material interests of a quantitative kind are involved, especially money in industrial disputes. "It is a fact of economic life that 'money is money.' . . . Money can only be divided into units; it cannot be reformulated into an arrangement that may be an improvement for both sides [1965:129]." This, in reality, is untrue. Such an assertion comes from the assumptions and over-simplifications of game and economic theory. Money, in fact, is not necessarily just money—except for some economists. It represents and can promote a variety of things. For instance, although it costs more arithmetically to pay higher wages, that can also "purchase" valuable prestige, good will, improved labor relations, or increased productivity. Moreover, to agree to pay higher wages may help to accelerate the negotiations and so to reduce other costs or remove uncertainties. Negotiators themselves recognize these facts so that they are not necessarily, nor even usually, compelled to accept a zero-sum definition of an entire dispute because of one particular attribute of a single issue (e.g., money). It would seem that zero-sum exists largely in the minds of some abstract theorists. Rather, negotiatiors may sometimes choose more or less deliberately to treat a particular issue (for instance, money or honor) in a distributive fashion for their own convenience in order to simplify and obtain a quick outcome. Occasionally, competitive rivalry forces the parties into zero-sum assumptions. Even so, there are most probably some associated values, recognized or not, that afford additional gains and losses or confuse the question as to which party actually won in the end.

Rather than pursuing a zero-sum interpretation of their dispute, negotiators become aware, by compulsion of the logic of the situation and the preferences of the opponent, of the multiple attributes of an issue and its connection with other issues in dispute. They perceive that overall there can be both gains and losses and that there can, on balance, be gains for both parties. That is, there is most likely to be an integrative outcome, quantitatively and qualitatively. By a process of exploration through cumulative clarification of their preference sets, parties are able to discover and devise possible outcomes from which both stand to gain (though not necessarily equally) or to lose. Concession and compromise are still required but "new alternatives are accepted of such a kind as to render it extremely difficult to discern the balance between concessions made and concessions received [Lasswell 1937:147; quoted in Walton and McKersie 1965:128]."

For example, the division of a disputed piece of land between peasant farmers may appear, prima facie, to be a distributive, zero-sum operation. It would, however, be extraordinary if that were really the case and if the solution were not an integrative one. In such instances (drawing on my experience of Arusha disputes), the division may be such that the person receiving the smaller portion gets a part where the soil is more fertile, or where there is irrigation water, or a part that is complementary to his existing landholding. Simple spatial division can be accompanied by arrangements, say, to make more irrigation water available or to put in a new access track. The parties might agree to cooperate in developing joint facilities on the land for mutual benefit. Always there is the opportunity to tie the division of the land to outcomes on other issues in the dispute.

An example of an integrative solution in industrial negotiations is taken from Walton and McKersie:

> The union had demanded that more weight be given to experience in promoting people in the clerical area. The company had been planning primary reliance upon test results which the union claimed favored the junior employees. A satisfactory solution was reached when the company proposed that a certain number of points, prorated according to service, be added to each test score; thereby achieving a blend of ability and seniority [1965:131].

Thus the outcome was a compromise between conflicting criteria, but it was not an either–or kind of resolution.

An integrative outcome not only requires a degree of coordination and trust between the parties, but also engenders coordination and tends to

reduce competitive rivalry. Indeed, success in creating an integrative solution, even on a relatively minor issue, can be a turning point in Phase 4. In
this phase, the parties are not only narrowing differences, achieving some
outcomes, and simplifying their mutual problems. They are also developing coordination, together with increased appreciation and acknowledgment of each other's preferences. The positive results of their changing interaction encourages confidence, tolerance, and a greater readiness to consider real possibilities and to make concessions. There is increasing
avoidance of that kind of interaction typical of Phase 3 where conflict is
emphasized. A stock of joint capital is, as it were, built up that allows the
parties to go on better equipped to tackle the remaining, more difficult
issues.

That is not to say, however, that the parties eschew all competitiveness, all mistrust and manipulation. Demands are still reinforced by
threats and sweetened by promises. Bluff and deception continue as each
party attempts to alter the other's expectations and evaluations. Both sides
try to conceal their minimal requirements and working targets. Commitments are made, alleged, or adhered to that prevent a party from making concessions and put the onus on his opponent.[9] There can be hard
bargaining even when the parties agree that they are not far apart on some
issue and that, therefore, an outcome is probable. Packages can be sharply
queried and argued. Misunderstanding, mistrust, and animosity are not
altogether absent or suppressed. New, unforeseen difficulties produce
bursts of hostility, even recurrence of interpersonal attacks. Tension persists as it continues to be necessary to revise preferences, reduce expectations, and grant concessions. Nevertheless, as Phase 4 proceeds,
negotiators come to control themselves more carefully in order that a still
somewhat precarious reorientation is not upset and, therefore, that the impetus toward agreement is not halted.

In effect, then, in Phase 4 the negotiators have to make the change of
orientation from emphasizing differences to more positive and conciliatory
approaches toward agreement, and they have to deal with problems of
multiple criteria in some workable form, however rough and ready. From
the empirical evidence available, it appears that the most common modus operandi combines two strategies: the gradual elimination of issues
together with trading and packaging. Discussion, argument, and tentative
proposals shift from one issue to another and from attribute to attribute of
particular issues. Each party tends to be unwilling for his opponent to concentrate too restrictively on one or two issues at the possible expense of ignoring others that may become important as information accrues. Quite

---

9. A useful, brief review of such tactics is given by Young (1975:310ff.).

typically, therefore, and sometimes confusingly to the observer, the parties' attention moves from one feature to another and on to another, later returning to an earlier one. One might think that the parties are talking at cross-purposes, not listening to or heeding each other. That might be the case, of course, but (in this phase, in contrast with Phase 3), it is more likely that there is effectively a process of exploring potentialities. By examining and reexamining the various issues in the light of accumulating information on demands, offers, strengths, and possibilities, interconnections are more clearly seen and trading opportunities detected. Trades and packages are proposed, considered, and reformulated. As issue is withdrawn as it is acknowledged to be unimportant or a hindrance, or in order to gain reciprocal withdrawal or concession by the opponent and to show a conciliatory attitude. There is a gradual simplification as some issues are disposed of. Particular outcomes are agreed upon, ostensibly only tentatively and dependent on outcomes yet to be reached on other issues. Once made, however, they tend to be permanent. That is not inevitable, of course; nevertheless, as the parties are succeeding in narrowing their differences and in building up working coordination, even some degree of trust, they are less and less likely to threaten such progress by going back on what has already been achieved. In practice, it seems that a negotiator puts issues out of his mind, once they have been dealt with, as increasingly he concentrates upon the remaining issues, their possible outcomes, and the strategy to be employed.

Gradually, therefore, the parties are able, with increasing knowledge and confidence, to identify the more obdurate issues in the dispute; that is, the ones on which agreement is seen to be most difficult, where demands and offers, even mutual understanding, are farthest apart. These will include two kinds of issues—those too important to be withdrawn if an acceptable resolution of the dispute is to be reached,[10] and those where the possibilities of an outcome continue despite persisting and considerable differences between the parties.

The obdurate issues are not necessarily the most "important" ones as might be measured either objectively in terms of interests and values or subjectively by the parties themselves at the start of negotiations. There is no necessary correlation between assessment of "importance" and the relative ease and order with which they are resolved. Both "important" and trivial issues can be withdrawn. Other "important" issues come to be seen as fairly readily resolvable as negotiations reveal little real difference between the parties. In industrial negotiations, the issue often assumed to be

---

10. Such crucial issues are most common in negotiations between parties who are locked into a persisting relationship, such as management and labor or close kinsmen.

important—wage rates—can often be resolved without too great difficulty, but a modification of the seniority system or extra paid vacations may turn out to be the ultimately obdurate issues. In a number of so-called land disputes among the Arusha, the obdurate issues were, in the end, not land but quite other matters, although land was inevitably important in the conditions of novel and acute scarcity of land in that wholly agricultural society. In other cases, of course, wages or land respectively have also been among the obdurate issues.

Issues become obdurate in the context of particular negotiations as the parties' preference sets develop and harden. The reasons for this are various. They relate to the nature of the issue itself, to the kinds of positions taken by the parties and to the relations between the parties as these have evolved during the negotiations. Stands may have been taken on irreconcilable principles and inflexible commitments so that to give way involves much more than simple concession and requires fundamental change. Parties may get locked, emotionally and symbolically, into mutual antagonism, fear of losing face, apprehension of the unknown results of making a change, or determination not to lose. Obdurate issues are often, in a sense, "public issues"—ones with public implications and reverberations, such as reputation, morality, and status, which are not easily compromised in public. Sometimes an issue is deliberately created and held obdurate by a party in an attempt to use it as a lever against his opponent to force him to a trade-off against another intractable issue.

Summing up the results of Phase 4: One way or another, differences between the parties have been reduced and some degree of coordination has been achieved and practiced. The obdurate issues have been identified and the parties are now faced with the necessity of somehow dealing with them in order to obtain final agreement on an outcome. There is strengthening anticipation that this can be done, and the negotiations move into another phase.

PHASE 5: PRELIMINARIES TO FINAL BARGAINING

With the parties' differences more starkly revealed and the issues reduced to a small number, the parties can come to final bargaining. Before that, they often (but not always) first engage in further explorations that can bring additional clarification and usefully set the stage for that bargaining. These preliminaries are concerned with one or more purposes: the search for a viable bargaining range, the refining of persisting differences, the testing of trading possibilities, and the construction of a bargaining formula. In some cases, these preliminaries are successful enough virtually to preclude the need or desirability of much bargaining thereafter. In other cases, issues are reduced to limited criteria that more clearly establish a practical bargaining situation.

A viable range for bargaining to an outcome for one or more issues is one within which both parties are willing to accept any outcome rather than have no agreement at all—that is, rather than accept the alternative of the status quo. If there is a viable range it means that to some extent, however small, the parties' separate expectations and preferences overlap, although within that range they disagree about exactly where the point of agreed settlement should be. This can usefully be illustrated by a highly simplified model in straightforward quantitative terms.

Let us suppose that one party can supply the other with some product he requires; there is disagreement only on the price per unit. If there is to be agreement, so that a transaction can occur, there must be some range of prices within which both supplier and purchaser prefer to settle rather than seek alternative transactions. The supplier seeks an absolute minimum price that is equal to what he can obtain elsewhere, less the cost in time, effort, transportation, and the like required to gain the best alternative. Say he can obtain $110 per unit elsewhere at a cost of $5; then his minimally acceptable price is $105. The purchaser seeks an absolute maximum that is equal to the price at which he could obtain the product elsewhere, plus the extra cost required to secure that alternative. Say he can obtain the product for $110 per unit at a cost of $5; then the maximally acceptable price is $115. There is then a viable range between $105 and $115 within which both parties would be satisfied. Any point within that range is, for each party, preferable to what can be obtained elsewhere. The parties still have divergent interests concerning the actual point of agreement because the supplier prefers something near $115 and the purchaser prefers something near $105. Nevertheless, if those facts are known to the parties, there is the possibility of an outcome advantageous to both. Subsequent bargaining could, though not inevitably, establish the particular outcome.

This little model is patently far too simple to be more than suggestive of what negotiators can attempt to accomplish. There are many real-life problems that it ignores but that negotiators usually cannot. One problem is that such precise quantification often cannot be obtained, not even on an attribute that is intrinsically measureable. The costs of obtaining the best alternative are often neither readily not reliably obtainable. Thus there is likely to be uncertainty about the outside limits of the viable range. Moreover, the question may arise whether or not the supplier would find it worthwhile to refuse a firm offer of, say, $104.90. Were this to set a standard for his selling price to a large number of other purchasers, he might well refuse; but were it a single, non-precedent-making transaction, he might agree if some associated compensations were to be added. In practice, the quantifiable attribute is likely to be linked with and so affected by other atrributes: for instance, the creditworthiness of the alternative purchaser, or the continued advantages of the business relationship between the two parties (say, one already supplies various products to the other or they are members of the same business or civic association). Some attributes are quantifiable only in rough terms, thus increasing the uncertainties. Some attributes are scarcely measurable at all and these, for that very reason, may be the ones on which agreement is most difficult to obtain. Therefore, although there could be tentative agreement on price, or on the viable price range, uncertainty and disagreement persist on the assessment of, say, quality control in manufacturing the product or the credit strength of the purchaser.

Another problem lies in the exchange of information. To know the limits of the viable range, each party must have good information on the other's alternatives and preferences. Where mistrust persists or while a party continues to hope for a better outcome, there may be a disinclination to be frank and to make admissions to his opponent. For instance, in the simple model, the purchaser is effectively telling the other that his maximal price is $115 and that he cannot afford to reject an offer that is below that. Yet he probably wishes to get a price that is well below his maximum. There is then an incentive not to be frank and instead to attempt to bluff the opponent into thinking that the maximum is lower than it is. There is also a possibility of persuading the supplier that his calculation of the minimally acceptable price is incorrect or that his alternative purchaser is unreliable now or in the future. In negotiations, as in politics, facts are seldom unequivocal, seldom free of subjective interpretation. If we assume that a party wishes to obtain the most advantageous outcome, or something quite near it, then the likelihood is that he will see advantage in restricting or manipulating the information he offers and that he will be disposed to suspect the validity of the information he receives.

Peters (1955:33 ff.) has described a case of industrial negotiations where the union party had an absolute minimal demand for a wage increase of 10 cents. The employer's failure to meet that would result in strike action. The employer did not know what the union's minimum was. However, neither the union leaders nor the employer believed that a strike would occur over a 2-cent difference between them; this in effect reduced the union's minimum to 8 cents. Earlier in the negotiations, the union had demanded 30 cents, and the employer had offered no increase at all. Later the union reduced its overt demand to 15 cents and the employer raised his offer to 3 cents. The union stuck at 15 cents in order to try to convince the employer that its absolute minimum was 12 cents, in the expectation that he would then offer at least 10 cents or possibly 11 cents in order to avoid a strike. The information that the union gave to the employer was intended to deceive because, it was believed, frankness would produce a lower outcome than the employer would otherwise accept.

Much depends on the amount of information already available to the parties. Additional information can come from elsewhere—a mediator or outsiders. A good deal depends also on the state of relations between the parties at this time and on their readiness to concede and compromise in a desire to conclude the negotiations. Together with the development of coordination and some trust, the parties may begin to press their demands less rigidly as a final outcome seems in prospect. Sufficing tends to become a main strategy if it had not been so before. Thus information exchange becomes freer with the aim of a satisfactory outcome, irrespective of whether it is the "best" obtainable. Negotiators become aware of this, despite continuing desires to conceal and to manipulate, as they struggle to discover a way out.

It is clear that a nicely calculated, viable range is seldom possible. Mathematical precision is but an abstract fancy that ignores the complex uncertainties of actual conditions.[11] Nevertheless, something like a viable bargaining range can be discovered in rough, general terms sufficient to allow the narrowing of concentration that is desirable. Such a range may be more or less agreed upon by both parties in order to obtain a limited working basis for bargaining. Alternatively, each party separately might make his own assessment, setting his own minimal and target demands against those expected of the opponent. This may indicate a range where overlap exists or where it might be induced. This too would provide a working basis in the face of uncertainty, although it means that the parties are working with differently assessed bases that may not coincide, neither of which is particularly accurate. They can, however, be adjusted as further probings bring more information. At least they are better than nothing and better than frustrated immobility.

For example, in an Arusha case, one obdurate issue concerned conflicting claims to a piece of land. By Phase 5, the mutual assumption had come to be that some division of the land was preferable rather than prolonging the negotiations or reverting to the status quo ante. One party, in his private consultations, made the assessment (acknowledged to be partly guesswork) that his opponent's minimal demand was roughly half of the

---

11. For example, the model of Iklé and Leites (1962), though usefully suggestive, is only reasonably workable because they chose to deal solely with "one set of mutually exclusive alternatives [p. 20]" that could be given in straightforward quantitative terms. These authors instanced the number of inspections connected with a disarmament agreement. That is, the viable range could supposedly be determined in easy, finite numbers.

land, if that portion were adjacent to his existing farm and included some of the better soil. The opponent's target (in the light of his readiness to accept a division) was thought to be about three-quarters of the land. The opponent had not admitted these limits but they were roughly deducible from his known interests and the information he had already given. Against this the party set his own anticipated limits: minimally about one-third of the land (sufficient to provide a paddock for livestock) and a target of about three-quarters. On this calculation, there was a viable range between one-half and one-third of the land going to the party (i.e., between one-half and two-thirds going to his opponent). Therefore the bargaining strategy was to aim for some outcome between those two points. This meant, of course, that the party had reduced his target in response to what he expected of his opponent and, in effect, he made no further attempt to persuade his opponent to make a larger concession. The calculation of the viable range took account, therefore, of the party's assessment of the relative strengths of the two sides.[12]

The second kind of operation preliminary to final bargaining concerns the reduction of the attributes to be considered in respect to obdurate issues. Where there are several atrributes, inconsistencies of assessment can occur or preferences can be uncertain, so that bargaining will be difficult and confused. To reduce the relevant attributes so as to facilitate bargaining is another act of simplification. It may mean that a party is, or feels he is, compelled to set aside some attributes of lesser importance in order to move toward bargaining. He expects and invites his opponent to reciprocate.

For instance, in industrial negotiations the issue described as the "wage rate" will certainly include many criteria: rates for different kinds of work and various kinds of overtime, rates for workers of different levels of seniority and skill, modes of assessing payment relative to productivity or to new machinery or new products, and so on. One (though not the only) method of simplification is for the parties to bargain over the issue in terms of a straightforward, across-the-board, percentage increase over current rates of pay—that is, leaving aside other features of wages and wage assessment. This a quite crude, though not uncommon in practice. It allows direct bargaining to occur over the percentage increase where the two par-

---

12. In the private deliberations of members of the party (which I was able to witness), these minima and targets were not made in fractional proportions but in terms descriptive of particular apportionments in relation to natural features and soil types. I have simplified for convenience here. In the end, the party agreed to accept a little less than half the land, thus gaining something over the minimum he had been prepared to accept if necessary. I should add that the party's calculations were not revealed to his opponent, nor was I privy to the opponent's deliberations.

ties are unable to agree on a more sophisticated treatment of the complex issue between them. It offers the possibility of an acceptable outcome. Less crudely, the parties might agree to take account of some other criteria as well, despite the prospect of lengthier and more difficult bargaining. They might do this because they wish to avoid the accumulation of unconsidered criteria and thus sources of future trouble.

Similarly in an African case where bridewealth debt is an obdurate issue, the two parties might agree to ignore criteria such as the amount already paid, the relative performance of associated kinship obligations and courtesies, and the state of marital relations. Most crudely, it might come down to straight bargaining on just how much more the son-in-law should pay.

A third preliminary operation is the examination of the possibilities of trade-offs. The reduction of attributes can be one form of this: We agree to ignore a certain attribute if you will ignore some other one, in a process of simplification. Trading can also occur between obdurate issues on the lines of a party offering to reduce his demands on one issue in return for the opponent making some concession on another. Thus the limits within which final bargaining has to occur are narrowed.

Fourth, the parties can attempt to find or develop a "formula" within which bargaining can occur, one that "contains and justifies outcomes acceptable to both parties and provides a series of referents of the specific details of the agreement [Zartman 1975:73]." Thus, rather than getting bogged down in details and in the problems of pure bargaining, the parties instead attempt to review their position, common ground, and objectives. The intent is to reconstruct the context of interaction, to pause, as it were, and reconsider the situation. There may be some refinement of persisting differences (as already described in this section), but more important, there is something like a recombination of the ideas, principles, and objectives that encompass the differences, so as to establish conditions and agreed limitations for bargaining. Certain features might be given added emphasis, whereas others are deemphasized or ignored. Questions are asked about what can be agreed to, what special considerations can be accepted as important for one or the other party, and what common principles are present or can be injected.

For example, in an Arusha case between half-brothers, the revealed obdurate issues were the inheritance of cattle, ritual prerogative, and a monetary debt. Reformulation contained an emphasis on the close kinship tie and common membership of the lineage founded by the disputants' grandfather. This posited that the disputants were locked into a persisting relationship of great importance to both, within a moral and symbolic penumbra highly valued in that society. There was reiterated agreement that one of the men, who was already married, had been allowed to take some of the father's cattle (in the father's lifetime) for partial payment of bridewealth, whereas the other disputant was unmarried, had not therefore taken any animals from the father's herd, and was in particular need of cattle so that he could soon marry. It was agreed also that some animals should go to each man, for economic and symbolic reasons. Concerning ritual prerogative, it was agreed to recognize that both men were dependent on and subservient to the dead father, now a dominant ancestor. Control of access to the ancestral shrine thus became less important than the fact that both men recognized and would have use of its spiritual potential. Finally it was agreed that the monetary debt was a secondary issue, the settlement of which should not be allowed to interfere with the crucial kinship, lineage, and ritual relations.

None of this formula was new. Indeed, these features had been insisted on by one or the other of the disputants in earlier phases of the negotiations. What was fresh was the rearticulation and reemphasis and the degree of agreement in principle. The details still had to be worked out but it was much clearer what the limits now were and what the pervasive values were that oriented subsequent bargaining. In fact, the bargaining over both cattle and the debt was hard and prolonged (requiring a special session of negotiations) and yet both parties were aware that eventual agreement was possible.

Zartman gave the example of the Vietnam negotiations in the early 1970s:

> Here the negotiations passed through two distinct phases, reflected in the two types of final documents that resulted. The first, from October 1970 to October 1972, concerned the American attempt to find a formula acceptable to both sides—freezing of the stalemate in place without removing either the North Vietnamese or the Saigon regime from South Vietnam—and selling it to Hanoi. The second, in the following three months, concerned a suspicious search for the details that followed from the agreed image [1975:73].

These four kinds of operation preliminary to final bargaining—the search for a viable range, reduction in attributes to be considered, agreement on trading between issues or between attributes, and the creation of a bargaining formula containing agreement on principles—are not, of course, mutually exclusive. Two or more may be combined in setting the stage for final bargaining and in clarifying and limiting the range of that bargaining.

Zartman has argued that the creation of a formula is the dominant operation in this phase.[13] He linked this hypothesis to the rejection of a

---

13. Zartman purported to apply this pattern to explain the entire process of negotiation and not merely the preliminaries to final bargaining. However, he has not separately considered earlier phases of negotiations. (See Zartman 1975 and 1977.)

most common assumption made by students of negotiations and bargaining: that bargaining is an incremental, concession-making process by which the parties gradually approach each other and converge at some final point of agreement. Zartman's view is that such incremental convergence is not generally true of actual cases and that, perhaps apart from obviously quantitative issues, it is scarcely a feasible endeavor. Unless he includes the three other preliminary operations within the creation of a formula—and there is little indication that he has—then he has overstated his case for the dominance of formula creation.[14] The search for and creation of an inclusive formula are, no doubt, often undertaken by negotiators prior to final bargaining, effectively leading to the practical success of an agreed outcome. It is clear, however, that ad hoc trading arrangements or the establishment of an approximate viable bargaining range can be successfully and usefully accomplished where there is no inclusive formula.

PHASE 6: FINAL BARGAINING

For the sake of clarity, I reiterate that bargaining consists of the exchange of more or less specific, substantive proposals (demand, offer, bid, etc., and their counters) about the terms of agreement for the outcome of one or more issues.[15] The proposals may refer to all of those terms, where until now differences between the parties have been marked, or they may apply to the settlement of details where a bargaining formula has already signaled agreement in principle. By Phase 6, both parties should have well-formulated preference sets and fairly clear expectations of each other. Culminating learning and adjustment are still required, but, with the obdurate issues established and clarified, the parties are emphasizing the potentiality of ultimate agreement.

A bargaining proposal by a party is either a determined reiteration of his known position or a concession toward the opponent. To say that every bargaining proposal is a "real" one, specifically intended as a possible resolution of differences, is overstating the case. Some proposals are interim statements and offers of information about a party's inclinations. For instance, reiteration of an existing demand might carry the message, "I will

14. Research, specifically directed to investigating this problem, might be revealing and it might indicate also under what conditions a particular operation is employed by negotiators. Zartman's view appears to derive from his own particular interest in, and knowledge of, international negotiations. It may be that the creation of a formula is the dominant mode of operation in such negotiations (even if not in other kinds), although the possible reasons for that are unclear.

15. See my earlier discussion of the analytical distinction between negotiation and bargaining in Chapter 3, pages 69–73.

not shift until you first make a concession." A concession may indicate a degree of movement, an expression of willingness to compromise, and an invitation to the opponent to reciprocate and show goodwill. Such proposals are chiefly intended, and so understood by the opponent, as part of a series and a positive trend aimed at some as yet unclear point of agreement. Nevertheless, bargaining proposals do contain the real possibilities of a final agreement.

There are a number of possible situations in which negotiators find themselves at the start of final bargaining, largely as a result of what has previously happened in the preliminary operations in Phase 5.

In one situation, the bargaining range may have been so narrowed that the advantages to be gained from bargaining have become small, even trifling, given the degree of agreement already achieved. Learning and coordination (and even cooperation) in Phases 4 and 5 have produced a joint disposition to compromise and a joint expectation of agreement, as well as a desire to complete negotiations without delay. What remains to be done is a clearing up of minor details and a joint commitment to the culminating outcome.

In another situation, the bargaining range may have been narrowed, or the bargaining formula may have already established much agreement in principle and orientation, but the details of terms need to be worked out. Persisting antagonism, remaining uncertainties, and apprehensions and perhaps the suspicion that remaining details contain implications for the future can make final bargaining protracted and tough. Yet the essential outcome is scarcely in doubt since its real basis has been created and agreed upon.

In a third bargaining situation, although something like a viable bargaining range has been discovered, albeit roughly and with unclear limits, considerable differences may remain between the parties. In principle, any point within the range is mutually preferable to no agreement, yet considerable gain or loss of advantage can still result from final agreement on a particular point. For the large business firm, employing thousands of workers, each cent per hour per worker can mean a large sum in annual expenditure. Each cent less can represent a loss of prestige to the trade union leaders who are subject to criticism and pressures from rivals within the union. For a peasant farmer desperately short of land, each few square yards represents invaluable crop production, and perhaps prestige and self-image, that cannot be ignored.[16] In situations of this kind, bargaining is

---

16. I have in mind the Arusha situation with population densities well over 1000 persons per square mile. The positioning of a field boundary a couple of yards either way over a lengths of 50 yards or more would involve an area that is not negligible to a man farming only 2 or 3 acres (cf. Arusha Case 6 in Gulliver 1963:190).

usually difficult, therefore, and sometimes there is failure to reach an agreed outcome when, in a sense, the parties have come so near to each other and have accomplished so much. Nevertheless, the realization by the parties that an agreed outcome is possible, that within the viable range it is preferable to no agreement, is usually sufficient to keep the bargaining going and ultimately to encourage concession and successful convergence.

In a fourth bargaining situation, it may be that no viable range has been discovered and it may well not exist. Here, although the parties are deliberately working toward agreement and are making "real" proposals for an outcome, their preference sets and expectations are still not altogether clear. It is not obvious to the parties how preferences can be modified nor how far it is tolerable to do so as against what the opponent might still be persuaded to concede from his current demands. There remains a good deal of ignorance on both sides, probably as a result of continuing antagonism that has interfered with success in preceding phases. What would the opponent be prepared to accept rather than face no agreement? And what would the party himself accept in that case? Bargaining continues as the two parties continue to learn and adjust, weighing their respective preferences and strengths and probing by offering some concession in order to see the opponent's reaction and response. It may be that they come to find themselves in what has been called a "pure bargaining" situation where, in a sense, the actual outcome is, and is recognized to be, more or less arbitrary. The parties then may become locked into aggressive, competitive conflict that is not susceptible to reasonable resolution (Kerr 1954:239; Stevens 1963:136) and can only be dealt with by a jump to some point on which both can agree.

What, then, is the predominant mode of behavior and interaction in the final bargaining phase? Certainly it still remains possible for the parties to create some new, integrative outcome of the kind previously described (pages 150–151) or to move to an outcome through the trading of items between them, or to work out the details of a previously agreed formula of accepted principles. All these may involve rather sudden jumps toward agreement rather than an inching toward compromise. Nevertheless, it seems that in this late phase of negotiation, the most prevalent mode of behavior is in fact bargaining by concession making toward convergence on some point of agreement. I state this with some diffidence since the available data are insufficient to support it quite convincingly. It is possible that I am too greatly influenced by that majority of theorists who have assumed, with little questioning, that bargaining constitutes convergence by incremental concessions. Similarly, descriptive writers have been quite persuasive as a result of their focus on wage bargaining in industrial disputes. However, my own experience of negotiations in interpersonal disputes in Africa convinces me that such incremental convergence is the most common mode for both quantitative and qualitative issues.

This view has been denied by Zartman (1977:75 ff.) in asserting the dominance of the mode in which details are implemented within an agreed formula. He himself, however, has noted that incremental convergence may occur in "wage bargaining . . . aid and trade figures . . . disarmament inspection stations and sizes of truce teams . . . boundaries and cease-fire lines [1975:71]." One could add many more examples, such as the sizes of payment of compensation of many kinds or of African bridewealth debt. Moreover, qualitative issues are, empirically, subject to incremental convergence where there are points of possible agreement that lie somewhere between the parties' demands and are discoverable by some kind of concession making.

For example, with an issue so immeasurable as public reputation and honor, one party might demand complete vindication and restoration of his prestige while his opponent denies all responsibility for any loss to the party. There is often, and perhaps always, a range of more or less discernible steps between those two extremes. That range might go something like the following, where A and B are the disputing parties and their respective, initial bargaining positions.

A. Refusal to accept any responsibility for loss of reputation (honor, prestige) by B and/or denial that such loss has occurred
   1. Admission of partial responsibility for injury to B's reputation
   2. Admission to total responsibility for that injury while acting under the stress of provocation by B
   3. Same as 2 but excluding B's provocation
   4. Step 2 or 3 plus tacit apology by A
   5. Step 2 or 3 plus public (formal) apology by A
   6. Step 2 or 3 or 5 plus ritual performance (and its expenses) by A to promote restoration of B's reputation
   7. Step 2 or 3 or 5 or 6 plus payment of compensation by A—nominal amount
   8. Same as 7 but substantial amount
B. Demand for complete admission by A of his responsibility for injury to B and for public apology, ritual performance, heavy compensation, and promise of future good behavior

Steps 1 to 8 might already be more or less known to both parties because cultural conventions define them for such an issue. In such a case, the parties do not necessarily use every step available. For instance, A might concede to 1 and then jump to 5; B might edge from his initial stand through 8 to 7. The final outcome might then be 6. On the other hand, these steps could emerge pragmatically as the two parties seek to converge on a point of agreement, perhaps also reaching 6.

My conclusion is that, although there are several possible modes of behavior in this phase, the predominant one is some form of convergent concession-making. That convergence may come through a gradual inching toward agreement (typical of bazaar haggling but with a far wider application than that) or through substantial concessions to or near the final outcome. Therefore it is the convergent mode that is the principal focus in the rest of this discussion of Phase 6.

It might be supposed that one or both parties will make concessions from their current levels of demand and offer until an equilibrium point is reached where the parties agree. It is sometimes that simple, as in marketplace haggling, but more often there are complications of multiple criteria so that the parties may be making concessions on different attributes and different issues. The principal questions, however, are how and why concessions are made, by which party and when, and what concession means to the opponent. Among theorists there have been two main lines of argument on the nature of concession making. One is that concession is made by the party that is less willing to risk further conflict (the possibility of no agreement or lengthy delay in reaching an outcome). Harsanyi has quite emphatically asserted this, following the lead of Zeuthen (1930):

> at any given stage of bargaining the next concession must always come from the party *less willing* to risk a conflict. . . . [This] is the only decision rule consistent with the expectations (subjective possibilities) that rational players [i.e., game-theory maximizers] can entertain about each other's bargaining behavior, in accordance with the principle of mutually expected rationality [Harsanyi 1977:12; italics in original].

The second line of argument is that a party's demand at any time is directly dependent on the expected future rate of concession by the opponent. If the opponent is expected to make a large concession, for whatever reason, then the party's demand hardens and his own inclination to make concessions decreases, and vice versa. The expected future rate is based on the opponent's past concessions. Siegel and Fouraker (1960), Coddington (1968), and Cross (1969), among others, have adopted this kind of explanation although they differ in some significant features.

Both arguments (here greatly simplified) are, in general, persuasive. It is probable that both have considerable bearing on the bargaining process and the explanation of the determination of an outcome. However, it would not be easy, and is probably impossible, to substantiate either at the moment or to give either appropriate weight by reference to the actual be-havior of negotiators. There is an acute shortage of empirical data. Nor have these theorists attempted to substantiate their arguments. These argu-ments remain assertions based on certain abstract assumptions, although they are stimulative of thought and reveal features of potential importance.

In any case, it seems possible that a bargainer might gain advantage over his opponent who assumes that either or both arguments are true. Thus a party could seek to convince his opponent that his (the party's) assessment of risk is low and his willingness to face it is high and/or that his future concession rate will be low. Cross (1969:190) has argued that if a party unduly delays concession with the intention of bluffing his opponent, he faces the danger that he may be compelled eventually to make a large concession. That would then persuade the opponent that the party is weak or afraid of risk and that therefore further concession can be expected. Thus the opponent would harden his own demands and reduce or stop of-fering concessions—the reverse of the party's intentions. This certainly could occur. On the other hand, if the party's stratagem is successful, he may never have to make any large concession because the opponent will first increase his concessions. Moreover, the party might also use other tac-tics to persuade the opponent that the risk of deadlock is higher than he had thought—higher than in fact it is.

However, the variables, the multiple criteria, and the uncertainties are all likely to be such that propensity to take risk or the expectations of the opponent's concession rate are not only difficult to assess but they are com-plicated by other features. In any case, a bargainer may act "nonrationally" under the stress of negotiations and the perplexities of assessment. If, therefore, the opponent attempts to deduce "rational" implications from that bargainer's behavior, he will necessarily reach incorrect conclusions. A bargainer strongly motivated by, say, antagonistic rivalry might ignore considerations of risk and of damage to his other interests—foolishly perhaps, but in practice quite possible—and with unintended advantageous results to him should the opponent read this as a sign of strength rather than of foolishness.

In bargaining, to make a concession can imply a number of different meanings according to context. Usually it is at least an invitation to the opponent to reciprocate. The party who makes a first concession is not necessarily the one less willing to risk conflict. He may be the more percep-tive one who more clearly foresees the danger of deadlock injurious to both parties. He may be signaling that "real" concessions should begin by mak-ing a first move, and that may be an attempt to control the interaction. Concession may truly indicate weakness, of course, but it can also come from and be seen as a show of confidence. Making a concession can be an experimental venture—to discover what the opponent will reply and what that reveals about his expectations or his desire for a speedy outcome. Concession can be, in effect, a kind of preemptive bid almost compelling the opponent to reciprocate more than he thought he would. Concessions can be made on issues that are of little importance to the party, although his opponent may not be fully aware of that.

For instance, in an Arusha case one issue in final bargaining was a claim for compensation for injuries. Throughout the negotiations the accused party had denied responsibility. Quite suddenly he admitted his culpability, with much rhetorical flourish. This was, he claimed, a most generous concession, more than the evidence warranted. He wished, he said, to have the matter settled, as it now could be if the injured party would make an equally generous concession: a withdrawal of his demand for compensation. The accused party was conceding what he had previously refused and still would have preferred not to, but in the context of final bargaining, he was conceding less than he expected to gain reciprocally—the concession from his opponent not to require payment of compensation. The other party, somewhat taken by surprise, was rushed into conceding and made no further claim. Afterward, in retrospect, the injured party told me that he thought he had acted too hastily and had conceded more than he need have done. His opinion was probably correct but that does not alter the way the bargaining actually went.

A well-known stratagem is that a party makes a demand for something about which he cares little, merely to be able to concede on it later in apparent weakness or generosity. The opponent may detect the bluff if his assessment of the party's preferences has been correct. Sometimes he does not detect it or is confused by it. Elsewhere (Gulliver 1975a), I have recorded an Arusha case in which this stratagem was quite successful. The major issue was the ownership of a piece of land, newly vacated by a tenant, that lay between the farms of A and B. Each claimed the whole of it. In a third session of the negotiations, A began to assert that not only did B not have a valid claim to the vacant land, but he did not even have proper right to the farm he already occupied. A alleged that he himself was the rightful owner of that farm. B, whose rights to his farm were not altogether clear, feared that he might now be in difficulties he had never foreseen. In simulated magnanimity, A withdrew any claim against B's farm. In fact, A had no real intention of claiming that farm; he probably could not have succeeded had he tried, once B was able to summon other supporters and witnesses. However, B allowed himself to be flustered by the possibility of being compelled, without preparation, to defend his rights. His relief at escaping the apparent danger put him at a disadvantage. Were he not to offer concession and accept compromise over the vacant land, he could appear greedy and ungenerous. Although other factors were also involved in these negotiations, A's stratagem was partly the reason why he eventually gained the larger share of the vacant land.

Such bargaining behavior cannot easily be explained by reference to propensity to take risk or to expected concession rates. It seems more realistic to see the explanation in terms of successful bluff and false concession.

Another aspect of the analysis of concession making and its outcome has been the attempts of contemporary theorists to discover determinate solutions to bargaining, not merely general explanations of bargaining behavior: "Indeed a theory not yielding a determinate solution cannot even explain how the players can ever agree on *any* specific outcome at all, and how any player, bargaining with another player, can rationally decide to make or not to make any particular concession to him [Harsanyi 1977:4; italics in original]." I do not dissent from Harsanyi's quite typical opinion. However, there is not yet any theory that is both inherently (i.e., conceptually) persuasive and directly applicable to the real-life circumstances in which actual bargainers work. In my view, we cannot explain how bargainers jointly settle on a particular outcome. Nor can we assume that a bargainer does "rationally decide" to make a concession or to accept an offer. Instead, we must reject the notion of complete rationality and its conceptually associated notion of maximization. As I have suggested earlier, a negotiator can scarcely know what a maximal outcome might be, but in practice, he is often prepared to accept something that appears to be satisfactory under the circumstances. How, when, and why something is regarded as satisfactory is not a wholly rational decision, at least not in the theoretical and conceptual sense.

The variable factors involved, including apparently inchoate subjective ones, are so numerous and permutational that an actual bargainer cannot "rationally" deal with them, especially in the face of his opponent and under the stress of negotiations. Indeed, he may be truly reasonable in not attempting to do so, thereby avoiding frustration and an inability to make any decision at all. The experience of observers of actual negotiations is that bargainers frequently plump for an outcome with a suddenness that defies explanation. Parties who have been fencing with each other and refusing to make substantial concessions abruptly jump to joint agreement. One explanation of this is that, in the face of the apparent impossibility of reaching a rational decision, the parties go for some conspicuous but arbitrary point. Schelling (1960:68–74) has characterized such a point as having an "intrinsic magnetism"; that point is patently obvious and offers a resolution. Examples are splitting the difference, taking a neat round number, or following a natural divider of land such as a stream. There is an implication here that not only is such a point conspicuous but that it no longer greatly matters to either party precisely where the agreed point is. Agreement per se has become more important than the particular point of agreement. When there is no obviously conspicuous point, it may be possible to create one (a common tactic by mediators) by increasingly focusing discussion and attention on something between the two current demands. It is not unknown for bargainers to toss a coin in order to decide the undecidable. A mediator or an outsider might be asked to suggest a point. There can be recourse to supernatural power through divination or oracular pronouncement.

One problem in all this lies in the rationalizations that bargainers themselves make, especially after the event. It is commonplace that bargainers claim to have obtained the best result possible. This kind of self-congratulation, backed by justifying argument, scarcely proves anything. Bargainers often need to convince themselves, their supporters, their constituency, or the world at large that they have done well. Even a "poor bargain" is often explained away in this fashion. The bargainer emphasizes some elements of the outcome and deprecates or disregards others. In many cases, it is useful and even necessary that each party should believe that it has won, or at least not lost. The rationalization may amount to a claim that the outcome, whatever its defects, was the best possible under the circumstances. Among the Ndendeuli, the rationalization tended to be that the bargainer had gained what he really wanted in the end, whatever the opponent may have gained—another kind of "best." The point is that these ex post facto explanations by participant negotiators give little real evidence of the reasons for the decisions made and the outcome reached.

My conclusion is that, in real-life conditions, it is not possible to foretell the particular outcome in negotiations by reference to specified rules of behavioral interaction and rational choice, nor is it possible retrodictively to perceive an outcome as specifically determined. Outcomes are inevitably the result, in part, of nonrational choices in what might otherwise be impossibly difficult situations to resolve.

PHASE 7: RITUAL AFFIRMATION

Once begun, negotiations produce some outcome.[17] Not all outcomes require formal affirmation. The culmination of the negotiations may be an impasse or breakdown such that the outcome is a return to the status quo ante or something near that. The parties merely separate or they continue

---

17. See my discussion in Chapter 3, pages 77–79.

their conflict through other means. However, an outcome prescribing novelty of some kind is universally given some kind of formal affirmation to make it clear and to mark and seal it. The novelty may be a positive acknowledgment and reassertion of the status quo or it may be a reallocation of resources, rights, status, and focus of action. Sometimes the conclusion of final bargaining is followed by a reiteration of the full terms of the agreement that have been reached on the various issues. This not only precludes misunderstandings but it can put the outcome before witnesses if that seems desirable. Thus neutral spectators, representatives of the community, members of the constituencies to which the parties belong, or specialist observers who record and disseminate information (e.g., news media) are informed. In literate societies, the outcome might be recorded in documentary form and, in some cases, this may acquire the status of a legal contract, as in industrial negotiations in many countries, in marriage settlements, land deals, and similar outcomes. All this is principally a matter of clarification and insurance.

The particular form adopted (often culturally prescribed) is also, in part, a ritual act. If the dispute is at all important to the parties and at all complex in its issues, final bargaining is followed by some symbolic action of affirmation. The simplest form of this is hand-shaking, embracing, kissing, and the like. Beyond this, there may be a taking of oaths, participation in specific ceremonial or in religious performance such as prayer, sacrifice, libation, and address to supernatural powers. Commensal drinking and eating by the parties is common, at least in non-Western societies. There may be exchange of tokens or gifts, even of hostages, and perhaps festive pleasure-making. The nature of the parties and of their relationship is important here. If they are, for instance, two disputing neighbors, they may go about their daily business after some simple affirmatory act such as embracing and a little drinking together. If the two parties are, or represent, distinct groups within the society, or discrete sectors of an important group, they are more likely to engage in public, ostentatious performance. This is because the terms of their agreement affect many other people, perhaps even the organization of the community.

The point of importance, however, is that the outcome is marked in some form or other and there is an expression of collaboration and agreement. The negotiations have been concluded and there may be a good deal of amity. On the other hand, a persisting antagonism and a number of disagreements may remain; the parties may be bitter rivals still. For the moment, however, there is agreement, whether limited or broad, and a mutuality in the achievement of an outcome, and the parties act in ritual fashion to demonstrate this. Since in many cultures, enemies and persons in dispute with one another do not shake hands or drink together, then the performance of these acts proclaims that, temporarily or more permanently, they are in satisfactory agreement.

These kinds of ritual acts may be instrumental as well as expressive. The purpose can be to establish actions against possible default from the terms of the outcome. Hence there is the public announcement to, or the notification of, superordinate authority (the Department of Labor, the judicial authority, the ancestors, etc.) or the involvement of supernatural forces. Thereafter, other persons and other forces will be involved should default occur.

PHASE 8: EXECUTION OF THE AGREEMENT

Where some positive action is required to put the outcome of negotiations into effect, the execution of the agreement may be handed over to specialists such as administrative or judicial officials, political leaders, lawyers, or a standing committee. Something of this kind may be especially required when the agreement is applicable to the behavior of the parties, or members of their constituencies, over a period of time such that behavior needs to be monitored or provisions made to deal with alleged infringements of the agreement.

However, if the agreement refers to some once-and-for-all allocation of resources and rights, the positive action takes another form. In nonliterate societies, but not only there, the agreement is generally put into effect immediately, or as soon afterward as possible, thus precluding delay and possible default, particularly when there is no machinery to deal with such problems. For example, as the negotiations end, often as part of the formal affirmation of the outcome, the compensation payment is handed over, the land boundary is marked, the formal apology is made. The whole affair, or as much of it as possible, is thus completed beyond doubt. In some African societies, participants have commented to me most favorably on the efficacy and value of doing this. The whole problem of enforcement or the possibility of reopening negotiations can be avoided. Moreover, the intervention of outside parties, such as governmental or judicial authorities, can be prevented and evaded when that is desired.

FLEXIBILITY AND PROCESS

The developmental model of negotiation, as it has been outlined in this chapter, was presented diagrammatically in Figure 5.1 (page 122). It is a generalized, ideal-type model constructed after reality. It was not intended, as it stands, to describe or to be rigidly applied to any particular empirical case of negotiations.

Essentially, the model depicts a series of phases that are sequential, interconnected, and overlapping. The notion of phases as an analytical tool by which to examine social processes is not, of course, a novel one. It has long been used by historians and is well established in the social sciences. Neither does it constitute a new approach to the study of negotiations. Although some writers have used it explicitly (e.g., Dunlop and Healey 1953; Douglas 1957, 1962; Stevens 1963; Stenelo 1972), it is implicit, but relatively unexplored, in much of the literature. The number of phases identified and their analytical limits and content are, in a sense, arbitrary, or at least they depend on the intentions of the writer and the particular emphases required. There are several ways of cutting up the cake, so to speak, each offering its own advantages. For example, the three-phase model of Douglas emphasizes the interactional differences between, and the critical shift from, "establishing" and "reconnoitering" the negotiating range to "precipitating the decision-reaching crisis" (Douglas 1957). Clearly, this identifies a major watershed in the total process; it corresponds approximately to the shift from Phase 3 to Phase 4 in my own model. Douglas' model is relatively simple and straightforward and therefore it has distinct advantages. However, I have deliberately chosen to present a more complex model, containing more phases, specifically to give attention to a number of other subprocesses of importance. It would, no doubt, be possible to refine the model further and to present more phases of interaction, and that might be useful for some purposes.

My model inevitably contains elements of both ordinary chronological time and what may be called conceptual time. It is obvious that negotiations occur through some period of chronological time—hours, days, weeks—from the precipitation of the dispute to an eventual outcome. Moreover, it is valid to say, for instance, that the search for an arena must come very early or that final bargaining occurs near the end. Yet neither is absolutely inevitable. Although an arena may be agreed upon without much difficulty, that decision is often subject to and must await discussions about the agenda. The arena may be subsequently changed (including changes of ground rules and composition of parties) right up to the end in order to accommodate difficulties that arise.[18] Similarly, final bargaining,

---

18. For example, among the Arusha, whether negotiations are to occur in a patrilineal moot or a parish assembly depends on whether or not important agenda items are defined as coming within the kinship domain. That decision is related to the kind of team the disputants wish to recruit and to the influence of relevant notables. Where impasse threatens later in the negotiations, the parties may seek a different arena, and thus different ground rules and teams, as a way of dealing with that problem (Gulliver 1973:Chapter 9). Whether negotiations should

or parts of it, may be accomplished to a considerable extent during the course of earlier phases. Parties may find, when the obdurate issues have eventually been identified and clarified, that in effect they have already achieved the basis or formula for a bargained outcome.

Other, intermediary phases can, in particular cases, stretch over more or less the whole chronological period of the negotiations, or they may begin, fade out, and begin again later. A recrudescence of competitive antagonism or a potential deadlock in Phase 4 (narrowing of differences) can induce a return to Phase 3 as the parties resume an emphasis on differences and reexplore the range between them. Parties sometimes operate and interact with the orientation of one phase vis-à-vis certain issues and another orientation concerning other issues. Failure of coordination and difficulties of transition from one phase to another can produce a situation in which the parties are each focusing (or trying to) on a different phase, in perceptual ignorance or in pursuit of their separate interests and purposes.

Each phase in my model represents an analytically distinguishable set of interaction, exchange of information, learning, and, in effect, purpose of the negotiators. These sets are indicated by the brief descriptive labels given to each phase and their elaborations in the expository sections of this chapter. Yet even in the generalized descriptions—and especially with the introduction of apt illustrations—it was noted that the limits of a phase are not altogether clear.[19] Two or more phases may overlap, as I have shown. This is crudely indicated in Figure 5.1 (p. 122), but overlapping and the interconnections of phased action are more complex and variable than can be represented on a diagram.

The model of Figure 5.1 might be analogous to a series of well-designed stepping-stones across a stream, each one solid and firm and a comfortable stride from the next. Some actual cases of negotiations fit that model quite neatly, but that is uncommon. Therefore, if the model is to be useful for the understanding of real-life social interaction, it must allow for considerable flexibility of application. The stepping-stone analogy is far too rigid because reality requires that a person should sometimes be able to have a foot on two stones simultaneously and that it be possible to go over the same stone twice or to step on a more distant stone before a nearer one.

To be frank, I wish to avoid the charge that this developmental model is "incorrect" or not useful because it does not fit closely the processual sequences of a specific empirical case. It is not expected to do so in a precise

---

begin and continue at the place (home, office, boardroom, etc.) of one of the parties or on neutral ground presupposes certain dispositions, attitudes, and expectations, and these may change later and require a change of arena.

19. The question of the identification of phases and their limits is elucidated further, with reference to the alternations of antagonism and coordination, in Chapter 6, page 184.

fashion. The situational factors, internal and external, bearing on the human interaction are too complex and variable. The apparent confusion in real-life negotiations—often troublesome to the observer and analyst— reflects the untidiness of actual social behavior. It cautions against insistence on a too neat and coherent model.

On the other hand, these phases do represent something like chronological periods that tend to link sequentially. Despite all proper caveats concerning chronology and with full recognition of the possibilities of overlapping phases, there nevertheless remains a general and significant correlation between chronological time and the sequence of phased sets of interaction and purpose. Although the model can only be a first approximation, it provides an essential guide. I must confess an inability to produce a model that can fully contain the general disposition to follow chronological time while allowing for the necessary flexibilities. It is, however, fundamental to the model that it attempts to disentangle the complexity of social interaction while revealing a pattern of general progression and cumulative achievement by the negotiators. Most important, the pattern reflects the reality of a general, overall trend from relative ignorance, uncertainty, and antagonism toward increased understanding, greater certainty, and coordination. Were there not such a trend, the negotiations would fail, as indeed sometimes occurs. Douglas has remarked, in reviewing her experience of industrial negotiations: "The one conclusion that has survived with greatest hardiness throughout all surveys of the data is that movement, orderly and progressive in nature, stands out as a staid property of the collective-bargaining situation which terminates in agreement [1957:70]."

The model says nothing about the absolute or relative time spans of the phases. These vary considerably according to situational factors, just as the total length of negotiations ranges from hours to years. In particular cases, a phase may be truncated by a quick achievement of its effective purpose. For instance, the choice of arena may be nonnegotiable or unproblematic, or final bargaining may be quite brief. Conversely, those and other phases can be prolonged as the parties get caught in repetitive, unproductive interaction and as antagonism fails to be modified by coordination.

Logically, the model presents a total process of negotiation that is ultimately "successful"; that is, an agreed outcome is positively achieved for all issues. Obviously this does not mean that all actual negotiations are "successful" in that sense. In practice, one party, or both, may never have intended to shift from the status quo or may never have sought any other outcome. Apart from such intransigence, there can be breakdown at any time, from inability to find an arena to failure of bargaining. Negotiations stop. Thereafter, they may be abandoned altogether or resumed later, or the parties may seek an alternative mode of action by which to deal with their conflict. It should be added, perhaps, for the benefit of critics of functionalism, that there is no intention or implication that the model specifies movement from equilibrium to renewed equilibrium. I see no usefulness in positing equilibrium at either end of the process.[20]

The process of negotiation depicted in this model can be usefully compared with other social processes, for the essential patterning is not unique. For anthropologists, an obvious and interesting parallel in some respects is the marriage process, especially as it is formalized and ritualized in many non-Western societies. There is a developmental process in which two principal parties—the bride's and the groom's, however defined—begin at a social distance, with some strangeness and even overt antagonism and mistrust, and gradually come together through a sequence of stages. They adopt new roles as affines, recognizing interdependence and coordination through the establishment of the marriage and their common interests thereafter. The bride and the groom themselves follow a similar and connected process as they move into a new relationship and new statuses. These processes may stretch over a period of days, months, and even years. They are routinized and often highly ritualized. Each stage symbolizes and is instrumental in the achievement of a limited purpose within the total process. This pattern, like that of negotiation, conforms to that partial definition of ritual as a standardized, irreversible process leading to a final conclusion. In the marriage process, more rigidly than in negotiation, one stage cannot be undertaken until the preceding one has been completed; once it is accomplished, the way is open to the next stage. There is order and regularity, an internal logic and an achievement of limited goals, step by step to a final outcome.[21] Comparable cumulative social processes are, for example, a Roman Catholic mass, the passage of a bill through a legislature, or the undergraduate career in a university.

Although, in contrast, negotiation is less formalized, less structured, and less overtly ritualized, and the phases not so clearly separated or irreversible, the processual similarities are worth noting. This is not the place to suggest a general theory of social processes. My immediate aim is more limited: to illuminate further the nature of the process of negotiation.

---

20. I have in mind familiar anthroplogical criticism of the partially similar model of political process constructed by Swartz *et al.* (1966:38).

21. For example, among the Jie of Uganda there were 15 defined and named stages of which 11 were notably ritualized. The whole process took a minimum period of about 5 years to complete. At the end, in the outcome, the couple had become fully husband and wife, affinal relations had been set, bridewealth transfers had been completed, and the basis of future close cooperation was established (Gulliver 1953).

Simply, I wish to emphasize the patent fact that it is easier and often essential to proceed in some orderly fashion so as to facilitate the movement from the initiation of a dispute to a final outcome. Were the disputants to go to court, they would come under the organizing authority of an adjudicator who himself operates within an institutionalized structure of rules, procedures, and roles with a more or less clear idea of due process. Thus the dispute and the disputants are brought within this structure such that the movement leading to a decision and outcome follow a recognized pattern. In negotiation, there is much less structuring and clarity, yet the process there too is ordered. It is not haphazard and arbitrary. Indeed, in one sense, the process is one of creating structure and order. The sometimes disparaging dismissal of negotiations as, for instance, "informal procedures," quite misses the point and only leads to failure to examine them carefully. More helpful are those writers, usually in the field of industrial negotiations, who refer to "the rules of the game" (Kerr 1954:237) or the "rules for play" (Stevens 1963:27). Similarly, Hyman (1972:57) has suggested that negotiation involves "the creation of an artificial social situation."

How far do participant negotiators themselves recognize the processual pattern and their position in it at a particular time? Among regular and professional negotiators and mediators, there is a marked awareness, according to Douglas and other reporters. My own experience of Arusha spokesmen and counsellors (who were repeatedly leading or influential in negotiating parties) indicates a similar conclusion. They quite often alluded to a particular phase, to kinds of behavior appropriate or inappropriate in it, to its purpose, and to the results expected from it. Moreover, even less practiced and less articulate negotiators are not unaware of the pattern, for they do not behave arbitrarily. One might almost say that the situation scarcely permits them to do so. It seems clear, for example, that in the previously cited case of the Ndendeuli bridewealth claim (page 131), the two parties were tacitly agreed that until agreement was reached on agenda definition they could not proceed further. Similarly, in the case of the Pilkington strike (page 127), failure to reach agreement on the agenda meant inability to agree on an arena for negotiations and effectively produced a deadlock.

It is a simple fact that unless there is due process—a more or less recognized, regular pattern of expectations and behavior—there is most likely to be chaos and failure. Attempts to short-cut the processual pattern, through ignorance, inexperience, and the desire for haste, can lead to serious difficulties, more prolonged negotiations, damage to interests, and perhaps breakdown. Douglas (1957:79–80) has reported an amusing, pertinent example. An energetic businessman, fearful of delayed production and lost sales, personally intervened early (in Phase 3) in the contract negotiations with his employees. He made a firm offer of a wage increase of 10 cents an hour. The union leaders at that time were asking for an 8 cent increase. His intention was to finish the negotiations there and then so that his business could return to immediate, uninterrupted production. The mediator in the case privately advised the businessman not to act so precipitately—indicating his professional, experienced awareness of due process and of its usefulness. The advice was ignored. The union representatives refused the offer. Soon after, the negotiations broke down and the workers went on strike. Eventually, after disruption of the firm's production, there was a settlement of 10 cents an hour.

The mediator commented afterward that the workers obtained "2c. above what they . . . were gonna get. Because it was thrown on the table at the wrong time. If he had *waited* and let negotiations go their usual course, his timing had been right, 'twould've settled for 8c. The union would've been happy and he would've been happy [Douglas 1957:80]." The mediator's argument was that the employer could have obtained a smaller wage increase (which he presumably preferred) more easily and quickly, without a damaging strike, had he allowed the "negotiations [to] go their usual course" and to follow the expected pattern.

A number of factors seem to have been important here. The union representatives felt that they had not had enough time to exchange and assess information so as to explore the field before proceeding further. They had had insufficient opportunity to present their own case to the employer's representatives and to show their constituents that they were acting as responsible leaders. The employer's sudden wage offer was virtually an ultimatum. "There'll be no considering. You'll take it or else," he declared. Yet this was in an early phase when possibilities and relative strengths were being initially examined. There was, therefore, no opportunity to discover if the employer was withholding important information, if he could be induced to increase his offer, and what other implications there might be. The union party had no time to reconsider and reorganize expectations and preferences. They were taken by surprise. They were also suspicious that they were being tricked and (in the mediator's view) resented the attempt to short-cut the negotiations. Because the recognized pattern was not followed, it would seem, they were uncertain where they stood and what was possible or feasible. Therefore, they would not and could not be pushed into accepting any offer at all, not even one that was above their current aspirations.

Cross (1969:95) has observed that, at first sight, it might seem that it is always possible for an arbitrator to propose an outcome that would be, for both parties, preferable to the cost and effort of further negotiations. Since in most cases the parties will eventually agree on an outcome, why not suggest it straightaway? Were this to be done, however—as Cross correctly noted—each party would assess the arbitrator's award by comparing it *not* with what might be obtained at the end of negotiations but with what the party expects to gain at the beginning. Almost inevitably, therefore, each party would consider the award to be inadequate; each would think he could have obtained a better outcome. By short-cutting the negotiations, the parties are unable to work through the process of learning and the essential adjustment of expectations and preferences that are necessary precursors to an acceptable and agreeable outcome. The parties need to experience that process and gain the experience of each other and of themselves and others so that they come to accept a particular outcome as satisfactory.[22]

---

22. Compare the remarks of Vickers and Douglas, quoted on pages 81–82.

6

THE DYNAMICS OF NEGOTIATION

The pattern models presented in the preceding chapters deal with the processual features involved in the negotiation of disputes. These models are principally concerned with the exchange of information between the negotiating parties and their interpretation of the information received. This induces the negotiators to formulate and adjust their expectations and preferences and in turn may induce modification of demands and offers concerning the issues in dispute. Such modification makes it possible for the parties to converge toward an agreed outcome acceptable to both. The models purport to show, primarily, the processes by which all this occurs. What the models do not consider, however, is why these processes continue and why an outcome is achieved. Neither the causes of convergent movement nor the sources of constraints and persuasions that induce the parties to change their expectations and demands have been systematically considered. Although much is implicit in the processual analysis, a full explanation requires the clearer identification and assessment of the variable factors that in interconnection, contribute to the determination of the convergence and thus of the outcome.

The causes of convergence are undoubtedly the most problematic aspect of negotiation. In general, analysis and theory in the social sciences continue to be unable to provide, in any satisfactory way, a determinate explanation of complex, interconnected variables that have a marked qualitative and subjective content. In a survey of the results of theoretical and descriptive work on negotiation by social scientists, Zartman realistically concluded that "despite all claims, there is not yet a satisfactory theory of negotiations and, perhaps even more important . . . there is still no explanation in terms of operationalizable variables that can be applied to real cases [1976:18]." That is a fair assessment in my view. The discussion in this chapter, however, does not attempt to provide such a theory and explanation, for I have no expectation that a determinate theory is possible in the near future. Rather, my intention here is to examine some of the factors that are involved in the determination of a negotiated outcome in the light of the processual models of cognition and interactional behavior. Thus, what I present is no more than an approach toward a general theory. Anything more ambitious seems only to be achievable at the expense of considerable simplification, and thus distortion, of the obvious complexity of real cases.

First I examine the processual dynamics within negotiation; that is, the dialectical interaction of contradictions between crucial factors in negotiation that appears to operate as a persisting propulsion of the process toward an outcome. Second, I examine the significance of power and of norms, in an endeavor to formulate some way of conceptualizing their contribution to negotiators' convergence and a negotiated outcome.

PROCESSUAL DYNAMICS

Each of the two principal general processes in negotiation—the cyclical and the developmental—has an internal dynamic of its own that is logically generated and sustained within the process itself. Continuing interaction within each process is propelled by varying conjunctions of opposites in intrinsic contradiction, and that, analytically speaking, is what keeps negotiations going and provides the potentiality of movement to an agreed outcome between the parties in dispute.

In the examination of the repetitive exchange of information and learning in the cyclical process, the dynamic was shown in the form of persisting dilemmas.[1] There is a need to receive information in order to learn about, and therefore take account of, the opponent's expectations, demands, strategy, strengths, and weaknesses. In receiving information, however, a party is at the same time unavoidably subject to the pressures of persuasion and coercion from his opponent, which he might otherwise wish to avoid. In complementary fashion, there is a need to give information to the oppo-

---

1. See Chapter 4, especially pages 83–85.

nent so that he may know and understand the party's demands and strengths, and to endeavor to persuade and coerce him to shift his expectations and demands. There is an additional need to give information specifically in order to be able to receive information in return from the opponent. In giving information, however, there is a risk of revealing, and being compelled to reveal, more than the party might wish. Thus neither party can merely give such information as he alone might choose but also, and sometimes predominantly, that which the opponent desires. In short, the needs to give and to receive carry ineluctable liabilities. In order to counteract those liabilities there is a persistent, strong motivation to give and to receive further information.

Information exchange is thus conditioned by the needs of both parties in interaction and interdependence. Each message received from the opponent creates a need and desire to respond; each message given to the opponent stimulates a response from him. In choosing to act in some particular way, a party provokes and intends to provoke reaction from the opponent. His reaction in turn provokes succeeding reaction from the party. Thus, there is a persisting force, arising from the dilemmas of exchange, that propels the continued, cumulative exchange process. Such positive interaction toward an ultimate outcome is not, of course, inevitable; people are not automata impelled by social forces and deadlock may occur or one party may default. Yet there is a marked propensity for exchange to continue as it is propelled by the intrinsic dilemmas that continuously confront the negotiators.

The dynamic of the developmental process, although comparable in principle, is somewhat different in form. The intrinsic contradiction here is between, on the one hand, the recognized conflict in which the parties seek different objectives at each other's expense and, on the other hand, their need for joint action in order to achieve an outcome in circumstances wherein neither party feels able merely to impose his own demands upon the other. This fundamental contradiction in the situation inevitably creates dispositions of antagonism and coordination that are evident in contrasting modes of interaction. These dispositions alternate inversely in relative dominance and suppression throughout the negotiations.

By *antagonism* is meant some degree of more or less overt conflict, competitiveness, mistrust, and opposition between the parties as each recognizes and emphasizes the differences between them, guards his own interests, and seeks to make them prevail over the interests of the opponent. Antagonism may, sometimes or even all of the time, include hostility and animosity. Conversely, *coordination* means a combining in unavoidable interdependence for the sake of concerted endeavor and action by which agreements are sought and in which common purpose, interests, and

181

values are emphasized. Coordination may include trust, amity, and cooperation, though often it does not; nor are these qualities essentially required in order to reach an outcome. By definition, since the parties have entered into negotiations, they have accepted a common purpose—to obtain an outcome—and they began coordination by agreeing that there is a dispute between them and that they can examine it in some coherent way. Yet at the same time, there is recognition that conflict and differences exist between them.

Prima facie, it would appear that, on the whole, there is likely to be greater antagonism in the earlier phases of negotiations than in the later ones or at the end when a final outcome is reached. Coordination appears to grow as negotiations proceed because it is seen to produce some result, because of the experience each party acquires of the other and of their joint circumstances, and because of the growing commitment to reach a conclusion. There is, it may seem, a general trend in which antagonism diminishes, without necessarily disappearing, and coordination grows without becoming perfect. However, although the process of negotiation could be characterized descriptively in this fashion, to do so would be to oversimplify and so to distort and obstruct understanding. The relationship between antagonism and coordination is more complex and the actual interaction between the parties does not follow such a straightforward, lineal pattern. Instead, there is a fluctuating relationship that, moreover, is not merely an empirical condition but can be seen as a dynamic, propelling force.

The crucial fact is that throughout the developmental process there are successive alternations of the relative dominance of these opposing dispositions of antagonism and coordination, irrespective of the absolute intensity of either through time. When one disposition is dominant, the other is temporarily suppressed. As either becomes dominant in the parties' interaction, it engenders its opposite and itself becomes subordinate, temporarily diminished in intensity and expression. In the context of negotiations, were either disposition to remain dominant there would be little or no movement toward an outcome. Of course, there is no absolute inevitability of alternation; the parties do sometimes reach an impasse, a deadlock, where antagonism remains dominant. Nevertheless there are good reasons why alternation should continue and deadlock be avoided and why, therefore, the cumulative process itself should continue toward an agreed outcome.

Before examining those reasons and thus the nature of the dynamics of the process, let me first give a brief descriptive account of the pattern of these alternations. Summarily, that pattern, also shown in Figure 5.1, is as follows:

Phase	*Dominant Disposition*
1. Search for arena	From antagonism to coordination
2. Agenda formulation	From antagonism to coordination
3. Exploration of the range of the dispute	Antagonism persists (possibly increases)
4. Narrowing differences	From coordination to antagonism
5. Preliminaries to final bargaining	From coordination to antagonism to coordination
6. Final bargaining	From antagonism to coordination
7. Ritual confirmation	Coordination remains

With the recognition of a dispute, antagonism is dominant as conflict is acknowledged and as unresolved differences are recognized. In Phase 1, the search for an arena gradually or quickly suppresses the antagonism as the parties need to find agreement on that initial issue and as, therefore, they must coordinate their efforts toward that accepted end. With that accomplishment,[2] the parties revert to a predominant antagonism as differences are articulated in the discussions to formulate the agenda and to define the issues contained in it. To complete that task with the necessary minimal success, the parties must again come to emphasize coordination for their evident mutual purposes. Phase 3 begins with a reversion to antagonism; the parties give strong emphasis to their differences and they display hostility and perhaps downright animosity (both intergroup and interpersonal). During this phase, while exploring the area of conflict between them and expressing the outer limits to their demands, the dominance of antagonism continues. Sometimes the level of antagonism rises toward the end of that phase as differences between the parties become clearer and are more emphasized. The beginning of Phase 4 is marked by a reversion to coordination as the parties begin to try to narrow their differences and to obtain some limited joint decisions. The emphasis shifts to common interests, overarching values, and reciprocal concessions. Antagonism is suppressed, hostility is suspended, and conflict is avoided in the concern to discover mutually acceptable solutions. This phase ends as the obdurate issues begin to emerge more clearly and as further resolutions are resisted. Antagonism becomes dominant as differences and conflict again become emphasized. Phase 5 opens with a reemphasis on coordination, with the agreed need to find ways to deal with the obvious obdurate issues. Antagonism is likely to regain dominance as the difficulties and dif-

---

2. Where an arena is prescribed and unavoidable, and thus no joint agreement and decision is required, the parties in effect start in Phase 2 with antagonism dominant.

ferences become more apparent but it finally gives way again to coordination as the basis is laid for final bargaining. That bargaining in Phase 6 begins with antagonism dominant, but final agreement is reached through the renewed growth of coordination. Confirmation and ritualization of the agreed outcome—Phase 7—is, of course, strongly marked by coordination as the mutuality of agreement is symbolized and accentuated, whatever the degree of antagonism that may persist underneath the overt accord.

Two features of this pattern must be stressed. First, antagonism results from the recurrent reemphasis of conflict and differences between the parties. It is not the cause of them. On the other hand, coordination leads to the accomplishment of particular mutual purposes and tasks. It is not the result of those. This distinction is important in the understanding of the relationship between the two opposing dispositions.

Second, the beginning of each phase is marked by the dominance of the disposition and mode of interaction that was subordinate at the end of the preceding phase. Indeed, it is this change and the concomitant changes of purpose and concern that create and identify phase change and thus, in effect, the phases themselves. This indicates that the phases of my developmental model are not, therefore, merely the constructs of the observer; rather, the phases arise out of the dynamics of the interaction itself.

The preceding summary description clearly oversimplifies the interactional fluctuations of the dominant dispositions, for these are rather more complex in most real-life negotiations. In all phases, there are three significant complications to be recognized. First, as already mentioned, although a disposition is not dominant at a particular time, it is not altogether absent. Currently subordinate dispositions persist, though temporarily diminished or suppressed, and continue to modify the process. Thus antagonism is, to some extent, tempered by continuing coordination, and coordination is conditioned by persisting antagonism. Second, within any phase (even Phase 3) there can be lesser fluctuations between the two opposites. These may be quite rapid or frequent within the broader pattern of a phase. This is perhaps especially marked in Phase 4 (narrowing the differences), where coordination dominates at first and for most of the rest of that phase. Yet antagonism may erupt in interim bargaining on particular issues and in the recurrent appearance, gradual emergence, and recognition of the obdurate issues. Each time, more or less deliberately, the antagonism is suppressed and the differences are passed over in the endeavor to continue to discover limited resolutions and to reduce the number and complexity of the issues in dispute. Therefore, each time antagonism threatens, efforts are made to restore coordination. Similar fluctuations, however, also occur in other phases as the parties attempt to manage their unavoidable contradiction.

Third, phases often overlap, as noted in the exposition of the developmental model. It is now possible to see more clearly what this means. Since a new phase is signified by the obtrusion of the disposition that is subordinate toward the end of the preceding phase, this means that the dominance of one disposition is directly counteracted by its opposite, which is coming into prominence. One might put it that antagonism and coordination compete: hence the frequent problems of phase transition. Not only are the parties shifting to a different and fresh purpose but they may be simultaneously compelled to be both antagonistic and coordinating. Thus the beginning of a new phase is often characterized by confusion as, in effect, the two parties endeavor to do two contradictory things at the same time and to express and act upon opposing dispositions and modes of behavior. One fairly common solution to that dilemma is for some members of a party to take a lead in and represent antagonism while other members are the proponents of coordination. An example of this was given in the Arusha bridewealth case cited earlier (page 133), where the role of the elder brother of the father-in-law was to express antagonism toward and to emphasize differences with, the party of the son-in-law, while the role of the father-in-law himself and some others was to emphasize coordination. Although this kind of strategy may be successful, it can cause troublesome dissension within the party itself insofar as it allows expression of real differences between members and is not merely a strategy used to overcome processual problems.

Why do these alternations of contrasting and opposing dispositions occur? What is their significance in the process of negotiation? Explanation must begin from a reiteration that both antagonism and coordination are inherent in negotiation. Sheer, persistent antagonism alone would produce little or no movement toward agreement and an outcome. Indeed, it might not allow the initiation of negotiations at all or, once begun, it would deny the possibility of the interdependent discovery of common interests and values and the potentials of joint decision. Instead there would be frustration. On the other hand, coordination is not required by itself, rather it is the means with which to grapple with the conflict that engenders antagonism. Thus, the dominance of antagonism, that is the emphasis on differences between the parties, means relative disregard for coordination and for the opportunities for joint action toward an outcome. Yet antagonism creates and re-creates the basis for such action. Conversely, the dominance of coordination and joint action means a relative disregard for the differences that constitute the dispute itself. In practice, the parties have to deal *both* with their differences and with their need for joint action. One breeds the other. Having completed a phase in coordinated action, the parties can build upon this by returning to their differences. Having explored and emphasized their differences, they can return to coordination so as to deal with some aspect of them. Indeed, it is not only that they can do this; they are in a sense compelled to do so, for, given the agreement to negotiate, each disposition requires the other to fuel it. A simple analogy is that of a person walking: first one foot, then the other. To advance the right leg is virtually to compel and propel the left leg forward in response.

For example, the agreed choice of an arena cannot be achieved without coordination. When that joint decision has been made, there is then the need and desire to use the chosen arena, and to use it is to begin to express differences in the antagonistic mode. Those differences—relating to agenda formulation and issue definition—then require a return to coordination for their resolution. With agreement there, the parties must begin to examine the consequences of their joint decisions on agenda issues by detailing their differences, showing their strengths, and making their demands. Refusal to shift from one disposition to the other simply creates deadlock, immobility, and failure. Too great and too long an emphasis on coordination threatens the neglect of a party's own interests and objectives, so he returns to his differences with his opponent. Conversely, persisting dominance of antagonism threatens the need for coordination and the possibility of movement toward agreement. It is not possible to emphasize both dispositions simultaneously because they are opposites, and it is not possible to discard either if movement toward an outcome is to be maintained.

This is the intrinsic, dynamic propulsion contained within negotiation as a process of interaction. The separate, successive phases are bound together by cumulative achievements, but the whole process is given persistence and movement by the basic contradiction between the parties' conflict and their need for joint action. This contradiction generates opposing dispositions that, in alternating dominance, give the possibility of continuous impetus toward some final agreement and outcome. That propulsion is linked with and reinforced by the simultaneous forces of propulsion within the cyclical process, coming from the dilemmas inherent in the giving and receiving of information.

POWER AND NORMS: PROBLEMS OF EXPLANATION

The internal dynamics of the process of negotiation, as described in the preceding section, provide an essential but not sufficient explanation of the causes of convergence and the nature of a jointiy agreed outcome.

Three other factors must be taken into account, factors that overlie the processual dynamics and give them direction. First, there is the endeavor by the parties to use the resources available to them that afford each some negotiating strength and a means of exercising persuasion and coercion upon the other. This is usually described as power. Second, there are the parties' references and appeals to norms (rules, principles, morals, values— oughts), which are claimed to set standards by which disputed issues can be assessed, and indicate the proper allocation of rights, obligations, and objectives. Third, there is the impingement of the outside world upon the parties in their negotiations—interested third parties and macrosocial conditions and trends that offer resources to, and impose constraints on, the parties. In the present section, I examine some of the problems of analysis and explanation relating to power and norms in order to provide the basis for an operational scheme that takes account of power, norms, and outside factors.

It is easy to state, in general terms, that power or norms, or some combination of both, are the determining factor in the parties' convergence on an outcome. However, it is much less easy to understand the actual operation of power and norms and to explain a negotiated outcome in those terms. Most certainly, scholars have been in considerable disagreement in this matter, such that there has been little consensus, even though a great deal can be learned from their discussions and differences.

In seeking an explanation of the shifts in expectations, preferences, and above all demands by the negotiating parties, and of the "causes" of convergence to an agreed outcome, the majority of writers have used some notion of power. In fact, negotiation has been conceived of as a power struggle with the outcome determined by the relative strengths of the two parties in context. This has been particularly marked among students of industrial negotiations. Long ago the Webbs stated that case quite frankly: "In so far as the issue is left to collective bargaining there is not even any question of principle involved. . . . The issue is a trial of strength between the parties [Webb and Webb 1902:184]." More recently, Stagner concluded that "there is only one single type of industrial conflict, namely conflict over power [1956:291]." Stevens wrote, "Within some limits, for variation, the basic determinants of the outcome of collective bargaining negotiations are the determinants of the basic power relationships which underlie the conflict in industrial relations [1963:132]." For such writers, who are concerned principally with the issue of wage rates, power and its determinants are essentially economic in their source. Thus, the power of a trade union to go on strike, and so to disrupt the firm's production schedule and profits, is limited by the workers' ability to go without work and wages during a strike period and is set against the ability of the firm to withstand a strike or to avoid its economic consequences (e.g., to absorb losses, to supply from inventory, to hire nonunion labor, or to switch production to another plant). From this point of view, negotiation consists of the discovery and the working out of the relative power of the two parties. Some other writers in this field (e.g., Flanders 1970; Levinson 1966; A. M. Ross 1948), while acknowledging the importance of purely economic factors, have wished to include also political and institutional factors that enhance or reduce the power of either party. That is, they wish to take account of noneconomic factors as well, such as legal restrictions, reference to patterns and standards in the same or another industry or area, and the force of ideas of equity or justice.

A difficulty with this kind of approach is that the notion of power is not made altogether clear; nor is it obvious precisely how power is to be assessed (by participants or observers) and precisely how it operates to produce a particular outcome. There have, of course, been numerous attempts to define the concept of power. None seems to have achieved general acceptance and none seems altogether satisfactory in coping with intrinsic difficulties. In lieu of attempting to survey the whole field, two can be mentioned by way of illustration. One influential definition has been that of Thibaut and Kelley (1959). For them, power is the ability of one person or group to affect another person's or group's outcomes such that the degree of power comes to be the potential range of outcomes that one can determine for the other (cf. Gruder 1970:113 ff.). More simply, Zartman (1974:396, following Dahl 1969) suggested that power might be defined as "the ability of one party to cause another to change behavior in an intended direction." With some such definition in mind, many social psychologists have very largely accepted the predominance of power in determining the outcome of interaction between individuals and groups, almost to the point of tacitly taking this predominance for granted. Thus, those analysts have concentrated on the mechanisms by which power is exercised. Consequently, there has been a considerable number of studies of threats, promises, deterrents, inducements, commitments, the use of status differential, and the like. Nevertheless, despite some useful results in detail, there has been indifferent success in understanding power itself. As Zartman has observed, specifically with reference to the Swingle symposium by social psychologists (1970): "Power is recognized, typologized, summarized, and left hanging in midair in pieces—a great half step forward [1974:396]." Those writers have been concerned with the variety of means by which power is exercised rather than with power itself.

Conversely, other writers, usually more purely theoretical and conceptual in their approach, have ignored power altogether in their determinate formulas. For example, both Pen and Coddington simply omit power from consideration without discussion. Such theorists have instead gone for concession rates, adjustments of expectations, propensity to take risk or to avoid conflict, and utilities. In his well-known solution of the bargaining problem, Nash effectively rules out power by his assumption of symmetry and his concern for justice and a "rational," collective, maximal outcome. One feels that it would be a crudity to introduce the factor of power into so urbane and elegant a solution.

Some theorists have explicitly denied the significance of power, or at least, they have seen difficulties of definition that, they believe, make it an impossible concept to use. Cross (1969) is probably the clearest in this respect. He deliberately rejected the notion of power because he thought that no satisfactory definition could be found for it as an independent and therefore possibly causative variable. For him, power in the purely bargaining context can be perceived and interpreted only in terms of the outcome. Thus, if a party can alter the outcome in some degree it has power, and if it can alter it to a greater degree it has greater power. But, Cross noted, such a definition is tautologous, equating "more power" with "better payoff," so that we merely have the conclusion that "he did better because he was more powerful." Power then becomes a dependent variable, not an independent, determinant one. As a result, its conceptual use removes the capacity to explain what happens since power can only be seen in the result, the outcome (p. 145). "A definition of power . . . cannot contribute anything to an analysis if it is simply taken to be synonymous with or descriptive of the outcome [p. 17]." In addition, and what looks like an equally serious difficulty for Cross in his endeavor to produce a determinant economic theory of bargaining, there is the apparent impossibility of quantifying power and so rendering it usable. Moreover, as he points out, if a party having "more power" means that every cost imposed on the opponent is at less cost to that party, then it is preferable to study the costs themselves and to ignore power. That procedure, in his opinion, is too complicated to accomplish effectively and therefore he discards it as a possibility.

Zartman is no less critical of the concept as it has commonly been used. "An explanatory theory in terms of power is . . . merely a theory that explains the causes of convergence [to an outcome] in terms of the causes of convergence [1974:396–397]." Similarly, Schelling has written,

"Bargaining power," "bargaining strength," "bargaining skill" suggest that the advantage goes to the powerful, the strong or the skillful. It does, of course, if those qualities are defined to mean only that negotiations are won by those who win. But, if the terms imply that it is an advantage to be more intelligent or more skilled in debate, or to have more financial resources, more physical strength, more military potency, or more ability to withstand losses, then the term does a disservice. Those qualities are by no means universal advantages in bargaining situations; they often have a contrary value [1960:22].[3]

In sum, there appears to be considerable ambiguity and great operational difficulty in using the concept of power to explain the nature and causes of shifts in parties' demands and offers and of their convergence on an agreed outcome. Common sense continues to suggest quite strongly that something we might designate as "power" is in practice operative; nevertheless, it is extraordinarily difficult to pin down.

Before attempting to grapple with this problem further, it is useful to turn to the significance of normative rules and values in the determination of a negotiated outcome. My contention will be that it is not merely helpful to consider norms in conjunction with power but it is an essential step for the development of explanation. In this matter of norms, as with power, there has been rather little consensus among students of negotiations.

Economic theorists, from Zeuthen onward, have given little attention and importance to normative rules and values. They have simply ignored them or perhaps taken them for granted, rather than positively rejecting them as significant factors. Where there has been reference to norms, they have been explained (or virtually explained away) merely as the means for rationalizing interests, power, and the outcome that is determined by power. For instance, Bloom and Northrup wrote, "Man prides himself on his rationality. Explanations are needed to fortify wants or demands, and to gain support for them. Every battle must have its slogans. The slogans should not, however, be confused with the practical realities of union–management wage determination however important they might be in crystalizing those realities in the form of policies [1958:322–323]." Reynolds (1954:575) asserted that arguments based on prevailing standards are "merely rationalizations" pressed into service to support demands for concessions that need justification. That justification seems, in his view, to be mainly for the benefit of nonparticipants in the negotiations since references to norms are "public relations arguments" (cf. Stevens 1963:71 ff.).

Such explanations, quite common among social scientists and "practical men," relegate norms to a position of minor importance while giving critical importance to the role of power. Yet such proponents of power recognize that reference to norms is quite usual in negotiations and is of some importance to the participants. This raises the questions, then, as to what exactly is happening and why. It seems to suggest quite strongly that

---

3. This and all subsequent quotes cited to Schelling (1960) are reprinted from *The Strategy of Conflict* by T. C. Schelling by permission of the publisher, Harvard University Press. Copyright © 1960 by Harvard University Press.

the invocation of norms is potentially useful to negotiators because it can impose pressure in some way on the opponent and on others who may be concerned with the outcome. Ryder (1956:353), though accepting the predominance of power as the determinant of a negotiated outcome, emphasized also the effects on the opponent of references to norms: They are a means by which a party softens up his opponent, undermines his position, promotes the doubts of self-questioning, and weakens his resolve, thus making him more susceptible to the exercise of power. This suggests that pure power plays needs to be, or at least can be, usefully reinforced by norms and normative assessment. This means, then, that norms have some degree of strength and weight of their own and that, therefore, they do make some contribution to the determination of an outcome.

This is not the place for a full-length consideration of the nature and significance of normative rules and values in social interaction, for that would require investigation of a complex and long-standing problem that goes far beyond present needs. It would indeed require a book to itself. Instead, I wish to make a few pertinent points that lead to the proposal that normative correctness, or claims to that evaluation, give strength to a negotiator's demands and to his resistance to those of his opponent. That is, my contention will be that norms are a source of some degree of power, a resource that is drawn upon by a negotiator along with other resources to which he has access.

First, some norms have an accepted, intrinsic character in that they tend to be more or less unquestioned. They symbolize moral and cultural values of prime importance. They indicate proper social behavior that is held to be ethically superior to amoral or immoral behavior. Therefore, such norms are likely, though not inevitably, to be constraining, and the party who has conformed to them may have powerful support against his opponent who has contravened them. Second, however, because norms exist, specifically or ambiguously and vaguely, beyond the immediate context of any particular negotiations, they refer to the society at large that envelops the negotiators, or to some sector of it that may or does impinge on the negotiations. Reference to norms, therefore, is reference to the wider social domain. It is acknowledgment that there are other people out there, ranging from a generalized public (with its "public opinion") to particular groups and individuals, who need to be assuaged, placated, and perhaps persuaded. Thus, norms refer to, and represent in shorthand form, sets of interests and distributions of power and status in society. To invoke such norms, and to claim to conform to them, is not only an acknowledgment of their importance per se but an attempt to make use of them by showing that a party's past behavior and present demands concur with, and are supported by, those interests and power. The implication, or perhaps downright assertion, is that the opponent ought morally to accede to the demands and also that his own and outside interests are best served if he does. Thus, it is urged, refusal to accede will be disadvantageous to the opponent, for he invites the possibility of adverse interference from the outside, now or later, should he refuse. The party's intention may therefore be an attempt to prevent or minimize outside interference by making his demands and the norms congruent. That is, he seeks to conform, or claims to conform, to the evoked norms. Alternatively, evocation of norms may be something of a bid to recruit outside support, potentially or actively, in order to strengthen the party's demands. Such an attempt, either to forestall adverse interference or to invite it advantageously, may apply principally to the negotiations in progress and to the demands and assessments being made there. In addition, there may be reference to the ongoing social life of the participants and to their future relationships, needs, and prospects in the wider society that have bearing on the current negotiations.

In brief, there is the possibility (though perhaps seldom the certainty) of gaining and using negotiating strength through claims to conformity with normative rules and values that are taken to be axiomatic and/or to represent the acknowledged social order. Thus a party attempts to persuade his opponent of the legitimacy and morality of his demands and to gain outsiders' approval and support. This does not, of course, deny the obvious possibility of the deliberate (and also unconscious) manipulation of norms; for instance, by selective emphasis on those that seem most supportive, by particular interpretation and biased application, by virtually inventing a norm to fit the demand ex post facto, and by the exploitation of attitudes and emotions associated with the symbolism of the norms. There is no need to ignore manipulation, or altogether to disregard the arguments for rationalization. Presumably a party considers it useful to rationalize. Nevertheless, whatever the expected advantages of the strategy, it is likely that in the process of demonstrating alleged congruence between norms and demand, there will be, as well as some manipulation of the norms, some constraints on and modifications of the demands themselves in order to make the fit more plausible and therefore more acceptable. However, it would be incorrect to perceive all evocation of norms as merely manipulation and rationalization. Even if negotiators themselves are unimpressed by normative conformity—and the evidence does not support so gross a conclusion—they are often constrained to conform, or at least to conform more than they otherwise might, because they need to appear to accept and adhere to the rules, standards, and values of their society.

Furthermore, it is obvious that when a dispute is initiated, there is allegation by at least one of the parties that certain rights have been infringed or denied. Such allegation presupposes open or tacit reference to norms that define those rights. Thus the dispute begins in terms of norms, whatever else may also be involved. Moreover, although the opponent may argue from nonnormative premises, he is virtually compelled to seek to deny the alleged infringement by a different interpretation and application of the same norms or by the invocation of others. As previously shown in discussion of agenda formulation, there is often more than one way of defining issues in dispute. However, once there is some agreement on definition, as eventually there must be if negotiations are to continue, this will be at least partly in terms of some set of norms that then provide a framework within which further negotiations occur. An example was given of a dispute between a father-in-law and a son-in-law where, eventually, it was agreed that the principal issues lay within the rights and obligations of affinal kinship rather than within those of marriage. Although affinal norms were not altogether clear, yet they provided the framework within which the main lines of negotiations developed thereafter.[4]

That is to say, the dispute itself (or at least some of the issues that are disputed) is defined in part by a normative framework that both parties more or less accept in the situation. That definition is, of course, affected and augmented by the preliminary recognition of other potential power available to each party: access to resources, differential status, external support, ability to reward or punish, and the like. Such a framework—in effect, the imposition of a certain constraint and control over the scope of the negotiations—is likely to offer certain perceived advantages to one party and possible disadvantages to the other. The point here, however, is that the framework and the definition are and must be in normative terms, and that means that the parties are in part constrained by the agreed and accepted norms. Moreover, their expectations are significantly affected by those norms.

The general conclusion from the preceding summary discussion is that normative correctness affords a possibly stronger position for a party. It is a potential source of negotiating strength. This being so, there is no need to set norms against so-called power when we are examining the causes of convergence to an outcome in negotiations. Unfortunately, this has too often been done as if it were a case of either–or: either norms (rules, values, standards, principles) or power (economic and physical resources, status, political strength, etc.). Instead we may recognize the potential strength of both; or rather, we may recognize normative correctness (or claims to it) as one kind of resource that affords power, which the parties may attempt to use in order to persuade or coerce each other. It is possible that norms are

---

4. Discussion of agenda formulation and definition of issues is on pages 126–135. The dispute cited—an Arusha bridewealth case—is given on page 133.

seldom, perhaps never altogether, convincing on their own in negotiations, either in the formulation and modification of a party's preferences and demands or in inducing the opponent to modify his demands.[5] "Pure power" by itself may seldom by solely convincing either, or only in rather special circumstances. Analytically, it is preferable in any case to avoid a distinction between norms and power and instead to look for all the kinds of resources that are available to each party. Then it is necessary to examine how and how far the potentials of those resources are actually exercised in the negotiating interaction, how the various resources reinforce or conflict with each other and how certain resources of one party counteract or prevail over those of the other party.

THE CASE OF THE HERDSMAN'S THEFT

The operation and interconnection of various kinds of resources available to, and used by, the parties can be brought out initially through the examination of negotiations in a relatively simple dispute; that is, one in which the variables are relatively few and straightforward. The following dispute occurred among the Arusha of Tanzania.[6]

A middle-aged man, Ngatieu, came to an arrangement with his cousin, Moruo, his mother's brother's son, whereby Moruo would keep and herd on his farm Ngatieu's four cattle and three goats. This was a quite common kind of arrangement in that country at that time and it included the provision that Moruo should take the milk of the animals and would in due course receive a calf for his services. There had been no particular problem in making the arrangement, and both were satisfied with it.

Two months later, after an absence from the country, Ngatieu visited Moruo's farm and discovered that one of his animals—a steer—was missing. Moruo, the herdsman, reported that it had strayed and could not be found. Ngatieu was suspicious of this unlikely occurrence and was disinclined to believe the story without further investigation. Making in-

---

5. Critical points in negotiations may, however, turn on normative issues. An example comes from an Arusha case where the dispute concerned a man's seduction of the girl betrothed to another man. The accused denied any offense and wanted the girl's father to agree to marriage, ignoring the preexisting betrothal. In a moot attended by many neutral spectators, the betrothed man and his supporters insistently challenged the accused to deny the immorality of his seduction of the girl. Eventually the accused and his supporters had to concede the norm and his breach of it. This set the stage for subsequent negotiation of compensation and other issues. In effect, the accused could not, in public, withstand the recognized, valid assertion of his normative offense (Gulliver 1963:261–262).

6. This case was originally reported in summary form as Case 22 in Gulliver (1963:253).

quiries locally, he soon learned that Moruo had slaughtered the animal and sold some of the meat for cash in order to meet a debt to a neighbor. Ngatieu returned to the farm and accused Moruo of theft. Fairly quickly, Moruo admitted to his offense. He adverted to his need to pay off the outstanding debt as his explanation and offered to replace the slaughtered beast and to pay a sheep to Ngatieu in addition.

Among the Arusha, it is commonly agreed that when a stolen animal is slaughtered (i.e., when the animal itself cannot be returned), it should be replaced by an equivalent animal together with a compensation payment of three more animals of the same kind. If the offender is a kinsman of the owner, the compensation should be two animals. Since theft of livestock was considered a most serious matter, the Arusha thought this compensation was entirely proper. Thus, Moruo's offer was well below normative standards. Ngatieu angrily refused his cousin's offer but Moruo refused to increase it, saying it was all he could afford and that Ngatieu, as a kinsman, should not press him so hard.

Ngatieu departed from the farm with the matter unresolved but left the rest of his animals in Moruo's charge as before. He first discussed the matter with his close associates—his near patrilineal kinsmen—and then, accompanied by one of them, went to consult with the counsellor of his lineage.[7] The counsellor agreed to take up the matter with the counsellor of Moruo's lineage and to try to arrange a meeting between the two parties in order to negotiate a settlement. Eventually it was agreed by the counsellors, and confirmed by the two principals, that a small conclave should be held at Moruo's farm. Ngatieu went there accompanied by his counsellor, one of his brothers, and a more distantly related but notable member of his lineage. They met Moruo's party, comprising Moruo, his lineage counsellor, a paternal cousin, and another kinsman who was an influential neighbor. No other people were present in Moruo's house for the counsellors had agreed that a small, private meeting was more likely to achieve a speedy and satisfactory resolution. Either party, however, could have sought a larger, more formal, and public encounter had this been considered more advantageous in the circumstances.

Moruo opened the negotiations by immediately admitting to his offense and offering (as he had previously) to replace the slaughtered steer and to pay a sheep in compensation. Ngatieu, fully supported by his own party, refused the offer and demanded the standard two steers as compensation. Eventually, after some 2 hours, it was agreed that Moruo should

---

7. In each maximal lineage the male members chose one of their members as a permanent spokesman who, inter alia, gave advice and acted as advocate for any member involved in a dispute (Gulliver 1963:101).

replace the steer and pay compensation of a male calf. Both of these animals were formally handed over to Ngatieu immediately, with the other men as witnesses. The rest of Ngatieu's animals were driven over from the nearby field and paraded before the men with the explicit intention of identifying them. It was also agreed that Moruo should deliver a "friendship gift" of beer to Ngatieu's house and that formal ritual reconciliation and consolidation of the agreement should be performed. Moruo provided a young goat for that purpose and the ritual was carried out on the spot. The meeting concluded as the assembled men ate some of the goat meat and drank a little beer. Ngatieu and his party returned to their homes leaving Ngatieu's animals with Moruo under the original herding arrangement.

In analyzing this case, with the intention of providing an approximate explanation of the final outcome, it is useful to begin by setting out the issues in dispute together with the initial goals of each disputant. It should be noted that each party was, under the circumstances, well informed of the other's position and preferences. There was, therefore, little need to exchange factual information. The issues and goals were as follows:

1. Compensation for theft. Both parties agreed on the replacement of the stolen steer. Ngatieu sought full, normative compensation; Moruo, as his initial offer showed, aimed to pay rather less than that.

2. The herding arrangement. Both desired to continue this because of the advantages it offered. However, whereas Moruo desired merely a continuation of the status quo, Ngatieu wished to reinforce it in order to inhibit further breach by Moruo.

3. The public reputation of Moruo. As far as possible, Moruo wished to avoid the damage that might come from an open breach with Ngatieu; Ngatieu had no desire to spoil Moruo's reputation so long as he obtained other satisfactions.

4. The kin relationship. Both disputants desired to continue the advantages of their prescribed, close kinship link if acceptable terms could be discovered on the other issues.

The framework within which the negotiations were conducted was established by certain normative rules and values. These were accepted by both parties without disagreement or difficulty. There was not, however, full agreement on the interpretation of the norms. Briefly, the normative framework was as follows:

1. Taking and using another person's property without his consent was wrong. It was especially serious when the theft concerned livestock and in that case an equivalent animal (same sex, age,

quality) should be given to the owner by the thief, together with a payment of three other animals, or two others if the men were kin.

2. The terms of the herding arrangement of the sort involved here were of an unexceptional, customary kind, freely accepted by both men. The herdsman received recognized rewards for his services and he owed a responsibility to care for the animals in his charge and to report to the owner any occurrence of importance in respect to them (e.g., pregnancy, sickness, disappearance, death).

3. Acknowledged kinship between two men postulated mutual trust, assistance, and good faith. Therefore a herding arrangement was most preferable between kinsmen. Although not agnatically related in this society where patrilineality was emphasized, the two men were close kin and were peers generationally and by age, so that the kinship obligations were strong and symmetrical.[8]

The first two sets of norms clearly afforded resources of strength for Ngatieu. Moruo did not dispute them. He was plainly guilty and did not attempt to deny that during the negotiations. Ngatieu himself had done no wrong nor was he accused of any. Moruo did not seek to deny the applicability of the norm of compensation. Instead, he claimed (with reference to another norm) that he could not afford to pay the full amount specified. This, however, was rejected as visibly false since his animals were to be seen in the nearby field. Thereafter he concentrated on the interpretation of the agreed kinship norm. He claimed that, because they were close kin, Ngatieu should be lenient and show "friendliness." This was a claim to a normative resource of some strength, for a man should be forgiving and generous to an offending kinsman. Not to do so is to risk the appearance of meanness and hardness. Ngatieu countered with the arguments that a kinsman especially should not act in bad faith as a herdsman and that the norm of compensation by a kinsman was not only commonly recognized, but also it was not denied by Moruo himself. These normative arguments, however, were somewhat blunted by Moruo's normative claim. The tendency to give way to that claim reinforced Moruo's principal negotiating strength and conversely, it accentuated Ngatieu's weakness.

Ngatieu needed to have his livestock herded away from his own mountain farm. Some years previously, he had kept his smaller herd on his farm. As the number of animals doubled, he had made a herding arrangement with his sister's husband so that he could hoe up his small piece of

---

8. In this particular case, there were opportunities for mutually advantageous economic exchange arising from the fact that the two men lived in different ecological areas (mountain slopes and peripheral, lowland plains respectively) in which crops and harvest times differed (Gulliver 1962:437).

pastureland to make a new coffee garden. Later, Ngatieu had quarreled with his brother-in-law and was compelled to remove his animals from the latter's farm. Moruo was his only kinsman who had sufficient pasturage to accommodate additional livestock.[9] The only other alternative was to make a herding arrangement with a nonkinsman, but this was disliked by Arusha because the arrangement was more difficult to monitor and enforce (unsupported by kinship) and nonkin sought higher rewards for their services. Moruo was well aware of Ngatieu's dilemma. During the negotiations, the matter was not explicitly referred to nor did Moruo openly threaten to end the herding arrangement if Ngatieu refused to make concession on the compensation issue. Yet the matter was known and its importance recognized by the participants, and Moruo was able to hint delicately at this. Only if strongly compelled would Ngatieu have removed his livestock and made some other arrangement. This was the crucial factor and it was so obvious that Moruo did not need to emphasize it. It did not give an absolute strength, of course, since there was at least an alternative available to Ngatieu, though a considerably less favorable one. Moreover, by diplomatically not emphasizing Ngatieu's dilemma, Moruo was able to avoid angering Ngatieu further to the point perhaps where, in emotional stress, he might have precipitately withdrawn his animals and so removed Moruo's negotiating advantage.

There was, however, weakness for Moruo in respect to the herding arrangement; that is, Ngatieu had a certain strength also. There were distinct advantages to Moruo also in continuing the herding arrangement—most obviously, the rewards for his services as herdsman and the goodwill as a kinsman. Both parties were aware of this. Ngatieu knew, too, that Moruo was hoping to make similar herding arrangements with other men. Because of this Moruo had concern for his public reputation insofar as an open breach with Ngatieu might prevent or make more difficult (i.e., less advantageous) such further arrangements. There may also have been other considerations (I do not know) regarding his public reputation that helped to induce Moruo to raise his offer and to show willingness to compromise.

In addition, during the negotiations Ngatieu threatened to take the dispute to the local government court should Moruo continue to refuse to pay a larger compensation. Had Ngatieu done this and had the witnesses to

---

9. Ngatieu and his other kinsmen lived on the mountain slopes where population densities were close to or more than 1000 people per square mile. Land was scarce there and farms were small. The new desire, and need, to grow coffee and other intensive cash crops had led to a general decrease, often disappearance, of land reserved for pasturage. The minority of men who had migrated to the peripheral, lowland plains, off the naturally more favored mountain slopes, had larger farms in which larger areas could be retained for pastures. Most of these men herded livestock for mountain-dwelling kinsmen.

Moruo's offense given their undeniable evidence, Moruo would most probably have received a prison sentence. On the other hand, the court did not recognize the Arusha rule about compensation and would have awarded no more than the replacement of the slaughtered animal, and even that was uncertain according to some recent precedents. Moreover, Ngatieu would have gained the most undesirable reputation of forsaking Arusha procedures for dealing with disputes in favor of the court of the disliked, alien, colonial government, at a time when the Arusha people and that government were in radical conflict characterized by a great deal of mutual ignorance and mistrust. This attempt at exercising strength through threat was, therefore, in the opinion of Moruo's party, no more than a bluff. Ngatieu told me later that he had had no intention of going to court. He did not attempt to emphasize the threat and he said that he had only made it in order to express more vividly his exasperation and indignation to Moruo's party. The latter appeared to have received the message correctly and so to have been persuaded not to exacerbate Ngatieu further; therefore he was more inclined to increase the offer of compensation.

One other matter is relevant and was important for Ngatieu. Not only did he desire to continue the herding arrangement but he wished to reinforce it. This he achieved by gaining the consent of Moruo's party to the performance of ritual reconciliation. That consent was, in part, a trade-off against Moruo's payment of a smaller compensation. It was, moreover, difficult for Moruo to refuse to undergo the ritual if he wished to demonstrate his readiness and intention to conform to the normative standards of herdsman and kinsman thereafter. Such ritual was not always performed at the conclusion of negotiations between kinsmen and it carried a muted suggestion that the future behavior of the offender was in some doubt. The ritual not only reaffirmed the bonds of kinship but also alerted supernatural power that, it was believed, would severely punish any further infraction. Probably Moruo believed in the efficacy of this power, at least sufficiently to be wary thereafter. But he was also given warning by all those present that he should behave correctly in the future, so that in the event of another offense his position would be weakened.

This relatively simple dispute case turns out to be rather less simple when analysis is made of the variety and nature of the resources, strengths, and weaknesses involved in the process of moving to an agreed outcome. It remains simple in that the framework of the relevant norms was clear and accepted, but manipulation and reinterpretation was attempted with some degree of success by Moruo's party. These norms did not, however, encompass all the interests of the disputants. In particular, they did not deal with, nor specify appropriate behavior for, the interests that each had in continuing the herding arrangement under the circumstances. Thus other negotiating strengths came to bear on both the application of certain norms and the mode of the continued arrangement.

Therefore, even with so simple a dispute, it is impossible analytically to allocate with any degree of certainty and exactness the relative weights of negotiating strengths, normative and nonnormative. Indeed, it is scarcely possible to disentangle them in terms of their effectiveness in the modification of demands on particular issues within the dispute or in the production of the outcome. There was multiplicity both of strengths and weaknesses and of issues to be negotiated. This means that, in dealing with actual cases of negotiation, we cannot resort to the common theoretical simplification of a single resource for power and a single issue to be resolved. There is the great difficulty that we cannot produce any straightforward equation of the sort that the exercise of such and such a strength (from a resource of potential power) caused a particular change in the demands of the other party. That kind of equation would ignore the dialectical process of interaction in negotiation as well as the real problems of double multiplicity. Moreover, as the foregoing case shows, it seems certain that the parties themselves were not able to make the distinction clearly and that, therefore, they did not altogether try to do so. This being the order of complexity of a relatively simple case, then it must be even greater for a more intricate one—that is, a case in which there are more items in dispute, where norms are unclear or conflicting and their application more contested, and where other resources of potential power and weakness come from a wide variety of factors. In short, all this throws most serious doubts on the notion of power (or strength) as a set of particular causes producing specific effects in the alteration of demands and offers in the real-life context of actual disputes and their negotiation.

To say that is, perhaps, to lay oneself open to accusations of denying the possibility of analysis and, as it were, throwing up one's hands in despair at the complexity of social interaction and behavior. That is not a conclusion that I wish to suggest. Therefore the question arises: What kind of operational scheme can the social scientist adopt that will allow analysis of empirical cases beyond mere description—analysis that may produce improved understanding of what happens, how, and why? The outlines of such an operational scheme are considered in the following section.

NEGOTIATING POWER: AN OPERATIONAL SCHEME

Somehow, an operational scheme of analysis that purports to help explain the causes of convergence upon an outcome of negotiation has to come to terms with the notion of power. However, if power is to be defined as something like the ability of one party to cause another to change behavior in an intended way, then we must take most seriously the objection to the common assumption that the distribution and use of power explains convergence. As we have already seen, it has been rightly pointed out (by Cross and others) that such a notion of power is only knowable in the result, the outcome, rather than in the process. Therefore, that conceptualization of power is not helpful to the explanation of process. Yet the commonsense idea of power as something like a lever, or superior strength, is hard to renounce. One way out of the dilemma is to distinguish between the potential and the actual ability to affect another's behavior. Clearly, a potential to do something is not necessarily an ability to do it successfully, and for several reasons. The two reasons to be emphasized here are, first, that the possessor of the potential may not appreciate it or, if he does, he may nevertheless not attempt to use it; second, in the context of negotiations, the attempt to exercise the potential may be partly or wholly countered by the opponent's exercise of his potential. To illustrate this crudely: The possessor of a big stick has the potential to hit another and subdue him with it. He may decide not to use it, perhaps because he dislikes violence, but, if he does attempt to use it, he may find it unavailing because his opponent has skill in dodging, wears a steel hat, or hits back even harder with a larger stick.

Thus we may start from the various *resources* available to each party in negotiations that afford *potential power*, putting the prime emphasis on the resources that provide a possible basis for action. Next we need to examine the exercise of potential power, the endeavor to translate it into *persuasive strength* in the dynamic context of interaction and interdependence in negotiation. This means, first, that a party must be able to communicate the expected or alleged strength so that the opponent may be able to learn and to adjust. Second, it is to be expected that the attempt to exercise strength is resisted and counteracted to some greater or lesser extent by the opponent's exercise of his own strength. Third, the exercise of strength inevitably carries costs: the expenditure of resources together with whatever costs the opponent may be able to impose. Fourth, the reaction of the opponent and the imposition of costs are likely to induce a reconsideration by the party: for instance, whether to persist, or desist, to modify the approach, or to attempt a different one. Similarly, the opponent too reconsiders and then acts again. There is, unlike most game-theoretical kinds of situation, a dynamic, changing condition rather than once-and-for-all decisions and determinants of power. Eventually, however, some outcome is reached from which the effective distribution of persuasive strength might, perhaps, be deduced. Until that time, there is a process of trial and testing as some, most, or even all of the power potential is translated into attempted strength. In that process, various means are used to exercise strength (e.g., threats, promises), but these themselves are not strength, nor power; they are merely the ways of attempting to use it.

Potential power exists in a wide variety of resources, depending in the particular case on the nature and context of the dispute, the relationships of the disputants with each other and with other people and their position in the society. As suggested previously (page 193), it is neither necessary nor useful to make any primary distinction between resources of a nonnormative kind (economic, physical, political, etc.) and those of a normative kind (rules, standards, values). The dividing line between the two is often unclear; in any case, all resources offer potentials for power that combine, or can be combined, in the actual attempt to exercise persuasive strength against the opponent. "Resources" is, in fact, a loose concept intended to cover anything that, in context, offers potential power in the negotiations. Thus resources range over economic and physical assets of many kinds, the relative status of the disputant and his supporters and their skills and experience, the degree of support that a disputant can recruit and the unity in purpose and policy of the party so formed, the support of influential outsiders concerned with their own interests and values, and normative correctness vis-à-vis the society at large, particular sectors or individuals within it and the opposing party in particular. No useful purpose is served by an attempt to enumerate or classify the full range of possible resources, not only because that range varies a good deal cross-culturally but also because available resources depend so heavily on the context of a particular dispute.

It is, however, useful and pertinent to interpolate and to refer more explicitly to the impact of the enveloping society upon the process of negotiation and on its outcome. Although this most important aspect will not be treated in full detail, I wish to indicate an approach, an orientation, and a mode of analysis in line with the operational scheme being outlined in this section. For the most part in this present study and for quite deliberate purposes of exposition, negotiations have been treated as if they constituted a more or less closed system. This is but an analytical strategy, for it is abundantly clear that the outside world impinges on and in various ways affects the interaction between the parties and the results they achieve. This impingement can most usefully be perceived and analyzed as augmenting, depleting, and modifying the resources available to the disputing parties—that is, their potential power. On the one hand, the parties seek to select from the outside those resources that seem advantageous and supportive to them; on the other hand, they may be subject to some unavoidable influences that affect their potential power and so their strengths and weaknesses. Thus one or both parties may be induced, even compelled, to modify behavior, adjust expectations, and alter demands. Either party may be encouraged to maintain and perhaps to harden his position vis-à-vis the other. That is to say, expectations, preferences, and objectives are established in the outside world or some significant sector of it; indeed, they are at least partly established by that outside world and may be reinforced by it. Moreover, resources that are available to the parties come from the outside world and the means by which they are controlled and used are conditioned by it.

In addition, however, there is frequently some direct interference by particular third parties who seek to influence the course and outcome of negotiations for a variety of reasons related to their own interests and values. Such third parties may reinforce or weaken other resources available to a negotiating party and third parties may interject further resources that counteract those of both disputants. Moreover, there are macrosocietal conditions and trends, such as the state of the economy, political developments, or prevailing ideologies, that create and foster standards and assumptions. The negotiators draw on these, or merely accept them, in setting their own expectations and preferences concerning the issues in dispute and in confrontation with the opponent. These conditions, or the perceptions of them, exert influence through the negotiators' own direct experience of and participation in the society. Such conditions are also mediated by particular individuals who have, or take it upon themselves to have, concern for the negotiators and for the outcome of their negotiations. For instance, it seems clear that the size and strength of wage demands (that is, expectation about perceived outcomes) by a trade union are affected by such conditions as the rate of inflation, business profitabilities, the degree of success of recent trade union action, and the kind of support to be expected from pressure groups on behalf of both the trade union and the employers.

The potential power coming from these external sources depends, of course, on the nature of the dispute and the disputants. To assert categorically, as sometimes is done, that external impingements are the real, effective determinants of a negotiated outcome is surely to prejudge the issues involved, with a macrosociological bias. It has by no means been sufficiently demonstrated to be invariably the case nor has it been adequately shown how these external factors enter into and operate within the negotiation process. It seems preferable to adopt a more cautious approach by which, for particular negotiations, those external factors are considered, first, as resources of potential power to the disputing parties. This will allow examination of the interplay among all relevant resources and their actual effects on the negotiations.

Obviously in some cases, external factors are fundamental and quite unavoidable, in effect leaving the negotiators little more to do than to find agreement on the details of the outcome. Seldom, perhaps never, are external factors altogether unimportant, but quite often negotiators are able to ignore or minimize some of them. Moreover, it is not to be assumed that the enveloping society is simply homogeneous with integrated and consistent interests and values. Therefore, depending on the kinds of issues involved and the status of the disputants, it is most probable that each party can find some resources of potential power, although each is likely to be subject to contraints and imposed weaknesses.

In any case it is often highly difficult and sometimes virtually impossible to distinguish clearly between what might crudely be called external and internal resources and potentialities for power and for constraint and persuasion by one negotiating party against the other. The sources of these potentialities are not altogether discrete. They overlap and interconnect in various degrees and in complex ways. This being so, although certainly we must not neglect the potential impact of the outside world in various forms, we can best treat that impact as part of the totality of resources available to the negotiators rather than as a separate set of factors.

Reverting now to the main operational scheme for the analysis of power, it is most important to note that potential power is not necessarily usable, persuasive strength. Some potential may not be perceived by a party at all, whereas other potential is untapped because of the assessed difficulty and costs of attempting to use it. More or less deliberately, a party attempts to assess his power potential and to weigh it against that of the opponent as it is or becomes known. Resources offer not only potential power but, relative to the opponent, potential weakness. For instance, economic resources offer potential in a number of ways but they may impose liabilities and weaknesses at the same time. The wealthy party may be able, perhaps, to hire specialists' advice, to attract a larger number of supporters, and to make more attractive promises for compliance by the opponent. But he may have to pay more heavily and he may also have much more to lose, more than a poorer party; or, conversely, the opponent may be even wealthier or it may be foreseen that destructive competitiveness might develop. Similarly, a party may have available some alternative opportunity to that which the opponent might be persuaded to offer—a potential resource that is—but that alternative may carry additional or different costs and disadvantages that he seeks to avoid if possible. Thus the alternative opportunity suggests certain weaknesses as well as strengths. This was illustrated in the case of the herdsman's theft: The owner of the animals could have sought another herdsman from among men with available pasturelands. This was a clear possibility, but he was disinclined to take it up because of its perceived, relative disadvantages. Thus the alternative opportunity was, on balance, a source of weakness since those disadvantages were also known to the opponent. Yet its existence did set limits to the demands of the herdsman and was to some extent a source of usable strength. Again, normative correctness may offer potential power but at the same time it may restrict the opportunities for action by the party who invokes it. For instance, a landholder may have the clear normative right to evict a tenant, but this may carry the normative obligation, say, to pay that tenant compensation for improvements made to the property. It is, then, necessary to set the advantages against the costs. It may, of course, be possible to try to exercise the advantage of normative right (to evict the tenant) while avoiding or reducing the normative liability. But that, too, may involve additional costs.

Usable persuasive strengths are, then, a matter of perception and of assessment and both of these vary as the negotiations continue. They have to be used and therefore in effect tested. They are exercised through a variety of means that have been much considered by social scientists: threats, promises, appeals to and claims of normative correctness, the supply of edited information, reference to the interests and values of outside groups and individuals, the offer of trade-offs, the attempt to persuade the opponent of his faulty perceptions of his own best interests, skill in presentation and argument, and so on. These are, however, the means of attempting to exercise usable strength and not, despite much of the literature, power or strength itself. The two must be kept separate in analysis. That is to say, in confronting our fundamental problem of explaining the convergence upon an outcome, an excessive concentration on the means (such as threats and promises) tends to obscure the resources of potential power and usable strengths that are more important. A party may be induced to modify its demands as a result of a threat or promise, or whatever, but the more basic lever is the resources of usable strength that lie behind those means and make them possible.

It is scarcely necessary at this point in the study of negotiation to reiterate the fundamental dynamic of interaction and interdependence between the parties. The point here is that potential power is exercised, tested, reassessed, and exercised again in that interactional context. There is no straightforward exercise of strength that produces a certain effect on the opponent, inducing him to modify his demands in some degree. There is not a linear cause and effect, or stimulus–response process, in any simple fashion. There are convincing general reasons for rejecting that kind of conceptualization, as systems theorists and others have well argued. Briefly, the so-called "effect" or "response" reacts back on the "cause" or "stimulus" such that it becomes virtually impossible to perceive what is cause and what is effect. Instead we should, in general, conceive of a dialectical, processual interaction and relationship between the variable resources in action that initially have potential to induce changes by either party. In particular, in the examination of a specific case, it is essential to look for and appreciate the probings of each party as strengths are put forward, reactions made, reassessments considered and applied. Any attempt at contraint by one party is itself affected by the opponent's interpretation of and reaction to it, by his own input of constraint, and by the changing expectations of both parties. In the event, in action, what appears to be potential power may turn out to be much less efficacious or indeed nugatory if it is resisted by the strength in practice of the opponent, or if the latter, rationally or not, refuses to learn and/or is willing to accept the costs. There is the story of the old lady, confronted by an assailant with a gun, who, so incensed by the affront to her dignity and unaware or disregardful of the danger of being shot, jabs the man with her umbrella and drives him off. His power potential is great and he confidently tries to use it, but the old lady refuses to learn; as it were, she refuses to accept his message, ignores the possible costs, and so wins the contest. She might, however, have lost if the assailant really had used his gun, the potentially powerful resource, or if she had rationally been afraid of it.

Effective persuasive strength eventually emerges through the interaction and becomes evident as parties modify their demands toward convergence. This could, if one so wishes, be presented as a kind of final balance sheet in which relative strengths and weaknesses are totaled to give the end result of the outcome. Such a balance-sheet conception merely offers that notion of power, previously rejected, that is knowable only in the result: "He who wins is more powerful." Similarly, it is necessary to get away from common assumptions that social scientists have made, perhaps under the influence of Weber's notion of *macht* ("imperative control"), by which a person or group is seen as exercising control over certain others so as to produce some intended effect of compliance. That too, at least in the context of negotiation, inclines one to take an end-result viewpoint rather than encouraging an examination of the processes through which the end result is in fact achieved. Negotiations are the interplay of relative strengths as they work, through both antagonism and coordination, toward an outcome. Analysis of specific cases is likely to produce a picture that is somewhat messy and incomplete, certainly less attractively straightforward than the simpler cause–effect, power–submission model. It is most probable that it will often be impossible to relate particular strength with particular effect with any certainty, as in any multiple-factor situation, of course. It is virtually certain that we cannot discover all the answers; for example, did a party properly assess its power potential and adequately convert it into persuasive strength? Did a party modify some demand directly in response to a threat or promise or some other exercise of strength by his opponent?

The conversion of potential power into effective persuasive strength through the negotiator's interaction is an inherent part of the processual models of negotiations. What has been outlined here should be taken in conjunction with those models. Together there is an orientation and some analytical tools with which to approach the closer examination of power in particular empirical cases. It should be possible to sharpen the tools of analysis and obtain improved understanding so as to develop more generalized, theoretical propositions. It is bound to be a slow and halting procedure, for there is a great deal to be done in this kind of approach before more sophisticated theory can emerge with adequate support. It is not a prospect that will appeal to those anxious to get more directly and quickly to definitive and determinate results. One must genuinely sympathize with that view, as expressed for example by Zartman: "If political scientists are ever to do more than add to the large number of studies in political history on individual negotiations, and both understand and explain what goes on beyond the unique event (past or present/future), both theory and analysis need to be further developed [1974:398]." I would add that, whatever may be the condition in political science, anthropologists and sociologists could advantageously enlarge the number of studies of particular negotiations of varying kinds, particularly over an adequate range of sociocultural contexts. It continues to be important to emphasize the persisting need for improved analysis of the cases that are available and to encourage the improved reporting of case materials. The analytical tools suggested here should facilitate this so that we may reach a much stronger position from which we may develop general theory more effectively.

7

MEDIATORS: TRIADIC INTERACTION IN THE NEGOTIATION PROCESS

So far in this study, negotiations have been deliberately described and analyzed as if they occurred between two disputing parties alone. That is the basic and simplest case. In some instances, however, there is intervention and participation by a third party who is not himself a disputant.[1] That is, there may be a mediator in the negotiations who, throughout or in certain phases, acts in some ways to assist in the endeavor to reach an agreed outcome. A mediator has no ability to give a judgment or to make a decision binding on the disputing parties; that is, he is a facilitator but not an adjudicator. This distinction is clear in general and for most real-life cases. There are only a few exceptions. Occasionally mediators virtually take control and make effective decisions; for instance, when the disputants have reached a sustained deadlock, they may be prepared to accept a third party's judgment rather than face failure to find an outcome at all. Sometimes an adjudicator may voluntarily relinquish control and seek only to improve communication between the disputants and to use persuasion. In either case, the change in role may be temporary at some stage in the

---

1. The third party may be a single individual or several persons acting more or less together. For simplicity of exposition, unless otherwise stated, it is assumed that a single person is involved and therefore third-person-singular pronouns are used (cf. page 81).

negotiations, though it can be more permanent. Nevertheless, and despite this important caveat, the two roles and the processes within which they occur—negotiation and adjudication—are analytically distinct, and in actual situations they are effectively different. The distinction was well made by a professional mediator who became chairman of the New York State Mediation Board: "Mediation and arbitration [i.e., adjudication of one kind] have conceptually nothing in common. The one involves helping people to decide for themselves; the other involves helping people by deciding for them [Meyer 1960:164]."[2]

The process of mediation and the roles and strategies of mediators have been rather neglected in studies of negotiation; consequently, there is a good deal of confusion and misapprehension conceptually and analytically. In a review of the topic, with particular reference to Western industrial negotiations, one social scientist wrote,

> One might reasonably assume, in the light of the extensive literature and the considerable amount of practical development of the collective bargaining process that has occurred, that studies of the dynamics of the mediation process would be most plentiful. In actual fact, the exact opposite is true. Mediation is perhaps the least studied subject in the field of industrial relations [Rehmus 1965:118].[3]

Although, since the time that was written, there have been new and important contributions to the subject,[4] mediation still remains a poorly understood process. The most comprehensive study of industrial negotiations to appear in recent years (Walton and McKersie 1965) contains no treatment of mediation. This neglect is not confined to the industrial field, however. Iklé's stimulating study of international negotiations (1964) has rather scanty mention of the topic. Druckman's social psychology symposium (1977), the symposia edited by Swingle (1970), the work of Zartman (1976, 1977), and the analytical work by Bartos (1974) contain little of direct consequence. In general, game theorists appear to ignore the possibility of mediation, and no more than secondary consideration has been given to it by the bargaining theorists in economics. Schelling's influential study

---

2. This and all subsequent quotes cited to Meyer (1960) are quoted with permission from *Industrial and Labor Relations Review* Vol. 13, No. 2 (January 1960). Copyright © 1960 by Cornell University Press. All rights reserved.

3. This and subsequent excerpts cited to Rehmus (1965) are reprinted from "The Mediation of Industrial Conflict: A Note on the Literature," by Charles M. Rehmus, Vol. IX, No. 1 (March 1965) by permission of the Publisher, Sage Publications, Inc.

4. Some of the more recent contributions have been made by Douglas (1955, 1962), Eckhoff (1967), Young (1967, 1972), Walton (1969), Fuller (1971), Simkin (1971), Edmead (1971), Gulliver (1977).

(1960) devotes but two pages to mediation, although there are a few passing references to it elsewhere in his book. On the other hand, some legal writers seem to have assumed that mediation is almost synonymous with negotiation, or at least they have not carefully considered the differences between negotiation with and without mediators (e.g., Fuller 1963, 1971). Others have confused the issue by taking mediation to be something like a form of adjudication where the mediator's award holds good only if accepted by the disputing parties (e.g., Allott *et al.* 1969; cf. Gulliver 1978:49).

In addition, quite strong cultural stereotypes and subjective, dogmatic assumptions have been proffered as fact and analysis. For example, one psychologist has seen the nondirective, impartial catalyst role as being crucial to third-party intervention (Muench 1963). In fact, without careful and detailed examination of mediators' actual roles and behavior, it has frequently been assumed that mediators are or should be merely catalysts or that they are and should be impartial or neutral. Another writer has emphasized that third parties have, or should have, "the objective of changing the relationship between the parties from a destructively competitive win–lose orientation to a cooperative collaborative problem solving orientation [Fisher 1972:81]."

It is clear, however, that the roles and aims of actual mediators are much more varied than these instances indicate and it is important to discover what the range is and why in real-life practice mediators vary in what they intend and do. The problem of doing this is exacerbated because in Western societies there has been a good deal of resistance to the possibility of analyzing and understanding the nature of mediation. Its practitioners in particular seem to have wanted to sustain an intuitive mystique about it. As one American professional put it, the mediator "has no science of navigation, no fund inherited from the experience of others. He is a solitary artist recognizing, at most, a few guiding stars and depending mainly on his personal power of divination [Meyer 1960:160]." Describing Swedish practice, C. C. Schmidt has written, "Each mediator has his own technique and his own methods of conducting negotiations, restricted only by his particular temperament and the circumstances involved [1952:52]."

Douglas (1962:100 ff.) has documented the considerable differences of opinion on issues relating to a mediator's role, strategy, and tactics among professional industrial mediators in the United States. She quoted Cyrus Ching who, as director of the United States federal mediation service reporting to Congress, wrote, "Each mediation problem is unique because the parties and particular issues are always different [p. 109]." Although this statement is, of course, perfectly true in that all social situations are in a sense unique, it ignores general patterns and common variables. It represents a viewpoint, not unjustifiable among practicing professionals, that emphasizes the nuts and bolts rather than the overall structure. For instance, it is obviously important to ask when a mediator should remain silent, and for how long, and when should he interrupt and intervene; yet it is rather less important than some of the professionals think while they are immersed in the details of their jobs. Moreover, their particular concerns seem to have led to an overemphasis on the social psychology of mediation with a neglect for the pattern and processes of negotiation.

These are, of course, culture-bound arguments and polemics. Yet anthropologists, with their intrinsic, cross-cultural concern, have not offered anything much better. They have scarcely looked for, let alone disclosed, the sociocultural range of mediator's roles and strategies or the determinants and implications of third-party intervention. The ghost of the neutral (or impartial or disinterested) mediator tends to haunt the scene, even where that is probably a myth in practice. Alternatively, or sometimes simultaneously, the mediator has been loosely depicted as more or less dictating solutions to the disputing parties, as being some kind of noninstitutionalized adjudicator operating at a low level of social organization and as somehow playing an extraprocessual role prior to adjudication. Careful description and first-level analysis of mediation and of cases of mediators acting within negotiations are quite rare. The most cursory references to mediators occur in the literature—who mediators are, how they come to the role, what they do—so that we do not have adequate data for a variety of cultures and societies.[5]

Finally, in this brief introduction, it is well to note that some confusion may have occurred because the term *mediator* has been used, sometimes quite loosely, in numerous ways. Probably the most common usage outside of the study of negotiations has been with reference to "the more general roles of providing a link between sectors of a society, with functions of innovation of practices and communication and interpretation of ideas [Firth 1965:388]." The term *broker* seems preferable in that context and it has become fairly widely established in anthropological writings. (See, e.g., Mayer 1967; Paine 1971.) There are important differences in the two kinds of role that makes it necessary that the two be kept analytically distinct; yet

---

5. Anthropological neglect is most obviously apparent in the well-known, general works dealing with dispute resolution. For example, apart from his excellent synthesis and reinterpretation of the data on the Ifugao go-between, Hoebel (1954) gave only passing references to mediation and no systematic discussion. As S. F. Moore (1969b:275) has pointed out, "negotiation and bargaining seems to have no place in Bohannan's scheme," and this applies also to mediation (Bohannan 1967: Introduction). The contributors to Nader's symposium (1969a) also ignored the topic (apart from my own essay), and there is no index reference for *mediation* or a near synonym in Pospisil's theoretical study (1971).

both the similarities and differences would, no doubt, yield fruitful comparison.

In this chapter, I examine the statuses, roles, and strategies of mediators and the processes of mediation within the framework of the general theory of negotiation that has been presented in the preceding chapters of this book. I maintain, however, that instead of examining mediation as a separate, autonomous topic, as some writers have done, it is essential to consider it as an integrated part of negotiation. As Stevens has stated,

> an analysis of mediation is not possible except in the context of a general analysis of bargaining negotiations. That is, unless the investigator has some theories about the agreement process in negotiations, about why and in what ways the parties do (or do not) reach agreement, it is difficult to see how he can analyse the contribution of the mediator to the resolution of conflict [1963:123].

My approach is largely that suggested by Schelling when he wrote that a mediator "is probably best viewed as an element in the communication arrangements or as a third party with a payoff structure of his own who is given an influential role through his control over communication [1960:44]." In taking this approach, it is necessary to recognize that the degree of control over communication can vary quite considerably from case to case and to emphasize that the mediator very often introduces interest, values, and perceptions of his own that are not altogether coincident with those of either disputing party.

TRIADIC INTERACTION AND THE STATUS OF THE MEDIATOR

The intervention of a mediator turns the initial dyad of a dispute into a triadic interaction of some kind. The disputing parties retain their ability to decide whether or not to agree to and accept proposals for an outcome, irrespective of the source of the proposals. Yet clearly the mediator exercises influence in some degree, whether he remains largely passive or virtually controls the exchange of information and the learning process. He himself interacts with each party and with both together, and they may communicate to and through him. He becomes a party in the negotiations. He becomes a negotiator and as such, he inevitably brings with him, deliberately or not, certain ideas, knowledge, and assumptions, as well as certain interests and concerns of his own and those of other people whom he represents. Therefore he is not, and cannot be, neutral and merely a catalyst. He not only affects the interaction but, at least in part, seeks and encourages an outcome that is tolerable to him in terms of his own ideas and interests. He may even come into conflict with one or both of the parties.

What a mediator can do, what he chooses to do, and what he is permitted to do by the disputing parties are all much affected by who he is in the particular context and why he is there at all. His relationship to the parties and to the issues in dispute and his position in the enveloping community are crucial variables in the triad. Some of the more common and generally significant statuses of mediators are briefly described subsequently. Concrete actuality may be more complex and less specific than the apparent clarity of the analytical types depicted. Therefore, they are not proposed as a watertight set of categories, nor are they altogether mutually exclusive. Rather, the intention is to emphasize particular characteristics that have a significant bearing on a mediator's participation. Some casual references are made to ethnographic examples for purposes of illustration.

The status of the mediator can initially be examined according to whether he is supposedly disinterested or acknowledged to be an interested party. By *disinterested* (or, alternatively, impartial) is meant that a mediator is not directly related to either disputing party and his own interests are not directly touched by the dispute or by possible outcomes. A disinterested status may derive from an institutionalized role in a society, such as the Nuer leopard-skin chief, a Pathan saint, or a professional agent of an established board of mediation or conciliation, as in some American states. Part of the person's role is an obligation and readiness to act as mediator as a result of his social and cultural distinction from disputants, their supporters, and interests.[6] Alternatively, the disinterested status may derive from the context of the dispute and therefore, in a sense, it may be casual and transitory. Disputants may choose or be willing to accept someone of acknowledged prestige or ability who is not directly concerned with the issues and the potential outcome. He might be a distinguished elder, a socially eminent person, or one of recognized sagacity.[7] The choice might, however, be some person who stands outside the structure of the society in some way—the "stranger" (Gluckman 1965:101) whose interests are separate from the principal groups, categories, and relationships that con-

---

6. Bailey has shown that the minimal definition of a Pathan (Pakistan) saint entails the characteristics of being learned in Islamic law, having mystical power, and not being the tenant of a chief (Bailey 1972:32). One might say that a saint stands outside of the basic power struggles and alliances of Swat Pathan society and is also above them, though that is something of a simplification.

7. For example, the "prestige-mediators," *kong-chhing*, among the Singapore Chinese (Freeman 1957:179–180), the Ifugao big man of *kadangyang* rank (Barton 1919), or the Iranian bazaar mediators, *kadkhodamanesh* (G. Thaiss, personal information).

stitute the community. Such a person has little or no extrinsic prestige or influence and by definition he is supposedly disinterested in the outcome. Moreover, he can perhaps be blamed by the parties for any disadvantages contained in the outcome. A fourth kind of avowedly disinterested mediator is the expert who can bring some sort of special knowledge and training to the negotiations: a lawyer, a technical specialist, a priest, or a genealogical expert.

In constrast, mediators may be quite clearly interested parties when their own interests make them concerned with the resolution of particular issues in dispute and with the disputants themselves. For example, the man who holds land adjacent to some disputed farmland may wish to know who his neighbor is to be, and with some urgency. He may have to coordinate with him over mutual access paths or a common irrigation channel. A tenant may wish to know to whom he should pay rent and from whom he can claim certain rights. Uncertainty can be disadvantageous or even downright harmful, so that such a person wants an early outcome so that he can get on with his own activities. He may not care much, if at all, what the outcome is so long as there is one; therefore he is acceptable as a mediator. Similarly, in international affairs, a country that might be affected if its neighbors were to go to war over their dispute might therefore act as mediator in order to prevent hostilities dangerous to it.

It can happen that a third party is not only interested in encouraging the resolution of a dispute but he is positively partial to one of the parties. Despite or even because of his known partiality, he may be acceptable as a mediator, though this may be as a last resort when negotiations appear to be heading for a breakdown or when it proves necessary to get them going at all. Elsewhere I have described an Ndendeuli case with a partial mediator and a comparable case has been recorded in a Jordanian Arab village.[8] Sometimes such a mediator emerges from among the members of one of the disputing parties as he perceives possibilities and needs for compromise that his principal is not yet willing to accept. He does not renounce his partiality altogether, but he is able to exert control over the communication and bargaining.[9] An interesting example of obvious partiality comes from San Francisco. There the Labor Council and its Executive Committee—an association of local trade unions and clearly a pro-labor body—was able successfully to act as mediator of last resort when industrial negotiations were nearing breakdown and a strike was threatened. This intervention

8. For the Ndendeuli case, see Gulliver (1971:145 ff., especially p. 148); for the Jordanian case, see Antoun (1972:78 ff.).

9. An example is given in the Ndendeuil Case 4 (Gulliver 1971:163 ff.).

was institutionalized in practice with the approval of the local employers (Liebes 1958:798–799). Sometimes anyone is better than no one at all.

Another type of mediator may emerge in situations where the two disputing parties are involved in some network of relations so that there are people who are structurally intermediate between them; that is, more or less equally linked to both. For instance, there is the man who is kinsman to both, or a political or economic ally of both, or a member of a lineage collateral with the lineages of the disputants.[10] The rationale here is that, being connected to both parties, such persons have divided loyalties and obligations and may therefore be tolerably acceptable to both. From the individual's point of view, he agrees to mediate because his interests are likely to be affected by the dispute and he seeks to protect them. He wishes to maintain his advantageous relations with both parties, and also with others in the same network, but this he finds difficult so long as they are in unresolved conflict. He therefore seeks to encourage and facilitate active negotiations and a speedy conclusion to the dispute. He also desires an outcome that damages as little as possible his own interests and his valued association with each disputant. But he may seize the opportunity to try to gain credit, prestige, and leadership and to improve his status with the parties.

However, the mediator can be in some sense a representative of a community to which both disputing parties belong: lineage, village, association, political or religious group. In that case, he is most likely to be a person of prestige, even a recognized leader, in that community, such as a member of the upper class or the headman in a traditional Chinese village (Cohen 1967). He may be a local politician, an administrative officer, a police officer, a lineage head. He acts as mediator in order to assist his fellow members of the community but also in order to influence and pressure them so as to restore peace and adequate working relations. He may take the opportunity to impress, both on the disputants and other members, the moral norms of the community and its common interests and needs. Although he can be helpful to the disputants, he commonly has the interests of the community, and perhaps his own particular interests in it, very much in mind. He may well be inclined to put those before the interests of the two parties. For instance, a quick settlement is often sought by such a mediator in the interests of the group or of its leading members. This can be at the expense of one or both parties if speed is given preference over a more genuine resolution of some important dispute. Apart from such intention, the mediator can take the opportunity to seek prestige or public attention by his efforts. He can use his temporary role to win advan-

---

10. For example, the Lebanese *waasta*, as described by Ayoub (1965:13).

tage and reputation as against his competitors for influence in the group, as Ndendeuli big men sometimes did (Gulliver 1971:187). There may be the opportunity to gain the indebtedness of one or both parties as a result of his services. In all this, the parties do not necessarily suffer. Often, however, their interests and preferences are in some way distorted or disregarded, depending on the strength of the mediator's influence and manipulation and his own perceived interests at the time. Indeed, it might be that such a mediator chooses a divide-and-rule strategy. He could attempt to lead the disputants to an outcome that leaves the dispute essentially unsettled, thus weakening their relations with each other, dissipating their resources and enhancing his position, or that of his subgroup, within the community.

One way or another, then, it is highly probable that a person can and does gain advantages from taking the role of mediator. I suspect that the truly disinterested, impartial mediator is in fact rather rare. He may perhaps be quite impartial toward the two parties but be quite partial toward his own interests, sometimes at the expense of one or both disputants. We should maintain a healthy cynicism here and inquire what is in it for the man in the middle. Even the professional mediator who claims impartiality likes to gain a reputation for his ability and success as that is judged by his superiors; he may get an increase in salary, a promotion, or more interesting cases in the future. It seems evident that a Pathan saint, the conventional mediator between chiefs in Swat society in Pakistan, could gain prestige, land, and followers as the result of his successful mediation. An Ifugao go-between in the Philippines, and probably a Nuer leopard-skin chief, could acquire wealth and supporters in much the same way.[11] Structural intermediaries, such as the kinsman of both parties, have obvious interests to protect and foster.

It strains credulity unnecessarily to believe that these kinds of interests and rewards do not affect the potential manipulations that are available to mediators, whatever their status, in the exchange of information and the learning–adjustment process in negotiations. The strong, Western, cultural stereotype and moral notion of the purely impartial mediator is neither invariably correct in practice in our own society nor valid cross-culturally.

---

11. On Swat Pathan saints, see Barth (1959) and Bailey (1972:28 ff.). Bailey has suggested that some saints may have gained such high rewards from mediation that they themselves could have become like chiefs, possibly losing their ability to continue as acceptable mediators. On the Ifugao, Barton wrote, "It is greatly to the interests of the monkalun [go-between] to arrange a peaceful settlement, not only because he usually receives a somewhat larger fee in such cases, but because the peaceful settlement of cases in which he is a mediator builds up a reputation for him, so that he is frequently called and so can earn many fees [Barton 1969:88–89]." On the Nuer leopard-skin chief, see Evans Pritchard (1940:163 ff.) and Howell (1954:passim). The Nuer data are most unsatisfactory and have been used in contradictory analyses (Greuel 1971; Haight 1972).

Yet these presuppositions seem to have given an idealistic, ethnocentric bias to social scientists' accounts of mediation. It is more correct to assume that the supposedly impartial mediator is probably seeking some degree of advantage beyond that of the disputing parties, and we need to take account of this in seeking to understand the significance of mediation and triadic interaction. Thus, it is necessary to inquire what, if any, are the additional interests involved and how they affect the mediator's intervention and the outcome of negotiations. The mediator may be on the side of the angels, exercising his manipulative influence for the greater good of the community or on behalf of the wronged or the weaker party, or he may be much, even primarily, concerned with his own interests. Either way his assessment of the situation and his choice of strategy and tactics will be affected and may significantly alter the process of negotiation and its outcome.

Some mediators are, no doubt, as impartial as is possible and strive to maintain that attitude throughout. Yet so many mediators in so many contexts are effectively interested parties. In fact, as I have indicated, their suitability and acceptability for the role are often overtly founded on recognition of that. Disputants may hope to gain the benefits of the mediator's facilitation without surrendering much if anything to his perceived interests. They may be more or less successful in this. Often they are not, however, and often they are aware that they are not and cannot be altogether successful. But it can still be thought worthwhile by a disputant to accept this as an additional cost of the negotiations if the mediator's intervention is considered helpful in an otherwise threatening situation. Sometimes there may be little choice in the matter when it is exceedingly difficult to refuse the intervention of a mutually linked third party or a representative of the common group. Of course, if the mediator is expected to be partial to one of the parties, then that party probably welcomes his participation.

The important point is that in examining mediation we need to take full account of the mediator's interests. This means that we have to consider three—not merely two—sets of interests, preferences, learning, strategies, and action choices in a triadic structure. The manipulation opportunities available to a mediator can be considerable, just as each party has such opportunities vis-à-vis his opponent. Each party similarly may seek to manipulate the mediator, for he too can be induced to act in ways thought to be advantageous to a disputant.

For example, one strategy of a disputant is to accept the intervention of a mediator in the expectation of persuading him of the validity and strength of one's own demands or of the reality of one's commitment to a stand in order to gain his influence upon the opponent. The mediator may become, perhaps unwittingly, a kind of ally. Another strategy is sometimes adopted by a party who foresees the inevitability of giving way in large part to the opponent's demands. By agreeing to mediation he may be able to put the blame on the mediator, using him as a scapegoat. Thus a Nuer man could claim that he would have used his weapons aggressively, as the ideal Nuer should, but that out of deference to the prestige and sanctity of the leopard-skin chief he reluctantly accepted a peaceful, mediated settlement, though he and everyone else may have been wanting that anyway. In other words, the presence of a mediator offers a way to save face or a way to make concessions without too obviously appearing to show weakness. As an American mediator explained, the parties may lock themselves into a position where "they can't retreat and they do not themselves wish to fight." The mediator may then be blamed for the necessary reduction of demands or the breaking of earlier commitment. A negotiating team representing a larger constituency (such as trade union or lineage leaders vis-à-vis their co-members) may wish to demonstrate to its constituency, and perhaps to a wider public, that the mediator forced it to give way. Alternatively, the aim may be to show that the mediator could obtain no better terms than the team itself could, so exonerating it from failure to gain its full demands. In these kinds of circumstances, the mediator is being used, with or without his knowledge and consent.

ROLES AND STRATEGIES OF MEDIATORS

If a mediator participates in negotiations, he must operate within the processes of communication and learning and the developmental pattern of overlapping phases that have been described previously. What he can do and how, and the strategies he adopts, are affected by those processes and must be reasonably congruent with them if he is to be effective. For instance, it can be useless or even harmful if he seeks to emphasize the narrowing of differences during the phase when the parties are concerned with expressing the extent of their differences. Rather he should assist them in that concern so that in due course they may move on purposefully to the next phase. In general terms, a mediator, whatever his status and strategy, facilitates and to some degree influences, even controls, the exchange of information, the concomitant learning, and the consequent readjustment of perception, preferences, and choices. He can, therefore, affect the flow of information both in quantity and content. He can also attempt to deal with problems of conflicting information and discrepant perception and perhaps with overabundant information that, by its bulk and complexity, adds to the difficulties of deciding preferences and of dealing with multiple, incommensurable criteria.

A general proposition is that a mediator is most needed and most useful during the transition from one phase of negotiations to another, or during transition back to an earlier phase. At these times the disputants are necessarily involved in substantial shifts of attitude, expectations, aims, focus, and the kinds of information exchanged. These shifts can be gradually achieved as a function of learning, but often the parties find real difficulties in reorienting and adjusting their interaction so that the negotiations run into frustrating deadlock. Of particular difficulty is the transition from the phase of emphasizing differences and exploring the outside limits of demands (Phase 3) to the phase of narrowing differences and emphasizing agreements (Phase 4). That is a shift from opposition, mistrust, and perhaps hostility to coordination, some degree of trust, and even cooperation. It is the principal watershed in the whole process of negotation, although all transitions are intrinsically problematic for the negotiators.

That general proposition is not intended to deny the obvious fact that mediators do operate and can be effective during a single phase. Information exchange can bog down in sterile repetitiveness, interpersonal relations between particular negotiators may interfere adversely, and misunderstandings may grow from faulty signals and inadequate interpretations. Sometimes one or both parties play to the gallery rather than dealing with each other or they may become overinvolved in intrateam problems. A mediator may enter the negotiations more or less from the start and so be available during all the phases. Where that is the case, it is likely and probably most effective that he varies his strategy in accordance with possibilities and requirements.

It is necessary to avoid an assumption of *the* role of *the* mediator, whether in description or prescription. Dogmatic assertions of that kind, unfortunately not uncommon, are misleading and stultify careful analysis. Empirically and logically the roles and strategies of mediators vary widely. Cultural precepts bar or hinder some strategies and enjoin others. Negotiators request or tolerate some but not others. Mediators differ in status, accorded prestige, and influence and in their skills. The sociocultural and situational context of particular disputes and their negotiations, as well as the nature of particular phases, affect the possibilities open to a mediator.

For the purposes of exposition and clarification, mediators' roles can conveniently be described on a continuum representing the range of strengths of intervention. This continuum runs something like this: from virtual passivity, to "chairman," to "enunciator," to "prompter," to "leader," to virtual arbitrator. These terms are not proposed as principally typological but rather as useful indices along that continuum: Actual roles and associated strategies can be displayed as more or less resembling, more or less near to, one or other of these indices. This, of course, states nothing about the effectiveness of the strategies. In the following brief survey some examples are given as illustrations. Comprehensiveness is not possible and would in any case be excessively tedious. Rather, the intention is to indicate something of the range of strategic roles of mediators.

By his very presence, a quite *passive mediator* can encourage more positive communication and interaction between the parties, stimulating the continuation or the renewal of the exchange of information:

> A wise mediator once said that the mere presence of an outsider in collective bargaining negotiations, regardless of anything he says or does, brings about a change in the behavior of the parties at the bargaining table. This is true enough, and where the parties are hopelessly deadlocked any change in behavior is presumably for the better [Rehmus 1965:118].

Because he is there, the parties are often constrained to observe minimal courtesy to each other, to reduce personal invective, and to listen and respond with some relevance. A party may feel it necessary to explain and justify his case, directly or indirectly, to the mediator because he is there at all or perhaps because he is perceived in some sense as a "generalized other [G. H. Mead]." Thus the parties restate their arguments, perhaps rethinking them, and they may find the opportunity of starting or restarting to learn.

Deliberate passivity has been an effective strategy on occasion, for example, for some American industrial mediators. They attend a meeting between the two parties, sit and say nothing and seek to show no particular reaction to what is said and done. One mediator related that he silently made volumnious notes on the proceedings while offering no comments whatever (Peters 1958:767; see also Douglas 1962:101). Another has told how he chain smoked, slumped in his chair, with his eyes carefully kept away from the negotiators. I have witnessed a similar performance by an Ndendeuli mediator, although in that instance passivity seemed to come from a disinclination to become involved and committed rather than from a deliberate strategy to encourage more positive interaction between the parties. Yet the effect was much the same. Deliberately or not, the strategy can be effective when an impassse arises because positive information is not being exchanged nor evident possibilities explored as a result. One major reason for each impasse is interpersonal hostility between members of the two parties, accompanied perhaps by an intentional policy of ad hominem abuse. Sometimes a party attempts to frustrate negotiations by such behavior and by refusal to give information and engage in exchange. The mediator's presence may prevent continuation of these kinds of actions.

However, a mediator is not always a free agent who is able to choose his own strategy; he can be more or less forced into some line of action by the disputing parties. Thus passivity may be partly the result of the parties effectively denying the mediator active participation. This occurs, for instance, where the mediator has been thrust upon them and they seek to ignore him in their intensive preoccupation with each other or perhaps in collusion to reject third-party interference. Yet even in such cases, the mediator's presence can still result in some change in the parties' interaction. Indeed, such collusion or the recognition of at least some common interest may provide a new starting point.

A more active participation by a mediator produces a role something like that of *chairman*. That is, in addition to the possible influence of his mere presence, he keeps order and tends to direct procedure. His actions are tolerated and accepted because he can give suggestions for order and coherence that engender coordination. At a minimum, this may help to prevent a threatening breakdown of communication and movement. Schelling has illustrated this vividly:

> When there is no apparent focal point for agreement . . . [a mediator] can create one by his own power to make a dramatic suggestion. The bystander who jumps into an intersection and begins to direct traffic at an impromptu traffic jam is conceded the power to discriminate among cars by being able to offer a sufficient increase in efficiency to benefit even the cars most discriminated against; his directions have only the power of suggestion, but coordination requires the common acceptance of some source of suggestion [Schelling 1960:144].

An additional implication here is that the mediator who is once accepted and found useful as coordinator may be more readily acceptable thereafter when further difficulties arise. He has shown his value and may be more trusted and listened to.

The chairman role can be extended beyond this. The mediator may announce and reiterate points of agreement, giving emphasis to them: for example, agreement by the parties to ignore an issue or to define it in a certain way or to settle it and remove it from further contention. More positively, the mediator may make procedural suggestions: to settle the immediate or overall agenda, to have separate caucus meetings for each party or a conclave between principals, to introduce new evidence or witnesses. He may actually take over procedural organization such as arranging the time and place of further meetings, calling for breaks in a particular session or curbing excessive interruptions, irrelevancies, and repetitiveness. He may suggest new or renewed concentration of focus where information and attention have become diffused or where there are problems of overabundant information.

In all this, the mediator may continue to be impartial to either party, seeking only to improve coordination of exchange. But this kind of strategy offers opportunities to influence the direction of negotiations and to favor one party, or to push toward the quickest outcome available more or less irrespective of merits. There are distinct possibilities for manipulation. A party may be unaware of what is being done or he may feel constrained, even relieved, to accept it rather than face deadlock or extended argument of indeterminate result.

A mediator goes beyond the role of keeping order and facilitating procedure—perhaps ignoring that kind of action—when he acts as *enunciator* of rules and norms relevant to issues in negotiation. This can take the form of clarification and emphasis of general rules and norms or the identification of particular ones relevant to the context. The intention is to remind the parties of what they have temporarily forgotten or neglected, which might provide a basis from which to move toward agreement. It reminds the parties, too, of the moral community to which both belong; and it articulates what may have been left unclear and obstructive between the parties. For example, in an Arusha inheritance dispute, a senior co-member of the disputants' lineage stated at successive times during the negotiations: "We are all one lineage with one ancestor," "Brothers should not quarrel," "Property should be shared equally," "Unmarried men have more need of cattle than those who have married," and "Irrigated land is more valuable than other land but not twice as valuable."

The choice of norms, the particular juncture when they are expressed, the way this is done and kind of emphasis given must—often quite purposefully—affect the learning process. It may be done impartially or at least with that intent, or it may be deliberately partial and manipulative. Enunciation directs and interprets the information exchanged, influencing the perceptions, preferences, and demands of the parties and implying certain lines of coordination and agreement. The parties are not bound to accept the norms so propounded nor to adjust their expectations and demands accordingly. Yet the party who has been denying some rule is likely to be put at a disadvantage when the mediator in effect supports his opponent. In any case, the parties may welcome the clarification of some rule that offers some prospect of progress.

Sometimes a mediator is expected to act as enunciator: the respected elder, the ritual expert, the lawyer. In a sense he represents the wider community and the rules it embraces. He is mediator because he has special expertise and prestige. He is not, as such, making judgments for he still leaves it—as he has to—to the two parties to follow up the implications of the norms and their mode of application to the particular circumstances of the dispute. Of course, some of the issues in dispute may be scarcely susceptible to normative assessment: for instance, the level of wages, the degree of respect owed to a person, the division of blame between husband and wife, the weight of allegedly extenuating circumstances. On the other hand, even if the enunciated norms are fairly specific, the parties still have to reach an agreed outcome. Moreover, a party may deny the validity of the specified rule or he may intend to ignore it. Thus, enunciation of norms and rules may be sign posting, offering possibilities to the parties, or it may be more manipulative than that as a mediator carefully emphasizes certain directions and ignores others. He may favor one of the parties in this manner but he does not dictate. His role is limited. At most he is concerned with assisting in establishing some rules of the game within which the parties can seek some actual outcome.

In the role of *prompter*, a mediator makes a more positive contribution, although his suggestions remain tentative and limited. He does not seek to insist on his opinions, at least not overtly, nor to take control of the negotiations. Rather, he attempts to clarify information and interpretation and to encourage coordination between the parties. For example, the mediator as prompter asks for a restatement of a party's argument or of particular demands and requests further information in support of them. He might himself restate an argument so as to bring out the principal points in order to obtain reaction. Typical prompter's statements are "Am I right in saying that your position is thus and thus?" "As I understand it, you are saying this and this." He may realize that one party just does not apprehend the meaning or significance of what the other party is saying and so he attempts an interpretation. He persuades a party to respond directly to the opponent's points, trying tactfully to stem irrelevancies and to dissipate smoke screens. He seeks to encourage the parties to talk about the same thing at the same time, to follow a relevant pattern of exchange. He attempts to gain and maintain focus on what he perceives to be the chief priorities of each party so that each can be clearer about what these are and their implications for himself and his opponent. The prompter may in this way be able to discover and help reveal a viable range for some issues within which both parties would be prepared to settle. Such a viable range is often obscured by bluffing demands and denials, by inflated expectations and by the reasonable unwillingness of a party to commit himself immediately to something that he would, in the end, prefer rather than get nothing at all. Arguments can become so diffuse that concentration and perspective may have been lost. In any case, where the variety of issues, or the range for particular issues, is wide, the mediator's careful questioning and suggestions may produce some acceptable and useful focal point around which further exchange can concentrate. This suggestion of a focal point, or an area of salience, may be particularly valuable where there are no accepted standards for assessing the range—say, of honor—and when items are incommensurable—say, chalk and cheese (cf. Iklé 1964:213). The prompter may be able to suggest packages of issues to be considered together where trading among them seems feasible.

The strategy of the prompter is probably most effective at the beginning of Phase 4 of negotiations, when differences are being narrowed and coordination developed, and in Phase 5, the preliminaries to final bargaining. Parties can find themselves in set positions from which it is difficult to emerge in order to make concessions to the opponent. They may be arguing past each other. They may be genuinely unable to see where there is common ground or how to proceed at all. False fronts may have been so thoroughly developed as the result of the earlier tactics that the parties have become affected by their own extreme positions and bluffs, to the point of losing perspective about their expectations. They deceive, or at least influence, themselves, as well as each other by their own rhetoric. The prompting mediator may be able to cut through the undergrowth or to indicate to the parties how this can be done. He does this not so much by offering his opinion as by orienting the parties' attention and efforts so that coordination becomes possible.

In the role of *leader*, a mediator more or less directly injects his own opinions and recommendations. He offers evaluation of the information from, and the preferences and demands of, either party. He may be able to suggest or endorse the basis for agreement on an issue or propose a package deal. Sometimes these are suggestions that the mediator believes a party would like to make, or at least have discussed, but the party himself fears to raise these suggestions lest they seem to indicate weakness or too great a readiness to concede, or because the implications are unclear. Thus a party may be relieved that the mediator says what he himself cannot. Coming from the mediator (even perhaps at the private instigation of the party) such a suggestion can be ignored or repudiated should it seem threatening as a result of the opponent's reaction to it. The party is not committed by the mediator's suggestion, as he might be were he to make it himself, but he can take advantage of it should that appear advantageous. An American mediator has called this "trying on for size" (Simkin 1971).

However, a leader is not limited to suggesting what is already a possibility in the mind of a negotiator. The parties may not be able to see where and how they can shift. They may overestimate the costs of concession or they may be unprepared to consider the implications raised. Here the mediator can try to force the issues that the parties avoid. Whether and how far the parties are willing or can be persuaded to follow the leader's suggestions are in part dependent on how far they feel unable to move otherwise, how far they tacitly welcome his initiative, and the degree of influence the mediator carries. Where the costs of continued negotiations are high and the disadvantages of persisting disagreement are intolerable—that is, where some outcome is on the whole better than nothing—the mediator's leadership is likely, sooner to later, to be strong and perhaps decisive. This is particularly the case where the disputants are in something like a bilateral monopoly relationship: close kin, sedentary neighbors, employer and employees. The compulsion to reach an outcome is marked insofar as the continued relationship is important and unavoidable to both. If that relationship is involved with other mutual interests—such as both parties being members of the same group or network sector—the felt need for an outcome is correspondingly greater. The mediator's leadership is probably enhanced if he is a co-member of the same social unit.

For example, in an Ndendeuli case, a man sought the return of his wife and child from her father's hamlet where, it was alleged, she had begun a liaison with another man. The father-in-law denied knowledge of, or complicity in, a liaison but he demanded payment of further bridewealth by the husband and a promise of future good treatment of his daughter should she return. The husband denied liabilitiy for bridewealth and rejected the implications of his past mistreatment of the woman. Although some associated minor issues had been disposed of during the phase of narrowing the differences, the two disputants and their supporters became stuck in the repetition of their conflicting demands and seemed in danger of returning to open antagonism. The mediator (co-neighbor and kinsman of both disputants) then suggested that the son-in-law should pay additional bridewealth, and the father-in-law should admit to harboring the wife and not acting vigorously enough in preventing a liaison. Such an admission carried an obligation to pay compensation to the husband. The son-in-law agreed to this but his father-in-law refused the package proposal. The mediator and the son-in-law virtually ignored that refusal as the mediator directed attention and discussion to the question of bridewealth payment. He gave his opinion that the size of the payment should be rather less than the father-in-law had demanded. He said that he favored approximately what had been claimed by the father-in-law, less the amount of compensation due the son-in-law. Without much difficulty he headed off any further discussion of the supposed liaison, leaving the parties to discuss the details of a fairly small bridewealth payment and the return of the wife.

In considering the range of possibilities for a mediator's role, it is important to reiterate that the third party does not necessarily, nor even usually, adopt a single role and strategy and then stick to it throughout the negotiations. Most commonly, he changes his strategy to fit the changing circumstances and requirements of both the disputants and himself. A dominating person as mediator might attempt to lead throughout, but the parties may frustrate his initiatives when they think he is pushing too hard and is ignoring their wishes and needs. He may be compelled to change strategy, even to retire altogether, while the parties work their way through a phase of interaction or as they examine together the consequences of the mediator's earlier suggestions.

Leadership is most usually needed, most tolerated, and most influential in transitional periods (change of phase, overlapping phases), in the phase of narrowing differences where stalemate is a growing danger, and in the phase of final bargaining over the obdurate issues. In general, these are times when the parties meet the greatest difficulties and therefore may be willing to accept positive and direct suggestions. At other times, a mediator chooses, or is compelled, to lapse into passivity or to act as chairman. Later again the mediator might emerge as enunciator or prompter or he might resume as leader, as that seems possible, acceptable, and potentially effective. Thus there is not only a range of mediational strategies but, in a particular case, mediators may and frequently do vary their strategies as negotiations proceed.

It should be emphasized that these different strategies are sometimes less easily and clearly distinguishable in practice than analytical exposition might suggest. To reiterate: They are proffered as indices along a continuum representing varying strengths of intervention and associated tactics and manipulative potentials.

A special case occurs when the mediator acts as *go-between*, with the parties physically separated and not in direct communication. A go-between may be no more than a straight messenger, although this tends to be unlikely because of his obvious opportunities to control and add to or detract from the information he carries. In conveying messages to and fro, he can change their content, emphasis, and strength. He can usually add his own interpretation, with or without informing the recipient. He can add new messages and he can offer his opinion. Each party is highly dependent on him and often has little means of knowing just how far the go-between is manipulating the information. A go-between may be passive, a chairman, or an enunciator, but he tends to become a prompter or leader, especially if negotiations are going poorly or if, for his own reasons, he wishes deliberately to affect the outcome.

The classic anthropological examples are the Philippine Ifugao *monkalun*[12] and the go-betweens in premarital negotiations in many societies. A similar situation is created in any negotiations when a mediator can arrange to isolate the parties temporarily for separate caucus meetings while

---

12. See Barton (1919, 1930:50–53) and Hoebel (1954:114 ff.). The leadership of the *monkalun* is evident in the only detailed case given by Barton (1930:65 ff.; see this book, page 30), though it is uncertain whether that is a record of an actual case or Barton's fictional construction based on his experiences.

he moves from one to the other. This may be done to stop mounting aggression and futile, frustrating confrontation.[13] The mediator, using one or another of the strategies, may be able to induce either party to reconsider his position, expectations, demands, and tactics. A party may be willing to be more frank with him, and he with them, in the absence of the opponent. He may be able, with or without approval and consent, to suggest fresh demands or offers of one party to the other. He may acquire an improved understanding of each party's real, anticipated minimal requirement and so perceive if there is a viable range within which both would settle. He may be able to discover or engineer a point of agreement that neither party had hitherto foreseen.

An example has been given by Peters (1958:765, 768) where the wage level was the obdurate issue in an industrial negotiation. Management had stuck at a 5-cent increase but the union persisted in demanding 25 cents, with a strike deadline a few hours away. In caucus the union party confidentially admitted to a 12-cent minimum. Then, separately with the manager of the business, Peters advised him to make a final best offer. This turned out to be 15 cents. Agreement was assured where before it had seemed most unlikely.

THE RATIONALE OF MEDIATION

The reasons for the appearance and participation of a mediator have already been suggested. They can be conveniently summarized before going on to consider why mediators do not invariably appear in negotiations.

In some societies a mediator is regularly imposed on the disputing parties by the community, through its leaders or by others who feel constrained to intervene, on the grounds that all disputes between members potentially or actively affect other members. Disputants than have no right to complete self-sufficiency even though adjudication of their conflict is not imposed. The more highly integrated the community, the greater the compulsion, morally and materially, for intervention. Such is the case, for example, in Moslem villages of the Middle East or in traditional Chinese villages (Cohen 1967:71). The parties have little or no choice, though they may be glad to have the expected assistance.

Elsewhere, and probably more commonly, mediators are available and the disputants are encourage but not compelled to accept them.[14] In any

---

13. A case example of such a strategy is given by Douglas (1962:22–23).

14. In the United States and Canada, governmental agencies have professional mediators available. These agencies or political leaders may urge the parties to agree to mediation but there is no authority to compel this.

case, the disputants themselves may agree to invite a mediator for the help he may give. A threatened deadlock may endanger the prospects of an outcome where neither party wishes this to happen. The need for assistance is recognized and the mediator may be able to find a way out. Where concessions are unavoidable, he can be made a scapegoat or a face-saver. He can be used to demonstrate that a party has indeed done all that is possible in the circumstances. Either party may hope to gain the mediator as an ally.

In other situations, the parties are sometimes prepared to tolerate the intervention of a third party whose interests are manifestly involved in the dispute and its outcome, where that party takes the initiative and seeks participation. This is a matter of recognizing his legitimate concern and the importance of his relations with the disputants.

In actual cases, there is often some combination of these reasons. The mediator can be welcomed and used, or tolerated and largely ignored. Explanations for the presence of a mediator are not in general principle difficult to understand, both emically and etically, though the implications and consequences of his intervention are often quite complex in particular cases. It seems less easy to understand why mediators do not always appear. Indeed, it has sometimes been assumed that they inevitably do appear and negotiations are equated with mediation. Probably in the majority of societies and in most negotiations, mediators do intervene, either from the beginning or at a later point. Yet this is certainly not inevitable or universal. In the United States in 1968, mediators operated in only 15% of private sector, industrial negotiations.[15] Among the Arusha, mediators seldom appeared in negotiations between men of different lineages or age-groups and not always in intragroup disputes. Ndendeuli negotiations usually precipitated a mediator (typically the common kinsman) but he could be excluded by the parties or he himself might refuse the role for fear of committing himself too greatly in a situation of divided loyalties and interests. In many societies, negotiations concerning marriage arrangements or marital disputes occur regularly or sometimes without third-party intervention. The parties are polarized and outsiders are positively unwelcome in what is considered none of their business. Certainly not all international negotiations involve mediators. There is no opportunity for the imposition of mediation by a relevant community, and although there may be groups whose interests are concerned in some way, the disputing parties can ignore them.

One suggested explanation has been that there is always mediation in effect—if not by some individual directly then by an "implicit mediator."

---

15. See Simkin (1971:52). He also stated that "at the remaining 85% of the bargaining tables the parties negotiated without any outside assistance." It is possible that in some, but by no means all, of these cases informal and unrecorded mediation did occur.

Barkun, for instance, has written that implicit mediation is "shared values without a physically present mediator," and that "system-preserving values themselves constitute an *implied third party* [Barkun 1968:106; italics in original]." Such a view confuses things that analytically should be kept separate. Obviously, virtually all pairs of disputants share some values, probably very many. These are important in a number of ways in negotiations. They provide some common frame of reference and a basis for discussion; they symbolize significant connections between the disputants and between them and others; they symbolize the community to which both disputants belong and their rights, obligations, and statuses there; they may link seemingly disparate issues in the dispute. They exist, and they are appealed to and used (and also ignored and abused) in every case of conflict between two people or groups, whether that conflict runs on or is dealt with by adjudication or by negotiation with or without a mediator. They are part of the subject matter of communication and learning. The point surely is that although all negotiations involve some shared values, only some negotiations involve actual mediators.

Barkun also wrote that "in the most simple societies or the less complex outer reaches of a society, implicit mediation is the standard procedure [1968:146]," and referred for support to the comparative study of Schwartz and Miller (1964). This patently ignores the fact that actual mediators regularly operate in some simpler societies (whatever "simple" may mean), and one cannot say that industrial negotiations without mediators ocur only in the "less complex outer reaches" of contemporary Western societies. There are implications in Barkun's argument that the absence of actual mediators is connected in some causal sense with less complex social systems and perhaps too that disputes themselves are less complex and less requiring of mediators in such systems. It is therefore worth emphasizing that highly complicated disputes in Western countries are negotiated and settled without a mediator, even though national political and economic interests may be touched. It may be that, with the assistance of mediators, such negotiations would be more effectively or expeditiously conducted, but we cannot merely assume that and it would be a difficult hypothesis to test. However, the parties in such cases have been quite unwilling to cede any freedom of action and to accept mediation, and for whatever reason it has not been forced upon them. They have doubtless been influenced by expressions of public opinion that have become part of the content of their exchange of information. Yet they have been able to continue in their primary concern, on their own, to influence each other and to reach a mutually acceptable outcome.

A different case for implicit mediation could perhaps be made with reference to expressions of public opinion and the statements of fact and opinion by political and other leaders, news media, and the like. Yet this kind of attempted influence, like common values, is nearly always present to some extent, whether or not an actual mediator participates. Such outside influence is probably best regarded as part of the information that becomes available to the negotiators, affording them resources of potential power. How that additional information is perceived by a party and used in an attempt to affect his opponent is then worked out in the course of the negotiations.[16] Sometimes a particular exponent of allegedly public opinion or of some interest group does become a mediator, even though he is not a participant in negotiation sessions. For instance, a politician might meet with each party separately to examine his position, the available information, and possible outcomes. That person might act as go-between. He could make positive suggestions, either privately or in subsequent public statements.

The sophistry of implicit mediation does nothing to help explain the absence of actual mediators in some negotiations. It avoids the problem instead of coming to grips with it. Rather, we need to ask three questions. First, does the relevant community, through its leaders or otherwise, insist that disputants are not entirely free agents and therefore impose mediation? Second, do the disputants want third-party intervention because of its expected advantages to them? Third, are the disputants willing to recognize and entertain the legitimate interests of a third party in their dispute and its outcome? If the answers to all three questions are "no," then a mediator is most unlikely to appear. This seems empirically to be the case in the instances cited, although the reasons behind the answers and the sociological implications vary from society to society and from case to case.

---

16. On the significance of outsiders to a dispute and its negotiation and to the distribution of potential power to the parties, see pages 202–204.

8

TWO CASE STUDIES

In the preceding chapters, my essential approach to exposition, analysis, and generalization has been to start from the empirical data provided by real-life situations and case studies of actual disputes and their negotiations. Thus, as far as possible, this study is based on concrete material, and although only a relatively small proportion of the material has been given in the book, throughout I have illustrated and exemplified the analysis and the concepts by references to parts of actual cases. Moreover, with a cross-cultural orientation, I have used illustrations from both small-scale societies and complex Western industrial situations. In the present chapter, I provide more comprehensive accounts and analyses of two cases of negotiation, from the time of unresolved, private disagreement and the emergence of acknowledged dispute to the achievement of an agreed, final outcome.

My intention is to illustrate further the analysis and generalizations previously presented. In particular, empirical data are given in some detail in order to demonstrate the major processual patterns in negotiation: first, the development of successive phases of interaction between the negotiating parties as information exchange, learning, adjustment of expectation and preferences, and changes of purpose occur; second, the alternation of antagonism and coordination as predominant responses to the intrinsic contradiction between conflict and the need for joint action; and third, the evolution of the relative persuasive strengths of the two parties as these emerge out of their respective potential power.

It must be reiterated that such apt illustrations, as these cases are, can be no more than further exemplification of my analyses. These illustrations cannot in any sense prove the correctness of my results; they may, however, help to substantiate and clarify them while demonstrating how my paradigm can be applied to actual cases of negotiation. On the other hand, no two case studies can illustrate all the analytical points and generalizations that have been made in previous chapters or are possible within the framework of the paradigm, and in the two following cases I do not attempt to accomplish that.

Deliberately I have chosen one case from a small-scale African society and the other from an American industrial situation in order to demonstrate that, despite differences in the social, cultural, and economic context as well as inevitable differences in many details, essentially the same processual patterns are evident. In each case, the dispute occurred between parties who were significantly involved in ongoing, mutually advantageous relationships such that negotiations were concerned with both the reorganization and the continuation of the relationship. In both cases, negotiations continued through to a final, agreed outcome and thus extended over the full series of developmental phases.

In the following accounts of the two case histories, the beginning of a new phase in the negotiations is noted. The beginning of a period of antagonism is marked by (A), an increase in antagonism by (A+), and the beginning of a period of coordination by (C).

A DISPUTE BETWEEN NEIGHBORS IN ARUSHA

Materials for this case were collected during the course of my own field research among the Arusha of northern Tanzania, both by personal observation of the negotiations in a public moot and by discussions with the principal disputants and others before and after the moot. The negotiations took place in 1957.

THE EMERGENCE OF THE DISPUTE

Lashiloi and Kinyani were unrelated neighbors. Each was about 50 years old and head of his own autonomous family that included an unmarried, adult son, and other younger children. They were co-members of the age-groups then in the age-grade of junior elders—the "executive" age-group particularly active in the public affairs of the community ("parish") in

234

which they lived. Thus, both were mature, well-established men. However, neither was an acknowledged "notable"; that is, they were not especially influential among their peers and neighbors (Gulliver 1963:25 ff.).

Each man had undisputedly inherited his farm from his own deceased father. Between their two farms there was a somewhat smaller farm of about 2½ acres, the ownership of which had been in question for a long time. This farm became vacant after the occupying tenant, Ngatio, died and his widow and children went to live in another parish with Ngatio's brother, who made no claim to continue the tenancy. It was generally agreed in the neighborhood that Ngatio was only a tenant and Ngatio himself had never claimed more than that. There was disagreement, however, as to how the tenancy had originally been established and who was now the rightful owner of the newly vacant farm. Some 10 years previously, when Ngatio had inherited the tenancy from his father, Raiyon, at the latter's death, the fathers of Lashiloi and Kinyani had each claimed sole ownership. Although neither had sought to interfere with Ngatio's tenancy at that time, each had demanded recognition as Ngatio's landlord. Negotiations failed to produce any resolution of the matter, and it seems fairly clear (from local informants' accounts) that neither claimant had wished to push the issue to a conclusion that might have endangered otherwise good and valued neighborly relations. Since then and until his recent death, Ngatio had made irregular small gifts of farm produce to both of his neighbor–kinsmen (and later, to their heirs, Lashiloi and Kinyani). Such gifts had indicated his status as a tenant and their acceptance had demonstrated recognition of his good standing. Ownership of the farm had remained undetermined.

During the few months after Ngatio's death, the farm lay vacant. Both Lashiloi and Kinyani grazed their livestock on it and their wives took fruit from the banana grove and did some desultory maintenance work. However, it was apparent that this situation could not persist; good agricultural land was involved and, in Arusha country, land had recently become scarce and valuable as a result of very high population density (about 1000 people per square mile), an inability to expand into new areas, and new cash crop cultivation. Moreover, both Lashiloi and Kinyani were eager to enlarge their existing farms, especially since each had an adult son who would soon marry and require land for a separate homestead.

According to Lashiloi, his grandfather, Loton, had granted the original tenancy to his (Loton's) sister's son, Raiyon, the father of Ngatio. Kinyani claimed that the tenancy had been given by his grandfather, Kosa, to Raiyon, Kosa's daughter's husband (see the genealogy in Figure 8.1b). Since the event had occurred some 70 years previously, there were no written records nor were there surviving witnesses to the transaction.

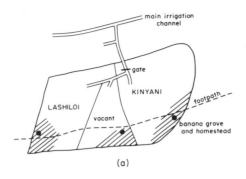

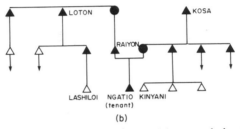

Figure 8.1. A dispute between Arusha neighbors: (a) map of the farms; (b) skeleton genealogy.

Until the time of Ngatio's death, relations between Lashiloi and Kinyani had been friendly and tolerant, with the casual cooperation typical of good neighbors. Any disagreements had been easily dealt with by amicable adjustment. After Ngatio's death, relations gradually deteriorated. Disagreement over the disposition of the vacant farm escalated to the point of open quarreling. In addition, other disagreements developed and were not resolved. Kinyani complained that several times Lashilio's goats had wandered onto his land and had damaged the growing crop; his demand for compensation was refused. Lashiloi complained that Kinyani had at various times withheld or interrupted the supply of irrigation water to Lashiloi's land, thus endangering his onion crop. Lashiloi also complained that Kinyani had harshly beaten his herdsboy son, but Kinyani counterclaimed that the son had trespassed on his land and, without permission, had operated and damaged the gate that controlled the flow of irrigation water. Lashiloi accused Kinyani of illicitly using supernatural power that threatened severe illness or death to members of Lashiloi's family. The two men had discussed these complaints several times but argument had ended in angry accusations and intransigence, so that relations became effectively cut off.

NEGOTIATING THE DISPUTE: PHASES 1 TO 4

Lashiloi forced the crisis that initiated the public dispute. At a meeting of their age-group that had assembled for other purposes, he made a claim to the whole of the vacant farm and demanded that Kinyani refrain from improperly interfering with his irrigation water. Kinyani strongly denied the claim and rejected Lashiloi's demand but he refused to accept offers of mediation by members of the age-group. Afterward, he went to consult with his lineage counsellor,[1] who lived in the same parish. His counsellor agreed to approach the counsellor of Lashiloi's lineage.

Phase 1. The two counsellors, with the consent of Lashiloi and Kinyani, agreed to convene a partrilineal moot. (C) There was no real problem in deciding the arena. Kinyani had already made it clear that he did not wish the intervention of co-members of their age-group (apparently apprehensive of their pressures in favor of Lashiloi, the more popular man), and he had shown his preference for a moot by choosing to consult with his lineage counsellor. Lashiloi saw no reason to contest the choice of a moot since he could expect strong support from his patrilineage. Moreover, in so important a matter as land, a moot was often preferred to a purely parish arena (Gulliver 1963:197). The obvious place to hold the moot was the vacant farm itself.

Such a moot posited that each disputant recruit a party of patrilineal supporters composed of members of the inner lineage (the smallest recognized kin group) and those members of the maximal lineage and clan section who lived fairly near and who agreed to participate. Lashiloi's party consisted of 12 men, among whom he, his counsellor, and his father's brother's son were the more prominent speakers in the negotiations. Kinyani's party included 10 men, of whom, he, his counsellor, and the counsellor of a collateral lineage were the leading members.[2]

Phase 2. The initial concern of the moot became the establishment

---

1. A counsellor was selected by the adult males of a maximal lineage to act as their permanent spokesman, advisor, and public representative. (See Gulliver 1963:101 ff.)

2. The parties were constituted as follows. Lashiloi's party: father's brother, two father's brother's sons, father's father's brother's son (from the inner lineage), the lineage counsellor, three members of the maximal lineage living in the same parish, and two members of the maximal lineage living elsewhere. Kinyani's party: two brothers and two father's brother's sons (from the inner lineage), the lineage counsellor, two members of the maximal lineage living elsewhere, a counsellor of a collateral lineage, and one member of a collateral lineage living in the same parish.

and clarification of the issues in dispute. At first, this was not dealt with deliberately. Lashiloi spoke first, giving a list of his allegations and demands in some detail. Kinyani followed in the same way until he referred to a sum of money that Lashiloi allegedly owed him. Lashiloi and his counsellor interrupted. They denied the debt and pointed out that, in any case, it was not a matter under consideration in the moot. (A) Kinyani rejected this contention and his counsellor declared that "we are not going to be told what we can talk about by Lashiloi." The counsellor went on to say that the debt was important and long overdue; he added that it was Lashiloi who had raised a petty issue by alleging that Kinyani had slandered him. After some exchanges, it was agreed that each party should be free to introduce any issue that was considered important. (C) "This is a dispute between age-mates who are neighbors. If we do not talk about everything they will not be able to live in peace," said one of Kinyani's supporters (the counsellor of the collateral lineage). Silence from both parties signified acceptance of this resolution and then the same counsellor reiterated Lashiloi's complaints. He was followed by Lashiloi's counsellor, who announced Lashiloi's complaints. After a few modifications, these were accepted by both parties. In all, 16 issues were identified. (These are set out summarily in Figure 8.2, together with the reference symbols used in the following description of the negotiations.)

Phase 3. Kinyani's counsellor then remarked that the important issues were those put forward by his party, whereas those of Lashiloi were petty or false and intended only to cause trouble for Kinyani. (A) This comment brought protesting cries from Lashiloi's side and Lashiloi himself came to stand in the open space between the two seated parties. He was allowed to speak at length with little interruption or comment. He began by declaring that his own complaints were the important issues and that Kinyani had so far refused to consider them. Then he repeated his allegations and demands one by one, going into details and justifying his claims. Finally, he referred briefly to Kinyani's demands and rejected all of them, saying that each was too unimportant to call for serious attention. "Kinyani says these things because he is unfriendly, because he dislikes me. Have I not been a good neighbor? Have we not worked together? Have I not helped him? [details of some occasions of this]. He says these things because he wants to take my land [i.e., the vacant farm]. It is not his estate [i.e., inherited property]; it is mine, the estate of my grandfather, Loton, who was the big man here long ago . . . Kinyani says bad words because he has not good [true, legitimate] ones."

Lashiloi returned to sit with his party and Kinyani came to stand in the central open space. His speech was similar to that of Lashiloi; he set out his complaints in detail and sharply rejected Lashiloi's demands. Kinyani was

Figure 8.2. Summary agenda of the negotiations.

Issues Raised by Both Disputants
  I. Land: Alleged hereditary right to the vacant farm
    1. Claimed exclusive ownership of the farm
    2. Claimed exclusive use of the land for agricultural and other purposes

Issues Raised by Kinyani
  II. Trespass: Alleged trespass and damage to crops by Lashiloi's goats
    3. Demanded compensation for damages
    4. Demanded promise by Lashiloi to control his goats in the future
  III. Gate: Alleged damage to his irrigation gate by unauthorized use by Lashiloi's son
    5. Demanded payment of costs of repairs
    6. Demanded recognition of his sole right to operate the gate
  IV. Debt: Alleged a long-standing debt of money owed to him by Lashiloi
    7. Demanded immediate payment in full

Issues Raised by Lashiloi
  V. Water: Alleged interruption and denial of irrigation water by Kinyani
    8. Demanded acknowledgment of his right to regular supply of water from the main irrigation channel
    9. Demanded compensation for damage to crops resulting from interruption of water supply
  VI. Supernatural: Alleged illicit supernatural act by Kinyani on the vacant land, aimed at him and likely to harm him and his family
    10. Demanded performance of ritual purification by Kinyani (including provision of sacrificial goat) to lift the threat from supernatural forces
    11. Demanded payment of compensation
  VII. Violence: Alleged that his herdsboy son had been severely beaten by Kinyani
    12. Demanded apology for illegitimate violence
    13. Demanded compensation for injuries to his son
  VIII. Slander: Alleged public slander of his reputation by Kinyani
    14. Demanded recantation
    15. Demanded apology
    16. Demanded compensation for injury to his reputation

---

followed by his counsellor who concentrated on the land issue and gave his version of the history of the tenancy. Although it added little to what Kinyani had already said before and during the negotiations, the counsellor claimed to give it greater validity because he, as a counsellor and a senior elder, knew the facts better than Lashiloi and his supporters. The counsellor then asked two elderly men to affirm his version. One was the oldest surviving member of Kinyani's maximal lineage and the other was the father-in-law of another member. After they did so, Lashiloi's counsellor spoke, apparently in great indignation, though this was largely contrived as a matter of planned tactics.[3] He dismissed the evidence of the two old

---

3. To make my own position clear: I was friendly with Lashiloi who had become a valued informant and sometime assistant. Because of this, I was allowed to sit in on the private

men: "They are only retired elders. They are feeble. Old men forget." This produced shouts of protest from Kinyani's party but the counsellor ignored them and continued to speak. "I am the spokesman of Loton's lineage. I knew Loton when he was a big man [some details about Loton]. And I remember the things of those days. I am not an old man and my age-group is not that of the old men [i.e., the retired elders]. But you, Oloreng [Kinyani's counsellor], and you, Kinyani, you are still young men who should listen to us, your seniors." From this act of asserting superior status, and thus superior knowledge and experience (quite typical of the behavior of an Arusha toward men of a junior age-group, though not necessarily effective), the counsellor went on to describe the legitimacy of Lashiloi's claim to the land. He ended his speech by accusing Kinyani of deliberately making a false claim because of his greed for land.

When the counsellor returned to his party, Kinyani stood up amid his own party and, ignoring the land issue and the previous speaker, reemphasized his other complaints. He was followed by his brother who went into details about the alleged damage to the irrigation gate (Figure 8.2, III). He explained that Kinyani, and their father previously, had always controlled the irrigation water.[4] He said that there had never been trouble before and, moreover, that Kinyani was well known to be properly careful in not taking too much water from the main channel, which had to supply many other farms. It was Lashiloi, he said, who was greedy for water because he had begun to cultivate more land than before and was therefore demanding more than his fair share. He concluded with more invidious remarks about Lashiloi.

Exchanges went on in this fashion for some time. Usually a member of one party, then of the other, monopolized the proceedings. Occasionally a witness was called to corroborate some statement or one party cross-examined a speaker from the other. However, there was virtually no attempt to make counteroffers to the opponent's demands. Rather, each

---

discussions of Lashiloi's party before the negotiations. During the moot, I sat as a neutral, along with a number of nonparticipating spectators. Kinyani was less well known to me and, as a friend of Lashiloi, I was not privy to his thoughts and plans. My field assistant, however, was able to discuss the dispute with Kinyani, though not with the freedom that I enjoyed with Lashiloi.

4. Because of the lay of the land, water came from the main channel to the men's farms by a takeoff channel. This channel divided into two just inside Kinyani's farm boundary, leading to Kinyani's and Lashiloi's land respectively. (See Figure 8.1a.) This meant that Kinyani could control the flow to Lashiloi's farm. He had constructed a rough wooden gate that could close the takeoff channel or direct the water to either farm.

speaker simply continued to deny the allegations against their principal and to deprecate the other's demands as grossly exaggerated. Occasionally, one party's interruptions and interjections temporarily interfered with a speaker from the other party, and there were several outbursts of anger. (A+) One of these outbursts, which included a threat that Lashiloi's supporters would go and break up Kinyani's irrigation gate, was quickly suppressed by Lashiloi's counsellor. He declared that, although such violence must not occur, it was Kinyani's actions and continued rejection of Lashiloi's legitimate demands that were responsible for the understandable indignation of Lashiloi's supporters.

Phase 3 to Phase 4. A distinct shift in the nature of the negotiations began rather abruptly when Kinyani's counsellor offered a "package deal": Lashiloi should consent to withdraw issues 9, 12, 13, 14, 15, and 16 and Kinyani would agree to 8 and would withdraw 3 and 4 (Figure 8.2). Then, added the counsellor, "We can talk about the land."

Lashiloi refused the offer peremptorily. Discussions were renewed on other issues but without proposals for concessions or counteroffers. Then Lashiloi said that he would withdraw the issues relating to the allegation of slander (14, 15, and 16). The slander had been well substantiated by witnesses but Kinyani had merely denied the charge and had made no other response to it. Lashiloi now declared that the matter was "not a big one—a matter of foolish words. We can forget it. We have both spoken many words that are not true when we should have remained silent." (C) Some of Kinyani's supporters made approving noises; Kinyani himself made no response at all and his silence signified his acceptance of Lashiloi's offer. These issues were not referred to again during the negotiations.

Phase 4. Thereafter, as the parties continued to bring up the various issues for discussion, a new orientation became obvious. There were more concentrated exchanges—with direct replies and counterreplies—rather than, as previously, merely a demand by one party and its rejection by the other. There began to be tentative counteroffers and probings for concessions. From this time, there was little personal attack against either principal disputant and the parties concentrated on the issues themselves.

Following Lashiloi's withdrawal of demands relating to slander, the other issues were reintroduced into the negotiations in the following order (reference numbers are to the agenda items summarized in Figure 8.2 [p. 239]). For the sake of simplicity, references are given only to the initiating party in the name of the principal disputant although various members of either party initiated renewed exchanges and discussions (K, Kinyani; L, Lashiloi).

Issue	Initiating Party	Nature of Exchange
1: Land	Kinyani	Exchange of views
10,11: Supernatural	Lashiloi	Exchange of views; L concentrated on the supernatural danger threatening his family.
5: Gate	Kinyani	Exchange of views
8: Water	Lashiloi	Exchange of views
7: Debt	Kinyani	Exchange of views
10,11: Supernatural	Lashiloi	L offered to withdraw 11 if K would agree to 10. K rejected this.
1: Land	Lashiloi	Exchange of views
6: Gate	Kinyani	Exchange of views
12,13: Violence	Lashiloi	Exchange of views
4: Trespass	Kinyani	K insisted that trespass and violence issues were essentially connected; he proposed that L should concede on 12 and 13 (no mention of how much) and then he would "think about" 4 (i.e., possibly offer concession).
13: Violence	Lashiloi	For the first time L named a specific sum of money for compensation. K rejected the demand after discussion.
8: Water	Lashiloi	L insisted that water and violence issues were essentially connected and asked K to make definite offers on these. K refused.
6: Gate	Kinyani	K argued that gate and water issues were essentially connected. He demanded L's acceptance of 6 in return for his acceptance of 8. L refused.
12,13: Violence	Lashiloi	Exchange of views. L admitted that no real harm had been done to his son (13) and K admitted to his error in chastising another man's son (12). *Issues resolved: 12,13.*
7: Debt	Kinyani	K agreed to withdraw this issue although reiterating that the unpaid debt still existed. L accepted this. *Issue withdrawn: 7.*
5: Gate	Kinyani ⎫	K successively offered minor concessions that
1: Land	Kinyani ⎬	were not acceptable to L unless the water
10: Supernatural	Kinyani ⎭	issues (8,9) were dealt with at the same time.
8,9: Water	Lashiloi	K proposed to accept 8 if L would withdraw 9 and agree to 5. L tentatively agreed on 8 and 9 but not on 5.
6: Gate	Kinyani	K demanded L's acceptance of 6 if K were to concede on 8 and 9. L refused.
1: Land	Lashiloi	Exchange of views but no new proposals.
3,4: Trespass	Kinyani	L admitted trespass by his goats but held that damage to K's crops was negligible. L offered to make a small "gift" of beer if K would make a similar "gift" for issue 9. K agreed. *Issues resolved: 3,4,9.*
5,6: Gate	Kinyani	Both refused to make requested concessions.
1,2: Land	Lashiloi	L proposed that he be recognized as owner of the land (1) while there should be a sharing of its use (2). K rejected this.
8: Water	Lashiloi	L insisted that this issue be settled before anything further be considered. K refused.
5,6: Gate	Kinyani	K insisted that these issues be settled first.
8,10,11: Water; supernatural	Lashiloi	L reiterated need to settle 8 and also 10 and 11. K rejected this.

242

Issue	Initiating Party	Nature of Exchange
6: Gate	Kinyani	K reiterated his earlier insistence. L again refused.
1: Land	Lashiloi	L proposed a division of the land. After exchanges K agreed. Both parties almost immediately agreed to a dividing line where a footpath ran through the middle of the vacant farm. Tacit agreement (no discussion) that each man should have exclusive use of his portion of the land (2). L proposed that, with this division of the land, K should accept L's demand for acknowledgment of his uninterrupted right to irrigation water (8). K agreed. *Issues resolved: 1,2,8.*
6: Gate	Kinyani	L rejected K's demand and also K's assertion that this issue was the most important one remaining.
10: Supernatural	Lashiloi	K rejected L's demand and L's similar assertion about issue 10.
5: Gate	Kinyani	L rejected K's demand and made no counteroffer.
11: Supernatural	Lashiloi	K rejected L's demand.

This effectively ended Phase 4, with the obdurate issues now identified. These issues related to the matter of the irrigation gate, raised by Kinyani, and to the allegation of illicit resort to the supernatural, raised by Lashiloi. No substantial concessions or new proposals had been made on these four issues, although all others had been withdrawn or resolved in agreement. (A)

ANALYSIS OF PHASES 3 AND 4

In what was, analytically, Phase 3, exchanges between the parties predominantly comprised the repetition and exposition of demands by each party. Neither party attempted a reasoned reply to the other's demands but merely rejected them as unwarranted and unacceptable. The major exception to this was on the issue of land ownership (issue 1). Here, each party gave detailed explanations of the legitimacy of his claim by referring to his grandfather as the original owner who had granted the initial tenancy of the disputed farm. There was little agreement in these explanations nor were concessionary proposals suggested by either party. During this phase, considerable animosity was expressed by members of each party toward the other and there were attacks on the characters of each of the principal disputants.

The shift to Phase 4 began with Kinyani's first proposal for a package deal. For a time there was an overlap of orientations, purposes, and kinds of interaction, but fairly quickly Phase 4 interaction became dominant. After Kinyani's first attempt, in effect (but perhaps in deliberate purpose) to shift from the emphasis on differences (Phase 3) to the narrowing of differences (Phase 4), there was some hesitancy. Then Lashiloi responded with his unilateral offer to withdraw the issues concerning slander. He clearly expected Kinyani to make some reciprocal concession, although for the moment he was disappointed in that. By now, however, it was obvious to Lashiloi's party that some issues were fairly trivial and that they stood in the way of dealing with the more important and/or difficult ones. Thereafter, a number of trends developed.

First, although the parties continued to range over the whole field of their dispute (as they had in Phase 3), they increasingly engaged in exchanges that explicitly considered each other's views. They made direct responses to each other's demands and suggested tentative offers of concessions from previously inflexible stands. Second, in this shifting from issue to issue, each party continued to raise and emphasize these issues relating to his own demands. Third, the parties began to search for connections between different issues: what package deals might be possible and what concession from the opponent was required against a party's own possible concession. Fourth, as some issues were disposed of, by withdrawal or by an agreed resolution, the parties' focus narrowed on the remaining issues. Fifth, both parties began to acknowledge that the outcomes already reached on some issues demonstrated the growing potentiality for further agreement and for an ultimate, positive outcome to the negotiations.

Withdrawal of an issue expressed, usually overtly, "friendliness"—a readiness to be generous and cooperative and a desire not to prolong the negotiations. Withdrawal also suggested, tacitly or explicitly, an expectation of reciprocity from the other party. Some bargaining occurred on the details of agreements but this was conducted in mild fashion and was not the principal way an outcome was achieved on an issue. Rather, effective package deals were arranged in which each party largely accepted the opponent's demand: issues 7, 12, and 13; issues 3, 4, and 9; and issues 1, 2, and 8.

Some issues turned out to be trivial or at least they were treated as such where it seemed advantageous to do so. Whether they were originally considered to be trivial by the interested party is difficult to say. Some were certainly precipitated in the emotional heat of the moment when they were felt to be important, although assessments may have changed by the time negotiations began. For example, Lashiloi was angered by Kinyani's slander during arguments over the land. Kinyani called him a liar, a thief, an ungenerous age-mate, and an untrustworthy neighbor. These were accusations against his reputation that Lashiloi could not easily ignore. However, by the time negotiations began, Lashiloi was prepared, if necessary, to overlook the slander, especially since other age-mates had assured him that they themselves took no account of it: Kinyani was known to be rather irascible and exaggerated in his speech. Yet Lashiloi decided to put the issues into the negotiations lest (as he told me) people might think he was afraid to defend his reputation. His willingness to withdraw these issues, as a show of "friendliness" and of readiness to search for agreement, indicated their relative triviality. It appeared that Kinyani also perceived this since he did not reciprocate immediately to what he considered to be almost no concession at all by Lashiloi.

Lashiloi attempted to continue his initiative in narrowing the differences by offering to withdraw another issue (11: compensation for the illicit use of supernatural power by Kinyani) if Kinyani would concede on issue 10 (performance of ritual purification). Again Kinyani refused to match the proposed concession and the parties resumed their examination of other issues. Lashiloi then made a further proposal for a reciprocal arrangement: his withdrawal of issue 13 (compensation for injuries to his son) in return for Kinyani's acceptance of 12 (apology for violence to Lashiloi's son). Kinyani now agreed, and soon after made a linked concession in withdrawing issue 7 (repayment of debt)—a sign of his readiness to cooperate.

Kinyani then offered several small concessions but Lashiloi refused to reciprocate until Kinyani agreed to accept his demand on the issue of irrigation water (8). Ever since that issue had emerged in the original disagreement with Kinyani, it had been important to Lashiloi. By this time, however, Lashiloi had decided that it was crucial because of Kinyani's refusal to yield. Briefly, the position was that Lashiloi had recently begun growing onions as a dry season, cash crop. This enterprise depended on a reliable supply of irrigation water, but Lashiloi had had no reason to expect that his neighbor would seriously interfere with this. Lashiloi (like Kinyani) had inherited his grandfather's original rights and responsibilities in the main irrigation channel and he was an accepted member of the semiformal association that maintained the channel. Kinyani's actions in withholding water and interfering with the timing and quantity of its supply were, therefore, quite illegitimate. Those actions were, apparently, an angry reaction and retaliation against Lashiloi during their disagreements and quarrels, although even before that he had sometimes been dilatory in opening the subordinate channel that ran to Lashiloi's farm. This had caused Lashiloi much anxiety since it endangered his new agricultural venture. Moreover, Kinyani had threatened, before the negotiations, to continue his interference if he did not obtain satisfaction from Lashiloi on other matters. Lashiloi considered that moral norms and public opinion were clearly on his side; nevertheless, he remained apprehensive of Kinyani's troublemaking and threat that, if implemented, would inconvenience him and perhaps damage his enterprise. Therefore, Lashiloi desired his rights to a regular supply of water to be acknowledged publicly by Kinyani.

By this point in the negotiations it had become apparent to Kinyani (and perhaps always had been) that he would have to give way on this issue; morally, he was patently in the wrong and it had been made clear that public opinion supported Lashiloi's demand—neighbors, including a spokesman of their common age-group, had affirmed Lashiloi's rights to water. Kinyani also realized that good neighborly relations with Lashiloi would be impossible as long as Lashiloi had any doubts about his water supply. Yet Kinyani wished to delay concession in this matter in order to threaten Lashiloi. His intention was to force a link between resolution on the water issues (8 and 9) and agreement on issues that were important to him, namely those concerning the irrigation gate (5 and 6); as a second possibility, he hoped to induce Lashiloi to withdraw issues 10 and 11 concerning Kinyani's alleged use of supernatural power. He was less successful than he had hoped, however, for Lashiloi refused to budge on issues 5 and 6, partly through failure to appreciate their significance to Kinyani. Lashiloi also refused to concede on issues 10 and 11 because he saw them as too important to consider concession at that time. The most Kinyani could achieve in the circumstances, therefore, was to arrange a trade with Lashiloi: Kinyani conceded on issue 9 (compensation for crop loss due to interruption of the water supply) and Lashiloi conceded on issues 3 and 4 (trespass and crop damage), with the exchange of "friendship gifts" of beer (i.e., not overt compensation payments).

Further exchanges were unproductive and there was a return to acrimony and failure to respond to each other's arguments. Lashiloi's lineage counsellor broke through the potentially threatening, stultifying interaction by a specific proposal that the two disputants divide the vacant farm between them. This proposal was prompted by the fact that, as the negotiations had proceeded, Lashiloi's party had given up expectations of obtaining the whole of the disputed land. Kinyani was not informed of this nor did he know that Lashiloi's party had private doubts about Lashiloi's hereditary claim to the land. Finally, this proposal to divide the land was in accord with what had been Lashiloi's minimal objective throughout: to acquire that part of the vacant farm adjoining the area of his own farm that was watered by the irrigation subchannel.

The counsellor's initiative appeared to take Kinyani's party by surprise, although such a proposal had always been an obvious possibility, with many comparable precedents in Arusha country. Possibly, Kinyani and his supporters had allowed themselves to concentrate too much on other issues (particularly on issues 5 and 6 concerning the irrigation gate) and had not adequately clarified preferences and expectations about the land issue. In any case, Kinyani was somewhat rushed into agreeing to the proposal (as he admitted afterward) and into accepting the subsequent proposal from

Lashiloi's party that the land be divided where a footpath crossed the vacant farm (see Figure 8.1a [p. 236]—a conspicuous line for the new boundary. This division gave Lashiloi the portion he required, but it also gave Kinyani the advantage of securing the house, banana grove, and some arable land, which could provide the basis for a new homestead and farm for Kinyani's son, who was soon to marry. Thus, both disputants gained tolerable satisfaction. Lashiloi immediately capitalized on the consequent euphoria to induce Kinyani at last to accede to the demand that he acknowledge Lashiloi's water rights (issue 8).

FINAL BARGAINING AND OUTCOME: PHASES 5, 6, AND 7

With the resolution of the land and water issues, four issues remained outstanding. So far there had been little flexibility or potential concession on any of them. These issues were Kinyani's demand for payment of the costs of repairs to his damaged irrigation gate (6) and for Lashiloi's acknowledgment that Kinyani had sole right to operate that gate (5); Lashiloi's demands for Kinyani's performance of ritual purification to remove the threat of supernatural danger (10) and for compensation for that illicit threat (11).

Concerning the irrigation gate: Kinyani was very proud of his wooden construction in place of the usual impromptu mud dam that most Arusha farmers made. After several years of use, some of the wood needed to be replaced and the whole gate had to be refixed in the walls of the channel. Kinyani held that this was because of damage caused by Lashiloi's son who had operated the gate clumsily and without permission. During the moot, Lashiloi denied responsibility. The wood was partly rotten, he asserted, and his son would not have had to operate the gate at all had Kinyani allowed a proper flow of water. In any case, Lashiloi said, no such gate was really necessary. It was clear that Lashiloi quite failed to recognize the extent of Kinyani's pride in his construction. Lashiloi perceived the issue to be a petty one on which Kinyani unreasonably put considerable importance. Thus, Lashiloi was piqued by Kinyani's insistence on the unimportant, and Kinyani's obstinacy was reinforced by Lashiloi's disdainful reaction.

The alleged supernatural offense had occurred during altercations over the vacant farm and other matters. According to Lashiloi, Kinyani had seized a handful of soil from the land and flung it at Lashiloi, saying, "This land is not yours. You will be hurt." Lashiloi interpreted this as an illicit performance of the ritual act of olemwua—an act that should only be performed with the formal, public approval of the leading members of the two parties of the disputants and under their supervision. When performed legitimately, Arusha believed, a wrongful claimant and members of his immediate family would become severly ill or die (Gulliver 1963:290). Since at the time of the alleged offense there was no formal dispute between Lashiloi and Kinyani, no such permission could be given. In addition, if Kinyani had performed the ritual act, it expressed intense animosity and a wish to harm Lashiloi. Kinyani, however, persistently denied that he had acted in the way alleged. He claimed that he had merely been emphasizing points in his argument by throwing down stones and soil.

As far as I could ascertain, neither disputant had foreseen that these issues would be the most difficult to resolve.[5] Materially, the damage to the gate was not great—a matter of two or three shillings for some new wood. Lashiloi had expected Kinyani to withdraw his demand or to be content with a token payment. However, Kinyani's pride was involved and Lashiloi failed to see that. On the other hand, the supernatural offense, if in fact it had occurred, was most serious since Arusha in general and Lashiloi himself believed in the grave threat involved. Therefore, he ardently desired Kinyani to remove the threat by appropriate ritual performance.[6] He also wished to obtain a public promise of future good neighborliness that would be part of the ritual. However, Kinyani would not admit to so heinous an offense nor to the personal animosity that it implied. I also suspect that Kinyani's obduracy was reinforced by his genuinely hurt pride concerning the irrigation gate and perhaps, too, because he felt that he had been unduly rushed into agreement over the land issue. He wished to demonstrate that he was a strong man and one not to be trifled with—a point that my field assistant and another, neutral neighbor indicated to me.

Phase 5. Before they came to bargaining on these four outstanding issues, the two parties reexamined and reexchanged views on them. (C) Initially, nothing new emerged since both parties remained overtly inflexible. Each repeatedly insisted that his own demands be accepted first, before the other's were considered. (A) There were expressions of some antagonism as each accused the other of unnecessary rigidity, insufficient goodwill, and deliberate attempts to prevent completion of the negotiations. Eventually, however, a member of Lashiloi's party initiated what turned out to be a breakthrough. This man was a member of Lashiloi's maximal lineage (i.e., a distant but acknowledged kinsman) who lived in the same parish and was

---

5. At the beginning of negotiations, Lashiloi had given the highest importance to the issues of water supply and land rights. I do not know which issues he or Kinyani had expected to be most obdurate.

6. Strictly speaking, since the agreement had been made to divide the disputed land, Lashiloi had proper right to his portion and was not, therefore, liable to supernatural danger for illegitimate possession. Nevertheless, he still believed himself to be under threat because the forces that had been released by Kinyani's ritual act remained at large and might still attack him.

a member of the same age-group as both disputants. Hitherto he had said little except to give vocal support to Lashiloi and other speakers of Lashiloi's party. Now he made a short speech from where he sat among Lashiloi's party. He spoke of the need for friendliness and peace between neighbors and age-mates. He added, "We have come a long way on the path, so now we can go to the end. The end is not far and we shall be foolish to turn back now." He said that both parties could give way a little in order to reach final agreement. (C) This theme was taken up by the counsellor of Kinyani's collateral lineage (a supporter and influential man, resident in an adjacent parish but not acknowledged as a kinsman). This counsellor commended the previous speaker, agreed with him, and virtually repeated his remarks. Then he suggested positive reciprocity between the parties, asking Lashiloi to reduce his demands so that Kinyani could reduce his. This proposal brought cries of approval from some members of both parties, although not from either Lashiloi or Kinyani. One of Lashiloi's supporters called out that the proposal was a good one and its proposer was a "big man" (i.e., implying that he was both an influential and a sensible man). Lashiloi's counsellor added that both disputants should reduce some of their demands. Then he, Lashiloi, and the latter's paternal cousin whispered together for a few moments after which the counsellor repeated his modification of the original proposal. He added that it would not be easy to carry out and that Lashiloi was not going to give up his legitimate demands. Kinyani's party made no reply, signifying agreement.

Thus, the principal was established that the parties should trade concessions on their respective demands in order to move to a final agreement. It is significant that this agreement in principle, the essential breakthrough in Phase 5, was the result of concerted efforts from members of each party who were not closely related to the principal disputants. Although each was an undoubted supporter of his own party, they were not involved in the interpersonal relations and disagreements between Lashiloi and Kinyani. Thus they were freer to make tentative suggestions that the disputants themselves and their closer supporters could repudiate if they seemed dangerous or useless. On Lashiloi's side, at least, this was not a deliberately planned strategy. His supporter, acting independently and taking a more dispassionate view, was looking for a way out of a potential impasse.

Phase 6.   After a brief pause (in effect, marking the shift to the next phase), Kinyani called for Lashiloi to make the first concession. (A) Lashiloi refused this request and said that concession should come from Kinyani. Kinyani expressed disagreement but a member of his party called out, "Let us take only part of the money for the gate." Lashiloi agreed to that and asked how much Kinyani wanted. Kinyani's counsellor suggested half of the cost of repairs; but Lashiloi rejected that as too much. Lashiloi went on to propose that Kinyani pay "only a few shillings" in compensation for the supernatural danger—previously he had demanded "many shillings," but no specified sum. Kinyani demurred, saying that he had committed no offense; however, he offered to accept "only two shillings" for the gate repairs. He added that he expected "friendliness" (i.e., reciprocal concession) from Lashiloi. Lashiloi's counsellor shifted to the demand for ritual purification. If a final agreement were to be obtained, he said, it would be fitting if the two men combined in an act of ritual friendship by the sacrifice of a goat. "Perhaps," he said, "a goat can be found." This seemed to me, but apparently also to members of Kinyani's party, a most ambiguous proposal. Was the ritual to be one of formal purification? Who was to provide the sacrificial goat? (In Lashiloi's original demand it was assumed that Kinyani, as the offender, would provide the necessary animal.) The proposal was discussed for some minutes until Lashiloi's cousin said that "our lineage" might find a small goat for the sake of friendship. (C) This was immediately accepted by Kinyani who offered to make a gift of beer to Lashiloi. There was a pause and whispered consultations within each party. "All right," Lashiloi called out, "I will give Kinyani one shilling to help him repair his gate."

There was no reply. Men began to stand up and move about. One or two crossed over to talk with members of the other party and, as I overheard, at least one of these spoke on a matter of no relevance to the negotiations. The negotiations were finished,[7] although in fact two outstanding matters remained. First, no mention had been made of Kinyani's demand to have sole right to operate the irrigation gate and thus to control the flow of water (issue 6). This was allowed to lapse, although Lashiloi told me afterward that he and his son would not attempt to use the gate so long as Kinyani did not interfere again with the water supply. Second, no time had been fixed nor details arranged for the ritual performance; indeed, it remained unclear exactly what form the ritual should take. Instead, the arrangements were made by the two principal counsellors before they left for home and it was agreed that the parties should meet 3 days later at Kinyani's homestead. Kinyani was to slaughter the goat supplied by Lashiloi; each was to feed the other symbolic pieces of meat and both were to swear friendship. Kinyani would produce the promised beer on this occasion.

---

7. The moot had begun at about 11 A.M., and ended a little after 5 P.M. My field assistant thought that final bargaining was made briefer and easier than it might have been because the assembled men were anxious to return home for evening chores and because they did not wish to return another day to continue the moot. He was probably correct in this opinion. There was, therefore, incentive to complete the negotiations that day when so much had already been accomplished.

Phase 7. All this was done as arranged on the agreed day. (C) After the ritual performance, each counsellor in turn announced that there was no longer any quarrel between the two neighbors. They said that each man now legitimately owned that portion of the vacant farm as had been agreed; thus, no one any longer feared danger to himself or his family because of wrongful seizure of that land. This nicely took care of Lashiloi's fears without directly specifying Kinyani's responsibility for those fears. The two neighbors, former disputants, drank beer out of the same gourd and then all the assembled men drank beer and consumed the rest of the goat meat.

In conclusion, I wish to reemphasize a number of points. First, the dispute and its negotiation were carried out between two men who were neighbors and also co-members of the same formal age-group. That is, there were clear norms and values that predicated amity, trust, toleration, and cooperation between these men. Moreover, there were real practical advantages to be gained if friendly neighborliness could be reestablished. Both men were well aware of all this and, outside of emotional stress, neither wished to prolong the dispute. Thus, if necessary, both men were prepared to give way on most of the issues rather than accept a mutually disadvantageous status quo. Whatever their initial preferences and assessments when negotiations began, it was gradually discovered that some issues were in fact more or less trivial and that mutual concessions were possible and satisfactory on other issues.

The restoration of good neighborly relations was more important to Kinyani. His inner lineage (closer patrilineal kin) was relatively small and its members were geographically dispersed. As a result, Kinyani found less help and support from them than he otherwise might and ideally should have. He found it necessary, therefore, to depend more on his neighbors. Lashiloi, on the other hand, belonged to a large and strong lineage with several of its members living nearby, and he was a good deal more popular among his age-mates than was Kinyani. This meant that his need for good neighborly relations with Kinyani was not quite so important.

Second, Kinyani was clearly in the wrong by interfering with the supply of irrigation water to Lashiloi's farm, and this fact was emphasized to him by neutral neighbors' comments during the moot. However, since he could affect Lashiloi's new agricultural venture, he hoped he could still gain persuasive strength from this threat. He was frustrated by Lashiloi's unshakable determination to safeguard his economic interests by taking a stand on normative grounds.

Kinyani would also have been morally guilty if he had performed the illicit ritual act that released dangerous supernatural forces; it was never determined that he had done so, however. In any case, it became necessary for him to agree to ritual reconciliation so that Lashiloi might be freed from his persisting belief that genuine and serious danger existed. Indeed, it was this belief that ultimately induced Lashiloi to make final bargaining concessions.

Third, Lashiloi failed to appreciate Kinyani's subjective evaluation of the issues of the irrigation gate—at least until final bargaining. Had he realized their importance to Kinyani, he perhaps could have conceded in the matter and so disposed of it earlier, in Phase 4, along with the other resolutions achieved at that period. Moreover, had he done so, his own position concerning the supernatural forces would, in the end, have been much stronger. As it was, he had to make concessions there in order to obtain concessions from Kinyani on the gate issue—that is, in order to reach a final outcome by bargaining.

Finally, concerning the disposition of the vacant farm, both men considered themselves to have a genuine hereditary (i.e., normative) claim. Privately, Lashiloi admitted that his own claim—and probably Kinyani's too—was not altogether justifiable since no one could any longer know what the original ownership had been. Kinyani appeared to be more convinced of the validity of his claim and was, perhaps, less prepared to compromise. Lashiloi became willing, in Phase 4, to accept his private, minimal requirement and, by taking the initiative and making a proposal first, he was able to secure this fairly easily. Kinyani and his supporters must have realized that a compromise division of the land was a possible outcome, in view of the precedents in the country in that period, but they failed to prepare themselves and to adjust their expectations. Quite possibly, despite the obvious boundary potential of the footpath, Kinyani might have obtained a larger share of the land had he acted more decisively. On the other hand, he was reasonably satisfied to gain a portion that suited his need to provide a new farm for his son.

NEGOTIATING A NEW CONTRACT:
AN INDUSTRIAL DISPUTE IN THE UNITED STATES

The data for this industrial dispute and its negotiations are recorded in Selekman *et al.* (1950:444–471). These data are provided in the form of a partial verbatim account of exchanges between the negotiators, augmented by summary accounts of other episodes. The record is therefore incomplete in detail, and there is no direct information concerning the formation and adjustment of expectations and preferences by either party. For these reasons, the presentation and analysis of this case are less detailed than those for the preceding Arusha case. However, it is still possible to apply the developmental model to these industrial negotiations and to analyze the structure of the empirical events in a case that is an example of the most common kind of industrial dispute in the United States. In this analysis, I deliberately omit consideration of the detailed content of the issues in dispute in order to focus on the processual patterns that developed in the negotiations.

THE EMERGENCE OF THE DISPUTE

The Process Workers of America (henceforth referred to as U) represented employees at three of the plants of the Industrial Processing Company (henceforth referred to as M) in Tennessee, Georgia, and Kentucky. On January 8, 1948, U sent a letter to M requesting a meeting to consider wage revision. This was a legitimate procedure under the terms of the existing employment contract. At that time, the contract had approximately 8 months to run. M agreed to a meeting, whereupon U asked for a separate meeting to consider a special wage adjustment for mechanics. This second request was rejected by M. When the two parties met on February 3, U demanded a general, 25% increase in hourly wages and a special adjustment for mechanics. In support of these demands, U referred to the company's increased earnings, increased productivity, and the rising cost of living. M rejected both demands on the grounds that the company already paid standard wages and that the economic future was unclear. M made no counterproposals.

There followed a period of unrest in the largest of the three plants as employees (apparently on U instructions) refused to work overtime or to give the customary help in minor emergency repairs. As a result, there were temporary interruptions of operations in some departments. M appealed directly to the employees individually by letter, promising no loss of jobs for those who disregarded U instructions. M also informed U that although it was prepared to meet with U, there could be no wage increase while economic conditions remained poor. After further appeal to U to cease encouraging work stoppages and other alleged "intimidations," production reverted to normal on March 23, after some 6 weeks of partial and periodic interruptions.

Two weeks later, in reply to U's renewed request for a meeting, M suggested that it would be "confusing to workers" to discuss both a wage increase and M's new pension play proposals at a single meeting. This plan had been pending for some years and, in the previous year's contract negotiations, M had agreed to submit its reformed scheme to employees. M proposed an early meeting to consider this scheme and a later meeting in June to consider wages and to negotiate a new contract. A few days later, a major competitor, during contract negotiations, granted a wage increase of 11 cents an hour to its employees. Again, M refused a meeting to discuss wages prior to the commencement of the new pension plan. At a meeting on April 22 to consider that plan, U objected to some of its provisions and to the fact that the plan had not emerged out of collective bargaining between U and M. On April 30, U repeated its written request for a meeting on wages, asking that this be held not later than May 10. M agreed to meet on May 13. Before that meeting occurred, M granted an 11-cent increase at three of its other plants that were not involved in these discussions.

Thus the preliminaries ended as M finally agreed to enter negotiations. The preliminaries had largely centered on the issue of a wage increase, although M persisted in its desire to get the new pension plan into operation. It seems clear, however, that M wished to postpone a wage increase as long as possible and eventually to link that with agreement on a new contract; M therefore attempted to avoid active negotiations as long as possible. When the negotiations eventually began, there was no joint understanding on the issues that were to be discussed.

THE NEGOTIATIONS

There is no suggestion in the record that choice of an arena was a matter of disagreement. Therefore, it appears, the parties moved immediately into Phase 2 (agenda formulation).

Phase 2. At the meeting on May 13, there was, first, an altercation concerning the presence of M's stenotypist. (**A**) This was eventually settled when U agreed to take a copy of the stenotyped account of the proceedings. U then reiterated its wage demands and these were rejected by M. M offered the choice of either (a) the negotiation of a new contract or (b) an interim wage increase of 5 cents until the expiration of the current contract in August. U rejected (a) and M repeated its offer of (b), although indicating its preference for (a). U asked for an adjournment in order to consult with its members. Four days later, when the meeting resumed, U informed M that it was now prepared to negotiate a new contract. Again, there was altercation over the stenotypist who, however, remained in the room. The two parties sat from 10 A.M. to 5 P.M. without talking. The next day the silence continued for 3 hours, after which time U said that it would report to its members. (**C**) The following day, in a meeting with a federal conciliator present, U proposed 18 changes in the current contract and M proposed 6 changes.[8] Thus, the agenda was agreed and the way opened for further negotiations.

---

8. U proposals referred to an unspecified wage increase, automatic checkoff, increase in shift differentials, overtime rates, paid holidays, vacations, rehiring provisions, and certain

Phase 3. At the next meeting on May 20, the parties recapitulated their respective proposals. (**A**) M rejected all of U's demands for fringe benefits. The discussion then focused mainly on the issues relating to the application of seniority within a plant. There was considerable disagreement and no overt shift in demands by either party. Eventually, M offered a wage increase of 11 cents an hour, together with withdrawal of other issues, if agreement could be reached on the seniority regulations. U agreed to consider this. Discussions at the following meeting again centered on seniority issues, with no changes by either party. Finally, U announced that it would ask its members to consider a 5-cent wage increase and to leave negotiations on a new contract until nearer the end of the present one in August when U would be able to "use their economic power."

The company was notified by letter from U that workers had agreed to accept the 5-cent increase. In a written reply, M accepted this but repeated its offer of 11 cents if a new contract could be agreed upon before June 8. In a further letter, U indicated its continued preference to allow the current contract to remain: U accused M of earlier stalling tactics to delay a wage increase but agreed to "one more meeting" in view of possible changes in M's demands. The parties met on June 8 and both reiterated their earlier positions. A proposal by M to set up a joint committee to study the seniority question was rejected by U. (**A+**) The meeting degenerated into verbal hostility and negotiations were broken off. U sent formal notice to M that it would recommence negotiations for a new contract not earlier than August 11 (2 days before the expiration of the current contract). M replied that this constituted a threat of strike action. In order to try to avoid this, the president of the company wrote to a senior official of the CIO (to which U was affiliated) asking for his intervention. As a result, the principal U and M negotiators met with that official. Eventually, after further protestation to him, by M, he obtained U's agreement that negotiations should resume on July 31.

Phase 2. At this meeting (held on neutral ground in a hotel), the agenda was reconsidered. (**C**) U submitted its earlier demands and added six others. These related to union shop, improved pension plan, wage equity adjustments, probationary employees, overtime pay, and seniority protection. M responded that these demands were excessive: "You are really asking for everything," said M's leader.

Phase 4. After a recess, M repeated its earlier demands and offered a further 6-cent wage increase (in addition to the 5-cent increase already given). (**C**) At M's request, U then explained its first issue—union shop and

---

clauses in the pension scheme. M proposals related to equal-work-for-equal-pay provisions, limitation of seniority rules for promotion and transfer of employees, and the deletion of job-rate adjustment.

checkoff. Rather than give an immediate rejection, M proposed that this issue be held until later. However, because U did not wish for such postponement, the checkoff issue was discussed and, in the end, an agreement was reached. Issues relating to shift differentials and vacations were examined and then held over (i.e., rather than rejected) since no agreement seemed imminent. U then accused M of making changes in the pension plan in accordance with U's earlier suggestions but without acknowledging their source. (A) M accused U of advising workers not to join the new pension plan. This was denied by U, who suggested that M could resort to buying more editorials in the local newspaper in order to promote its proposals. Further discussions produced no change.

At the resumption next day, M agreed to submit to its legal advisors U's proposals concerning the pension plan. Demands relating to vacations were examined and left without agreement. M agreed to four minor, noneconomic proposals and rejected one, whereas U withdrew one issue. (C) M then proposed the deletion of the contract clause permitting the arbitration of wages during the life of the contract, but U refused to agree unless M would accept substantial wage adjustments. M rejected that package suggestion. On the following day (August 2), M raised the issue of the application of seniority rules to intraplant transfer of workers. Each party made proposals that were unacceptable to the other and, after lengthy considerations, it was agreed to leave the issue for the time being. M then announced its rejection of U's proposals concerning the pension plan, although promising to consider them further. U accused M of deliberate procrastination on the wage issue in order to save itself a quarter of a million dollars. This was denied by M, who also rejected U's demands for a wage increase above the offer of 11 cents that was already on the table.

The next day, M again raised the issues relating to seniority. Proposals and counterproposals were considered but without any significant concession by either party. U insisted that seniority and the associated issue of the reemployment of laid-off workers was "the all-important thing." Thereafter the parties discussed issues relating to job-rate adjustment, equal-pay-for-equal-work regulations, and adjustment of inequities in wages. There continued to be little or no change by either party. At U's request, M repeated its wage offer of 6 cents in addition to the 5 cents earlier. U demanded that this offer be either made retroactive or increased in size. M refused these demands and also a U proposal for more paid holidays. Finally, despite U's further insistence, M refused to offer anything above the 6-cent increase in wages, although it expressed some willingness to consider wage-adjustment problems if the general wage rate could be settled first.

The following day (August 4), M rejected a U proposal concerning seniority. U then reiterated its principal demands: union shop and checkoff, extra paid holidays, seniority regulations, vacations, wage adjustment, and a wage increase to be retroactive. M rejected all these demands. (A) Deadlock was reached and this continued into the next meeting held the day after, despite the participation of a federal conciliator. There followed a week without meetings between the parties, during which time each set out its position and demands on the outstanding issues: M in letters to employees and U in bulletins and statements to the press.

Negotiations were resumed on August 13 (the day the old contract expired).

Phase 5. U proposed that the less important, minor issues be taken first, leaving monetary issues to the last. (C) This was accepted by M, who also agreed to start with the pension plan issue.

Phase 6. After considering the parties' respective proposals, a compromise was agreed upon. At U's suggestion M raised the next "lesser" issue: equal pay for equal work. U asserted that this also raised the issues of job-rate adjustment and suggested a trade-off between the two issues. No agreement was reached here and attention moved to the seniority issues. (A) Failure to reach agreement led to renewed expressions of antagonism and the U leader suggested an adjournment because of this.

After a recess for dinner, the U leader admitted to some internal disagreement within union membership and said that there was a fear of the developing possibility of a plant shutdown by the company or of a strike, which would be costly to both the company and the workers. In order to avoid this threat, U proposed a compromise on the seniority issue: that the company should state its intent to follow as far as possible U's proposals on this issues. (C) M agreed to consider this, saying that although it was prepared if necessary to "suffer the worst" it desired to avoid further deterioration of the dispute.

The following day (August 14), the seniority issue was resolved by U's acceptance of M's earlier proposal, together with M's declaration of its future policy in principle, as proposed by U. Disagreement on the wording of that policy statement produced renewed antagonism. (A) The conciliator sought to promote agreement by suggesting his own wording but this was not immediately acceptable. After a recess for lunch, the parties discussed and reached agreement on wage adjustments in terms of M's earlier proposal. (C) In return for this concession by U, M agreed to give a 5-cent "inequity" increase of wages to mechanics (i.e., above the proposed general wage increase). M agreed to U's proposals relating to union shop and checkoff. U then offered to accept M's wording of the seniority policy statement if M would agree to the general wage increase being made retroactive to May 25 (the date when a similar increase was made in the other plants of the company). M offered to make the increase retroactive to July 25. U asked for a recess and on return still demanded May 25. M rejected this, recessed, and then offered the date of July 9. U accepted.

ANALYSIS

The structure of this industrial dispute and its negotiations evolved during three successive periods. First, disagreements under the terms of the existing contract were eventually transformed into an acknowledged dispute. Second, in the early negotiations the parties were not agreed as to what their dispute was about. Agenda formulation produced overt hostility and the subsequent exchanges led to a deadlock and suspension of the negotiations. Third, the resumption of negotiations, with a modified agenda, led to the production of a new employment contract.

Disagreements between U and M arose when U sought wage increases under the provisions of the employment contract and M wished to implement its new pension plan. Each party, in its own interests, attempted to block the other's objective. U attempted to strengthen its demands by encouraging disruption of operations at the largest of the three plants concerned. Although this show of strength does not seem to have been effective, it demonstrated and perhaps exacerbated the antagonism between the parties. A business competitor's grant of a wage increase to its employees reinforced U's demand, but at the same time M was determined to link a wage increase with concession by U concerning the pension plan. M then granted a wage increase to its employees in other plants, thus making it clear that a similar increase was available to its unionized employees in the three plants concerned if M could obtain satisfaction on its own requirements. M's strategy prolonged the disagreement for about 4 months before negotiations got under way, although by that time there had been numerous exchanges, mainly by letter.

When negotiations began, high antagonism immediately showed itself in the altercation over the presence of the stenotypist. The wage issues were dominant but M sought to widen the dispute by making a wage settlement conditional upon agreement on a new employment contract. M's threat was that if a new contract could not be produced fairly quickly, there would be only an interim wage increase well below the obvious standard set by the business competitor and accepted by M in its other plants. This threat induced U to accept the enlargement of the dispute to include a new contract. During this initial period the parties were dealing with the scope of their dispute and with agenda formulation. With growing antagonism, these first exchanges ended in several hours of deadlocked silence. Agenda discussions were resumed with the assistance of a mediator (federal conciliator) and agreement was reached.

This agreement led into Phase 3 of the negotiations. Antagonism grew as a prime conflict developed: U wished to delay negotiations on a new contract until nearer the time when the existing contract expired, with the expectation that, at that time, M would be more amenable to making concessions in the face of a strike threat. M wished to avoid that situation and it attempted to pressure U to work for an early agreement on a new contract by making a full wage increase dependent on that achievement. U refused to shift, presumably perceiving greater advantage in delay, despite the smaller interim wage increase that entailed. As a result, an impasse was reached and negotiations were suspended.

M's apprehensions about last-minute negotiations as the old contract ran out were indicated by the private initiative of the company president. He had little success, however, since negotiations were resumed only a week or so earlier than they otherwise might have been. Negotiations started again in the context where both parties now accepted the necessity of producing a new contract, including the issues relating to wage increases. The previous agenda was quickly modified (return to Phase 2) and this led straight into Phase 4: narrowing differences and making partial agreements, with a joint emphasis on the need to establish and maintain coordination. Tacitly (so the record indicates) the parties wished to suppress the antagonism that still persisted, which, unless controlled, could interfere with movement to agreement on a new contract before the old one expired. Failure to accomplish that meant the threat of a strike. The shift to Phase 4 was shown by the first overt efforts to examine possibilities for agreement as the parties ranged over the issues involved. Some issues were resolved but others were left for further reconsideration. Possibilities of later concessions were implicit, rather than an emphasis on differences; conflict between the parties was played down. Nevertheless, antagonism could not be altogether suppressed despite these efforts at coordination, and after some limited successes in reaching agreements, open antagonism reemerged and impasse was reached. By this time, however, the obdurate issues were revealed to both parties.

After a week's delay (while both parties resorted to public propaganda), negotiations resumed on the day of the expiration of the old contract. Fairly easily, the parties agreed to a proposal by U (Phase 5) by which "lesser" items were to be dealt with first (pension plan, seniority, equal pay for equal work, job-rate adjustment), leaving the monetary issues for subsequent consideration—these were the various wage issues, apparently agreed to be more difficult to resolve. This agreement provided a plan of procedure as the parties prepared to enter final bargaining.

The phase of final bargaining (Phase 6) began with the parties reaching agreement on the pension plan issue. An attempt by U to create a package deal (equal pay for equal work and job-rate adjustment) was unsuccessful, and further conflict over the seniority issue produced an increase in overt antagonism. U reemphasized the possibility of the failure of the negotiations and the threat of a strike. To avoid this, U proposed a compromise over seniority: acceptance of M's demand if M would agree to state publicly its intention in principle to follow as closely as possible U's demands in the matter. This became acceptable to M, although the persisting antagonism showed in the disagreement over the wording of M's statement. U then accepted M's demand on wage equity adjustments in return for M's acceptance of U's demand for a special wage increase for mechanics.

On the issue of wage increases, it had long become obvious that M would concede a general increase compatible with the increase already established elsewhere. U's efforts to obtain a larger increase were not prolonged, and U could not exert negotiating by strength by offering concessions on other issues against M's agreement on a wage increase. All that could be done was an attempt by U to link its acceptance of M's wording of the public statement on seniority with M's agreement to make the wage increase retroactive to the date such an increase had been made in M's other plants. It seems doubtful that the tactic was successful: M's final concession on retroactivation (smaller than U demanded) appears to have come as much from a desire to conclude the negotiations and to avoid further threat of a strike or other industrial disturbance.

SOME ANALYTICAL IMPLICATIONS

Both of these disputes emerged out of refusals by each party to meet the demands of the other. Dyadic adjustment of disagreements proved impossible but at the same time the status quo was unacceptable. In each case, as in all disputes and negotiations, the two parties were situationally interdependent in that each could only expect to achieve its requirements and aims insofar as the other could be induced to meet them. Although each party made his demands, supported by whatever arguments and persuasive strengths seemed available, appropriate, and useful, the eventual outcome had to be the result of joint decision by the two parties. Negotiations were, therefore, processes through which the parties gradually adjusted their expectations, preferences, and demands. Some demands came to be perceived as unimportant and could be withdrawn or quietly dropped; some demands were modified to a point where they became acceptable to the opponent, sometimes in conjunction with trade-offs; and some demands were so resolutely and more or less inflexibly maintained that the opponent was eventually constrained to accede to them. These changes from the initial situation were the result of information exchange and learning; issues were clarified and their implications for one or both parties became increasingly understood and taken into account as the negotiations developed. Despite obvious differences in detail and in sociocultural context, the processual, phase patterns of the development of negotiations were essentially the same although there were, of course, variations in the timing and persistence of each successive phase. Moreover, this similarity of pattern and process was not fundamentally affected by the fact that the Arusha negotiations lasted only 6 hours in a single session whereas the American negotiations went on, with interruptions, for about 3 months in 15 sessions.[9]

At the same time as changes in preferences and demands were being made, and in intimate association with them, the potential power available to each party was effectively transformed into persuasive strength and inducement. On the one hand, potential power was derived from resources and capabilities available to each party (e.g., the possibility of a strike by workers or the withholding of a wage increase by management; Kinyani's ability to interfere with irrigation water and so with Lashiloi's cultivation of Lashiloi's normative correctness relating to his water rights). On the other hand, the practical effectiveness of potential power was worked out between the parties through their interaction. Moreover, outside factors impinged on the relative strengths of the parties and thus affected the outcomes they eventually constructed (e.g., the business competitor's wage increase set an unavoidable standard; in Arusha, neutral neighbors endorsed Lashiloi's water rights and his belief in the threat of supernatural danger).

The necessity of joint decision-making in negotiation, as I have noted previously (Chapter 6, pages 181–186), contains a basic and intrinsic contradiction: that is, the contradiction between conflict and differences between the parties and their unavoidable need to participate in joint action to achieve some agreement and resolution of their dispute. Antagonism resulted from that conflict, although coordination was essential for joint action. These two dispositions, or modes of negotiating interaction, alternated in their relative predominance, as indicated in the case studies. However, it should be clear from those accounts that whenever coordination was being emphasized antagonism nevertheless remained, sometimes interfering with the effectiveness of coordination and at other times resuming overtly after an interim success of coordination. In complementary fashion, while antagonism predominated, the need for coordination persisted such that antagonism was blunted and had in the end, as it were, to give way to renewed coordination. The shifts from one disposition or mode

---

9. It should be noted that some Arusha negotiations extended over many weeks and numerous sessions (an example is given in Gulliver 1963:208 ff.) and that some American industrial negotiations have been rather quickly concluded.

of interaction to its opposite marked distinct phases of interaction and effective purpose. However, there were also fluctuations within a phase, particularly as antagonism broke through into a period of emphasis on coordination.

The potential alternative to continuing negotiations and their intrinsic contradiction was to break off and either accept the status quo or seek substitute sources of satisfaction for a party's requirements. However, in the American industrial case, the two parties were virtually locked together in unavoidable bilateral monopoly. For the workers to find other employment was almost impossible in what were largely company towns, leaving only the undesirable alternative of moving elsewhere to find jobs. For management, perhaps the recruitment of other, more amenable workers and the closure of the plants were possibilities; the record has no mention of these or of the difficulties that might have been involved, nor is it reported if management actively considered these options. In fact, all the evidence indicates that both parties fully recognized that each needed the other, so that ultimately and ineluctably they had to work out some kind of tolerable resolution of their immediate differences in order that individually they might continue to pursue their vital interests: for the employees, to have employment, earn wages, and so maintain a livelihood; for the management, to ensure a labor force in order to continue production and profit making.

In the Arusha case, the two disputants were linked as neighbors and as co-members of the same formal age-group, in virtue of which they had the strong possibility of a mutually advantageous relationship that would serve the particular interests of each. In some contrast with the American case, it was not absolutely essential to the vital interests and objectives of either party that they reconstruct their relationship. Other options were available; each disputant could expect assistance and cooperation in a range of economic and other activities both from kinsmen and from other neighbors. Indeed, Lashiloi in particular could reliably expect these other people to meet his needs reasonably satisfactorily, although Kinyani's position was weaker since both his kinsmen and his neighbors were less supportive. Nevertheless, the certain advantages of good neighborliness (and the absence of disadvantages that could arise otherwise) were clear and strong enough so that the two men scarcely considered the possibility of ignoring them. Moreover, good neighborliness and good relations between age-mates were emphatically supported and encouraged by cultural values and ideology. In short, in each case both parties in their negotiations acknowledged the importance of reaching agreement in their dispute, however pronounced their antagonism.

The strength and operational significance of antagonism were directly connected with the nature of the relationship between the two parties within the structure of their respective societies and with the cultural values and ideologies that were involved. In the American case, although no complete breakdown of negotiations occurred, there were three occasions of impasse when antagonism temporarily prevented positive interaction and progess toward an agreed outcome. In the Arusha case, in contrast, no impasse developed nor was there real danger that this might have happened. There seem to be two principal reasons for this difference and they demonstrate further dimensions of the negotiation process. First, because the American parties were so locked in bilateral monopoly, within a socioeconomic structure that inevitably placed them in permanent opposition, the level of antagonism was high. The necessity of constructing an agreed outcome could not altogether override that continuing opposition. Each party knew that, whatever the immediate outcome, their opposition would continue. Only its opponent could provide each party with what was required, yet their interests were for the most part diametrically opposed and that situation would scarcely be affected by the particular outcome. Therefore, there was persisting suspicion between the parties that each would benefit at the other's expense. Thus, antagonism broke through and sometimes became irresistably dominant such that, temporarily, a return to coordination became impossible. The impasse that produced the lengthy suspension of negotiations for some 6 weeks was the most notable example of such an upsurge of antagonism; then the union party was determined to discontinue meetings until the time, just before the contract expired, when its strength could be expected to be greatest. This was a strategy of antagonism, rather than one of coordination and compromise.

This level of antagonism and the recurrent inability to control it (or, perhaps, the desire to allow it free rein in order to gain advantage) were not present in the Arusha case. There the two parties were not in structural opposition, although for the moment they were in conflict with one another. Indeed, once their differences could be resolved, they could and did expect to enter into cooperation and mutual assistance that offered the same advantages to each of these two neighbors. Thus, whereas both parties in the American case could look forward to continuing conflict and antagonism, whatever the particular outcome in the sepcific dispute, in the Arusha case both parties could look forward to a sharing in common benefits in their renewed relationship.

This distinction between the two cases should not be attributed to differences between American and Arusha societies per se. Although it so happened that the two Arusha disputants were not tightly locked into a relationship of structural opposition and antagonistic competition and conflict, this might have been the case. For instance, they might have been half-brothers disputing over inheritance, land rights, and other ongoing issues, or they could have been members of different and therefore persistently competing age-groups. Conversely, had the American dispute occurred between, say, two businesses in connection with formulating a contract to supply goods, where there were many alternative buyers and sellers, then the disputants would not have been locked into unavoidable, structural opposition and antagonism.

The second reason for the marked difference between the two cases lies in the pervasiveness of strongly emphasized, common values and norms in Arusha and the near absence of these in the American case. The Arusha people put a high premium on the importance, practically and ethically, of good relations, cooperation, and sharing between neighbors and between co-members of the same age-group. These values, as well as the real advantages they offered, permeated the whole dispute and its negotiations. Both disputants were well aware of them throughout and they were reemphasized by supporters and by expressions of public opinion. Common values were scarcely relevant in the American case; those that existed were not emphasized but rather were quite subdued by the overt antagonism of the parties' structured opposition.

9

CONCLUSION

Theory is always simpler than reality. Even when it seems terribly complex, it is still simplistic, as compared to the range of factors, operating as conditions, as means, or as ends in any actual concrete situation [Viner 1953:1].

SOME FURTHER PROBLEMS IN THE STUDY OF NEGOTIATIONS

The models of the processes of negotiation, of behavior and interaction among negotiators, are of course conceptual constructions and simplifications of complex social circumstances. These models, and the discussions and analyses accompanying them, provide a tentative, working paradigm based as far as possible on real-life conditions and aimed at improving understanding of those conditions. However, as Kuhn has pointed out, a paradigm "need not, and in fact never does, explain all the facts with which it can be confronted [1970:18]." My models, or paradigms, are intended as something like a first approximation, and there is no reason to think that my own particular approach and the emphasis it gives to certain kinds of factors will provide a complete treatment of negotiation. Indeed, I recognize that there are a number of other ways in which negotiation (or aspects of it) can be conceptualized and analyzed and where, therefore, the selection of and emphasis upon certain elements are rather different. Zartman has identified eight more or less distinctive approaches that have been adopted by social scientists.[1] Each of these has its advantages and its practi-

1. The eight approaches are labeled as historical, contextual, structural, strategic, personality-type analysis, behavioral skills focus, process variables analysis, and experimenta-

tioners have been able to make sensible contributions to our understanding both of negotiations per se and of some of the particular problems; I have been able to borrow liberally from many of the analyses that have been made by means of these other approaches.

However, it is evident that my models do not deal with some important matters, which, though directly relevant to negotiation, have been set aside for a number of reasons: My own interests have not encompassed them, the empirical data relevant to them are relatively poor, or it has not been possible, so far, to incorporate them into the models in a satisfactory way. Moreover, I have chosen—perhaps with subjective and experiential bias—to concentrate on certain factors and processes that seem to be particularly problematic and especially germane. It is useful, therefore, to note some of the issues and problems that have been more or less ignored in the present study in order to indicate further considerations that need examination and ought to be linked with my paradigm.

First, I have not considered the dynamics of discussion and interaction—negotiations of a kind—inside a negotiating team or party. Although my paradigm presupposes that negotiators are grouped into opposing teams, I have largely assumed that each team is structured monolithically, with a single mind, perception, and intention, almost as if it were a single person. Obviously, in actual situations this kind of assumption is generally false. The individual members of a team have their own interests and cognition and they must frequently differ in interpreting information, in formulating expectations, preferences, and strategy, and in deciding about tactics and the information to be proffered to the opponent. Quite often, some members of the team are less directly concerned and involved with the issues in disputes; they are, perhaps, participants primarily in order to fulfill obligations to the principal disputant and/or to an influential member of the team rather than because they have any keen interest in the dispute as such. Such members are likely to have little or no practical or emotional involvement in the issues or in the relationship with the opponent; consequently, they may take a more dispassionate view, or perhaps a less flexible one, of the negotiations and of potential outcomes. There may even be members of a team who, in reality, scarcely support the principal disputant or the team leaders—indeed, they may be positively antipathetic—and who have joined the team in order to meet overt obligations or, possibly, in order to subvert the leaders' position and success. In short, there are numerous reasons for joining and participating in a negotiating team and these lead to various kinds of support, involvement, and interest in the search for an outcome.

---

tion and simulation. These are not altogether mutually exclusive approaches. (See Zartman 1976:20 ff.)

In any case, however, there is no reason to suppose that the several members of a party can or do agree about everything all the time. This condition can, of course, lead them to a more thorough examination of preferences, strategy, the opponent's demands, and so on than the principal disputant or the team leader alone could achieve. Some experts are recruited for that very purpose—for example, lawyers, accountants, genealogical and ritual experts, and others with special knowledge and skills. On the other hand, internal dissension may weaken decisiveness and resolution, particularly if they become apparent to an opponent who makes use of them for his own advantage. A good deal depends on the nature of leadership within a team—the degree of influence (even authority) and deference accorded to the principal disputant or to the effective leader.[2]

Thus, the probability of genuine differences of perception and opinion, and the possibility of more or less serious dissension, require an elaboration of the cyclical model of the repetitive exchange of information and the associated processes of learning and adjustment, as described in Chapter 4. Moreover, the shifts from phase to phase (as described in Chapter 5) are most probably complicated by internal differences and problems within a party. In addition, the translation of potential power into actual persuasive strength must be affected by internal dissension and efforts to remove and conceal it. For instance, potential power may be dissipated because of disagreement within the party concerning its attempted use against the opponent.

These kinds of considerations have not been adequately examined by social scientists nor have their implications been incorporated into the analyses of processes of interaction between the negotiating parties. The most useful and extended treatment has been by Walton and McKersie (1965:281 ff.), who point out that intraparty "bargaining" is likely to begin in the prenegotiation period and to continue into the postsettlement period. They examine early attempts within a party to avoid incompatible expectations, later endeavors to revise expectations, and general efforts to rationalize and to obscure discrepancies in preferences and choices among members. However, their analysis is restricted almost entirely to problems arising between a party leader (the chief negotiator of a trade union of a business) and his constituency or organization. There is little on intraparty

---

2. In the case of an interpersonal dispute, the principal disputant is most likely to be accorded leadership, but he may be associated with or superseded by some other influential member (e.g., a lawyer or, among the Arusha, the lineage counsellor). Where the negotiating team represents a larger constituency, as in the case of a trade union negotiating committee, the leader might be the head of the local union branch or the visiting representative of the national union.

discussions, dissensions, and efforts to gain and sustain consensus and on their connections with, and effects on, the negotiations between the parties.

A second problem that has been ignored is the consequences for the process of negotiation when there are three or more parties. Throughout this study, I have assumed that negotiation occurs between only two opposed parties. This is because my own research experience and most of the ethnographic data (including those relating to Western industrial disputes) have largely concerned two-party disputes; these must surely comprise the majority of negotiations. Nevertheless, cases that include three or more parties are neither rare nor negligible, particularly in political and international disputes. In such cases, the dynamics of interaction among the parties and the lines and processes of communication are considerably more complex. Although, a priori, it can be assumed that sooner or later some kind of dichotomous alliance is likely to emerge, the processes and consequences of establishing a "two against one" kind of alliance must necessarily affect the approach to an outcome (Caplow 1968; Groennings et al. 1970; Riker 1962). Moreover, there are additional problems involved in intraparty decision-making and in the distribution of the proceeds of a final outcome. In any case, we cannot neglect the possibilities of more complicated alliance patterns during part or even all of negotiations in multiparty cases.

A third limitation of my study comes from the fact that I have focused almost entirely on the process of negotiation during the period from the overt initiation of a "dispute proper" or public dispute (see page 75) to the achievement of a final outcome and its confirmation and ritualization. This limitation raises conceptual problems concerning the starting point of the "dispute proper"; these are considered later. For the moment, I wish to direct attention to a rather different aspect. Elsewhere (Gulliver 1969) I have argued that, sociologically, the total case history of a dispute and its treatment includes more than the negotiations in a public domain, culminating in an outcome. Although for many purposes it is legitimate to concentrate attention on this particular period of social interaction, every dispute occurs in a cultural context and a social situation that have been previously established. Moreover, the outcome of negotiation inevitably has consequences for the disputants themselves and, most probably, for other people connected with them. That is to say, a dispute and its negotiations are an episode in the continuum of social life. Thus, there are three successive parts to a total case history: the prehistory of the dispute, the treatment of the dispute itself, and the consequences of that treatment and its outcome upon a range of people, their relationships and interests.

The prehistory contains three components. First, there is the sociocultural milieu: the generalized pattern of roles, relationships, and groups,

together with the enveloping rules, values, and expectations within which the disputants and associated persons operate. Second, there is the previous development, if any, of actual relations between the parties, including the particular rules, attitudes, conflicts, and expectations that have emerged and the involvement of the parties in common or overlapping networks of relationships and linkages. Third, there is the genesis and emergence of disagreement that led to the dispute. Some presentation of these is made in the subsequent negotiations, in the statements, claims, and counterclaims of the parties and in the evidence of witnesses. However, none of these is likely to provide a full or objective account or to furnish an adequate analysis of what happened and how that affects the negotiations. Nor can the outside observer expect to pick up and to take account of all the tacit assumptions and elliptical references during the negotiations. Thus, some matters of fact and cognition may remain unclear, even unidentified, although they affect the negotiations. This makes it difficult to trace and understand the flow of information and changing perceptions and expectations that begin before negotiations and continue thereafter.

After an outcome is achieved, it is put into effect, whether it leaves things more or less as they were or requires some significant adjustment of relationships and a redistribution of resources. One way or another, actual relations between the parties themselves are affected. Usually the negotiators are more or less aware of this and take account of it and mold the outcome accordingly, but they do not and cannot foresee all implications and consequences. Moreover, sometimes a particular dispute is an episode in the relations, or part of a series of encounters, between the parties. In that case, the dispute and its negotiations are affected by and contribute to the ongoing, wider process.

It should be unnecessary, perhaps, to make these rather obvious remarks concerning context and consequences of a dispute. Yet the neglect of their analysis and their implications in the literature strongly suggests the need for emphasis. Generally speaking, and with some notable exceptions, the presentation and analysis of dispute treatment—whether by negotiation or by some form of adjudication—have disregarded or given only cursory attention to these considerations. This has meant some inevitable defects in the understanding of the processes themselves as they are affected by both past and future. No less important is a relative failure to place the dispute processes and the outcome within the continuum of social life in the real world.

In a comparative survey of anthropological analyses of dispute processes, Starr, and Yngvesson concluded that it is necessary to "shift our focus of attention from the dispute itself (and the techniques for handling it) to the social processes of which the dispute is part." These writers were themselves especially concerned with "relative power and the use of scarce resources to create and maintain differences in power [1975:564]." Although there are other equally important aspects to be considered, I am not at all inclined to disagree with their general conclusions. Indeed, I have previously attempted a fairly detailed, diachronic analysis of that kind with reference to the negotiation of a sequence of disputes within an Ndendeuli local community (Gulliver 1971). Nevertheless, the analysis in the present book has largely ignored this wider context. Apart from a desire to set limits to the field of inquiry, my aim has been to examine closely the particular processes and techniques of negotiations by which disputes are handled and decisions are reached. This is because there has been some confusion and a relative neglect in the study of these particular processes from a real-life point of view and in cross-cultural perspective. It should be obvious, however, that a fuller understanding of negotiation will be achieved when they are considered in their full sociocultural context.

A fourth aspect of negotiation that I have almost completely neglected is the sociopsychological dimension. At least since the late 1950s, social psychologists have developed an extensive literature in the areas both of conceptual and theoretical work and of experiment and simulation in laboratory conditions.[3] The results and implications of this work have not been incorporated in this book largely because the social psychologists have concentrated on and emphasized aspects of negotiations that lie outside the sociological and cultural dimensions of these processes. It is clear, however, not only that the psychological elements in negotiation are intrinsically important but also that there is much overlapping with the sociocultural aspects. Here, I can only plead my need to maintain a particular focus in order to develop certain kinds of models and analyses. Although acknowledging stimulus from psychological work, I note the need, sooner rather than later, for a greater integration between the different kinds of inquiry.

In addition to these four neglected areas in my study of negotiation, there are a number of other aspects and particular problems that, although I have considered and discussed them, require more detailed examination and theoretical development. These are briefly mentioned as indications for further research and analysis. First, although frequent references are made to the strategies and tactics adopted by negotiators, we need to know a good deal more about these in actual cases: the empirical range, the reasons for particular choices, the implementation in practice, and the effects under

---

3. An early survey of this work was given by Sawyer and Guetzkow (1965). A partial review, with reference to the analysis of international negotiations, was made by Druckman (1973). More particular studies were made by Deutsch (1974), Druckman (1977), Rubin and Brown (1975), and Swingle (1970), among others.

different conditions. Second, there is the operation and significance of power in negotiation. I have outlined an operational scheme for this purpose, distinguishing between "potential power" and "persuasive strength" and focusing on the resources available to negotiating parties. This kind of working model, insofar as it has merit, needs to be further elaborated and related to the extensive general discussions on the concept of power. Third, that operational scheme also takes account of the impingement of forces external to the particular negotiations. Those forces are resources of power (or sources of relative weakness) for one or the other party, but they also affect the parties' expectations and assessments. There is still a real need, not sufficiently met in this study, to examine these external impingements in actual cases, as well as conceptually, in order to clarify their importance and to attempt more elaborate generalizations. Fourth, I have insisted that negotiations can be characterized (inter alia) as processes of information exchange that lead to learning. These processes have been treated in rather simple fashion, but undoubtedly they could be better understood—and therefore negotiations would be better understood—as a result of some applications of modern information theory. Fifth, the dimensions and processes of triadic interaction when a mediator participates in negotiation must be examined further. For instance, models of this interaction might be developed as a result of more detailed empirical investigation of mediators in actual cases. It would be most helpful to know more about mediators' strategies and their effects on the negotiating parties and on the outcomes that are reached. There remain in the literature rather too many unsupported assumptions (sometimes ethnocentric myths) concerning the roles of mediators. Such assumptions need to be carefully examined in order to justify or modify them. Sixth, the nature of the relationship between the disputing parties within the structure of their society affects the negotiations between them. This feature has not been emphasized in my exposition. One crucial aspect of this was noted in the comparison of the two detailed case studies in Chapter 8. There I indicated that antagonism is likely to be greater and less controlled when the parties are locked into something like bilateral monopoly—that is, where alternative sources to meet the parties' requirements are more or less absent and the parties are involved in unavoidable structural opposition. Further investigation of this variable would, in particular, provide clearer understanding of the alternation of antagonism and coordination and, therefore, of the intrinsic contradiction in negotiations between conflict and the need for joint action. Finally, I have strongly emphasized the importance of multiple criteria (both issues and their attributes) in disputes and pointed to the neglect of this crucial condition in most analyses of negotiations and to some of the ways in which negotiators themselves solve the inherent problems. Both empirically and conceptually, these problems and practical solutions require much more attention. When recognized at all in most theorists' models, they have generally been passed over. I have been able only to be suggestive of some of the ways in which multiple criteria can be incorporated into the general analysis.

FURTHER APPLICATIONS OF THE PARADIGM OF NEGOTIATION

For convenience of exposition and in order to sustain a particular focus of inquiry, I have assumed throughout this book that negotiations occur in some arena in the public domain and that they are limited to the attempt by two opposed parties to resolve a set of issues between them. In addition, it has been assumed that each party comprises a team. This focus has allowed me to construct models of the processes and variables that are involved. Furthermore, there is a presumption that the paradigm thus developed is applicable, mutatis mutandis, to the treatment of interpersonal disputes of all kinds, intergroup disputes, and international negotiations. This last presumption remains unproved, and ultimately perhaps unprovable, although sufficient evidence has been provided to give it prima facie validity as a working hypothesis. Nevertheless, there are possibly some distinctive differences between these various kinds of dispute and their negotiation that need an emphasis not given in this book.

There remain, however, a least two other kinds of social interaction in the context of conflict resolution that are often referred to as negotiation and might be brought within the same paradigm. One kind involves what I have earlier referred to as private "disagreement" within a social relationship that may be resolvable by "dyadic adjustment" rather than by resort to a public arena. The other kind is evident in "multiple negotiations": a series of successive or partly simultaneous negotiations that create, sustain, and change a particular area of social order among a group of people. I briefly examine these two kinds of interaction with reference to the paradigm developed in this book.

The developmental model of negotiation (Chapter 5) has its starting point where an unresolved private disagreement between two persons or groups is transformed into a dispute proper, or public dispute, as it is put into a public domain. This transformation occurs as the result of a crisis precipitated by the unwillingness of one or both disputants to accept the status quo (page 75). This has meant that I have been able to begin my description and analysis (Phase 1 of the model) with the search for an arena. Apart from the obvious advantages of clarity and simplification, this analytical procedure recognizes that to put a disagreement into a public domain is to put it into a different frame of reference and action. The disagreement, as it becomes transformed into a dispute, is given some kind of public recognition and is then handled by a procedure that involves other people as supporters and advocates of one or the other party. As this occurs, the issues between the disputants are often redefined and augmented—if only because others begin to participate in their explication and so begin to influence the disputants and affect their interaction and exchanges. Nevertheless, this analytical discrimination between private disagreement and public dispute introduces an element of rigidity and implies a distinction that is not necessarily so clear in the continuum of concrete social life. Quite commonly, the shift from private to public, together with the involvement of other people, is gradual. Moreover, it is probable that what can reasonably be called negotiations effectively begin while that shift is occurring. In short, where dyadic adjustment is not successful in producing an agreed resolution of private disagreement, the interaction between the disputants prior to entering the public domain becomes in effect part of, and blends into, the burgeoning negotiation process.

Apart from this refinement of the development of negotiations, however, I wish to suggest another and conceptual kind of connection between the processes of dyadic adjustment and public negotiation. My hypothesis is that where dyadic adjustment achieves an agreed outcome for the two parties, the process of interaction follows a pattern similar to that of public negotiation. It seems obvious that in dyadic adjustment, there is an exchange of information and learning, leading to the adjustment of expectations, preferences, and demands. There is clarification of the issues involved, equivalent to agenda formulation; there is first an emphasis on differences between the parties and some exploration of the dimensions of the issues, followed by attempts to narrow the issues and to resolve and/or to dispose of some of them. Finally, something very like bargaining occurs in order to reach an outcome.

Often, this processual pattern is rapidly followed and the blurring and overlapping of separate, analytical phases are much greater than those that occur in the public confrontations between two teams. Indeed, in many cases of private disagreement, the processes and culminating resolution are telescoped within the continuum of an ongoing relationship, or as a brief episode between two otherwise unrelated persons, as the disagreement is quickly resolved. Such telescoping should not be allowed to hide what effectively happens. Moreover, the processes are not invariably so nearly collapsed and may in fact be more or less prolonged so that the distinct phases of interaction are fairly clearly discernible. This is likely to occur when the disagreement is more problematic and its resolution is consequently more difficult.

Therefore, is should be possible to examine the dynamics within a social relationship—that is, within private, dyadic interaction and within the context of inevitable disagreements that must arise—in the framework of my models of negotiations. This means that in addition to, perhaps even in place of, perceiving a social relationship in terms of roles, rules, and content, we can also perceive it as the ongoing, cumulative results of more or less constant negotiation. That is to say, a social relationship can be seen as a problem-solving process or, more exactly, as a continuing sequence of such processes. These processes and their outcomes modify and direct the relationship. They constitute its dynamic as they produce adjustment, reinforcement, or even the cessation of its form and content. In essence, this is not a novel conception, for it has been more or less accepted in sociology and social anthropology. Nevertheless, the description and analysis of social relationships have tended to overlook, or underemphasize, this characteristic of ongoing negotiations. If we recognize what S. F. Moore has referred to as "the element of plasticity in social arrangements" and the associated "processes of situational adjustment [1975b:235],"[4] it is necessary that we consider these processes more carefully. My suggestion here is that it can be useful to examine them within the framework of a general paradigm of negotiation. Thus, insofar as social relationships are more or less fluid and flexible, and since they necessarily involve the need to deal with problems, uncertainties, and disagreements, then improved understanding of the processes of dyadic adjustment—of negotiations—will contribute to avoidance of older, more rigid constructions and stereotypes of social relationships as constituted by roles and rules. Indeed, it should prove possible to perceive a dialectic between the rules (and norms and values) and interactional problem-solving. On the one hand, there is no need to conceive of everything as up for grabs, plastic, and almost without form at all; on the other hand, we should not ignore the inherent quality of plasticity nor the proccesses of problem solving and their continuing effects on the relationship.

With this idea that particular social relationships involve recurrent negotiations that affect and in part determine and change their form and content, it is a logical extrapolation to the conception that negotiations, both private and public, contribute to and perhaps largely determine a whole social order involving many persons and the ongoing organization

---

4. S. F. Moore's essay (1975b) contains a stimulating discussion of some of the dimensions within which negotiations occur in social relationships and in social situations (see especially pp. 232 ff.).

of an interconnected set of social activities. Strauss *et al.* (1964:377) have suggested the term *arena negotiations* to refer to this. Here, we are concerned with the interrelations among an open-ended series of negotiations and their outcomes "whereby spheres of interests are demarcated, working procedures established and normative rules agreed upon [van Velzen 1973:597]." It is, however, not a matter of the creation of a social order as if that were a once-and-for-all process. Rather, it is necessary to emphasize the sustaining and adjustment, and even radical changing, of such an order through continued negotiations.

There was a great deal of interest in such multiple negotiations by social scientists in the 1960s and references continue to be made to some of the suggestive, pioneering work published in that period.[5] Yet analysis and conceptualization have not been developed much further. At least one reason for this seems to be the failure to examine more closely the actual processes of negotiations that are involved. My suggestion is that these processes can usefully be analyzed within the framework of a general paradigm of negotiations. This approach should then allow a better understanding of the ways in which particular outcomes are acheived. More important, it would facilitate improved appreciation of the exploratory processes and of the interplay of potential power and negotiating strength and the articulation, creation, and modification of values, rules, and precedents in these multiple conditions. Beyond that, and as result, we could then examine more carefully the interconnections between successive negotiations and their outcomes within the emergent, flexible, and changing social order.

---

5. Ongoing, multiple negotiations within a social order were examined chiefly in connection with hospitals and psychiatric situations by Roth (1962, 1963:1–62), Strauss *et al.* (1963, 1964), and Schatzman and Bucher (1964). Hall (1972) has advocated a similar approach for the analysis of a political order; Martin (1976) adopted the approach for the analysis of the social order in elementary schools.

REFERENCES

Allott, A., A. L. Epstein, and M. Gluckman
  1969 Introduction to *Ideas and procedures in African customary law*, edited by M.
         Gluckman. London: Oxford University Press.
Antoun, R.
  1972 *Arab village*. Bloomington: Indiana University Press.
Archibald, K. (Editor)
  1966 *Strategic interaction and conflict*. Berkeley: University of California, Institute of In-
         ternational Studies.
Aubert, V.
  1963 Competition and dissensus: Two types of conflict resolution. *Journal of Conflict
         Resolution* 7:26–42.
  1969 Law as a way of resolving conflicts: The case of a small industrialized society. In *Law
         in culture and society*, edited by L. Nader. Chicago: Aldine.
Ayoub, V. F.
  1965 Conflict resolution and social reorganization in a Lebanese village. *Human Organiza-
         tion* 24:11–17.
Bailey, F. G.
  1972 Conceptual systems in the study of politics. In *Rural politics and social change in the
         Middle East*, edited by R. Antoun and I. Harick. Bloomington: Indiana University
         Press.
Barkun, M.
  1968 *Law without sanctions*. New Haven, Conn.: Yale University Press.
Barth, F.
  1959 *Political leadership among Swat Pathans*. London: The Athlone Press.

Barton, R. F.
  1919   *Infugao law. University of California Publication in American Archaeology and Ethnology* 15:1–186.
  1930   *The halfway sun.* New York: Brewer and Warren.
  1969   *Ifugao law* (new ed.). Berkeley: University of California Press.
Bartos, O. J.
  1967   *Simple models of group behavior.* New York: Columbia University Press.
  1974   *Process and outcome of negotiations.* New York: Columbia University Press.
Beattie, J.
  1957   Informal judicial activity in Bunyoro. *Journal of African Administration* 9:188–195.
Bishop, R. L.
  1963   Game-theoretic analyses of bargaining. *Quarterly Journal of Economics* 77:559–602.
  1964   A Zeuthen–Hicks model of bargaining. *Econometrica* 32:410–417.
Bloom, G. F., and H. R. Northrup
  1958   *Economics of labor relations.* Homewood, Ill.: Irwin.
Bohannan, P.
  1957   *Justice and judgement among the Tiv of Nigeria.* London: Oxford University Press.
  1967   (editor) *Law and warfare: Studies in the anthropology of conflict.* New York: Natural History Press.
Caplow, T.
  1968   *Two against one.* Englewood Cliffs, N.J.: Prentice-Hall.
Carter, C. F.
  1972   On degrees Shackle: Or, the making of business decisions. In *Uncertainty and expectations in economics,* edited by C. F. Carter and J. L. Ford. Oxford: Blackwell.
Chamberlain, N. W.
  1958   *Sourcebook on labor.* New York: McGraw-Hill.
Charsley, S.
  1969   *The princes of Nyakyusa.* Nairobi: East African Publishing House.
Cochrane, J. L., and M. Zeleny (Editors)
  1973   *Multiple criteria decision making.* Columbia: University of South Carolina Press.
Coddington, A.
  1968   *Theories of the bargaining process.* Chicago: Aldine.
  1972   On the theory of bargaining. In *Uncertainty and expectations in economics,* edited by C. F. Carter and J. L. Ford. Oxford: Blackwell.
Cohen, J. A.
  1967   Chinese mediation on the eve of modernization. In *Traditional and modern legal institutions in Asia and Africa,* edited by D. C. Buxbaum. Leiden: E. J. Brill.
Colson, E.
  1953   Social control and vengeance in Plateau Tonga society. *Africa* 23:199–212.
Columbia Journal of Law and Social Problems (eds.)
  1970   Rabbinical courts: Modern day Solomons. *Columbia Journal of Law and Social Problems* 6:49–75.
Cross, J. G.
  1969   *The economics of bargaining.* New York: Basic Books.
Dahl, R.
  1969   The concept of power. In *Political power,* edited by R. Bell, D. Edwards, and R. H. Wagner. Glencoe: Free Press.
Deutsch, M.
  1974   *Resolution of conflict.* New Haven, Conn.: Yale University Press.

REFERENCES

Doo, L. W.
 1973 Dispute settlement in Chinese-American communities. *American Journal of Comparative Law* 21:627.
Douglas, A.
 1955 What can research tell us about mediation? *Labor Law Journal* 6:545–552.
 1957 The peaceful settlement of industrial and inter-group disputes. *Journal of Conflict Resolution* 1:69–81.
 1962 *Industrial peacemaking.* New York: Columbia University Press.
Druckman, D.
 1973 *Human factors in international negotiations.* Beverly Hills and London: Sage Publications (Sage Professional Paper in International Studies, 02–020).
 1977 (Editor) *Negotiations: Social–psychological perspectives.* Beverly Hills and London: Sage Publications.
Dunlop, J. T., and J. J. Healey
 1953 *Collective bargaining.* Homewood, Ill.: Irwin.
Dworkin, R.
 1977 *Taking rights seriously.* Cambridge: Harvard University Press.
Eckhoff, T.
 1967 The mediator, the judge and the administrator in conflict resolution. *Acta Sociologica* 10:148–172.
Edgeworth, F.
 1881 *Mathematical physics.* London: Routledge.
Edmead, F.
 1971 *Analysis and prediction in international mediation.* New York: United Nations (UNITAR PS No. 2).
Ellsberg, D.
 1975 The theory and practice of blackmail. In *Bargaining,* edited by O. Young. Urbana: University of Illinois Press.
Epstein, A. L.
 1971 Dispute settlement among the Tolai. *Oceania* 51:157–170.
 1974 (Editor) *Contention and dispute: Aspects of law and social control in Melanesia.* Canberra: Australian National University Press.
Evans-Pritchard, E. E.
 1940 *The Nuer.* Oxford: Clarendon Press.
Felstiner, W. L. F.
 1974 Influences of social organization on dispute processing. *Law and Society Review* 9:63–94.
Firth, R.
 1965 A note on mediators. *Ethnology* 4:386–388.
Fisher, R. J.
 1972 third party consultation: A method for the study and resolution of conflict. *Journal of Conflict Resolution* 16:67–94.
Flanders, A.
 1970 *Management and unions.* London: Faber.
Foldes, L.
 1964 A determinate model of bilateral monopoly. *Econometrica* 32:117–131.
Fortes, M.
 1958 Introduction to *The developmental cycle in domestic groups,* edited by J. Goody. Cambridge; Cambridge University Press.

Freeman, M.
  1957 *Chinese family and marriage in Singapore.* London: H.M.S.O.
Fuller, L.
  1963 Collective bargaining and the arbitrator. *Wisconsin Law Review 18*:13–46.
  1971 Mediation—Its forms and functions. *Southern California Law Review 44*:305–339.
Furer-Haimendorf, C.
  1967 *Morals and merit.* London: Weidenfeld and Nicholson.
Gluckman, M.
  1965 *Politics, law and ritual in tribal society.* Oxford: Blackwell.
  1967 *The judicial process among the Barotse of Northern Rhodesia* (2nd ed.). Manchester: Manchester University Press.
  1973 Cross-examination and the substantive law in African traditional courts. *The Juridical Review: The Law Journal of the Scottish Universities,* pp. 221–253.
  1974 *African traditional law in historical perspective.* London: Oxford University Press, for the British Academy.
Goldschmidt, W.
  1971 Independence as an element in pastoral social systems. *Anthropological Quarterly 44*:132–142.
Gouldner, A.
  1965 *Wildcat strike.* New York: Harper & Row.
Greuel, P. J.
  1971 The leopard-skin chief: An examination of political power among the Nuer. *American Anthropologist 73*:1115–1120.
Groennings, S., E. W. Kelley, and M. Leiserson
  1970 *The study of coalition behavior.* New York: Holt, Rinehart and Winston.
Gruder, L. G.
  1970 Social power in inter-personal negotiations. In *The structure of conflict,* edited by P. Swingle. New York: Academic Press.
Gulliver, P. H.
  1953 Jie marriage. *African Affairs 52*:149–155.
  1962 The evolution of Arusha trade. In *Markets in Africa,* edited by P. Bohannan and G. Dalton. Evanston, Ill.: Northwestern University Press.
  1963 *Social control in an African society.* London: Routledge (Boston: Boston University Press).
  1969 Introduction to "Case studies of law in non-western societies." In *Law in culture and society,* edited by L. Nader. Chicago: Aldine.
  1971 *Neighbours and networks.* Berkeley and London: University of California Press.
  1973 Negotiations as a mode of dispute settlement: Towards a general model. *Law and Society Review 7*:667–691.
  1975a A land dispute in Arusha, Tanzania. In *African dimensions,* edited by M. Karp. Boston: African Studies Center, Boston University.
  1975b Nomadic movements. In *Pastoralism in tropical Africa,* edited by T. Monod. London: Oxford University Press.
  1977 On mediators. In *Law and social anthropology,* edited by J. Hamnett. New York and London: Academic Press.
  1978 Process and decision. In *Cross-examinations: Essays in memory of Max Gluckman,* edited by P. H. Gulliver. Leiden: E. J. Brill.
Haight, B.
  1972 A note on the leopard-skin chief. *American Anthropologist 74*:1313–1318.

REFERENCES

Hall, P. M.
    1972   A symbolic interactionist analysis of politics. In *Perspectives in political sociology,*
            edited by A. Effrat. Indianapolis: Bobbs-Merrill.
Harsanyi, J. C.
    1977   *Rational behavior and bargaining equilibrium in games and social situations.* New
            York: Cambridge University Press.
Heath, A.
    1976   *Rational choice and social exchange.* Cambridge: Cambridge University Press.
Hicks, J. R.
    1932   *The theory of wages.* London: Macmillan.
Hoebel, E. A.
    1954   *The law of primitive man.* Cambridge: Harvard University Press.
Howell, P. P.
    1954   *A manual of Nuer law.* London: Oxford University Press.
Hyman, R.
    1972   *Disputes procedure in action.* London: Heinemann.
Iklé, F. C.
    1964   *How nations negotiate.* New York: Harper & Row.
Iklé, F. C., and N. Leites
    1962   Political negotiation as a process of modifying utilities. *Journal of Conflict Resolu-
            tion 6*:19–28.
Keirstead, B. S.
    1972   Decision-taking and the theory of games. In *Uncertainty and expectations in
            economics,* edited by C. F. Carter and J. L. Ford. Oxford: Blackwell.
Kelley, H. H.
    1966   A classroom study of the dilemmas in inter-personal negotiations. In *Strategic in-
            teraction and conflict,* edited by K. Archibald. Berkeley: University of California, In-
            stitute of International Studies.
Kerr, C.
    1954   Industrial conflict and its mediation. *American Journal of Sociology 60*:230–235.
Kirsh, H.
    1971   Conflict resolution and the legal culture: A study of the rabbinical court. *Osgoode
            Hall Law Journal 9*:335–357
Koch, K. F.
    1974   *War and peace in Jalemo.* Cambridge: Harvard University Press.
Kuhn, T. S.
    1970   *The structure of scientific revolutions.* Chicago: Chicago University Press (Interna-
            tional Encyclopedia of Unified Science, Vol. 2, No. 2).
Lane, T., and K. Roberts
    1971   *Strike at Pilkingtons.* London: Collins-Fontana.
Lang, D.
    1963   Profiles: A scientist's advice. *New Yorker,* January 26.
Lasswell, H. D.
    1937   Compromise. In *Encyclopedia of the social sciences.* New York: Macmillan.
Levinson, H. M.
    1966   *Determining forces in collective wage bargaining.* New York: Wiley.
Liebes, R.
    1958   Contribution of mediation to the development of mature collective bargaining.
            Labor Law Journal 9:797–800.

Luce, R. D., and H. Raiffa
    1957   *Games and decisions.* New York: Wiley.
Macauley, S.
    1963   Non-contractual relations in business: A preliminary study. *American Sociological Review* 28:55–67.
MacCrimmon, K. R.
    1973   An overview of multiple objective decision making. In *Multiple criteria decision making,* edited by J. L. Cochrane and M. Zeleny. Columbia: University of South Carolina Press.
Martin, W. B. W.
    1976   *The negotiated order of the school.* Toronto: Macmillan of Canada (Maclean–Hunter Press).
Mayer, A.
    1967   Patrons and brokers: Rural leadership in four overseas Indian communities. In *Social organization,* edited by M. Freedman. Chicago: Aldine.
McGrath, J. E.
    1966   A social psychological approach to the study of negotiations. In *Studies on behavior in organizations,* edited by R. V. Bowers. Athens: University of Georgia Press.
McMurry, R. N.
    1955   War and peace in labor relations. *Harvard Business Review* 30:48–60.
Meyer, A. S.
    1960   Functions of the mediator in collective bargaining. *Industrial and Labor Relations Review* 13:159–165.
Moore, P. G., and H. Thomas
    1976   *The anatomy of decisions.* Harmondsworth and New York: Penguin Books.
Moore, S. F.
    1969a Politics, procedures and norms in changing Chagga law. *Africa* 40:321–343.
    1969b Law and anthropology. In *Biennial review of anthropology,* edited by B. J. Siegel. Stanford, Calif.: Stanford University Press.
    1972   Legal liability and evolutionary interpretations. In *The allocation of responsibility,* edited by M. Gluckman. Manchester: Manchester University Press.
    1975a Selection for failure in a small social field. In *Symbol and politics in communal ideology,* edited by S. F. Moore and B. G. Mynerhoff. Ithaca, N.Y.: Cornell University Press.
    1975b Epilogue: Uncertainties in situations, indeterminancies in culture. In *Symbol and politics in communal ideology,* edited by S. F. Moore and B. G. Mynerhoff. Ithaca, N.Y.: Cornell University Press.
Morgenstern, O.
    1972   Thirteen critical points in contemporary economic theory: An interpretation. *Journal of Economic Literature* 10.
Muench, G. A. A.
    1963   A clinical psychologist's treatment of labor–management disputes. *Journal of Humanistic Psychology* 3:92–97.
Murphy, W. F.
    1964   *Elements of judicial strategy.* Chicago: University of Chicago Press.
Nader, L.
    1969a (Editor) *Law in culture and society.* Chicago: Aldine.
    1969b Styles of court procedure: To make the balance. In *Law in culture and society,* edited by L. Nader. Chicago: Aldine.

Nash, J. F.
  1950   The bargaining problem. *Econometrica 18*:155-162.
  1953   Two-person cooperative games. *Econometrica 21*:128-140.
von Neumann, J., and O. Morgenstern
  1944   *Theory of games and economic behavior.* Princeton, N.J.: Princeton University Press.
Northrup, H. R.
  1964   *Boulwarism.* Ann Arbor: University of Michigan, Bureau of Industrial Relations.
Paine, R.
  1971   A theory of patronage and brokerage. In *Patronage and brokerage in the East Arctic,* edited by R. Paine. Newfoundland: Memorial University, Institute of Social and Economic Research.
Patchen, M.
  1970   Models of cooperation and conflict: A critical review. *Journal of Conflict Resolution 14*:389-407.
Pen, J.
  1952   A general theory of bargaining. *The American Economic Review 42*:24-42.
  1959   *The wage rate under collective bargaining.* Cambridge: Harvard University Press.
Peters, E.
  1955   *Strategy and tactics in labor negotiations.* New Haven, Conn.: National Foremen's Institute.
  1958   The mediator: A neutral, a catalyst or a leader? *Labor Law Journal 9*:764-769.
Porsholt, L.
  1966   On methods of conflict prevention. *Journal of Peace Research 2*:178-183.
Pospisil, L.
  1971   *Anthropology of law.* New York: Harper & Row.
  1978   The structure of a society and its multiple legal systems. In *Cross-examinations: Essays in memory of Max Gluckman,* edited by P. H. Gulliver. Leiden: E. J. Brill.
Pruitt, D. G.
  1972   Methods for resolving differences of interest. *Journal of Social Issues 28*:133-154.
Rapoport, A.
  1964   *Strategy and conscience.* New York: Harper & Row.
  1966   Strategic and non-strategic approaches to problems of security and peace. In *Strategic interaction and conflict,* edited by K. Archibald. Berkeley: University of California, Institute of International Studies.
  1970   Conflict resolution in the light of game theory and beyond. In *The structure of conflict,* edited by P. Swingle. New York and London: Academic Press.
Rehmus, C. M.
  1965   The mediation of industrial conflict. *Journal of Conflict Resolution 9*:118-126.
Reynolds, L. G.
  1954   *Labor economics and labor relations.* Englewood Cliffs, N.J.: Prentice-Hall.
Riker, W. H.
  1962   *The theory of political coalitions.* New Haven, Conn.: Yale University Press.
Roig, C.
  1973   Some theoretical problems in decision-making studies. In *Political decision-making processes,* edited by D. Sidjanski. New York: Elsevier.
Ross, A. M.
  1948   *Trade union wage policy.* Chicago: University of Chicago Press.
Ross, H. L.
  1970   *Settled out of court.* Chicago: Aldine.

Roth, J.
  1962   The treatment of tuberculosis as a bargaining process. In *Human behavior and social processes*, edited by A. Rose. Boston: Houghton Mifflin.
  1963   *Timetables: Structuring the passage of time in hospital treatment and other careers*. Indianapolis: Bobbs-Merrill.
Rubin, J., and B. Brown
  1975   *The social psychology of bargaining*. New York: Academic Press.
Russett, B.
  1963   The calculus of deterrence. *Journal of Conflict Resolution 7*:97–109.
Ryder, M. S.
  1956   Strategy in collective bargaining. *Labor Law Journal 7*:353–358.
Sawyer, J., and H. Guetzkow
  1965   Bargaining and negotiations in international relations. In *International behavior*, edited by H. Kelman. New York: Holt, Rinehart and Winston.
Schattschneider, E. E.
  1957   Intensity, visibility, direction and scope. *American Political Science Review 51*: 933–942.
Schatzman, L., and R. Bucher
  1964   Negotiating a division of labor among professionals in the state mental hospital. *Psychiatry 27*:266–277.
Schelling, T.
  1956   An essay on bargaining. *American Economic Review 66*:281–306.
  1960   *The strategy of conflict*. Cambridge: Harvard University Press.
Schmidt, C. C.
  1952   Mediation in Sweden. In *Meeting of minds, a way to peace through mediation*, edited by E. Jackson. New York: McGraw-Hill.
Schmidt, O.
  1969   Conciliation, adjudication and administration: Three methods of decision-making in labor disputes. In *Dispute settlement in five western European countries*, edited by B. Aaron. Los Angeles: University of California, Institute of Industrial Research.
Schwartz, R. D.
  1954   Social factors in the development of legal control: A case study of two Israeli settlements. *Yale Law Journal 63*:471.
Schwartz, R. D., and J. C. Miller
  1964   Legal evolution and societal complexity. *American Journal of Sociology 70*:159–169.
Selekman, B. J., S. K. Selekman, and S. H. Fuller
  1950   *Problems in labor relations*. New York: McGraw-Hill.
Serrin, W.
  1974   *The company and the union*. New York: Vintage Books.
Shackle, G. L. S.
  1968   Foreword to *Theories of the bargaining process*, by A. Coddington. Chicago: Aldine.
Shubik, M.
  1975   *Games for society, business and war*. New York: Elsevier.
Siegel, S., and L. Fouraker
  1960   *Bargaining and group decision-making: Experiments in bilateral monopoly*. New York: McGraw-Hill.
Simkin, W. E.
  1971   *Mediation and the dynamics of collective bargaining*. Washington, D.C.: Bureau of National Affairs.

Snyder, R., H. W. Bruck, and B. Sapin
1962 *Foreign policy decisionmaking.* New York: Free Press.
Stagner, R.
1956 *Psychology of industrial conflict.* New York: Wiley.
Stahl, I.
1972 *Bargaining theory.* Stockholm: Economics Research Institute, Stockholm School of Economics.
Starkman, A. G.
1975 Rabbinical courts in North America today: An anthropological perspective. Paper presented at the 74th Annual Meeting of the American Anthropological Association, San Francisco.
Starr, J.
1978 A pre-law stage in rural Turkish disputes negotiations. In *Cross-examinations: Essays in memory of Max Gluckman,* edited by P. H. Gulliver. Leiden: E. J. Brill.
Starr, J., and B. Yngvesson
1975 Scarcity and disputing: Zeroing in on compromise decisions. *American Ethnologist* 2:553–566.
Stenelo, L. -G.
1972 *Mediation in international negotiations.* Lund, Sweden: Lund Political Studies, No. 14.
Stevens, C. M.
1963 *Strategy and collective bargaining negotiations.* New York: McGraw-Hill.
Stone, J.
1964 *Legal systems and lawyers' reasonings.* Stanford, Calif.: Stanford University Press.
Strauss, A., L. Schatzman, R. Bucher, D. Ehrlich, and M. Sabshin
1963 The hospital and its negotiated order. In *The hospital in modern society,* edited by E. Friedson. New York: Free Press.
1964 *Psychiatric ideologies and institutions.* New York: Free Press.
Swartz, M., V. Turner, and A. Tuden
1966 *Political anthropology.* Chicago: Aldine.
Swingle, P. (Editor)
1970 *The structure of conflict.* New York and London: Academic Press.
Thibaut, J., and H. H. Kelley
1959 *The social psychology of groups.* New York: Wiley
Timasheff, N.
1965 *War and revolution.* New York: Sheed and Ward.
Van Velsen, J.
1967 Procedural informality, reconciliation and false comparisons. In *Ideas and procedures in African customary law,* edited by M. Gluckman. London: Oxford University Press.
van Velzen, H.U.E.T.
1973 Robinson Crusoe and Friday: Strength and weakness of the big man paradigm. *Man* 8:593–612.
Vickers, G.
1972 *Freedom in a rocking boat.* London: Penguin Books.
Viner, J.
1953 *Internal trade and economic development.* Oxford: Claredon Press.
Walton, R. E.
1969 *Interpersonal peacemaking, confrontation and third party consultation.* Reading, Mass.: Addison-Wesley.

Walton, R. E., and R. B. McKersie
1965   *A behavioral theory of labor negotiating.* New York: McGraw-Hill.
Webb, B., and S. Webb
1902   *Industrial Democracy.* London: Longmans.
Wedderburn, K.
1969   Conflicts of "rights" and conflicts of "interests" in labor disputes. In *Dispute settlement in five western European countries,* edited by B. Aaron. Los Angeles: University of California, Institute of Industrial Research.
Whyte, W. F.
1951   *Patterns for industrial peace.* New York: Harper & Row.
Williams, G. L.
1945   Language and the law. *The Law Quarterly Review 56.*
Yngvesson, B.
1976   Responses to grievance behavior: Extended cases in a fishing community. *American Ethnologist 3:353-373.*
Young, O. R.
1967   *The intermediaries: Third parties in international crises.* Princeton, N.J.: Princeton University Press.
1972   Intermediaries: Additional thoughts on third parties. *Journal of Conflict Resolution 16:51-65.*
1975   *Bargaining: Formal theories of negotiation.* Urbana: University of Illinois Press.
Zartman, W.
1974   The political analysis of negotiations. *World Politics 26:385-399.*
1975   Negotiations: Theory and reality. *Journal of International Affairs 9:69-77.*
1976   *The 50% solution.* New York: Anchor Press.
1977   Negotiations as a joint decision-making process. In *The negotiation process,* edited by W. Zartman. Beverly Hills and London: Sage Publications.
Zeuthen, F.
1930   *Problems of monopoly and economic warfare.* London: Routledge.

INDEX

Williams, G.L., 24